Dance and Authoritarianism

Dance and Authoritarianism

These Boots Are Made for Dancing

Anthony Shay

intellect
Bristol, UK / Chicago, USA

First published in the UK in 2021 by
Intellect, The Mill, Parnall Road, Fishponds, Bristol, BS16 3JG, UK

First published in the USA in 2021 by
Intellect, The University of Chicago Press, 1427 E. 60th Street,
Chicago, IL 60637, USA

A catalogue record for this book is available from the British Library.

Copy editor: Newgen
Cover designer: Alex Szumlas
Production manager: Jessica Lovett
Typesetting: Newgen

Frontispiece: Aman Folk Ensemble performs Bunjevačko Momačko kolo. Author is in the center. (c. 1970). From the author's collection.

Print ISBN 978-1-78938-352-2
ePDF ISBN 978-1-78938-353-9
ePUB ISBN 978-1-78938-354-6

Printed and bound by Severn.

This is a peer-reviewed publication.

This book is dedicated with profound thanks to my friend and colleague John Pennington.

Contents

List of Figures

Acknowledgments

Scholarship is never the work of a single individual. The scholar owes the mentors, like Sally Ann Ness, who oversaw my dissertation process over twenty years ago and whose influence I still feel in my work. Her scholarly rigor set a model for me. The scholar is also in debt to the scholarship of many nameless colleagues who give insight to a new idea or a new perspective. One of the greatest joys of completing a book is to acknowledge and thank the many individuals who supported, participated in, and aided in the production of a study.

First, I want to thank Pomona College and the many gifted colleagues with whom I have had the privilege to work. I especially want to express my gratitude to John Pennington, the chair of the Dance Program. His dedication to the field of dance, dance education, and dance scholarship is beyond generous. The college also provided a generous subvention for the production of the book, as well as travel grants to research sites and conferences. I also want to thank my students who ask challenging questions that often spark the ideas that lead to the questions I pose in my studies. It is they who make me strive harder.

I am ever grateful to the artists and administrators at Lado, the State Ensemble of Folk Dances and Songs of Croatia, for their continuing support and friendship over the past 50 years. They keep me abreast of all of their activities through publications and other media. I am still in debt to the generosity of the Igor Moiseyev Dance Company and their artistic director, Elena Shcherbakova.

Over the past sixty years the dancers, singers, and musicians of the Aman Folk Ensemble and the Avaz International Dance Theatre have provided inspiration and friendship. It is because of my work with them that I learned what it means to found and direct a large-scale folk dance ensemble. That experience informs my insights into the ins and outs of how state dance companies are maintained, the daunting challenges they face, and the intricacies of the behind-the-scenes activities that contribute to their success.

Bill Montrose, a former participant in the folk dance world and a friend, generously read the entire manuscript, proofread it, and provided thought-provoking suggestions for its enrichment. I am truly blessed for his insights and the care that he gave to its final shape.

Philip Nix read several parts of the text and offered generous suggestions for its improvement.

I am very grateful to the three anonymous readers whose wisdom informs the book. They made thoughtful suggestions, many of which I have incorporated into the study.

Jessica Lovett, my editor at Intellect Books, has been tireless in her support and supportive at every stage of its birth.

To my spouse, Jamal, I am ever indebted for his love and care, and his presence, which in this time of pandemic when I pen these words, reminds me of the beauty and joy I find in these challenging times.

Introduction: Dance and Authoritarianism

This is a study about how dance and politics intersect. More specifically, it addresses how many elements of politics—authoritarianism, ethnicity, and nationalism—interact with dance, because I argue that it is in a variety of authoritarian regimes, perhaps more than any other type of political entity, in which dance is frequently an important propagandistic vehicle for the government and its ideology. No matter how an authoritarian regime may act in reality, it invariably has what it calls an "ideology" to justify its existence. "Ideology operates with images as symbolic vehicles" (Wedeen 2019: 164), and dance, as a non-verbal, embodied spectacle provides authoritarian regimes with highly idealized and politically positive images of the nation dressed in its Sunday clothes, redolent with ethnic and nationalist symbols, the massed dancers symbolizing mass political support for the state.

The former Yugoslavia is a good example: Following the savage ethnic strife and killing of World War II, especially between Serbs and Croats, Josip Broz Tito attempted to create a Yugoslav identity to replace those ethnic identities, with the symbol of the highway between Beograd and Zagreb called, not highway 1, but the highway of brotherhood and unity. Following the soviet model of the Igor Moiseyev Dance Company, the Yugoslav state founded three professional ensembles: Kolo in Serbia, Lado in Croatia, and Tanec in Macedonia.[1] These professional state folk dance ensembles embodied and symbolized "brotherhood and unity" (*bratstvo i jedinstvo*) through their all-Yugoslav programs, which included dances from all of the other republics, in addition to specializing in the dances and songs of their own respective republics. Unfortunately, Tito's dream of Yugoslavism perished as the various republics went their own ways in the 1990s. Local ethnic identities of Serb, Croat, Macedonian, Slovenian, and Bosnian Muslim triumphed over the newer Yugoslav national identity (Maners 2008; Shay 2002).

State-supported dance ensembles provide their respective regimes with spectacularized images and symbols of a "golden age" of the ethnic groups and nationalist aspirations the regime claims to represent and support. However much

FIGURE 1: The Avaz International Theatre performs *Dances from Serbia*. Choreography: Anthony Shay. Photo: D. Young. From the author's collection.

these dance companies claim that their mission is to preserve the nation's folkloric heritage, they are, in fact, political entities, specifically designed to provide a positive and spectacular image of a nation-state. This is a notion that Igor Moiseyev noted in his autobiography (1996). It is entirely predictable that the Moiseyev Dance Company (officially The State Academic Ensemble of Folk Dances of the Peoples of the Soviet Union) was Josef Stalin's favorite company (Moiseyev 1996; Shay 2019b).[2]

I have written about such intersections before (2002, 2016a, 2016b, 2016c, 2019b), but those studies were a more general investigation of the ways in which particular nation-states and a wide variety of political regimes underwrote, supported, and continue to support, the performances of staged folk, tribal and vernacular dances. Putin continues to utilize the Igor Moiseyev Dance Company to represent the Russian Federation in the same way that Stalin did for the former Soviet Union (Shay 2019b). This is specifically a study of how authoritarian governments, governments that in general have dictators as leaders, with their whims and caprices, utilize spectacularized dance performances, often by state-supported folk and traditional dance ensembles, to broadcast their ethnic and national agendas as idealized support for the state.

These governments do not want actual folk dance on the stage because actual folk dances often represent backwardness to dictators, who want modern, sleek, and spectacular versions of them to glorify their regimes and to appear modern and progressive. What viewers see is not actual folk dances, but spectacularized versions of these dances. The spectacularized staged versions often hold only a tenuous relationship with the actual folk and traditional dances they claim to be preserving. It is state-supported ensembles that provide these mini-festivals of national and regime pride. These ensembles are not merely popular with the leaders, but also with large segments of the national population who often view these dance ensembles that carry a "national" imprimatur as keepers of the ethnic or national flame. For this reason, authoritarian governments find these ensembles valuable for domestic propaganda.

When a state, like the authoritarian regime of the Islamic Republic of Iran, no longer maintains a dance ensemble, such propaganda can fail. The propaganda provided by dance is diffuse, nonverbal propaganda, applied with a light hand. When the Islamic Revolution occurred, dance and music were the first casualties, thus depriving the new regime of a valuable tool. Middle East scholar Narges Bajoghli notes "a sizeable number of Iranians are tired of the state's propaganda, and because of that, the regime confronts a crisis of credibility" (Bajoghli 2019: 5).

I call staged dances used in the overwhelming number of performances of state dance ensembles ethno identity dances to distinguish dances prepared for public performance from actual folk dances found in village and tribal settings (Shay 2016a). Ever since the first dramatic appearances of the Igor Moiseyev Dance Company in the 1930s, authoritarian regimes made, and continue to make, political and economic capital through the creation of professional folk dance ensembles, the creation of wide networks of festivals and amateur dance group performances, and tourist performances, made in the image of the official national company (Shay 2019b). National dance ensembles frequently symbolically serve to weld together disparate ethnic and political groups within multicultural, multiethnic nation-states like Mexico, the Philippines, and the former Soviet Union (Schauert 2015; Shay 2002).

The maintenance of these dance ensembles is expensive. More than any other type of government, dictators can act on a whim and demand the formation of such dance ensembles, especially as was the case with Serbia, Iran, and Uzbekistan. Many dictators, upon seeing the enormous political success of the Igor Moiseyev Dance Company, decreed the founding of dance ensembles in their own state (Shay 2002, 2019). In non-authoritarian states, many legislative voices have a voice in how state finances are spent, while in authoritarian states, frequently one voice—that of the dictator: Josip Broz Tito, the Shah of Iran, Josef Stalin—is sufficient. Thus, in this study we will look at the intersection of authoritarianism, ethnicity, nationalism, spectacle—the tools of dictators—and dance and music.

The use of spectacle, whether military or dance, is not a modern phenomenon. It is ancient. From the period of classical Rome authoritarian governments have supported spectacle in the form of dance and mass movement, to underpin their regimes. Members of the elite, including the emperor, underwrote the spectacularized appearances of pantomime dancers, because they had huge followings among the populace. (Jory 1996; Lada-Richards 2007; Shay 2014) "Contemporaries observed the importance of *panem et circuses* ('bread and circuses') for the Roman people" (Leppin 2011: 662). "Rome was a warrior state and the city became a theatre where elites competed for adulation and status, parading in state-sponsored triumphs and erecting monuments to their military prowess" (Cunliffe 2008: 365). These triumphs were funded by booty "and, in Rome, by providing an array of public amenities for entertainment [which included very popular performances by pantomime dancers] and leisure purposes" (Cunliffe 2008: 366). Historian Hartmut Leppin adds "this aristocratic competitiveness, which frequently expressed itself in underwriting of *spectacula* engendered a tendency to make games bigger and ever more inventive" (Cunliffe 2008: 661). Hollywood had a field day depicting these spectacles in box-office hit films like *Ben-Hur* and *Cleopatra*.

The court of Louis XIV was also famous for using dance as spectacle in glorifying the image of the king. Like ancient Rome, Louis XIV invested huge sums of money in the production of royal spectacle. (Cowart 2008; Nevile 2008; Prest 2008) For the participants of these lavish performances, in which Louis XIV himself starred, the proximity to the king and prestige of appearing alongside him, gave the participants financial and political advantages. Thus, spectacle and monumentality mark authoritarian dictatorships both historically and in the present.

Historian George L. Mosse states "Public festivals had become cultic rites during the French Revolution and this tradition foreshadowed German concern with the new politics a few decades later" (Mosse 1975: 7–8), and they became a central feature of Nazi rule. Mosse adds, "German mass politics and mass democracy moved in a world of myth and symbol, and defined political participation by means of cultic rites and settings" (Mosse 1975: 12), and these cultic ritual spaces were the perfect setting for hundreds of German peasants to appear in Nuremburg festivals and rallies, representing the Volk. (Giersdorf 2013; Von Bibra 1987: 56–57) The Volk indicated the "true and pure German People." The Nazis, all the way to the highest echelons, were obsessed with folklore, including folk dance, as a vital link between the government and the *Volk*. (Lixfeld 1994)

Mosse, who lived through the period in Germany, informs us that during the Nazi period and in the spectacles and festivals that the Nazi leaders supported to create political excitement, "folk music and folk dancing were practiced with increasing intensity" (1975: 135).

The specific use of spectacularized traditional folk dance, began in the late 1930s, with authoritarian regimes likes those of the Soviet Union, Nazi Germany, and Greece, and became so popular that they largely continue to this day. Beginning with the Igor Moiseyev Dance Company, which was founded in 1937 as a political and diplomatic vehicle for the former Soviet Union, governments of many stripes founded spectacular, state-supported professional dance companies for purposes of nation-building at home and creating good will abroad.

By focusing on dance I do not wish to imply that other forms of artistic expression were neglected by authoritarian regimes, especially if they lent themselves to spectacularization. On the contrary, authoritarian regimes attempt to control most forms of artistic expression, like music, sculpture, painting, theatre and architecture. In a few cases, particularly in some Islamic countries like Iran, dance can be viewed as shameful to perform in public.[3] For example, in Iran dance is a banned activity, even the word dance (*raqs*), which "was seen as the worst possible behavior of an undisciplined body in public, and symbol of all vice" (Stellar 2011: 235), is forbidden. Traditional solo improvised dance, for which the state can flog those who perform it even in private, has been replaced by the state with a clunky form of mass movement performances in ugly, non-functional costumes designed to cover any hint of human corporeal contours, which is, paradoxically called "harmonious movements" (*harekat-e mowzun*). The Iranian state oversees the performances, which are carefully controlled by the authoritarian theocracy of the Islamic Republic to guard against any whiff of sensuality. (For dance see Meftahi 2016; Stellar 2011) (For architecture see Bown 1991, for music see Buch et al. 2016; Randell 2005; Siamdoust 2017; Slobin 1996; national monuments Bown 1991; Mosse 1975; theater Van Steen 2015).

Authoritarian states, in particular, often believe that arts that do not further the regime's agenda are useless. In this study I am suggesting that many states, particularly of a more authoritarian cast, use dance politically, particularly folk dance and vernacular dance, which can serve as an instant icon of ethnic or national identity. These ensembles often feature large numbers of performers because, I argue, the large number of dancers symbolically represents mass support for the leader and the regime.

Because authoritarian states tend to regard the arts as utilitarian, that is, for positive representation of the state they support, specifically state-controlled, prepackaged arts whose primary purpose is propaganda. Nothing can be spontaneous or improvised in the performances. As I have stressed in other studies (2002,

2018, 2019), authoritarian political regimes lean toward the grandiose and the monumental—in architecture, in the arts, in music, and in dance. The use of spectacle works like a drug, as Guy Debord (2010) reminds us.

Prior to the founding of the Igor Moiseyev Dance Company, the first permanent spectacularized professional folk dance company, many of these governments, like the former Soviet Union, already supported widespread amateur folk dance activities such as elaborate festival events, which featured hundreds of thousands of participants. Nations like Greece, Nazi Germany, and Spain, during their periods as authoritarian states, held similar events throughout the 1930s. The Soviet government undergirded these activities by holding master classes and creating instructional manuals for teaching amateur artistic directors of thousands of new state-supported amateur groups to perform what was to become the "official" way of presenting folk dance on stage. (Filanovskaya 2016; Loutzaki 2008; Shay 2019b; Swift 1968; Tkachenko 1954)

The imprint of the power of dance, with thousands of dancers wearing colorful costumes and accompanied by often iconic folk dance music, as a field of political representation, was dramatically created by the Igor Moiseyev Dance Company that was felt throughout the world. Its stunning 1958 appearances in the United States at the height of the Cold War and in its subsequent performances at the World's Fair held in Brussels that same year inspired many nation-states to establish professional ensembles in emulation of the Igor Moiseyev Dance Company. Large repertory dance companies became the new, more efficient, less expensive way of providing spectacle and representation. The breathtaking impact of the Moiseyev performances provoked a reaction among many other nations to found similar professional companies in order to garner similar positive reactions to their own nation-states (Shay 2002, 2019). Unlike festivals, largely designed for domestic audiences, these professional ensembles were efficiently packaged, mini-festivals, ready-made propaganda and diplomatic vehicles for various regimes. In this dance ensemble format the state had an instant festival, a diplomatic tool at its beck and call, and performances by these spectacular ensembles dominated concert stages throughout the world during the second half of the twentieth century (Shay 2002) (Figure 2).

For the states that had joined in the founding and expensive maintenance of these dance companies, there often also accrued financial benefits in the form of touring fees and increased tourism, as well as positive diplomatic recognition. For example, by the mid twentieth century, Franco's Spain had become a pariah state. His regime utilized stylized folk dance, with charming young performers, to work his way back into the global diplomatic network (Martínez del Fresno 2014).

In my previous studies, while observing and noting their political impact, I focused more on the professional state-supported companies themselves—their structures, the technical aspects of their performances, and their repertoires as they

FIGURE 2: The Igor Moiseyev Ballet performs *Leto*. Choreography: Igor Moiseyev. Photograph courtesy of the Igor Moiseyev Ballet and Elena Shcherbakova, artistic director.

related to issues of representation—rather than the regimes that founded and sustained them. In this study I will focus equally on those regimes and governments as much as I focus on the companies and the genres of dance and music they perform in order to meet the political needs of the regime, and the dynamic created by this interaction (Shay 2002, 2016b, 2016c, 2019b). Because of the nationalist and ethnic underpinnings that support and justify both these dance activities and the existence of the regime, I will look in depth at how all of the threads intersect in the warp and woof of national patterns of nation-building, and the impact of dance and music in that project.

The Many Hues of Authoritarianism: Authoritarian States and Regimes

The first problem that I encountered in this study was that the term "authoritarian" appeared to cover far too much political territory to be any longer meaningful for this study. As political scientist Milan W. Svolik was able to claim as late as 2012: "Although growing at a fast pace, contemporary scholarship on dictatorships has so far generated only a fragmented understanding of authoritarian politics" (2012: 2).

"Authoritarian" governments ranged from well-known examples, such as Stalin's Soviet Union and Adolf Hitler's Nazi Germany, to Peron's Argentina and Franco's Spain, to the Shah's Iran, the Philippines under the iron rule of Ferdinand and Imelda Marcos, and Nasser's Egypt to the Kingdom of Saudi Arabia. In the latter states, even in the contemporary period as attested by CNN and the *New York Times*, authoritarian princes and kings, and authoritarian dictators and presidents from these kinds of nation-states can order people they do not like to be summarily killed. This coincides with Lisa Wedeen's vivid description of an "ascetic, austere, tanks-in-the-streets reality" because, as she states, "The unvarnished essence of autocracy [is]—its reliance on coercive power to squelch unrest" (2019: 19). And while some authoritarian regimes appear more benign, what characterizes all such governments is that violence can be used at any moment.

We are faced with a formidable array of nations that fall under the rubric "authoritarian," many of which have supported national folk dance ensembles. In East Germany "A great number of professional as well as lay ensembles were created. Their main field of activity was the research and performance of folk dance considered to be of East German or East European origin ..." (Jeschke and Vettermann 2000: 66). However, in many states, across a wide variety of political regimes, like Russia, Serbia, Croatia, and Bulgaria, they have maintained their usefulness to the current regimes and continue to exist.

Authoritarianism is fraught! "Authoritarian politics has always been a ruthless and treacherous business. For most dictators, merely dying in bed is a significant accomplishment" (Svolik 2012: 13). I had many questions about what constituted an authoritarian regime, because they come in so many sizes and shapes and a variety of flavors. What, for example, was the ruler's title? Dear Dictator? President? Your Majesty? Generalissimo? Turkmen father? Some of the terms, like "totalitarian," chosen to characterize both Stalin's and Hitler's regimes, were very slippery and imprecise.

> The evidence from both Germany and the Soviet Union strongly suggested that the vast majority of both populations, unaffected by the [prison and death] camps ... found numerous ways of going around its dictates when it was not, and, in general, was politically unengaged—namely, that the paradigmatic totalitarian states, however centralized and terrorist, were not totalitarian (or at least extremely unsuccessful in their totalitarian aspirations).
>
> (Greenfeld 2016: 69)

Nothing is total.

Potter's study of the arts (2016) in Nazi Germany demonstrates how, in spite of all efforts, the Nazi government did not have total control over art production, which varied greatly from genre to genre. Nationalism scholar Liah Greenfeld argues that a modern state is "a new form of government. In distinction to kingship, for instance, which is a personal government, state government is impersonal" (2016: 2). But I would argue that Adolf Hitler and Josef Stalin, and most other dictators like Trujillo and Franco, headed arguably modern states, and wielded even more power than Mohammad Reza Pahlavi, the Shah of Iran, who, unlike contemporary European monarchs, actually ruled. I would also argue that not only were their regimes personal, but they constituted personality cults, their ubiquitous photographs and statues constant reminders of their presence. I remember from my time living in Iran that one saw those images everywhere: on postage stamps, on money, in offices and schoolrooms, in all public offices, in restaurants and private businesses.

Even as Greenfeld argues that kingships were personal, by contrast I will argue that authoritarian governments of all stripes, whether fascist, communist, royal or dictatorships, are, in fact, personal as well. We know in the cases of Hitler, Stalin, and Nicolae Ceauşescu of Romania and Trujillo of the Dominican Republic that their rules were personal, bordering on cults.[4] We can even see the transition that Turkey under Erdoğan has been making over the past decade from democracy to authoritarian rule. His rule and imposing will are concomitantly becoming more and more personal; punishment in contemporary Turkey is meted out to the degree Erdoğan feels personally affronted or threatened. Indeed, he punishes whole classes of people—journalists, public school teachers, university professors, government bureaucrats—because their behavior touches him personally.

Choosing an accurate designation for the types of authoritarian government that has such powers of financing elaborate dance companies, grandiose architectural projects, and showy events became important to this study. Authoritarian regimes have a great deal in common. Nevertheless, they come in a variety of colors. That fueled a search for the proper term to describe more precisely the types of authoritarian regimes that would participate in such often micro-managed social engineering projects as dictating the directions which artistic productions would take. In questioning the use of the term "authoritarianism" for this study, I was not surprised to find that my colleagues in political science had also been criticising the use of the term "authoritarian" as too general, and the need to break the term down into subdivisions. I will borrow some of their better fruitful ideas for this study.

What I assert is that all nation-states, no matter the political stripe, need, encourage, and thrive on the nationalist and ethnic identities of their populations in order to survive. Sometimes nations, such as Germany, relied on the powerful emotions of German ethnic identity to spur German nationalism. By contrast, Franco had to quell and suppress, often with force, local identities (Catalan, Gallego, Basque) in favor of an overarching Spanish national identity. In both cases, traditional dance played an important role in constructing those identities and determining the fields of representation those dance events featured. Authoritarian regimes have a special craving to align themselves to ethnic and nationalist identities and to impress upon their populations the crucial support of the state through the manifestation of relevant national and ethnic identities. Dance colorfully fulfilled those aspirations. In the following chapters I will address nationalism and ethnic identity.

Consulting sources like the *Oxford Concise Dictionary of Politics and International Relations*, it becomes clear that terms like fascist, authoritarian, despotism, and totalitarianism are blurred and share some characteristics, and many individuals use them interchangeably. For this study, none of those terms struck me as precise enough to encompass the several case studies that I will use to illustrate the conceptual points that I wish to make regarding the intersection of dance and authoritarianism.

> Authoritarianism [is] a style of government in which the rulers demand unquestioning obedience from the ruled. Traditionally, "authoritarians" have argued for a high degree of determination by governments of belief and behaviors and a correspondingly smaller significance for individual choice. But it is possible to be authoritarian in some spheres while being more liberal in others. (Brown et al. 2018: 32)

Supporting my claim that the term "authoritarianism" covers too much conceptual territory, the authors add, "Authoritarianism has become simply a boo word" (ibid.). In describing the term "despotism," Brown et al. note "the use of the term has degenerated into a mere political boo-word, not really distinguishable from 'tyranny', 'dictatorship,' or 'absolutism'" (Brown et al. 2018: 154–55). Brown et al.'s characterization led me back to my original proposed topic: Dance and Authoritarianism, that is I could use the term "authoritarian" because of its long-standing meaning. Consulting one of my Pomona College colleagues in the Politics Department, Heather Williams assured me that the use of "authoritarianism" was widely understood in the field of politics and that I could use the term, which I will do, but with some subdividing.

However, because many states—authoritarian, communist, fascist, democratic, dictatorial, and contemporary kingdoms—fall back on nationalism and/or ethnic identities to control and justify their rule, I want to consider ethnicity and nationalism in all of the case studies that I undertake because they become so prominent, and relate to the dance part of the equation. Even as I focus on authoritarian regimes and their political use of dance to harness those ethnic and nationalist emotions to help prop up their regimes, I will consider where on the authoritarian continuum each regime fits.

I found two important sources to provide much-needed subdivisions that are suitable for this study: Steven Levitsky and Lucan Way's *Competitive Authoritarianism* (2010) and Houchang Chehabi and Juan Linz's *Sultanistic Regimes* (1998). *Competitive Authoritarianism* is a recent study of hybrid regimes that came into being after World War II. The term includes a number of different regimes. For this study, the rubric of competitive authoritarian regimes includes the authoritarian governments of Croatia, under Franjo Tuđman, and the Dominican Republic, which have recently found themselves on the road to democracy.

In *Sultanistic Regimes*, political scientists Chehabi and Linz have characterized such nation-states as Iran, the Philippines, the Dominican Republic as what I call "over-the-top regimes," by which I mean that the dictators self indulge in gigantic statues of themselves, or massive gatherings that celebrate their greatness. I would also class the last of my case studies, the former soviet Republic of Uzbekistan, in this category. Sultanistic regimes are, in reality, way over-the-top governments, like North Korea, that create jaw-dropping buildings and mass-movement events, designed to stun the observer with the power of the leader. These sub-divisions of authoritarianism give my study the specificity that will allow me to meaningfully analyze the ways in which dance intersects with authoritarianism, and how these various regimes, each singularly and particularly due to the character of the dictator, used dance as a diplomatic vehicle to send messages abroad, as well as to domestic audiences, and how dance became a vehicle for the construction of ethnic and nationalist identities in these states.

I heed the warning that Levitsky and Way issue: "Scholars should create new regime subtypes with caution" (2010: 13), even though they have three possible outcomes for their model. I will use the two subtypes that they and Chehabi and Linz offer, Competitive Authoritarian Regimes and Sultanistic Regimes, to apply to the case studies that I have chosen.

Competitive Authoritarianism: Hybrid Regimes

Levitsky and Way characterize competitive authoritarian regimes as "civilian regimes in which formal democratic institutions exist and are widely viewed as the primary means of gaining power, but in which incumbents' abuse of the state places them at a significant advantage vis-á-vis their opponents. Such regimes [and Levitsky and Way identify more than 40 countries] (2010, volume 16) are competitive in that opposition parties use democratic institutions to contest seriously for power, but they are not democratic because the playing field is heavily skewed in favor of the incumbents. Competition is thus real but unfair" (2010: 4). It should not be lost on the reader that a photo of their book shows the Russian police brutalizing participants in a political demonstration. Western observers of Putin's government are familiar with the naked force that he employs against his opponents. In the contemporary political scene, Putin's Russia illustrates the points that Levitsky and Way make: these governments do not hesitate to show their teeth and use violence against their own populations, while attempting to put on a show of democratic apparatus of constitutions and elections.

Levitsky and Way also consider Croatia as a former competitive authoritarian regime (1992–2000, 2010: 21–22), one under Stjepan (Stipo) Mesić that required the underdog democratic forces to wrest power from the often former authoritarian regimes forcing them to give ground to the new democratic forces because the political mechanisms to gain political power were in place under the façade of democratic institutions, as Levitsky and Way analyze them. They note that, in Croatia, "Parliament and the judiciary were strengthened after opposition forces had removed the autocratic Croatian Democratic Union (HDZ) from power" (2010: 81). However, in the end in Croatia, fate played a role: "yet it was Tuđman's death in December 1999 that created a real opening for democracy" (Levitsky and Way 2010: 116). According to Levitsky and Way, two months after Tuđman's death, with considerable outside pressure, the "2000 elections were considerably cleaner" because of outside pressure from Europe which "prevented the HDZ from resorting to outright fraud despite earlier signals that it would … The regime democratized after 2000. Croatia became the 'jewel' in the crown of the EU's strategy for South East Europe" (Levitsky and Way 2010: 117).

Sultanistic Regimes

I turn to H. E. Chehabi and Juan J. Linz, whom I quote at great length because their description of these types of regimes is so compelling, prophetically state, "Most of the regimes analyzed in these introductory chapters belong to the past. This poses the question whether sultanism is still relevant to an understanding of today's world." (1998a: 46).

> The ideal type of a contemporary sultanistic regime can be constructed as follows: It is based on personal rulership, but loyalty to the ruler is motivated not by his embodying or articulating an ideology, not by a unique personal mission, nor by any charismatic qualities, but by a mixture of fear and rewards to his

> collaborators. The ruler exercises his power without restraint, at his own discretion and above all unencumbered by rules or by any commitment to an ideology or value system. The binding norms and relations of bureaucratic administration are constantly subverted by arbitrary personal decisions of the ruler, which he does not feel constrained to justify in ideological terms. As a result corruption reigns supreme at all levels of society. The staff of such a ruler is constituted not by an establishment with distinctive career lines, like a bureaucratic army or a civil service, recruited based on more or less universal criteria, but largely by people chosen directly by the ruler. Among them we very often find members of his family, friends, business associates, or individuals directly involved in using violence to sustain the regime. Their position derives from their purely personal submission to the ruler, and their position of authority in society derives merely from this relation. The ruler and his associates do not represent any class or corporate interests. Although such regimes can in many ways be modern, what characterizes them is the weakness of traditional and legal-rational legitimation and the lack of ideological justification.
>
> (Chehabi and Linz 1998a: 7)

Earlier in the essay, I noted that authoritarian regimes frequently have an articulated ideology; primarily this is to provide a degree of legitimacy to the regime's existence. However, this is frequently window dressing for the regime, which frequently operates at the whim and caprice of the dictator, who feels free to act in whichever manner he chooses.

As I reviewed the examples of dance genres and dance companies and the regimes and governments that supported them, I realized that more than half of them fell under the classification of sultanistic regimes. I regard sultanistic regimes as a subset of authoritarian governments, largely characterized by dictators, by any name such as general or king, who make arbitrary decisions and who have unlimited funds at their disposal, since one aspect of their reigns is that they become kleptocracies, such as Russia and Romania. For example, various writers estimate that Rafael Leónidas Trujillo Molina at the end of his regime ended up with 60% to 80% of the Dominican Republic's total economy and became one of the richest men in the world (Crassweller 1966; Derby 2009; Mayes 2014). Today North Korea provides a remarkable example of a dictator who possesses total control over the economic resources of his nation.

Chehabi and Linz observed that, as with all typologies, none of these regimes fulfilled all of the criteria, and certainly there were governments, like Tito's Yugoslavia, which did not fall into this category. "As in the case with all ideal-typical concepts, no empirical reality fully matches all characteristics of a sultanistic regime" (1998a: 9). The reason for this is that sultanistic regimes not only exhibit the highly personal qualities characterized by the personality cult surrounding the ruler, as we will see in the models of the Dominican Republic, Iran, and Marcos's, and now Duterte's Philippines, but the ideologies expressed by these regimes have little to do with the actual administration of the government.

Authoritarianism and Dance

In the 1930s and beyond many Eastern European nation-states began to use dance for social as well as political purposes:

> Folklore, as well as folk dance started being used to define and unite the working class and to inspire artists to incorporate folk elements in their songs, tales, choreographic works, etc. This way of creating "new folklore" was very popular and was encouraged by the Russian government ... In just a few decades, folklore had gone from being a representation of traditions to a highly controlled means of creating a new Soviet culture.
>
> (Petkovski 2016: 173)

Historian Karen Petrone adds that, in the former Soviet Union in the 1930s, "Only controlled 'folk' customs such as wearing national costumes or performing dances were now permitted by Party officials" (2000: 41). After more than a decade of government repression of folk expression, the Soviet government now turned to folklore, especially folk dance, as a legitimate form of expression but, and this is important, not just any folk dance, folk dance in the form of ethno identity dance created by the government, in which Igor Moiseyev played a part (Shay 2019).

Chinese dance scholar Emily Wilcox chronicles a similar development in China: "Chinese dance, although derived from research into folkloric, traditional, or historical performance forms, is a modern concert dance genre that exists independently from these forms" (2019: 192). Thus, like Igor Moiseyev, professional dance choreographers have created a new form of ethno identity dance. Chinese dance scholars label the ethno identity dance "academic-style folk dance" as opposed to dance in the field, actual folk dance as "original-environment folk dance" (Wilcox 2019: 193). In other words, this is a new genre of dance that refers to original folk dances with which this newly created genre may have only the most tenuous relationship.

This brings up a final thought: Governments do not attempt to control that which is unimportant; clearly folk dance now became an important vehicle for government propaganda. As Wilcox notes, "Like most large-scale dance dramas staged by government-affiliated song and dance ensembles in twenty-first century China, *Maritime* is a high-budget production with a large and star-studded creative team and ample use of stage technology and special effects" (Wilcox 2019: 198). Authoritarian governments, in charge of state funding, find dance important enough to sink significant funds into its performance. In the case of China, we saw a vivid example in the 2008 Beijing Opening Ceremony in which dance and mass-choreographed movement played a central role (NBC 2008). Clearly, the Chinese government, like many other authoritarian regimes, regards dance as central to its positive image, and has spent lavishly on its training and performance for decades.

Many individuals think that spectacularized mass movement was a feature of Nazi Germany: "... at the end of the twentieth century, associated solely with the National Socialists for political indoctrination" (Burt 1998: 107). But, in the production of mass movement productions, the communist states also participated in similar military and gymnastic displays, which Igor Moiseyev, for example, helped to design, choreograph and stage (Shay 2019). Thousands of smiling peasants in colorful costumes performing regional folk dances were almost always a feature of these mass events. They stood as a symbol of popular support for the regime (Loutzaki 2008; Shay 2019).

In the same way that East Germany took over Nazi practices of mass folk dance and gymnastic mass movements, we also have, as in the case of Uzbekistan, one authoritarian regime, that of the Uzbek Soviet Socialist Republic of the former Soviet Union, like all of the former soviet republics, under central direction from Moscow, launching a state-supported dance company, Bahor. The subsequent successor regime, that of the authoritarian dictator/president Islam Karimov's independent state of Uzbekistan, saw its political and propagandistic uses, and continued to support it. The Philippine national company, Bayanihan, has also seen a succession of political rulers, some authoritarian, a few democratic, all of which have supported its existence, maintenance, and extensive touring programs, which provide diplomatic good will and keep the Filipino Diaspora, an important source of income, connected to the homeland.

In order to establish a state dance ensemble, a dictator, or an individual close to him, may order its foundation, and assign an individual to create it. By contrast, I do not think that it would be possible in the United States, or most other constitutional regimes, to establish such an ensemble without public debate (see Shay 2013).[5]

In authoritarian regimes, from Stalin to Trujillo, the rulers had direct input into the nature of dance that would be supported but, in others, they delegated this responsibility. In Iran, more than any other member of the royal family, the Empress Farah Pahlavi successfully launched and supported many popular art projects with public funds, including the Shiraz Arts Festival, cinema festivals and the purchase of visual arts, all of which enjoyed popular support and garnered favorable international recognition for Iran. She also supported the foundation of the Mahalli Dancers, under the artistic direction of Robert De Warren, an English-trained ballet dancer. The main point that I make here is that specific, well-placed individuals in authoritarian regimes, like the former Empress Farah Pahlavi, even though not politicians, have the power and authority to found elaborate folk dance companies and other projects in the arts.

Dance for the State

The nature of the dances that most of these rulers and their regimes sought were invariably folk and traditional, spectacularized in order to fit within their programs of monumentality. Some of these regimes, like China and Iran, supported classical ballet, especially narrative ballet with nationalist themes, because of what they perceived as its international prestige. Within the process of founding and maintaining these large ensembles, there exists a great deal of competitiveness: Each succeeding dance spectacle, such as Riverdance and Anatolian Fire, has strived for increasing degrees of spectacle and monumentality. The competition for demonstrating a powerful image of the nation and regime as youthful, athletic and pure is keen (Meftahi 2016a, 2016b; Shay 2002, 2019).

By contrast, contemporary or modern or postmodern dance, in order to produce meaning, must often rely on the content of the specific work, either through narrative or movement sequences to produce meaning. Recently, as I read the various contributions to the *Oxford Handbook of Dance and Politics*, I noticed that the majority of contributors addressed, almost exclusively, contemporary theatre dance and the various political meanings that performances of contemporary dance generated in different contexts. I understand that different genres of dance constitute different meanings and contexts when dance and politics intersect. The editors of the volume clearly state this: "Dance is not one; it is dispersed geographically and distributed aesthetically, and it is diverse genealogically, such that gathering movement practices under the banner of dance bears a politics of its own" (Kowal et al. 2017: 1), And yet, the editors focused largely on Western concert dance. Alexandra Kolb, the editor of an earlier collection, *Dance and Politics*, made the same choice, and states her reason: "The collection centres predominantly on twentieth- and early twenty-first-century Western stage dance, although some articles allude to developments outside and beyond it" (2011: xiii–xiv). I would argue that her decision may have limited its value by limiting the collection's focus to western or colonial political regimes where these dance genres are largely performed. By contrast, most authoritarian regimes support folk, traditional, or vernacular dance in spectacularized formats as more germane to their political agendas.

These studies demonstrate that we have ignored or forgotten Joann Kealiinohomoku's sage writing in her seminal article "An Anthropologist Looks at Ballet as a Form of Ethnic Dance" (1970):

> Let it be noted, once and for all, that within the various 'ethnologic' dance worlds there are also patrons, dancing masters, choreographers, and performers with names woven into a very real historical fabric ... It is instructive, however, to remind ourselves that all dances are subject to change and development no matter how convenient we may find it to dismiss some form as practically unchanged for 2,000 years.
>
> (1970 reprint: 35)

Kealiinohomoku reminds us that classical ballet and modern and postmodern dance genres are also "ethnic" dance forms because, like all other dance genres, they were created and performed within specific ethnic and historical cultural milieux. These dance genres are not acultural because they are performed in Asia or Africa. In China, classical ballet was imported and reworked into a political vehicle, following the Soviet example of the *dramballet*, the plots of which had to reflect social realism and be accessible and understandable to their audiences.

This study addresses the ways in which folk and vernacular dance genres have been pressed into the service of political regimes. "It's remarkable how prevalent is the assumption that dance draws up its skirts in panicked withdrawal from anything resembling real life" (Judith Mackrell, 2004 quoted in Kolb 2011: 1). This study addresses this "real life" issue, demonstrating how authoritarian regimes focus on dance as an important vehicle of propaganda for both domestic and foreign consumption. In a fervid belief in art for art's sake, my students are sometimes shocked to find that dance can serve as a political vehicle.

I was struck, in particular, by how many authoritarian regimes of various stripes—kingdoms, fascist states, communist states, dictatorships—often attempt to use dances of the peasantry and the working urban classes, not modern dance or ballet, to generate powerful symbolic meanings in their bid for mass support, or at least the appearance of political support, for their brutal regimes. Many regimes have utilized these dances because peasants and other rural populations, since Johann Gottfried Herder (1744–1803) enunciated the shape of Romantic Nationalism with its stress on collecting folklore, are believed to be the repository of pure and authentic national and ethnic identities. The appearance of colorfully garbed folk dancers twirling and leaping to well-known folk melodies stimulates instant visions of the specific nation or the specific ethnic group represented. Sociologist Bryan S. Turner points out, "Dance appears to have a fundamental, or at least an enduring relationship to national culture, if not to nationalism" (2008: 220).

This feeling still lingers and the continuing presence of state-supported folk dance companies and festivals of the festive state attests to this continuity.

The semiotic meanings that dances and the costumed dancer convey depend on the spectator, but they can be powerful. Dance performances have different kinds of audience reception. I want the reader to keep in mind that, however one can make some general observations, I have often experienced strong audience reactions to performances of several state dance companies that I have witnessed from other nation-states, in which the dance performances of state-supported dance ensembles elicit cries of "Viva, Mexico!". The sight of members of the Russian diaspora leaving a Igor Moiseyev Dance Company performance in tears because they have experienced Russia again, or Empress Farah Pahlavi addressing an Iranian audience after an AVAZ (Shay 2002) International Dance Theatre performance, telling them, "I never thought I would see Iran again, but tonight I have." During the many weeks that I traveled with Lado, the Croatian State Folk Ensemble, throughout the United States in 1992, I experienced, performance after performance, the degree to which diaspora Croatians ecstatically responded to their powerful performances. These are only a few examples of the degree to which performances of traditional dance can evoke strong feelings of ethnic and national identity (Figure 3).

Spectacle

Above all, these authoritarian regimes craved spectacle and monumentality, as studies of architecture in the former Soviet Union and Nazi Germany reveal. In this the two regimes did not differ; both dictators craved spectacle and monumentality to mark their careers, leave a legacy, and impress foreign states and audiences. The creation of large dance companies and large folk dance festival settings in huge arenas, like those in Nuremberg and Moscow, fall into this phenomenon of monumentality. As German studies scholar Pamela M. Potter observes, "The most compelling similarities between Stalinist Russia and Nazi Germany, however, lie not in their leadership but elsewhere: in the attention to spectacle and fanfare" (2016: 224). As an example of what I call monumentality or gigantism favored by authoritarian states, Potter notes:

> The Nazi chapter in architectural history is dominated by Hitler and Speer's hugely ambitious plans to rebuild Berlin as "Germania," drawing on ancient Greek and Roman prototypes in an effort to display global power. Massive structures were designed to dwarf not only the existing buildings in Berlin but also government centers elsewhere in the world.
>
> (2016: 28)

FIGURE 3: Avaz International Dance Theatre performs a scene from *Shatranj* (chess), a choreographic depiction of the exchange of backgammon and chess between the Indian and Sasanian (Iran) courts. Choreography: Jamal. Music: Ahmad Pejman. From the author's collection.

Massive structures and statuary became an important aspect of Stalin's imprint on the Soviet Union as well. His stamp on architecture can be seen in the "wedding cake" structures, like the University of Moscow, that still dominate the Moscow skyline. Monumentality was an important aspect of Trujillo's reign in the Dominican Republic, and continues to run amok, in North Korea and some of the sultanistic regimes of Central Asia, such as Turkmenistan and Uzbekistan.

It is striking that the two twentieth-century authoritarian regimes of Germany, that of the Third Reich and the East German Communist state both utilized folk dance in their fields of representation, illustrating my point of the use of folk dance by authoritarian governments of different stripes. Dance scholar Jens Giersdorf reminds us that both the Nazis and the East German communists utilized folk dance and mass choreographed movement to create identities and symbolized support for the regime. "The Nazis streamlined dance and physical culture by melding disparate ideas into a single-minded force, most notably through the extensive employment of folk dance and songs for education of the Hitler Youth" (Giersdorf 2013: 29). After the war, he chronicles how the East German Government turned again to spectacle, following ironically, both the Nazis and practices from the Soviet Union that Igor Moiseyev originated. "Leipzig became the center for these socialist mass choreographies ... the opening ceremony, which included more than ten thousand participants and was staged in the newly erected central stadium, eventually became the signature event for all these festivals" (Giersdorf 2013: 4). And, these mass movement practices sometimes involved the audience in the choreographed mass movements designed as a vehicle for creating a powerful, sometimes new, national identity.

Spectacle is created to be unforgettable. Those who saw the Igor Moiseyev Dance Company's dazzling displays have not forgotten them, especially during their first visit during the Cold War in 1958 when audiences were dazzled; no one in the United States had ever seen such spectacular dancing. Some of us remember the performances in great detail.

> His dancers, especially the men, could without exaggeration be described as sensational, capable of executing an exhausting number of split jumps, turns on the head or forearm, and of course, the signature step in which legs are kicked out from a squatting position—the *prisijadka*.
>
> (Reynolds and McCormick 2003: 254)

The West had never encountered such male dancing when the Igor Moiseyev Dance Company burst on to the scene as the opening act of the Cultural Cold War in 1958 in which dueling dance companies and musical virtuosi competed in a titanic cultural struggle. Their spectacularized performances of "folk dances" brought instant recognition of Russian identity and the audience received the message that the Igor Moiseyev Dance Company successfully sent across the proscenium stage that the peoples of the Soviet Union were youthful–athletic, and likeable–just like us (Hallinan 2013; Shay 2019b).

Monumentality

Monumentality is closely related to spectacle. A close look at the ways in which the dictators of the majority of these sultanistic regimes behave, almost always includes the construction of over-the-top statuary and architecture exalting the ruler, with their images plastered on every conceivable surface. Indoctrinated citizens, and those who managed to escape indoctrination, cannot escape the eyes of "dear leader" following them everywhere, including postage stamps, currency, photographs in almost every building, and textbooks at every level (see Lim 2015).

North Korea is, of course, a sultanistic regime par-excellence. Its citizens are subject to a constant barrage of reminders of the ruling family who have, perhaps even more than the Roman emperors, been deified, and the state has created a series of leader symbols. These "leader symbols," as political scientist Jae-Cheon Lim labels them, not only function to aggrandize the dictator himself, but also indoctrinate the population to idolize the leader. Lim notes "the people begin their daily work only after first cleaning the symbols of the leaders that are displayed in their workplaces" (2015: 27). While all of this appears like some Orwellian dystopia, it is not science fiction:

> The fanatical cults surrounding Kim Il Sung and Kim Jong Il, as demonstrated at the two funerals [in which hundreds of thousands of North Koreans rushed weeping to cultic statues of the dear leaders], are enigmatic to outside observers and may be the most unusual of North Korean phenomena.
>
> (Lim 2015: 2)

The Dear Leaders have personally involved themselves in how their symbols appear. "Kim Jong Il was very interested in learning about propaganda methods, including those of the Soviet Union and Nazi Germany" (Lim 2015: 11). With less budget than those two states, "Kim was also involved in creating cultural works (including films, plays, operas, and mass games), the main theme of which was the idolization of his father and family members. Furthermore, all important North Korean publications on art and literature have been published under the authorship of Kim Jong Il" (ibid.). Among those volumes, he "penned" *On the Art of the Dance* (1990). According to Lim, "most North Koreans believe that the fabricated facts of Kim's anti-Japanese struggle are genuine" (Lim 2015: 15). And, unfortunately, much more as well, which is the point of all of this expense. North Korea has a spectacularized state-supported folk dance ensemble that the reader can find in multiple examples on YouTube. Their performances are central to many of the mass gatherings in the capital.

Perhaps no authoritarian state has taken what political scientist Jae-Cheon Lim has termed as "Leader Symbols" to such a point of fanaticism (2015). No area of North Korean life is free of leader images.

The Festive State

In order to frame this discussion around dance and spectacle in the twentieth- and twenty-first centuries, I first turn to anthropologist David M. Guss's concept of "The Festive State," which the state-supported folk dance ensembles embody, perhaps even more than the creation of the state-supported festivals that Guss describes for Venezuela. Guss points out that "an important strategy for relocating festive practice in the sociopolitical reality in which it occurs has been to view it as cultural performance" (2000: 7) because "states too have always recognized the incomparable power of festivals to produce new social imaginaries" (Guss 2000: 13). Nowhere was this more evident than the history of festivals displaying colorful rainbow ethnicity through folk dance in the former Soviet Union, some of which Igor Moiseyev directed. Moiseyev Dance Company performances can be conceived of as instant festivals, portable and more manageable than the traditional festivals with thousands of performers and viewers. In order to make his new choreographic inventions of folk dance more effective, its "superabundance of symbols and meanings, [should] be shrunk as much as possible to a handful of quickly and easily understood ideas ... an icon of 'national tradition,' a borrowed image of difference made to stand for the nation as a whole" (Guss, 2000: 13). That the Moiseyev Company was a stand-in for the former U.S.S.R. as a whole, and currently the Russian Federation, cannot be in doubt. Unlike the ensembles of the former Yugoslavia, which dropped the repertoires of other republics, much of the Moiseyev repertoire represents the entire former Soviet Union, perhaps revealing Vladimir Putin's wish to reconstitute the Soviet Union.

These festivals are still popular. One can attend the annual Smotra Folklora in Zagreb or the Koprivshchitsa Festival in Bulgaria which is held every five years in which peasants from all of the nation-state appear on stages set up all over the city. Both of these festivals last for several days and are well-attended. The participants, dressed in festive clothing, frequently practice assiduously for their performances, some of them reaching nearly professional proficiency. There are touching moments offstage as well. I remember in Zagreb, in a park, one of the tamburica orchestras from Slavonia (Eastern Croatia) began to play and not only did the peasants dance, but more than a hundred of the spectators joined in the circle. In Koprivshchitsa several of the orchestras played informally in the evenings for the viewers to become participants.

In order to be effective as spectacle, "folklore had to be cleaned up. It would be colorfully costumed and dramatically rechoreographed. In short, it would be repackaged so that it could compete onstage with other art forms no matter how classical or refined" (Guss 2000: 114). Taking folk dance as inspiration, Igor Moiseyev created a new dance genre. The result of this manipulation of folk dance Guss points out:

> The aesthetic makeover required in order to translate these forms into national spectacles shares many features cross-culturally. The privileging of the visual, accomplished through colorful costumes and dramatic choreography, combines

> with technical excellence and virtuosity to present a cheerful, unceasingly optimistic world. This increased theatricalization abjures any mention of true historical conditions and replaces them with the staged creation of a mythic detemporalized past.
>
> (Guss 2000: 14)

Thus, Guss's concept of the festival and the invention of tradition allows us to understand the multiple cultural, political, and aesthetic levels that characterize the performances of these sunny, optimistic ensembles that dominated concert stages all over the world from 1950 to 2000. In an ironic note, since the Igor Moiseyev Dance Company features highly professional dances with movement skills no peasant would ever possess, one of the books about the company furnishes us with the raison d'être of the company, underscoring the points made by Guss:

> Folk art, whatever its form, is always on the side of good, always wholesome and optimistic. In folk-lore we find the vices denounced and held up to ridicule while praises are sung to man's better instincts ... Folk art, the art of the people, is a splendid means of educating the masses, for it can speak their own language, simple, colourful, and replete with wisdom.
>
> (Chudnovskii 1959: 23)

In other words, folklore makes us better people, a principle fully in line with the government's stance. As Jens Giersdorf pointed out for the state folk dance ensemble of Eastern Germany, the Erich-Weinert-Ensemble, built on the Moiseyev model, its very use of folk dance in general took on serious meanings: "The steps, turns, and holds in *Spinnradl* and all the other dances in the manual were never seen by the East German government as solely folk dance movements; they were also movements capable of carrying an ideological message and transforming practitioners into better East German citizens" (Giersdorf 2013: 32). Folk dance became a means to create a new, East German national identity.

Within the concept of the Festive State, I will then describe and analyze the dance ensembles and genres that I have chosen to investigate for this study. For all of these cases, the choice of folk and vernacular dances by the national state and particular dictators and their regimes becomes clear as Chudnowskii's passage above indicates.

Methodology

As a scholar, I most frequently assume the position of participant observer, drawing on my experiences as a dancer, choreographer, artistic director, and viewer of hundreds of performances for more than 50 years that give me insight to the effect that these performances have on the viewer. Seeing and experiencing these performances up close, and the effect they have on spectators, has been revealing to me both as a scholar and historian. I also draw on interviews with colleagues and colleagues within state dance companies and amateur dancers, an extensive clipping file, and academic works that have appeared, especially over the past two decades, benefitting from the research of many new dance scholars whom I often encounter in the context of scholarly conferences and with whom I exchange information.[6]

NOTES

1. I took the liberty to paraphrase "These Boots are Made for Walking and I'm going to Walk all over You," a very popular song written by Lee Hazelton in 1965 and recorded by Nancy Sinatra seemed appropriate for the title of this volume. Folk dancers frequently wear boots and so do dictators. Dictators often loved to wear military uniforms, including highly polished boots. The song lyrics seemed so appropriate to the topic. Indeed, Hitler, Franco, Trujillo, Reza Shah, the first Pahlavi king, and other dictators and rulers are often photographed wearing boots.
2. Realizing the enormous expense of subsidizing a professional ensemble, the Yugoslav state did not form professional ensembles in the other three states, Montenegro, Slovenia, Bosnia-Hercegovina. Instead the leading amateur ensembles like France Marolt in Slovenia acted as quasi-professional companies for official events. Croatian dance historian Stjepan Sremac notes that a professional ensemble was founded in Montenegro but was short-lived. (2009: 93).
3. Igor Moiseyev, who was the founding artistic director and choreographer of the first state-supported, professional "folk dance" ensemble, was trained at the Bolshoi Ballet, and he became famous for his staging of parades of athletes as well as creating ethno identity dances for ethnic groups participating in the festivals known as the *dekady* (ten-day festivals to display various ethnic and national groups in Moscow), as well as the all-union folk dance festival. He came to Josef Stalin's attention for these activities, winning first prize for a group of athletes that Stalin sponsored. (For Moiseyev's relationship with Stalin see Moiseyev 1996; Shay 2019.)
4. I want to qualify this statement. Certain tribal and folk dances, like the Saudi Arabian sword dance have positive meanings of tribal or political solidarity, as we saw in Donald J. Trump's reception in Riyadh in which the elite male dancers performed a ritual sword dance, and, as an honor included him. (Shay 1999, 2005, 2014) By contrast, dances, like belly dancing or Pahlavi-era film dancing, in which women display their bodies, uncovered, in front of men not properly related to them, can bring down clerical and public wrath.

5. I would argue that many of the states like Rumania, North Korea, and the former Soviet Union were not really communist states in the sense of actually following the practices set forth by Marx and Engels. They were simply more or less brutal dictatorships. On the other hand, Josip Broz Tito was a true believer in the communist system. When Tito wore dress uniforms, they were the real thing since he fought in and directed the Partisan struggle.
6. In 2013, I addressed the complex question of why the United States never founded a state-supported national folk dance ensemble.

1

Dance and Ethnicity

Introduction

Authoritarian states, perhaps more than any other, utilize ethnic and national identities as tools of population manipulation. Because ethnic identity and national identity can be linked, and often inextricably intertwined, in this and the next part of the volume I want to contrast and compare them. Ethnicity and national identities have many similar elements, and both phenomena can be accompanied by strong emotions. However, they are different. For example, there does not exist a single American ethnicity, but there does exist an American national identity. On the other hand, Japan has an ethnic identity as well as a Japanese national identity. Dance is linked to both in the form of serving as an element in the construction and maintenance of both ethnic and national identity for many individuals.

While dance may appear to be a relatively easy concept to understand, the concept of ethnicity is far more difficult to define: Theories and viewpoints abound and have increased exponentially over the past three decades, frequently in contradictory ways. Dance is inextricably bound to ethnicity. Like language and clothing, it frequently, but not always, serves as one of the visual markers of an ethnic group, particularly if the dancers wear iconic costumes (Desmond 1997). For example, Japanese classical dance genres like *bugaku* and *buyo* serve as markers of Japanese ethnicity. These genres are performed exclusively by the Japanese and they do not exist in other ethnic groups in the way that the polka can be found in the dance inventories of several ethnic groups (Hahn 2007; Pronko and Hall 2016; Sellers-Young 1993). However, solo improvised dance in the Persianate World, a cultural and historical concept, does not serve as an exclusive ethnic marker of Persian speakers in Iran. Rather, solo improvised dance is shared throughout the Persianate world, which includes speakers of a variety of languages and ethnic groups such as Persians, Pashtuns, Azerbaijanis, Armenians, and Uzbeks, among others (Shay forthcoming).

To illustrate my point, costumed dancing figures constitute symbols that frequently give instant visual evidence of an ethnic or national group. The hula girl, the female flamenco dancer, the Scottish highland dancer in his kilt, the Bavarian lederhosen-wearing German dancer, the Japanese geisha, the Bharatanatyam dancer—these are all iconic visual symbols, almost clichés, that signal in semiotic fashion to viewers all over the world ethnic and national identities. These visual symbols are found on tourist posters; travel guides; advertisements for food, drink, and other specifically ethnic items; television; and in many other media sources.

I could also name other dancing figures that signal ethnic and national identities, but they tend to be known to a narrower group, mostly to individuals who belong to the specific ethnic group in which they are well known: the Mexican charro and china poblana dancing around a hat, Filipinos dancing over bamboo poles, Croatian dancers in red and white full skirts whirling, and the Greek dancer in his full-skirted evzone costume all provide the knowledgeable viewer with instant recognition and sometimes powerful feelings of ethnic identity and pride (Shay 2002).

Many states, particularly those with a single or majority ethnic group, use dance as a vehicle to support the cohesion of the named ethnic group. In building ethnic cohesion, the state will concomitantly build feelings of nationalism and patriotism. Because dance, especially folk, traditional, and vernacular dance genres, constitutes a symbol of both ethnicity and the nation, state-supported dance ensembles furnish the state with a valuable tool for creating, and continually reinforcing, those strong emotions. Croatia currently has a negligible non-Croatian population, and the national ensemble, Lado, is widely seen as the "proud light of Croatian culture" (Lado 2019: 63, inside back cover). Many individuals believe that these ensembles guard and perform dances, songs, music, and costumes that stretch back to the beginnings of a specific ethnic group. It is important to look carefully at such claims of ethnic origins.

In speaking of prehistoric ethnic groups in Europe, historian Patrick Geary issues a caveat:

> Clothing and ornamentation certainly varied widely and may have been symbols of group identity. How certain members of a society dressed, what sorts of brooches or belts they wore, how they styled their hair could all have important symbolic meaning. What such meanings were is impossible to discern in retrospect. (2002: 76)

However, clothing and jewelry items, especially luxury trade products, discovered in the graves of a specific historic group may have been made elsewhere and traded into the society in which they were found and in which they took on new meanings. If Geary can assert that clothing and jewelry have left traces, how then can dance scholars and other writers claim to know the meanings of early dance when the evidence we have is a few paltry illustrations? Depictions and illustrations of prehistoric, and even historic, dancing can tell us precious little about what dance looked like and what meanings it may have had (Shay 1994, 1999).

Because of the complexity of the topic of ethnicity, I will divide the discussion into three sections. The first part constitutes introductory observations, the second will look into the fascinating topic of ethnogenesis, or how ethnic groups are born and morph over time, sometimes disappearing, and the third part is a more formal presentation of the elements of ethnicity, what I call the "contours" of ethnicity.

The topic of ethnogenesis is important because groups like Greeks, Iranians, Chinese, and Japanese, which have undoubtedly long histories, today largely stake the claim that their genetic makeup derives from ancient sources in an unbroken and, by extension, ethnically pure blood and kinship line and cultural continuity (Rutherford 2017). The ethnogenesis of a particular ethnic group is almost always shrouded in mythology because we cannot know the actual origins. I address this topic with a degree of specificity in the sections on Iran and Croatia, because many individuals in societies in which the origins of ethnic groups are not important find it difficult to comprehend the importance that individuals place upon it in societies in which ethnic identity is a core element of one's identity, and stories of ethnic and national origins, some historical some mythological, abound in these societies. Ethnic origins are sometimes so important that they appear in literature courses in school curricula (Ramet and Matić 2007).

In discussing ethnogenesis I will offer some arguments concerning the conditions of warfare, slavery, and massive human movements that contributed to altering and shaping current gene pools in major ways, and that is the reason I think many claims of ethnic purity and a single unbroken line of ethnic identity are in need of modification. When an individual was taken as a slave, they were ripped out of their former identity, including ethnic identity, and, in most cases, had to adopt a new identity just to survive. "The great divide in the Roman world lay between those who were slaves and those who were free" (Geary 2002: 64). In all of these cases, slaves—who made up a sizeable portion of the population, especially in Rome, Athens, and Baghdad, and could sometimes purchase their freedom—were ultimately assimilated into those populations. Many noncombatants of the losing side in the constant warfare among the Greeks, Romans, and other historic groups like the Aztecs, were sold as slaves. Thus, millions of individuals were forcibly taken from their original ethnic group and placed into a new context. They often produced children in the areas where they had been slaves.

It is important to remember that ethnicity is fluid and dynamic, not a static phenomenon passed uninterrupted from generation to generation. For example,

Iranian and Greek histories are frequently presented as if contemporary Iranian or Greek ethnic identities form an unbroken link to a glorious ancient Persian or classical Greek identity. Everyone assumes that they are directly linked to the past, that they are descendants of the nobility, the philosophers, the literati, and other great figures who made ancient Iran and Greece glorious, never coming from the peasants that made up the vast majority of the population and, not insignificantly, kept the elite fed (see Rutherford 2017, chapter 4). In contemporary Greece, "Greek identity not only in a political sense but with all the connotations of unbroken continuity with the classical past (and beyond) is an almost universally claimed possession" (Just 1989: 71), and "what *had* to be proved was that they were the very descendants of Pericles" (Just 1989: 84, emphasis in the original). "The lure of fame or infamy in your family is strong" (Rutherford 2017: 166).

Historian Walter Pohl notes, "It is self-evident that the Croats, Bulgars, and Turks of the early Middle Ages are not identical to the present-day nations with these same names" (2018: 19). In the same way, the Iranians and Greeks of the past are not the Iranians and Greeks of the present, a point that I cannot stress enough and, given the history of human movement and migration, widespread slavery and warfare, many of them may not even come from the same gene pool as those they claim as ancestors.

I also agree with archaeologists Ton Derks and Nico Roymans that "Ethnic identities are always constructed in close association with political systems. It is politics that define ethnicity not vice versa" (2009: 1). I would include, as well, social and economic systems that promoted widespread slavery and warfare. As I noted above, the concept that today's populations are direct descendants of past populations, as I observed about the Iranians and Greeks, defies the reality of history.

As part of the fluidity of ancient gene pools, "Despite frequent claims by ethnic groups to the contrary, all ethnic formations are intrinsically unstable and dynamic over time. Much of the dynamism is to be understood in close association with conflict, violence and changing constellations of power" (Derks and Roymans 2009: 1–2). That is the reason why, in constructing ethnic histories, I believe that insufficient attention has been paid to three of the most important impetuses of ethnic dynamism, that is, population movements, war, and slavery, which have dramatically altered gene pools and which I will briefly address in this portion of the introduction. In the ancient world incessant warfare, human migration, and the institution of slavery dramatically uprooted millions of individuals that originally began with a small gene pool (Bellwood 2013; Bradley 1994; Cunliffe 2011; Rutherford 2017; Wickham 2005). And yet, many people continue to imagine the past through the romanticized lens of unbroken ethnic origins.

What Is Ethnicity?

For many individuals, ethnicity is a basic component of identity that constitutes socially constructed differences between groups and determines insiders from outsiders: us from them. Ethnic identities can be self-ascribed or ascribed by others, and those two ascriptions may not match. For others, ethnicity has no meaning within our personal lives.

In this way Fredrik Barth's concept of the boundaries of ethnicity (1969) is useful: the boundaries that mark the differences between two or more ethnic groups, which differ situationally.

> The only thing I would add to the theories of Barth is that the criteria are not chosen at random. Language, religion, physical features, and common history are often recurring boundary marks. The notion of a common descent, though often fictitious, but mostly with a kernel of truth, always plays an important part in the perception of ethnicity. In Antiquity, the situation was not very different.
>
> (Van der Spek 2009: 102)

Some boundary markers, like language and religion, appear more frequently than others, such as dress or food ways, and, as Barth has indicated, each case is unique.

While the actual fact of ethnicity, as we understand it today, most likely existed prehistorically as an "us and them" phenomenon, according to John Hutchinson and Anthony D. Smith (1994) in their study of ethnicity, the word "ethnicity" was first employed in English in the 1950s and was not widely used until the 1970s. Ethnicity, in short, is about individual and group identity, but as such it is inextricably bound up with class, race, and nationalism, and this point cannot be stressed enough. Frequently, when individuals speak of ethnicity, they are actually discussing race or nationality. These subjects overlap significantly, especially in the United States where many Caucasian individuals can select an ethnicity for purposes of identity, even if that ethnicity has been reduced to reproducing one's Polish or Italian grandmother's recipes, but ethnic minorities are frequently perceived as racial as well as ethnic minorities, and many individuals have a perceived notion that racial identity is fixed (Rutherford 2017, chapter 5).

In public discourse and official government forms in the United States, the categories of race and ethnicity constitute confusing areas. Are Latino or Hispanic, Asian, or Native American racial or ethnic categories? These questions are important because state and federal largesse is frequently dispensed on a racial/ethnic basis, even though the notion of race has been scientifically discredited (Fenton 2003; Steinberg 2001; Waters 1990).

In this part, I want to define what I mean by the term "ethnicity," as the second of the three elements in this study of dance and authoritarianism.[1] First, I conceive of both ethnicity and nationalism in the plural: ethnicities and nationalisms because they are not a singular experience, but multiple experiences, and individuals and groups experience them differently. Unfortunately, we often think of and discuss ethnicity and nationalism as solely group phenomena, but groups are composed of individuals. I experience American identity differently than many other Americans, as well as friends that I know who are Iranian, Armenian, Mexican, Croatian, or Greek, and how they experience their feelings of ethnicity and nationality. These, I suggest, are experiences and feelings that are deeply embedded in belonging and identity.

All of this means that I do not want to lose sight of the individual within the theoretical and conceptual congeries of nationalism and ethnicity; each of us experiences the bundles of our identities differently.

> Western social science proceeds from the top downwards, from society to the individual, deriving individuals from the social structures to which they belong: class, nationality, state, ethnic group, tribe, kinship group, gender, religion, caste, generation, and so on. We have concentrated on these collective structures and categories and by and large have taken the individual for granted.
> (Cohen 1994: 6)

For this reason, I record some of my own reflexive reactions to the phenomena of ethnicity and nationalism to remind the reader that each of us, myself included, reacts to various phenomena as members of a particular society, family, ethnic group, and nationality, both similarly to others in the group or society and differently. I do not want to lose sight of the individual in his or her humanity within the social web of cultural meaning in their lives.

As I grew up in South Central Los Angeles, I did not feel that I had an ethnicity. I must not have been alone because I thought that ethnicity was

> an attribute of the Other. Ethnicity thus becomes something that characterizes other people rather than my family and I. We need, however, to remind ourselves all the time that each of *us* participates in an ethnicity—perhaps more than one—just like *them*, just like the Other, just like "the minorities."
> (Jenkins 1997: 14, emphasis in the original)

Thus, ethnicity is important because we are all implicated; we are all ethnic, although with the popularity of subscribing to Ancestry.com and other genetic analysis organizations, many people, at least in the United States, seem uncertain of their ethnic origins.

In the opening line of one of the first major scholarly works on the topic in English—"Ethnicity seems to be a new term" (Glazer and Moynihan 1975: 1)—the authors of the famous work *Beyond the Melting Pot* (1963), which dealt with issues of assimilation in New York City, turn to ethnicity to lay out how recently the multitude of dictionaries of the 1960s and 1970s used the term "ethnicity," or more often did not use it. Ethnicity in the United States has often become conflated with the term "race," a phenomenon with which many Americans still wrestle and which continues to divide many Americans. In this chapter, I argue that Americans have a national identity but not a specifically American ethnic identity.

Ethnicity is more difficult and slippery to define than nationality or nation; nations, with specific flags, anthems, armies, and the right to issue passports, have an "official" existence that ethnic groups do not have. And ethnicity has a deeply emotional component:

> The second argument that permeated our volume was that ethnicity was a subjective sense of loyalty based on imagined origins and parentage rather than something to be measured by objectively visible present cultural criteria or historical facts. This argument also remains
>
> (Romanucci-Ross and De Vos 1995: 13)

In the United States, at least, the term "ethnic" frequently served as a negative code word indicating non-white, or not white enough, and therefore was conflated with race, which, along with class, is the major divider of identity and privilege in American society, even today. Given the number of new volumes now available on the topic, I would suggest the term "ethnicities," in the plural, is more apropos to cover the number of variations of this phenomenon. Specifically in the United States to many individuals, ethnicity meant and, for some, continues to mean race: African American, Mexican American, Native American, Asian American and other non-white individuals constitute "ethnics." Through the early and middle part of the twentieth century the term "ethnic" held negative connotations in America and served as a code word to indicate less or lesser than white, extending to groups that are today considered white. In Hollywood and on Broadway, relatively liberal spaces, it meant that if you were Jewish, Latino, Italian, or Middle Eastern or appeared as not quite white, that is, if you did not look like Rock Hudson or Tab Hunter, you were limited in the roles available to you. That meant you were cast in character or villainous roles, if you were even employable. That was one of the more benign aspects of ethnicity in America, like not being able to join an all-white fraternity.

In the field of dance the term "ethnic" also carried negative connotations. The label "ethnic" dance meant reduced funding as not-mainstream ballet or modern dance, and you were not taken seriously. Katherine Dunham, with her Africanist Caribbean dances, labored under that rubric. I worked in that category for decades, and I have experienced the snobbery and lack of financial support that category entailed, in which dance organizations labeled my work, literally, as "other" (see, for example, Kaufmann 2004; Rumbaut and Portes 2001; Steinberg 2001; Stern and Cicala 1991).

Anthropologist Richard Jenkins states, "It is now anthropological common sense to consider ethnicity and nationalism in the same analytical breath" (1997: 11). I will depart from Jenkins's conclusion. Ethnicity and nationalism differ, even as they overlap. Ethnicity and nationalism are two different phenomena, interrelated but different. Ethnic and national identities sometimes coincide, as is the case in Japan, Croatia, or Greece, in which the vast majority of inhabitants are Japanese, Croatians, or Greeks. And sometimes they do not. Americans do have an American national identity, but they have different ethnic identities: I argue that there does not exist a single American ethnicity; the nation is too ethnically diverse to identify a single American ethnic identity that would cover nearly everyone in the United States. Where these two identities coincide, those who have alternate ethnic identities are frequently excluded from the national identity and participation as well. The case of the Koreans in Japan, being excluded from Japanese citizenship and treated as "the lower Other" (along with *Eta* [an untouchable caste] and Ainu), is well known to nationalism scholars (De Vos and Wagatsuma 1995); Serbs who were born and lived all of their lives in Croatia will always be Serbs (Gilliland 1995); Greeks who live in Turkey will always be Greeks (Just 1989). Ethnicity is an ongoing social process.

Ethnicity defines a group of people who believe, sometimes passionately and often erroneously, that they have a common history, descent, and other cultural traits such as religion, language, or dress that make them different from others. And they believe that these traits reach back to the beginnings of time, which is generally unprovable and which is why many governments spend large amounts of funding on archaeological sites and studies, ethnographic museums, and institutes of folklore: to prove that the current population, whom they govern, has deep roots in their current ethnic real estate and, thus, justifies the current nation-state and the regime that rules it. Sadly, some of the members of these ethnic groups are ready to kill for the details of that history (or pseudo-history) and cultural traits that appear to others of us as unimportant. In the United States, I have experienced Serbs objecting to the playing of a piece of music they understood to be Croatian, and vice versa. For them such minute ethnic differences matter.

Throughout most of my life, I had no sense of belonging to an ethnic group. After Ancestry.com became fashionable, I discovered that I was, genetically, 47% Irish, with significant touches of 27% British Isles, 10% Scandinavian

(Viking perhaps?), and 10% Iberian (whatever that means: Portuguese, Castilian, Catalan, Basque?) in my makeup. A trip to Ireland in 2018 did not impel me to take up Irish step dancing, or read poetry by Yeats, nor did my newfound genetic makeup make me feel that I was more Irish than I was before I knew that I had Irish ancestry. I did, however, purchase a beautiful Irish sweater that did not read "Kiss me, I'm Irish."

The definition of ethnicity, I will argue, like ethnicity itself, is fluid. I call the different elements the "contours of ethnicity" in order to cover many examples and to indicate that scholars through time understand its fluidity and dynamism. My definition of what constitutes ethnicity is crucial to this study because of the ways in which ethnicity and nationalism are interconnected and, sometimes, indivisible because they share many of the same elements of kinship, descent, shared living territory, shared language and religion, history, and other characteristics. In this way ethnicity differs from nation and nationalism: The latter has an official imprimatur; national identity is indicated in official documents of citizenship, while ethnic identity is frequently not indicated in those documents.

Ethnic identities historically precede national identities: "Nations, nearly all of which were formed on the basis of a dominant, 'core' ethnic group," constitute the current global landscape of nation-states (Kaufmann 2004: 1). I was, therefore, stunned when Liah Greenfeld, whose brilliance I greatly admire, stated: "Thus, there were *no ethnic identities before nationalism*" (2016: 36, emphasis in the original). Contra Greenfeld, in this study, I will argue that the notion of ethnicity, in fact, began at least before the period in which empires came into existence; "us and them" identities dominated these empires.

We cannot know when ethnicity became a fact of peoples' identities. Jonathan M. Hall points out what both ancient and modern ethnicities have in common: "Recent research into ethnicity in antiquity, drawing on comparative studies from social anthropology and social psychology, would suggest that there is nothing inevitable or primordial about ethnicity" but, rather, "ethnic self-identification responds to—and fluctuates with—specific historical circumstances ... [E]ntire ethnic groups may appear or disappear as a result of processes of social differentiation and assimilation" (2007: 53). Writers like Herodotus and Thucydides provide the contemporary reader with vivid descriptions of ethnic groups of their time, sometimes described as "barbarians," the Other: those who did not speak Greek or Latin.

Walter Pohl provides us with a case of the formation and disappearance of an ethnic group, the Avars (567–822), who for nearly a quarter of a millennium occupied Central Europe (today's Hungary and Croatia) and in doing so masked the development and expansion of another ethnic group, the Slavs, who did not disappear but rather expanded and prospered into the present, and ultimately, the Avars were assimilated by the Slavs (2018). Pohl characterizes the Avars as:

> A mixed group of steppe warriors and their families in flight adopts a prestigious name, victoriously moves across thousands of miles and founds an empire, and can thus consolidate itself as a people. When, after a quarter millennium, its identity and institutions lose their motivating force, this people disappears, apparently without leaving a trace. This is the history of the Avars in a nutshell.
>
> (2018: 397)

Pohl calls them "a political ethnos ... with a rather opaque ethnic background" (ibid.). Throughout his study he contrasts the Avars' existence with that of the Slavs who seemed to slip under the historic radar with few notices:

> Slavic life unfolded in local agrarian communities, which often succumbed to foreign rule but in the long term proved more resilient than the politics of their rulers. It was a simple life, with minimal investments in buildings, lasting forms of representation, or the cult of the dead, but without systematic taxation and rents ... The resultant lacunae in the archaeological record make it hard to trace the progress of the Slavs.
>
> (2018: 398)

And, as a result of the disappearance of the Avars as a distinct ethnic and political power, the majority of them did not, in fact, disappear but, rather, "were increasingly forced to accommodate themselves to Slavic ways of life" (2018: 400). All of this briefly describes the ethnogenesis of groups that came into being, not from those speaking a common language or sharing a common gene pool but through the circumstances of history that decreed the Avars would rise in glory, leave an historical and archaeological record, and "disappear" four centuries later but survive as part of the dynamic and shifting mass of ethnic groups that eventually formed into the linguistic ethnic groups that today constitute the various Slavic peoples and nations that occupy the vast reaches of Central and Eastern Europe. The Avars ultimately disappeared as an ethnic group, at the same time that the Slavs, with whom they were associated, succeeded by the ways in which they exploited the historical and geographic circumstances in which they found themselves.

In my conceptualization of identity, of which ethnicity is one element, each individual experiences each part of his or her identity differently at different times: for some individuals their religion or their language is their most important identity marker, whereas for others his or her sexuality, or his or her status as a parent, or their identity as a businessman or businesswoman. In other words, identities can be experienced as fluid, and each individual has bundles of identity markers. Each of these elements can surface at different times depending on context: one's country is attacked, one's religion is threatened, or one's sexuality is persecuted. These situations can trigger strong feelings within an individual, making him or her feel powerful identity emotions.

Recently in the United States, such emotions have been labeled identity politics. "It will take more than an academic treatise—even a score of scholarly works—before this nation is prepared to discard its ethnic heroes and racial villains" (Steinberg 2001: xi).

Elsewhere ethnicity was, and is, based on forms of difference other than racial phenotypes, such as religion and language. In instances where people speak the same or nearly identical languages, for example, Dutch and Flemish, Serbian and Croatian, Hindi and Urdu, religion looms larger as an ethnic marker of identity than other traits (Barber et al. 2009). All of these examples indicate that what constitutes ethnicity is historically contingent, and scholars of ethnicity and nationalism must be cognizant of this factor in their analyses.

Ethnicity and gene pools are constructed by historic events. In early modern Spain, to escape death, banishment, and persecution, many Jews and Muslims escaped to the New World in the guise of Spaniards. World War II witnessed a similar situational change of ethnicity as many Jews placed their children into different ethnic environments in order to survive. Some of them, especially if very young, remained in their new identities and married French and Polish individuals among whom they settled. Thus, the idea of common descent and the sharing of genes for many individuals in order to be a member of an ethnic group is patently false. Illustrating this point, many of the advertisements of the genetic analysis companies, like 23andMe and Ancestry.com, show how surprised individuals are when discovering their scientifically analyzed genetic makeup. I was one of them.

Livi-Bacci notes that "the current population of 6 million French Canadians descends, for the most part" (1992: 19) from the 5,000 intrepid French people who moved to and stayed in Quebec in 1608. This gives the reader a sense of how small the Paleolithic gene pool was from which many of us descended, not to mention the origins of specific ethnic groups.

What fascinates me as a scholar looking at ethnicity is how durable it is and how ethnic groups come into being (ethnogenesis) and how they can fade and completely disappear, like the Batavians (Derks 2009; Roymans 2009) or the Avars (Bálint 1989; Pohl 2018), or, conversely, how they continue, like the Iranians and the Chinese, albeit in new guises. Ethnicity is an us/them–we/they form of identity and as such has existed since groups of people needed to define themselves in terms of one another. Ethnicity is both self-ascribed and defined by others—in fact, without an Other, ethnicity cannot exist. As scholars, it is our task to identify the cultural boundaries that ethnic groups select for self/other differentiation. Most ancient societies that have left us records describe the others that surround them and, by doing so, define themselves as a special and unique people. To have an "us," there must also exist a "them."

Can We Theorize Ethnicity?

Sociologist Steve Fenton has stated "that there cannot be a theory of ethnicity, nor can 'ethnicity' be regarded as a theory" (2003: 2). To a large degree I agree with Fenton's assessment, because the salience of ethnicity as an element of identity varies from individual to individual, and even within the life of a single individual, group to group, historical period to historical period.

> The ethnicity of a collectivity that manifests itself in the form of an annual gathering of a few of its numbers to perform a dance or a ceremonial is different from ... situations [in which] it leads to violence and bloodshed.
>
> (Cohen 1974: xiv)

One reason it is difficult to theorize ethnicity is due to the fact that ethnicity can be lightly held or passionately embraced.

Other forms of identity, such as sexuality, class, religion, or profession, may be more important to some individuals than their ethnic identity. Psychologist Claude M. Steele notes that individuals can experience identity threat that can be directed at one's identity as gay or lesbian, African American, or a professor or medical doctor. When that identity is threatened, "it allows a given identity to 'invade our whole identity' " (2011: 76). Ethnicity, then, constitutes only one aspect of identity and, perhaps, not an important aspect. Therefore, I suggest describing and analyzing the *contours* rather than *theories* of ethnicity.

Another reason that ethnicity cannot constitute a theory is that the cultural markers, the boundaries, that we associate with ethnicity—symbols, language, religion, special clothes, dances, songs, and so on—vary widely. For many ethnic groups language is an important ethnic marker, while for others it is not. The same can be observed for other ethnic markers like religion, music, costume, ritual, or dance. In some cases, no such ethnically specific markers exist.[2]

Some societies are obsessed with ethnicity, which is frequently conflated with race, to the exclusion of almost all other concerns. As a result of the eight-century-long reconquest (*Reconquista*) of Spain from the Muslims, the Christians instituted draconian laws and forcibly converted or expelled all of the Jews and Muslims from Spain. Over the next two centuries following the fall of Granada, the last

Muslim kingdom, in 1492, the Spanish government and the Catholic Church disrupted the lives of thousands of individuals through forced conversions and expulsions. But they never fully accepted the forcibly converted and regarded them as traitors to the Catholic faith and *Espanidad* (Spanishness). They became increasingly obsessed with what the Spaniards termed "purity of blood," by which they meant one's identity as a pure-blooded Catholic Spaniard. Given the ethnic invasions and mixing that occurred in Spain over the two millennia prior to 1492, no pure "race" or "pure blood" actually existed on the Iberian peninsula (Carr 2000; Wickham 2005).

This obsession of "purity of blood" became the dominant theme in colonial Mexico, known as New Spain, during the process of *mestizaje*, the mixing of races that took place almost immediately after the Spaniards arrived in the New World where there existed few Spanish women. And the Spanish left "the constraints of Europe, sailing westwards to the Americas, taking with them slaughter, disease and Catholicism" (Cunliffe 2008: 476). Due to the joint decision by the Spanish crown and the Catholic Church that the native population was not to be enslaved (at least officially) and the decimation of staggering numbers of the Native New World population due to contact with European-introduced diseases like smallpox (Smith 1996), large numbers of African slaves were brought to Mexico to constitute a new labor force to replace the deceased Native Americans.[3]

The resultant mixture of white, African, and Indian populations brought into being the *sistema de castas* (the system of race mixture), an official classification system that became a dominant feature of life in the Spanish colonies, especially Mexico, one that still resonates into our own period. Anthropologist Kathleen Deagan notes: "This ultimately resulted in the formal institutionalization of race mixture into more than twenty-five categories that were explicitly illustrated in colonial Mexico by nearly 1000 paintings" (2001: 191). These *casta* paintings, as they were called, demonstrate "how race, as an organizing principle of colonial society, became the subject of a genre of painting that lasted an entire century" (Katzew 2004: 3). These paintings, generally created in sets, show the racial and ethnic permutations that result from miscegenation, depicting a man, woman, and child, and explicitly labeled, for example, A Spaniard and an Indian woman produce a mestizo. In order to show the wide variety of genetic possibilities, "most sets consist of sixteen scenes depicted on separate canvases or copper plates" (Katzew 2004: 5). The system, which attempted to preserve the prestige and power of the Spanish and creole elites through sumptuary laws and other controlling devices, was inherently permeable and unstable. Nevertheless, it impacted the lives of the entire population of colonial Mexico, determining social status, occupation, marriage partners, and residence.

The Spanish authorities became obsessed as well with the native dances and clothing and actively sought to alter them in both movement and meaning in order to conform to Spanish notions of proper dancing in a Christian context. In order to create a definitive rupture with African and Native American religions and cultures, they introduced the *morisca*, the dance depicting the battles between the Christians and the Moors (hence, *morisca*) that was "first introduced into New Spain by the conquerors towards the end of the XVI century" (Covarrubias n.d.; Stevenson 1952).

Of course, such preoccupations with race and ethnicity were not just historical, it could be found in the twentieth century as well in Nazi Germany, the American South, and the Republic of South Africa, which provide us with particularly egregious examples of the destructive policies of racial and ethnic obsession, codified on both social and legal levels (see Fredrickson 2002; Rutherford 2017). We turn now to the contours of ethnicity, the constituent elements of ethnicity, a human preoccupation in both historical and contemporary periods.

The Contours of Ethnicity

At this point, I will briefly discuss the ways in which I utilize and describe ethnicity for purposes of this introductory chapter and the way the term is deployed throughout the volume. First, ethnicity is about identity, both individual and group—it is a we/they–us/them consciousness au fond. It is about the human desire for belonging, about inclusion and exclusion, and about descent and history.

Second, ethnicity is dynamic, ongoing, and socially and historically contingent. As much as we and many contemporary Greeks would like to think so, modern Greeks are not the same as ancient Greeks as Lord Byron discovered (Crompton 1985; Hall 1997; Shay 2002, 2008c), modern Arabic-speaking Egyptians are not the same as ancient Egyptians, modern Iraqis are not the same as ancient Mesopotamians, no matter how often individuals and governments of those modern ethnicities attempt to hark back to the perceived glory of their forbearers in order to create powerful emotions of nationalism. As humans link themselves back into history, they romanticize what and who those Egyptians, Romans, and Greeks were: "These tendencies to project modern norms onto past behaviours have been exacerbated by the privileging of the Classical world, and the way in which modern western societies have styled themselves as the successors of Classical civilization" (Revell 2016: 5). How we look at ethnicity often tells us more about the present than the actual past, which classicist Louise Revell notes "has resulted in a mistaken familiarity with Roman culture" (2016: 4).

In fact these modern groups, even though they sometimes bear the same ethnonyms as earlier populations, are in essence different from those historic, in some cases prehistoric, populations in almost every way: religion, language, material culture, and all of the significant ethnic boundary markers that demonstrate perceived ethnic differences between populations. Unlike the Japanese, whose ethnic contours have been shaped through an evolutionary, largely unbroken historical process, other societies have experienced significant, often violent, ruptures with their past, which have resulted in the forging of essentially new ethnic identities, replete with new languages, religions, and new modern, national identities (De Vos and Wagamatsu 1995).

In other words, some ethnic groups are older than others, at least in their consciousness of an ethnic identity that separates them from other ethnic groups. That is not to say that what it means to be Japanese in the twenty-first century is the same as in the past. Rather it is to say that the Japanese have evolved from the past in a more continuous historical line, and some cultural markers, such as dance and theater, constitute an important link to the past that is generations deep.

By contrast, historian Fikret Adanir notes that "only at the turn of the twentieth century did a distinct [Slavic] Macedonian consciousness begin to develop" (1992: 170, see also Borza 1990; Kennedy et al. 2013). Today, following the collapse of the former Yugoslavia, which only after World War II officially recognized a Slavic Macedonian ethnicity, Macedonia constitutes a separate nation-state and a distinct ethnic group with its own distinct language. Since Macedonia has gained an independent existence, the Greek government has sought to impede the Macedonians from using the name Macedonia. They finally agreed on calling Macedonia as North Macedonia under the Prespa Agreement of 2018 (Cowan and Brown 2000; Just 1989: 80–86; Poulton 1995).

Third, ethnicity can have a powerful emotional component, which can appear in times of stress like war or the group is threatened in some way, as we witnessed in the former Yugoslavia when Slobodan Milošević radicalized elements of the population through poisonous ethnic rhetoric (Magaš 1993; Ramet 2006). The degree of emotional feeling toward one's ethnic group varies with the individual and the situation, and individuals like Milošević, Hitler, and Trump can alter that through wild-eyed but slyly planned rhetoric.

Ethnicity almost always contains a historical dimension of genealogical descent; most people conceive of their ethnicity as many generations deep, a shared history and a shared past, even though ethnicity can be permeable and not historically deep.

> Ethnicity is not innate, but individuals are born with it; it is not biologically reproduced, but individuals are linked to it through cultural constructions of

> biology; it is not simply cultural difference, but ethnicity cannot be sustained without reference to an inventory of cultural traits.
>
> (Curta 2001: 15)

Many individuals view ethnicity as biologically determined and believe issues of descent and historical depth constitute a basic reason that most people conceive of ethnicity as a basic element of their identity, even though each new generation has to learn from their grandparents and parents what it means to be a Navajo, a Hawaiian, or a Turk. Thus, ethnicity contains elements of social construction since it is learned, not merely inherited (Epstein 1978). Anthropologist J. A. Nagata pinpoints why so many social scientists prefer the socially constructed view of ethnic identity over the primordial:

> The primordial viewpoint leaves some social scientists academically uneasy, for they feel poorly equipped to handle such loyalties and sentiments, which seem to slip dangerously out of the world of tangible interests and groups into a half-world of emotion and unreason.
>
> (1981: 89)

In discussing the question of descent as an element of ethnicity, anthropologist Richard Tapper notes that among several Iranian tribal groups, "some tribal groups have no shared genealogy ... Yet other groups do not even pretend to common origins" but they nevertheless maintain "an ethnic identity of cultural-political separateness" (1989: 237). Clearly, for each of the many contours that scholars maintain must be present to constitute ethnicity, even such elements as basic as descent and genealogy, often fictional, various researchers find exceptions within the ethnic contours of specific groups. Within these contours of ethnicity, not unlike Barth's ethnic boundaries, such as Hawaiians, dance can figure centrally as an identity marker.

Language

Among the "cultural stuff" that constitutes ethnicity, I would argue that language is one of, if not the most basic element. Linguistics scholar Nicholas Ostler states that language "links its speakers into a tradition that has survived for thousands of years ... to stand on the shoulders of so much ancestral thought and feeling. Our language places us in a cultural continuum, linking us to the past" (2005: xix). This is a concept that nationalists espouse. Language is almost always listed as one of the vital components of ethnic and national identity. This is why so many nations maintain language policies and institutions to maintain "correct usage," to eliminate foreign words, real or imagined, and to create new ones. One need only follow the linguistic gymnastics being performed in the former Yugoslavia in which the former Serbo-Croatian is now Bosnian, Croatian, or Serbian, treated as separate languages.

> Sociolinguists of the future will have much to study in Croatia. Language planners in Croatia have put a great deal of effort into creating a linguistic norm which would crystallize and express the specifically Croatian national-ethnic identity and which would explicitly be something other than Serbo-Croatian (which they perceive as essentially Serbian).
>
> (Alexander 2006: 415)

I should be happy; I now speak three languages instead of one.

We think and act in a specific language. In the construction of ethnic identity "particular weight is often attributed to language ... [A] common and distinct language was the key to the perseverance of the Galatians' self-consciousness as an ethnic group" (Derks and Roymans 2009: 2). I argue that the ease with which contemporary Iranians can read the *Shahnameh* or Khayyam's quatrains (both composed in the eleventh century) gives them a heightened sense of their history and ethnic identity that links them to their historical past, in a way that modern English speakers, struggling to read Chaucer or even Shakespeare, lack. Speaking of Persian,

> Few, if any, other languages have enjoyed a continuous history of two and a half millennia as the primary vehicle for written communication. It is further distinguished from any rivals by its slow rate of change over such a long period and its maintenance of standard vocabulary and syntax over such a vast territory.
>
> (Spooner and Hanaway 2012: x)

Language, through the telling of stories and histories, links us to our past. And, for many, that past constitutes a precious legacy, linking their ethnic present to our ethnic past.

Language has been a basic identity marker throughout history: For the ancient Greeks and Romans, barbarians were defined as those who did not speak civilized languages, that is, Greek and Latin. "Romans loved to juxtapose themselves and their world against that of the barbarians" (Geary 2002: 65). Those slaves and other outsiders became successful only if they adopted and mastered the local language. For example, the singing slave girls of the Baghdad Caliphate were always non-Arab slaves who had to learn perfect Arabic, because music was a vehicle for language, and it offered these slaves the opportunity to escape their servitude (Shay 2014). "But the use of a language as a marker of ethnic identity is a property of all human groups recorded in ethnography and in our modern world"

(Bellwood 2013: 87). Personally, as a scholar and an artist, I discovered early that the knowledge of a language was the key to people embracing an ethnic identity and wanting to share their culture, the crucial distance between "in" and "out."

NOTES

1. The term "ethnicity" first appeared in the 1950s in the English language. It is first recorded in the *Oxford English Dictionary* of 1953 and one of the earliest compilations of articles under that heading states: "Ethnicity seems to be a new term" (Glazer and Moynihan 1975: 1; Hutchinson and Smith 1994: 4). Thus, by the time I had encountered the term, I had received my BA and three MA degrees, but, more importantly, I had been encountering the phenomenon of ethnicity for over two decades in my folk dance research.
2. For example, Eriksen cites anthropologist Michael Moerman's work among the Lue of Thailand:

   > They lived in close interaction with other groups in the area: they had no exclusive livelihood, no exclusive language, no exclusive customs, no exclusive religion ... Moerman was forced to conclude that "someone is Lue by virtue of believing and calling himself Lue and of acting in ways that validate his Lueness."
   >
   > (2002: 12)

3. Anthropologist Michael E. Smith notes that after waves of Old World diseases swept through the Aztec Empire by 1580, only 200,000 natives remained in the Valley of Mexico, a reduction of 88 percent of the population of 1519, when the Spaniards first arrived (Smith 1996: 287).

2

Dance and Nationalism: The Nation, the State, and the Nation-State

After authoritarianism, ethnicity, and dance, nationalism is the fourth and last topic I wish to address in some depth in this study because of its relation to authoritarianism. "I argue not only that nationalism, in all its diverse forms, is a dominant ideological narrative of the modern age, but also that to understand it fully one needs to analyse it as a dominant *operative* ideology of our times" (Malešević 2006: 6). All states, and almost all regimes, utilize strong feelings of nationalism when they are able because they need to know that, in case of national crises, such as war and invasion, they can depend on the positive emotions of the population toward the nation and the regime. Most authoritarian regimes, even more than democratic ones, rely on the emotions of patriotism and nationalism to save the state, if not the regime. Folk and other traditional dance genres often play a major role in instilling ethnic and national pride in the population.

In addition, as I noted earlier, nationalism often overlaps with ethnicity, and I will discuss this overlap in the following discussion. I will also demonstrate how, in modern states, the use of folk dance, with its ethnic references, serves as an important tool to instill feelings of both ethnic and nationalist pride.

As an example, Josef Stalin realized that the Russian population of the then Soviet Union would not lay down their lives for the communist regime and his dictatorship, but they would fight to the death for Mother Russia. He turned to Russian folklore and history, which the Soviet regime until that time had suppressed, as a vehicle to instill feelings of Russian nationalism; in order to achieve his aim, he had Igor Moiseyev create the State Academic Ensemble of Folk Dances of the Peoples of the U.S.S.R. (known in the West as the Igor Moiseyev Dance Company) and gave support to the Pyatnitsky Folk Chorus, performers of Russian folk songs. They were both so successful, and continue to be, that they also toured throughout the nation to bring inspiration and pride to the Russian-dominated Soviet military. I personally viewed a performance June 1, 2017, in Moscow and experienced the overwhelming enthusiasm of the Russian audience for the Moiseyev concert (Shay 2019b). The Croatian state folk ensemble, which I have viewed dozens of times over five decades, evokes similar enthusiasm among the Croatian public and its diaspora (Shay 2016c).

I would characterize nationalism as an inclusive discourse about group and individual identity and the nation-state and the individual's role within the nation. In creating citizens who believe in the special identity of the nation-state and loyally serve it, respective governments inculcate the citizens of their particular specific nation-state through various agencies—educational, military, artistic, and political—with strong, and patriotic, feelings about their nation. Nationalism scholar Elie Kedourie cautions,

> It may serve to distinguish nationalism from patriotism and xenophobia with which it is often confused. Patriotism, affection for one's country, or one's group, loyalty to its institutions, and zeal for its defense, is a sentiment known among all kinds of men; so is xenophobia.
>
> (1994: 49–50)

Nationalism, therefore, involves the feelings that an individual has for the nation-state in which one lives, although, I will caution, not everyone in a nation-state feels the same about it, and some individuals or groups, such as ethnic minorities, who live in a particular nation-state, may have negative feelings toward their nation. So, then, what is the nation-state?

Michael Billig, in his thought-provoking book, *Banal Nationalism*, states,

> All societies that maintain armies maintain the belief that some things are more valuable than life itself ... William of Normandy, speaking before the Battle of Hastings, exhorted his troops to avenge the spilling of "noble blood." To fight such matters appears "barbaric," or worse still, "mediaeval."
>
> (1995: 1)

Today, of course, we fight, with ever-escalating spilling of blood, with more lethal means for the nation, "whether to achieve national independence, or to defend the national territory from encroachment, or to protect the very principle of nationhood" (Billig 1995: 1). According to the authorities of many nation-states, that is the only entity worth dying for. Not everyone agrees.

Following nationalism scholar John Coakley's definition, "A state is a self-governing territorial entity with a central decision-making agency which possesses a monopoly of the legitimate use of force in ensuring compliance with its decision on the part of all persons within its borders" (2012: 11), I adopt Coakley's definition of state, which is simple, readily grasped, and will inform my arguments. It has the advantage of defining both historical and modern states. There is something "official" about a nation-state and, depending on the economy, there will be governmental buildings and employees, an official military in official uniforms, a flag, an anthem, currency, an educational system, a national theater, a national dance ensemble, and so on.

I use the terms "nation," "state," and "nation-state" as synonyms for purposes of this study; even though nation certainly refers to the people as "the French nation," many use nation in the popular usage as a territorial unit as I will do from time to time. Many consider the formation of nation-states to be inevitable and "natural." But we must not accept the commonly held myth. "Nations are not inscribed into the nature of things; they do not constitute a political version of the doctrine of natural kinds. Nor were national states the manifest ultimate destiny of ethnic or cultural groups" (Gellner 1983: 49). In fact, to a large degree, as Ernest Gellner suggests, nations and states, both historical and modern, are socially constructed entities, often supported by mythical origins and fictive genealogies promoted in order to build powerful feelings of patriotism and solidarity, in order to enable the nation-state to coalesce and survive.

Of the terms "nationalism" and "ethnicity," I will argue that nationalism, despite its complexities, is the easier of the two to characterize, describe, and analyze because it is official. In this study I will also argue that there are many kinds of nationalism and that, in addition to the modern nationalisms that scholars Ernest Gellner, Benedict Anderson, and Liah Greenfeld espouse, there also exist ancient and medieval nationalisms that not only share many elements of modern nationalism but also differ in intensity and degree of public participation, but otherwise have a great deal in common (see Plokhy 2006: 3 n.2).

As to modern national identity, nationalism scholar Liah Greenfeld, in her brilliant study (2016), has correctly stated, "Nationalism underlies all areas of modern reality" (2016: 4). From the passports we carry, the flags we salute, the anthems that make us rise and sing in a specific national language, to national armies wearing specific national uniforms with national colors in specific military environments, national flags flying from governmental buildings at home and abroad, and national language(s) at ports of entry and in government buildings like post offices, one can quickly understand the ubiquity of national identity in individual contemporary lives and its spread around the globe since modern times began after the French Revolution. In this chapter I will also posit that, in certain cases such as Iran and China, nationalism and the concept of national identity have ancient roots, depending on how one defines "nation." In this premodern conception, I join scholars Anthony Smith (1986) and John A. Armstrong (1982), who propose premodern roots for certain nations.

However, I want to warn readers that the creators of modern nationalisms frequently built the basis of a specific national identity on questionable and romantic historical and philological data: "From the nineteenth century on, nationalism sought its justification to no little extent in a misconceived view of the peoples of the early Middle Ages" (Pohl 2018: 3). For example, a question that still remains unresolved is whether or not the Eastern Slavs are three peoples—Belarusians, Ukrainians, and Russians—or one people who speak dialects of a single language. "The most politically loaded question is whether the East Slavic languages developed directly from a Slavic proto-language or whether there was an intermediate stage in the form of a common East Slavic language" (Plokhy 2006: 24).

The answer to that question hinges on whether the contemporary states of Belarus and Ukraine, or parts of them, rightfully belong to Russia or not.

Such questionable origin myths of nation continue to attract interest:

> In many eastern European nations, ancient and medieval origin stories were used to elaborate modern national myths; results of scholarship were incorporated into these myths in eclectic ways. Few European countries, though, developed such a variety of national origin myths as Croatia: migration or autochthony; prehistoric, ancient, or early medieval immigrations; Illyrian, Gothic, Iranian, or Slavic origins. Predictably, the creation of an independent Croat state and the war in Yugoslavia led to a resurgence of pseudo-scientific narratives of national origin.
>
> (Pohl 2018: 311)

And, from personal experience, I have met Croats who vehemently subscribe to all of these origins.

Certain nations seem to be fragile due to competing local or regional allegiances. I would therefore observe that there exist many states where national, regional, and local identities vie with one another for an individual's attention and affection, as in the Philippines and India. The former Soviet Union, Yugoslavia, and Czechoslovakia fell apart due to competing regional ethnic identities: the national identities lost, regional and ethnic identities won. Catalonia, Scotland, Flanders, Quebec, and other regional, ethnic-focused identities often make the news due to the fact that they want a divorce from the national entity in which they are located. Thus, nationalism, in all of its complexity, becomes a form of both individual and communal expression, but national identity, as I have just shown, can readily reduce to ethnic identities: The latter trumps the former in almost every instance. Folk ensembles like Lado adjusted their repertoires to meet the new realities in which they existed (Shay 2016c).

Various national states, of different complexities of political organization, especially those of authoritarian hue, look for tools and vehicles with which to create strong passions of patriotism and nationalism in the service of the state, and the symbolic support of folk dance performances and vernacular dance activities resulted in the creation of state-supported folk dance ensembles and systems of festivals that lend themselves to evoking strong feelings of nationalism because the performers in colorful folk costumes evoke iconic images of national identity. Nationalism scholar Gellner states, "The self-image of nationalism involves the stress of folk, folklore, popular culture, etc. In fact, nationalism becomes important precisely when these things become artificial. Genuine peasants or tribesmen, however proficient at folk-dancing, do not generally make great nationalists" (1994: 58). That is because, I argue, the dancing peasants do not represent the entire nation, but rather a local and regional portion of the nation. They often dance to represent local and regional pride; the government tends to use them as stand-ins for the total nation-state; their usefulness to the nation is as one of the colors in the ethnic rainbow that constitutes the nation and as a mass with all of the other regional folk dancers.

Each human being has a unique identity consisting of bundles of elements: gender and sexuality, marital status, age, religion, political belief, profession, ethnicity and nationality, language, among others. Identity is largely socially and contextually created, that is, each individual is born into a specific family, in a specific city or village, and into a specific neighborhood speaking a specific language or, as in my case, two languages; he or she has or does not have a specific religion and other cultural traits. They may be members of occupations that only certain ethnic groups occupy, even in premodern times. A good example is the Japanese *Eta* (*Burakumin*) that George A. De Vos and Hiroshi Wagatsuma describe and analyze and who have always served as a despised separate ethnic group, an outcast group that worked historically for centuries, and still today, with leather, as butchers and handlers of the dead, even though they are not physically distinguishable from the majority Japanese population (1995). In the De Vos and Wagatsuma analysis, the *Eta* bear many of the same social burdens as African Americans.

Why are such concepts as ethnicity and nationalism exclusively modern or premodern? "And yet, if one accepts modernist theorist Ernest Gellner's definition of the nation as a rough congruence between culture or ethnicity and state, then nations are not confined to modern times" (Gat 2013: 2). In this study, I will argue that nation creation and accompanying nationalist sentiments occur both in the modern period and in antiquity. To support my argument I turn to several scholars who look at the premodern roots of nationalist emotions. Archeologist Barry Cunliffe notes, "So it was that Rome was drawn on to conquer the disparate tribes and towns of Italy and bind the conquered, through rights of citizenship, into a nation state" (2008: 363). Even though Rome did not have the technical wherewithal to withstand the environmental overreach it practiced, it lasted nearly a millennium and, like the United States (which has not yet lasted three hundred years), facing its own disastrous environmental issues, the Roman Empire used Roman citizenship as a lure to bind its population to develop a national identity.

> Italy was now identical with the roman State, which after a period of cultural and social fusion provided the closest parallel found in antiquity to a large national state in the modern sense, with a universal language and a single system of local government and civil law.
>
> (Gat 2013: 120–21)

As in modern times, each premodern political entity has specific characteristics. Nevertheless, they can be usefully grouped for conceptual purposes.

Historically, many, if not most, people did not live in nation-states: Humans lived in hunting and gathering groups, small subsistence agricultural communities, tribes, villages, religious states and communities, city states, kingdoms, chiefdoms, empires, and all of the other settlement patterns that anthropologists have spilled much ink over attempting to describe and analyze. Perhaps that is why so many scholars of nationalism conceive of it as a modern phenomenon. But Azar Gat notes,

> Historical sociologists of the modernist persuasion hold that premodern empires were elite power structures, wherein the ruling elite were indifferent to the ethnic composition of its subjects. Yet this widely held view is highly simplistic, for very few historical empires, if any, were so construed or were ethnically blind.
>
> (2013: 5)

Rome serves as a good example of opening Roman identity to others.

> Rome had no policy of acculturation. Still, Roman acculturation throughout Italy had been steadily advancing, through Roman and Latin settlement, elite connections, military service, and the increasing attraction of belonging to the Roman state. And if ethnic differences in Italy were still noticeable at the beginning of the first century BC, they had practically disappeared by the end of that century.
>
> (Gat 2013: 120)

So great was the desire for Roman citizenship and identity that, even as Rome declined and was in increasing peril of barbarian invasion, "the fearful provincials clung to their Roman identity with greater fervor" (ibid.).

Nationalism scholar Greenfeld makes claims for nationalism as a modern phenomenon: "Nationalism underlies all areas of modern reality" (2016: 4). I will make more nuanced claims about the phenomena of nationalisms. First, I suggest that nationalisms, in the plural form, constitute a more suitable term because the nationalisms that exist in Armenia, Mexico, North Korea, Serbia, France, and the United States vary, often dramatically. I argue that, from experience living in other nations, nationalism expressed in Norway, Iran, and Croatia is significantly different from what I have experienced in the United States. For example, people who live in small nations, who have hostile neighbors that have historically threatened them, feel significantly different about their allegiance to their nation-state, often experiencing stronger feelings of nationalism about their nation-state than people in many Western European or North American nations. Certain smaller nations, like Greece and Serbia, have what Alkis Raftis, president of the Dora Stratou Greek Dances Theatre, characterizes as a "fortress identity" where the people feel threatened by outside forces that would potentially destroy national and ethnic identity (personal interview, February 16, 2000).

I will also argue that these modern nationalisms differ from premodern ones, and yet they hold much in common as the Roman example above illustrates. One reason that many scholars who think of nationalism as a modern phenomenon exclude it as an historical phenomenon, and eliminate the possibility of the nation as an historical entity, is because they claim that premodern political entities had only an elite population, with everyone else excluded, rather than large-scale participation in the decision-making process and, therefore, participation in "national" life did not exist (see Plokhy 2006). However, as seen in the Roman and other examples, by "212, the entire free population of the Empire was given citizenship" (Gat 2013: 120). Emperors now came from every former barbarian ethnicity. While I cede the point that mass participation through elections and mass communication, as we know it today, did not exist with universal suffrage or mass political movements, nevertheless, large segments of the population, mostly free males, did participate in Roman public life and eagerly embraced their new identity. If not a form of modern nationalism, Roman identity strongly resembled it in many ways.

Identities

Frequently, as individuals we regard the elements of our unique identity as "natural," that is to say, we regard our sexuality, our religion, our ethnicity, and other aspects of our identity as unchanging, and even as unchangeable. We feel that the elements of our identity are "natural" and inevitable. However, as individuals, we can change virtually every aspect of the elements that make up the bundles of identity markers, even though it might be difficult or unpalatable. Some elements are more easily changed than others: It is perhaps easier to change or evolve into a new profession or adopt a new political position than change to a new religion or adopt a new language or sexual status, and yet premodern individuals did. In this study, I consider national identity and national sentiment, especially in the context of nationalism, an emotion that is often deliberately created by political actors, often associated with national governments, as socially constructed and historically contingent.

In my conceptualization of identity, each individual experiences each part of his or her identity differently: For some individuals their religion is their most important identity marker, whereas for others it is their sexuality, parental status, identity as a businessperson, or specific ethnic group. In other words, identities can be experienced as fluid. Each of these elements can surface at different times depending on context: one's country is attacked, one's religion is threatened, or one's sexuality is persecuted. We are all capable of wearing multiple masks depending on the context. These situations and contexts can trigger strong feelings within an individual, making him or her feel powerful identity emotions (Figure 4).

FIGURE 4: Avaz International Dance Theatre performs a ruchanitsa from Thrace, Bulgaria. Choreography: Anthony Shay. Photo: D. Young. From the author's collection.

First, I conceive ethnicity and nationalism in the plural: ethnicities and nationalisms because they are not a singular experience, but multiple experiences in different societies and eras, and individuals experience them differently. I experience American identity differently than friends that I know who are Iranian, Armenian, Mexican, Croatian, or Greek feel and experience feelings of their specific nationalisms.

I suggest that ethnicity and nationalism were experienced historically and those identities, too, were experienced differently than modern ones. I will argue that ancient Rome, as I briefly described above, ancient China, ancient Iran, and ancient Japan also had many of the trappings of a modern state. Most scholars agree that nationalism is a modern phenomenon appearing at different times, a point from which I will depart. Many, following Ernest Gellner, begin the history of nationalism with the French Revolution. Liah Greenfeld compellingly demonstrates that English nationalism began with the decimation of the English aristocracy during the Wars of the Roses and the foundation of the Tudor dynasty (2016).

However, these are European examples, and I argue that too many of the examples that the modernist school of nationalism scholars use are European examples and that, to the detriment of their arguments, they have adopted a Eurocentric point of view, ignoring the existence of nations in the past that were located outside of Europe. They argue that nationalism originated in modern Europe, ignoring ancient Rome. They posit modern origins and majority population involvement in the nation-state with "true" nationalism. "Still, the national state was also quite prevalent during premodern times and outside Europe. Nations and national states can be found wherever states emerged since the beginning of history" (Gat 2013: 4).

I posit that historic national and ethnic identity differ in intensity and degrees of participation from modern forms of national and ethnic identity, but they contain the same essential elements to classify them as states and nationalistic sentiments. Populations from palace to peasant participated in these historic states and societies in various ways, and historical states, such as China, attempted to include the male freeborn population of all social strata into various levels of national and state participation.

> In reality, empires were indeed elite power structures, yet, at the same time, nearly all of them were grounded in and relied upon a dominant ethnic nucleus. Thus, ethnicity has always been highly significant in determining identity, solidarity, and political organization within and between states.
>
> (Gat 2013: 5)

Ancient Rome makes a good example through the manner in which it continuously widened the meaning of what it was to be Roman through the way in which it constantly extended Roman citizenship to ever-increasing populations.

As Roman power spread, becoming a Roman citizen became a highly desired status embraced by large numbers of individuals, throughout their unquestionably multiethnic empire. "Rome was the most successful city-state ever, owing primarily to its ability to transcend the inherent size limitations of the city-state and dramatically expand its citizen body" (Gat 2013: 75).

In opposition to Greenfeld, in this study I will explore the notion that ethnicity, in fact, began at least in the period in which empires and other premodern political entities came into existence, if not before, and that "us and them" identities dominated these empires. Writers of those periods provide the reader with vivid descriptions of ethnic groups, listed as "barbarians": those who did not speak Greek or Latin. However, individuals and groups who fell under Roman sway increasingly opted to speak Latin in place of their original language. "In the western Empire Latin came into conflict with a number of vernacular languages and eventually effected their death" (Adams 2003: xix).

As they expanded their influence throughout the known world, Romans, too, under the perceived threat of looming Hellenistic influence, attempted to define their own national Roman identity. In order

> to promote the collective ascendancy of the Roman ruling class, government encouragement of early Latin poetry as celebratory of national values, the plays of Plautus as a vehicle for conveying Roman attitudes toward Hellenism, and the simultaneous repression of Greek professors and cultivation of their subjects in the training of the young.
>
> (Gruen 1992: 2)

As we can see, the Roman government "promoting" symbols of Roman identity behaved in much the same way as twentieth- and twenty-first-century governments using propaganda.

A major point that I would like to make is that, while participation in democratic states is theoretically universal, the participation of the general population in authoritarian states like Franco's Spain, Hitler's Germany, and Stalin's Soviet Union were not that different from Rome because they lived in authoritarian dictatorships and had no say in decision-making.

Unlike the period of ancient Rome, almost everyone, even reluctant minority groups, in the contemporary world "belongs" to a nation-state, like a subject in some cases, or identifies with one or another nation-state as a citizen, and the resultant citizenship informs their sense of identity. So internalized is this concept of the nation-state to most individuals that most people live it as a fact of nature, thinking that every person in the world should belong to a nation. Thus, individuals have a national identity above or behind every other aspect of their identity.

This concept, as Roland Barthes suggested in *Mythologies*, is one of those things that everyone "knows" and no one questions, as if it were the "natural" order of social arrangements rather than an order that is socially constructed and historically contingent. The received idea is that everyone should belong to a nation, and love it, and be ready to sacrifice, and even die for it, which is an important aspect of nationalism. Such powerful feelings are so deeply embedded in many contemporary men and women that when a nation-state, like Belgium, fails or has the potential to devolve into its constituent parts, in this case Flanders and Wallonia (see Erdbrink 2016), or when Scotland, Catalonia, or Quebec wish to become an independent state through open elections to separate from Great Britain, Spain, and Canada, respectively, pundits and politicians raise a hue and cry about the imminent end of the world—that financial, political, and social chaos and collapse are around the corner, and there exist many individuals who agree with them. National identities are created identities, not a "natural" part of one's existence. This, however, does not mean that they are not real identities.

It is precisely because several scholars, if not a majority of them, attempt to create the notion that ethnicity and nationalism are, in fact, only modern phenomena that I address these issues in this study. I believe that ethnicity and nationalism occur in both ancient and modern societies, albeit with different intensities and technologies of communication, but with similar characteristics.

With the help of Azar Gat, I think it would be instructive to turn to the case of historical China, which I argue had many characteristics of a modern state. "China is one of the world's oldest civilizations and states, singular in having survived and exhibited a virtually unbroken cultural and political continuum since its inception" (Gat 2013: 93). Gat adds,

> Thus, the question of whether or not premodern China ought to be regarded as a national state should have been central to the controversy concerning the nation. And yet this question has been given only minimal attention on the very margins of a European-centric debate.
>
> (Ibid.)

Gat notes,

> Literary culture, mass education, and universal military service are famously regarded as the tools that forged modern national identity. Yet all of them were largely present before modernity in that fifth of humanity that China has always comprised. Since the time of the Tang Dynasty (618–907), China was uniquely ruled by a body of literate Confucian bureaucrats, the mandarins, a meritocracy selected through highly competitive examinations held in all the provinces and

> open to candidates of every class. To prepare people for the examinations, the imperial authorities established schools in the towns and villages ... Moreover, the imperial authorities stipulated that decrees of national significance would be read aloud in public gatherings held in every village.
>
> (Gat 2013: 95)

In addition, the Chinese government also maintained a standing army that all Chinese men (plus perhaps Mulan) were required to join. The military, in China and Rome, as in modern states, is a notorious environment for instilling powerful feelings of nationalism. Thus, not only did China have many of the requisites of a modern state, it probably surpassed those elements more efficiently than modern states like Afghanistan. Like the case of Rome, "Over time, the conquerors were irresistibly allured by and assimilated into Chinese culture" (Gat 2013: 98).

So, in this study I will argue that we can conceptualize both modern and premodern forms of ethnicity and nationalism, and that many of these states, both old and new, involved dance, patterned movement, and mass displays of movement in their political agendas.

> While fully acknowledging the tremendous growth of modern nationalism in response to the massive forces of transformation generated by modernity, I am closer to the view of those who criticize and reject the exclusive identification of the nation with modernity.
>
> (Gat 2013: 2)

I posit in this study that, as Gat notes above, one can notice perhaps an intensification and more general participation of the general population in the processes and manifestations of nationalism and ethnicity within a state, historical or modern. Nevertheless, ethnicity, in some form or other, has probably existed as an element in early individual and group human identity since prehistory, while nationalism has existed since the establishment of early states and, contra Greenfeld, even earlier than nationalism, not later. Gat notes, "Historical states are commonly classified into the following categories: petty-states, states, and empires. And in *all* of them ethnicity was a major factor" (2013: 3, emphasis in the original).

I claim in this study that since the inception of empires in the ancient world, if not earlier, ethnic and cultural identities constituted a major form of personal and group identity, named groups of peoples who must have had certain distinctive characteristics appear in some of the earliest writings of Mesopotamia, and the subject peoples of the Persian Empire are illustrated on the Apadana, the formal staircase of the Achaemenid palace at Persepolis, in remarkable ethnographic detail in their specific clothing. As we will see, by the Greek period, the known world was divided into a checkerboard of ethnic territories (See the maps in Cunliffe 2008). I will also argue that those identities were, as in modern circumstances, ethnic identities, historically and territorially contingent, and many writers such as Herodotus and Thucydides wrote extensively about those peoples and their ethnic characteristics in a proto anthropological style. And, yet, as we have seen, individuals also were able, despite their ethnicity, to become citizens in larger political, perhaps we might even say national, enterprises like Rome.

The widespread practices of slavery and warfare, among other behaviors, resulted in the creation, that is, the ethnogenesis, and disappearance of ethnic identities, as millions of individuals were torn from their original environments, and in order to survive they had to absorb and adopt new identities and languages.

> The ancient historical sources provide a wealth of detail that focuses on men and their motives as theatres of conflict around the Mediterranean. Armies and navies of increasing size confront each other, death tolls mount to massive proportions, cities are destroyed and landscapes devastated as the desire to dominate the land and resources of others outstrips the simple need to protect home and family.
> (Cunliffe 2008: 318–19)

As the Roman Empire expanded, so, too, did the numbers of peoples driven to new lands, killed, or captured and taken into slavery. Thus, archaeological finds of bodies wearing distinctively Greek or Roman garments may not have been originally Greek or Roman individuals but, through various circumstances, adopted a new identity through long years of living in a new environment as former slaves.

In this study, I also focus on the ways that Iranian history, as a non-European example, demonstrates that an Iranian or Persian identity existed both historically and in the present and, while the modern and premodern identities are not the same, they contain many, if not most, elements in common. I will also cite other instances such as China and Japan to illustrate and underscore these points, as these early empires have much in common.

Before Nationalism: The Case of Iranian Ethnic/National Identity

Upon entering Los Angeles City College in the fall of 1954, I encountered many Iranian students in my classes, and I began learning the Persian language and experienced an immersion into Iranian life, which changed my life and allowed me to enter a world I never knew existed. Among the first things that I learned from my Iranian classmates was that Iranians loved poetry to a degree that was different from anything that I had ever experienced in the English-speaking world;

poetry was quoted at appropriate moments, especially to advance the argument of the speaker. The second thing I learned was that, in contrast to my own existence, Iranians had a deep sense of their history and the antiquity, millennia deep, of their national/ethnic origins (*hoviyyat-e irani*), whereas mine did not stretch back two hundred years. Third, they emphasized that they were not Arabs; Iranians were different in every way. Iranian studies scholar Hamid Dabashi condemns this attitude as " 'Persian racism' against systematically ethnicized minorities. Persian racism against Arabs is echoed in Arab racism against Persians—a prolonged bourgeois binary that has dialectically sustained itself for generations within colonized minds mimicking European ethnic nationalism" (2016: 18). These attitudes were very much in evidence among Iranian students I knew, as it is in today's news in the invectives hurled across the Persian Gulf between Iran and Saudi Arabia.

The Shahnameh[1]

Almost from the beginning, I understood that the Persian language and the *Shahnameh*, the epic history of Iran in verse, constituted touchstones of Iranian identity, and I wondered at the degree that they venerated Persian and the *Shah-nameh*.[2] Perhaps better than any other scholar, Dabashi has articulated its meaning in Persianate culture and beyond:

> The *Shahnameh* is the surviving relic of many beautiful and exquisite tales informing bygone and forgotten empires. It is forever loved, beautifully written, ceremoniously read, happily recited, and then, generation after generation, memorized, performed, painted, praised, critically edited, and even revered by Iranian and other Persian-speaking people around the globe. People name their children after its heroes ... The original text of the epic is carefully researched, judiciously documented, impeccably preserved—every single word of it lovingly cherished, meticulously honored, thoroughly documented.
>
> (Dabashi 2019: x)

In short, the *Shahnameh* occupies a nearly sacred position within Iranian society and Persianate culture, beyond Shakespeare or any other author in the English-speaking world. It is through the *Shahnameh*, and its recitation in teahouses, palaces, marketplaces, and village squares to enthralled audiences (all male) for centuries, that non-elite Iranians imbibed in deep-seated feelings of Iranian identity.

During the composition of the *Shah-nameh*, Abol Qāsem Ferdowsi (c. 940-1020-25), the poet who set down, like Homer, to whom he is often compared, a multitude of a mix of mythological and historical tales that had circulated for centuries in ancient pre-Islamic Iran during storytelling events by bards known as *gosan* and *mobad*, understood the connection:

> *Basi ranj bordam dar in sāl-e si 'ajam zendeh kardam bedin parsi*
> (Thirty years have I labored [on the *Shah-nameh*]
> I revived ancient Iran with this Persian [language])
> (See Shahbazi 1991: 123, 124)

Three centuries before the appearance of Ferdowsi's *Shah-nameh*, the mighty Sasanian Empire fell before the Arab forces in 642 CE. The Arab victory was completely unexpected on both sides and dizzying in its rapidity. Sasanian Iran was in tatters and fell into chaos.

> The defeat of the Iranians by the Arabs in the course of the conquest has left a scar on the national Iranian historical memory. This was articulated in no uncertain terms by Ferdowsi more than a millennium ago, and has been part and parcel of the Iranian nationalist discourse to this day.
> (Pourshariati 2017: 464)[3]

The Muslims, the direct inheritors of the antique classical world, also inherited new or altered ethnic identities as a major form of individual and group identity. My classmates maintained a kind of imperfect knowledge of those empires, but they basked in their glory, and stressed their tolerance as opposed to Arab intolerance, as they perceived it.

> The empire was famously tolerant toward local ethnicities, customs, and cultures. And yet it was anything but ethnically blind. The formation of a Persian-Iranian national state, with its incipient cultural and linguistic core and national religion (Zoroastrianism), was superseded by imperial expansion. But it was hardly in question whose empire it was. There was clear hierarchy here: the Medes came very close to the Persians as co-partners in the empire, and other Iranian peoples constituted the next circle, quite distinct from the rest. This was not an abstract matter. Not only the royal house, but also the top provincial governors (*satraps*), generals, and other high-ranking officials were Persian-Mede and, second, Iranian … Darius I also reinforced the centrality of Persian identity as its official culture.
> (Gat 2013: 115)

Clearly, Iranians had a good idea of who they were, even if such evidence of ethnic consciousness does not align with contemporary ethnic identity. Iranian history scholar Neguin Yavari notes that following the Islamic conquest, "Iranians by and large shed their old customs and converted to Islam before the end of the tenth century, although myriad vestiges of Iranian culture and thought worked their way into the mosaic of Islamic civilization" (2014: 227).

Many contemporary Iranians attempt to read an anti-Islamic, anti-Arab nationalist attitude into the Ferdowsi past and his purported nationalist sentiments. Yavari notes that the sources of the period,

> do not suggest a political worldview imbued with nationalist or ethnic opposition to foreign rule. In any case the modern concept of nationalist aspirations cannot be applied to the study of group identity, communal bonds, and ethnic fraternity in premodern societies.
>
> (2012: 229)

She concludes, "The idea that Muslim or even Arab rule sought to suppress and obliterate the Iranian cultural or other legacy needs to be put to rest" (2012: 232). In other words, we cannot posit modern nationalistic thought of today, and many modern Iranians often express the idea that Arabs attempted to suppress Iranian identity and impose current attitudes on the past. Yavari's position is underscored by historian Mohamad Tavakoli-Targhi's findings in which he describes and analyzes the construction of modern Iranian nationalism. He found

> a secular national identity in the nineteenth century. Informed by *dasatiri* texts, many nineteenth-century historians represented the pre-Islamic past as a "golden age," which come to a 'tragic end' with the Muslim conquest... This invented past was used to project Iran's "decadence" onto Arabs and Islam and to introject desirable attributes of Europeans to the pre-Islamic Iranian Self.
>
> (2001: xiv)

Thus, we can see, as Yavari's and Tavakoli-Targhi's studies indicate, that what constitutes Iranian identity changes through time, and they correctly identified the same attitudes that I encountered in the 1950s among many, if not most, of the Iranians whom I knew.

The Shu'ubiyyah

In the beginning, the Arabs regarded Islam as an Arab religion, to the exclusion of all others, and non-Arab outsiders, branded as *mawali* (clients) who wished to become Muslim, for a long period, had to attach themselves to one or another of the Arab tribes to gain admittance to Islam. "Indeed from the 2nd/8th century onwards, the principal cultural language of Iran was Arabic and it had been openly adopted as such by the Islamicized Iranian aristocracy" (Lazard 1975: 603). Iranians and others had become second-class citizens.

This exclusive access to Islam bred great resentment among the non-Arabs who still retained memories of a glorious pre-Islamic empire, especially the Iranians. While whole populations such as Nabateans and Egyptians, through the adoption of Islam and the Arabic language, ultimately became Arabs, Iranians fiercely clung to their pre-Islamic identities, and they especially resented this second-class identity forced on them by the Arabs, whom they regarded as cultural inferiors. This new status resulted in a literary ethnic pissing contest, the *shu'ubbiyah,* in which Arabs and Persians traded literary barbs to establish their ethnic superiority over one another.

> The controversy of the *Shu'ubiyya* provides a striking demonstration of the extent to which the Iranians were aware of their own ethnic affiliations, when they came up against the Arabs. This "national" consciousness did not, however, manifest itself in the sphere of language ... *The arguments of the Shu'ubites were all conducted in Arabic.*
>
> (Lazard 1975: 603, emphases added)

It is little wonder then that individuals like Ferdowsi, who despite the fact that he was a Muslim, nevertheless, felt that his primary identity, that of an Iranian, was under threat and set out on his life's work: the creation of the *Shah-nameh*. And, over the 60 years that I have interacted with the Iranian community, both here and in Iran, one of the most important aspects of Iranian identity is that it is often held in tension with an Islamic identity.

Let me caution the reader, however, that, as we will see, such identity politics should not be equated to modern Iranian or Arab nationalism (see Browne 1902: 578; Busse 1975: 309), even though some modern writers make it appear in that light, and yet it indicates a consciousness of ethnic identity. In fact, historian Parvaneh Pourshariati suggests, in her words "heretically," that the last pre-Islamic Sasanian dynasty was riven along ethnic fault lines. The Sasanians, an ethnically Persian dynasty, in order to succeed politically, was forced to enter into a reluctant partnership with the great families of the former dynasty, the Parthian Arsacids. She claims that the Parthian families retained their old religion (*Mehr*) Mithraism, their Parthian language, and through these two major boundary markers, their Parthian ethnic identity, and when the confederacy collapsed, so too did the Sasanian dynasty[4] (2017: 453–63). As another example, Bertold Spuler writes: "Men of letters would deliberately emphasize their Persian ancestry and often defend Zoroastrianism, as well as Manichaeism, from more of a nationalistic conviction than a religious one. This development led ultimately to the Shu'ubiya, a specifically Persian national movement" (2015: 221).

I find Spuler's observation anachronistic in that while many Iranians, especially the elite men of letters (*adab*), had a sense of Iranian identity, I would not call it "nationalism," a far more modern, late nineteenth- or early-twentieth-century development, but perhaps something like it, a sense of Iranian identity. Nevertheless, the *shu'ubbiyah* became a sign of ethnic identity and indicates that the participants in it had a sense of ethnic identity, that is, being an Iranian, not an Arab. One indignant Arab writer of that period, Al-Jāhiz, characterized the Iranians as those "who swagger round and exalt the wisdom of the Sasanid emperors and Buzurgmihr, and the *adab* of Ibn al-Muqaffa' over that of the Prophet and caliphs, and even over that of the Qur'ān," all but claimed apostasy, which like the case of al-Muqaffa' could result in torture and a brutal execution, to indicate how heated the scene became between the ethnic groups (quoted in Yar-Shater 1998: 7 n.7). Hamid Dabashi notes: "The resistance to Arab domination and dynastic feudalism was relentless, uncompromising, multifaceted. The crowning achievement of this moral uprising against political defeat was the Persian language and Persian literary humanism" (2012: 50).

All of this intricate political and cultural posturing, which was taken very seriously during the eighth and ninth centuries by its participants, I describe to indicate that medieval identities had ethnic coloring, even if they do not fit into modern concepts of ethnic and national identities. "Nor should we minimize, much less ignore, the anti-Arab and pro-*mawāli* sentiments that crystallized in *Shu'ubiyya* rhetoric and gave expression to non-Arab Muslims' resentment at the Arab discrimination against them" (Yar-Shater 1998: 68). In an overwhelmingly social and religious environment, these expressions were perhaps proto-nationalistic or *ethnic*. While many Iranians today seem unaware of the *Shu'ubiyya* conflict, the *Shahnameh* occupies a central place in their lives. The *Shah-nameh* is truly an epic in verse.

> It is 50,000 lines long, and they are very long lines at that, each approximately equivalent in length to two lines of standard English iambic pentameter verse; compare this with, e.g., the 15,000 lines of hexameter verse of the *Iliad*.
>
> (Davis 2006: xv)

In fact, the *Shah-nameh* is longer than the *Iliad* and the *Odyssey* together (Davidson 1994: ix). Mirza Mohammad Ali Forughi, one of the leading scholars of Persian literature, as well as serving as prime minister, recognized its value: "Firdausī's [sic] *Shāh-nāma*, considered both quantitatively and qualitatively, is the greatest work in Persian literature and poetry ... our second obligation to Firdausī is for his having rescued from oblivion and preserved for all time our Persian language" (quoted in Arberry 1958: 46, 47).

The *Shahnameh* became central to modern national identity: "Identification with the ancient world of *Shahnamah* became a formative element of modern national identity" (Tavakoli-Targhi 2001: 99). Richard Cottam notes: "For the politically unaware, whose horizons are too limited to comprehend national history, much less nationalism, the *Shahnameh* creates a predisposition for a rapid infection with genuine nationalism" (1979: 27), giving the reader an indication of the centrality of this literary work to Iranian national identity.

This renewed interest in the *Shah-nameh* resulted in Iranians increasingly selecting their children's names from it, which "signaled an important aesthetic shift in the constitution of both personal and national identities" (Tavakoli-Targhi 2001: 98). Iranians seek their true (heroic) identities within its pages and oral recitation. More than twenty editions were published in Iran and India (where Persian was an official language until the 1830s) during the nineteenth century (Tavakoli-Targhi 2001: 97).

Persian literature scholar Olga M. Davidson locates some of its elements not "only to Parthian Arsacid times. Rather, they can be traced all the way back to the remotest Indo-Iranian and even Indo-European layers of the classical Persian language" (1994: 6). Certainly, I cannot make such claims of great antiquity, but the existence of bards singing epic songs can be identified in the earliest times in Iranian history and importantly through the *naqāl*, the storyteller, into the present.

> Because we do have evidence, thanks to Mary Boyce's [Iranian historian] survey of the Arsacid period and beyond, for thinking that the "book of kings" tradition was indeed a matter of oral poetry, we have a sound theoretical basis for positing the continuity of Indo-European traditions up to Ferdowsi.
>
> (Davidson 1994: 7)

Davidson characterizes the *Shah-nameh* as "a formal and traditional expression of how Iranian society views itself and how it wishes to be remembered through the ages ... it is a majestically vast poem concerned with the very identity of Iran as a nation" (1994: 9–10; 15). Today, in Los Angeles, many individuals in the Iranian community gather regularly to hear the *Shahnameh*.

Nationalism, Modern and European?

As I return to these topics, I find that many scholars deny the existence of nationalism before the modern era, often dating the emergence of nationalism to no earlier than the French Revolution. Ernest Gellner (1983) is among them: "The minimal requirement for full citizenship, for effective moral membership of a modern community, is literacy" (1994: 55). Many of the requisites, such as widespread literacy, do not exist in many modern nation-states like Somalia and Afghanistan, as well as nineteenth-century Iran, or in many early-twentieth-century Eastern European states in which nationalism ran rampant, as the nationalist-based violence of the Balkan Wars (1912–13) attests. I tend to side with scholars like Hugh Seton-Watson who proposes the notion of old and new nations:

> The old are those which had acquired national identity or national consciousness before the formulation of the doctrine of nationalism. The new are those for whom two processes developed simultaneously: the formation of national consciousness and the creation of nationalist movements.
>
> (1994: 134)

Perhaps the emphasis on the modernity of nationalism is connected with their notion that such identities originated in Europe. I wish to modify and question that scholarly position through my study of Iranian nationalism and national identity. I think nationalism, or at least a form of proto-nationalism or a form of nationalism that is not modern, but contains enough of the same elements to merit the category of ethnicity or nationalism as a basic aspect of individual or group identity, came into being much earlier than the French Revolution, as I am attempting to show with the Chinese and Iranian examples.

Certain individuals among people like Iranians, with long histories, have written tantalizingly of having a sense of ethnic or proto-national identity before the advent of modern nationalism—a sense of themselves as Persian that distinguished them from ethnic others. The discourse of Iranian identity was not limited to Ferdowsi. Two of the most important Iranian literati—Hafez (1326–1390), one of the greatest Iranian poets, makes references to a Persian identity in contrast to a Turkish one (see, e.g., 1994: 75, *ghazal* 5), and a century earlier, Jalal Ad-dln Rumi (1207–1273), Persian literature's most celebrated mystical poet, referred to "pārsā'i-ye ma-rā" (my Persian-ness) (Shiva 1995: 58). I am providing tantalizing hints that the consciousness of Iranian identity existed, but I cannot say with any certainty to what degree it existed among the Iranian population historically. Political scientist Richard W. Cottam is more certain:

> Iran, in fact, is an excellent example of a state in which national consciousness can be clearly identified for many centuries. But the importance of nationalism

> as a primary determinant of Iranian attitudes and political behavior is largely confined to the twentieth century.
>
> (1979: 5)

But Tavakoli-Targhi has described many of the elements of that nationalism (2001) which I described above.

Every scholarly commentator that I have encountered over the past 50 years acknowledges the connection between national identity and Iranian nationalism and the *Shah-nameh*. Literary scholar A. Shapur Shahbazi notes:

> The idea of "nationalism" as known today is a fairly recent European development which has spread into other countries. However, a people with a common background (descent, language, religion, and customs) living in a specifically determined and continuously maintained land naturally develops strong nationalistic bonds. Such ties had created an undeniable nationalism among the Iranians which became particularly powerful under the Sāsānians.
>
> (Shahbazi 1991: 123–24)

In the *Shah-nameh* Ferdowsi writes: "If it is not in Iran, let my own self not be (*na-bašad be Iran tan-e man ma-bād*) Calamity will it be if Iran is destroyed" (Shahbazi 1991: 125).

And, one must remember that, as Ferdowsi penned those lines, many Iranians of his time felt that, through the Arab conquest (642 CE), they were in danger of losing their national identity and being assimilated into Arab society, one of the driving forces behind Ferdowsi's composition of the *Shah-nameh*, which took over a quarter of a century to compose. As we saw the *shu'ubiyyah* was conducted in Arabic, and many of the Persian aristocracy were adopting Arabic. Shahbazi observes:

> It may be stated with fairness that no one has influenced the concept of Iranian nationalism as has Ferdowsi … But his greatest service was to stimulate and strengthen the pride in being Iranian so effectively that he prevented Iran from assimilation into an Arabic nation.
>
> (Ibid.)

Dick Davis states:

> The *Shahnāmeh* was then a direct product of the reappearance of a sense of Persian ethnic identity and worth, and as with most epics, the people celebrated are defined as being in conflict with their neighbors with whom they do not share ethnicity.
>
> (2006: xx)

One of the claims often made by nationalism scholars is that national sentiments begin among the intelligentsia and then percolate to the masses through print literacy and public education systems. More important to my argument, I would also suggest that generations of both literate and illiterate Iranians from peasant to palace listened enraptured to the *Shah-nameh* (1010 AD) of Ferdowsi, in which *shah-nameh-khani* or *naqāl* (reciters of the *Shah-nameh*) recited the epic verses nightly in the teahouses and palaces for years wherever Persian was and is spoken.

> Everyone who could read has always read the *Shāh-nāma*, while those who couldn't read would throng to listen with enjoyment to the recitation of its rhapsodes [sic]. Very few indeed were the Persians who were ignorant of these stories and didn't know the *Shāh-nāma* by heart.
>
> (Arberry 1958: 47)

The *Shah-nameh* is all about being Iranian. While not a distinctly modern Iranian identity perhaps, such literary references and the *shu'ubiyyah* that I discussed elsewhere indicate that some kind of awareness of an Iranian identity existed prior to modern Iranian nationalism and paved the way for a sense of modern Iranian nationalism.

More importantly, I find that some scholars even question the existence of ethnicity before the advent of nationalism; as Liah Greenfeld, they argue that ethnicity follows nationalism. In this study I will claim that ethnicity, or whatever we wish to call it, existed in prehistoric and early prehistoric times, perhaps not in its modern form, but with enough of the same characteristics (claims of common ancestry, descent, language, spiritual beliefs and practices, and common blood, among others) to merit the same subject category; it was, as now, a means of marking the differences between us and them (see Derks and Roymans 2009; Drinkwater and Elton 1992; Hall 1989, 2002; Jones 1997; Kennedy et al. 2013; Malkin 2001).

I think the appearance of the *Shah-nameh*, the *shu'ubbiyah*, and other literary responses that appeared in Iran in the centuries following the Arab/Islamic conquest reveals that sentiments of ethnic or proto-ethnic, nationalistic or proto-nationalistic sentiments resided among the Iranian population to the present. It reveals that these sentiments were not limited to a narrow, literate group of individuals, but to a multilayered section of the population of Iran.

I will assert in this study, as a major point, that since the inception of empires, if not earlier, in the ancient world, ethnic and cultural identities constituted a major form of personal and group identity; named groups of peoples who must have had certain distinctive characteristics appear in some of the earliest writings of Mesopotamia and the subject peoples of the Persian Empire are illustrated on the Apadana, the formal staircase of the Achaemenid palace at Persepolis, and other locations, in remarkable ethnographic detail in their clothing, at least as perceived by the ancient Persians. In their eyes, the processions represented in great detail represented "a tax paid by a subject nation" (Root 1979: 227). And, as in "the courts of Egyptian and Mesopotamian monarchs ... such displays clearly offered great potential for pictorial representations of imperial power ... a statement of the power of the king over the specific lands represented by the tribute bearers" (Root 1979: 229). Those representations were carefully observed depictions of ethnic differences that focused on the specific ethnic clothing worn by the tribute bearers, as well as the products and materials they carried, which were associated with specific geographic origins.

By the Greek period, the known world was divided into a checkerboard of ethnic territories. I argue that those identities were, as in modern circumstances, ethnic identities, historically and territorially contingent, and many writers such as Herodotus and Thucydides wrote extensively, in essentialist fashion, about those peoples and their ethnic characteristics in a proto anthropological style.

> By its very nature all written evidence is selected and distorted by its authors, but among the more reliable sources are the histories of Herodotus written in the mid-fifth century BC and of Thucydides written later in the same century. Both writers were close to the events they described and, while by no means free from bias, they strived for accuracy.
>
> (Cunliffe 2008: 270–71)

These writers wrote extensively about the Persians, as well as many other ethnic groups, in order to differentiate them from Greeks.

Nationalism and Modernity

Nations continue to come into existence. In 1993, what came to be called the "Velvet Divorce" resulted in two new nation-states: the Czech Republic and Slovakia. Following the breakup of Yugoslavia, independent states that had never existed before, such as Macedonia, Slovenia, and Bosnia and Herzegovina came into existence in the 1990s. The Republic of South Sudan, even more recently, in 2011, became a new nation. All of them came into existence due to severe breakdown of ethnic relations in Czechoslovakia, Sudan, and Yugoslavia. Nationalism is contextual: One can view nationalism on display during the Olympic Games or the World Cup, during which crowds of people celebrate their nations and in which people wear garments in their national colors and wear other national symbols, like Icelanders wearing faux Viking helmets, as compared to when people are going about their daily lives, going to work, cleaning house, and shopping. I feel less nationalism than many of my compatriots. Many of my neighbors display American flags and bunting on their houses on national holidays like July 4th; I never do. Thus, in any discussion of nationalisms, we must take into account individual differences of the experience of nationalism.

Greenfeld reminds us that the sight of attendees rooting for their national teams reminds us of

> the essential competitiveness of nationalism. Competitiveness indeed becomes the operative word, the lash that spurs us on to greater feats of productivity and innovation, lest we lose our place in the race to someone [or nation] more "competitive" than us.
>
> (2016: 5)

Her observation underscores the scenes we experience in the Olympic games among various national groups, some serious, some whimsical like the Viking horns.

I add, however, that national and ethnic identities, like so many other identities that each person bears, are socially constructed. National and ethnic identities coexist with a variety of other identities: Those can consist of professional identities, familial identities, that is, our identities as wife, mother, daughter, granddaughter, the belonging to a state or province, a city or town, religious identities, sexual identities, identification as an individual attached to a particular hobby, a dog or cat lover or breeder, a bowler, folk dancer, a bicyclist, a political identity, class identity, all of which sometimes become the most salient identity for an individual. Certain identities become salient in particular contexts. One's identity as a parent becomes crucial when the principal of the local school calls one in to consult about the progress of one's child. Class identity becomes important when one is excluded from the local country club or snubbed at a social event. Sexual identity was important when one did not have the right to marry if one were gay or lesbian, or when someone hurls a homophobic slur. My identity as a gay man, for most of my life, was far more important than my identity as a white man or as an American, because that is how I self-identified and the way in which my life was most threatened or, conversely, enjoyed. Other individuals have different identities that they consider more important.

Why is national identity and nationalism so prevalent? Social scientist Craig Calhoun answers that best: "There are global reasons why nationalism remains the central form of identity in which people pose their claims to sovereignty. The most important of these is simply the creation of the world system as a system of states" (1994: 320). Almost everyone today belongs to a nation-state; one cannot travel without documents issued by one or another nation-state (Figure 5).

FIGURE 5: Igor Moiseyev Ballet performs Gopak, a Ukrainian dance. Choreography: Igor Moiseyev. With permission from the Igor Moiseyev Ballet and Elena Shcherbakova, artistic director.

Most scholars of nationalism believe that the current system of nation-states began with the French Revolution, when the personal rule of a king or queen was replaced by popular participation in the politics of decision-making, and that marked the beginnings of civil society. Many scholars of nationalism also link the modern nation-state with modernity. Liah Greenfeld, when discussing nationalism, states,

> This above all, includes relating nationalism to *modernity*: such central elements of modern politics, society, and economy, as *democracy, class structure*, the *state* and *civil society, capitalism*, the institution of *science*, the processes of *secularization* and *globalization*, and the distinctively modern passions, sense of reality and of self.
>
> (2016: ix, emphasis in the original)

While I agree with Greenfeld that these characterize truly modern states and the nationalism found in them, I would argue that in the nineteenth century among the Polish nobility, if not the rest of the nation, there existed powerful, passionate emotions of romantic nationalism without capitalism, secularism, science, or the other trappings that she mentions. In the system of nation-states that Calhoun described above, there exist many contemporary nations like Afghanistan, Somalia, and Oman where barely any of the trappings of modernity described by Greenfeld exist.

As all scholars of nationalism attest, nationalism spread to different groups of people and different classes at different times. Greenfeld traced the various iterations of *natio*, a Latin term that was originally used to refer to foreigners and, therefore, disparagingly, barbarians living in Ancient Rome; centuries later it referred to students at various universities in medieval Europe, where they were foreigners, then later it referred to the rabble.

> Our concept of "nation" as a people, an inclusive, sovereign community with membership unaffected by divisions of class and status, thus equal, and a natural object of the members' loyalty and commitment, emerged sometime in the late fifteenth to early sixteenth century in England.
>
> (Greenfeld 2016: 11)

"Nationalism was fathered … by the War of the Roses" (2016: 12). That was the long war in which the two factions of the Plantagenets, the York and Lancaster lines, culminated in the battle of Bosworth Field, which resulted in the extinguishment of almost every blue-blooded person in England. The upper echelon of English society had to be replaced. "The commons had to be wooed, and its members encouraged, and practically invited to be upwardly mobile. Particularly intelligent and educated commoners answered the call early on, forming the new Henrician aristocracy" (ibid.). Such a huge societal replacement of the elite had not occurred in Europe before; in order to explain how people born as commoners could have moved up to their new elite positions, short of creating new genealogies, a new explanatory social institution had to be created because, prior to that time as Greenfeld eloquently described it, "It was no more possible to be born a laborer and to become a nobleman, than it is to be born a chicken and graduate into a human being" (2016: 13). As Greenfeld expresses it,

> One fine day one of them … had a eureka moment, it becoming clear to him that all English people were a nation. He shared it with others, and people in England found it easy to believe, because it explained the positive but confusing experience … their blood was red, but they in every respect lived the life of the blue-blooded, which was a fuller and richer, and more exciting life, in which, above all, they enjoyed dignity unknown to them before.
>
> (2016: 14)

I relate this intricate narrative (somewhat shortened) because I believe that Greenfeld presents us with the reason why nationalism has lasted for so long as a human experience that so many individuals share. Nationalism, and belonging to a nation, gives people dignity, a sense of belonging, of having an equal status to others. As Greenfeld explains, prior to the act of belonging to a nation and the dignity and sense of belonging it confers, few people had the experience of dignity, and once an individual experiences dignity, no one wants to give it up (2016: 16–19). Similarly, I would argue that the *Shahnameh* provided Iranians with a dignity in their existence as Iranians.

While Greenfeld explains in which ways many individuals cling to nationalism, Craig Calhoun shows that nationalism is a communal response to a sense of dignity: "Nationalism is the rhetoric of identity and solidarity in which citizens of the modern world most readily deal with the problematic nature of state power and with problems of inclusion and exclusion" (1994a: 305). In other words, does one belong to the extended family of the nation or not? "Nationalist claims are one genre of answers to the question of what constitutes an autonomous political community capable of 'self-determination' " (ibid.) and the term "self-determination" I equate with a form of communal identity in which people feel that they have agency and can make decisions regarding important communal issues.

Thus, as a concept that I address in this study, nationalism, alongside dance and ethnicity, is one of the most important. Traditional and folk dances have become an important tool in the arsenal of building strong feelings of nationalism in many nation-states around the world.

NOTES

1. Because Persian transliterations for famous works like the *Shāhnāmeh* appear in several ways, including in this work when I quote other writers: *Shah-nameh*, Shahnamah, Shah Nameh, Shahnama, and so on. I will use *Shahnameh*, to reflect contemporary pronunciation in standard Tehran Persian.
2. Iranian historians and literary scholars Touraj Daryaee and Parvaneh Pourshariati, in the Persian language BBC (July 2, 2011) program Pargār, cautioned that in approaching the *Shahnameh*, one has to keep several issues in mind: (1) Many versions exist in which copyists changed, added, or otherwise significantly altered the text. (2) While Persian is a relatively conservative language and a contemporary individual who knows Persian can read this 1010 CE document with relative ease, many words and phrases have changed meaning from the eleventh to the twenty-first century. (3) The text, including concepts of Iranian identity, could well have different meanings for people from the eleventh century than they have for people of the twenty-first century, and yet they still have meaning for Iranians of today. And above all, (4) The scholar must approach the

Shah-nameh as a verifiable historical document with care and check its contents against other contemporary documents of the Sasanian and early Islamic period with care. And yet, Pourshariati notes, "And it will show that the Shāhnāma is not merely one of the sources, but often the only source that provides us with details corroborating the information contained in some of the primary sources for Sasanian history" (2017: 14, emphasis in the original).

3. The transliterations that I use are contemporary uses of Persian. I avoid the use of the Library of Congress usage, because Persian transliteration is based on Arabic usage. I prefer the contemporary transliteration of Persian as it sounds to a contemporary Persian speaker from Tehran. Thus, *Shu'ubiyyeh, shu'ubiyya*, etc. characterize the spelling of this word as well.
4. Iranian historian Parvaneh Poushariati proposes the fascinating and "heretical" (her term) idea, completely upending our notion of Iranian history and backed by intensive research, that Sasanian Iran was in fact an empire in which members of the former Parthian Arsacid dynasty contributed to Sasanian success through various means of political cooperation. In other words, the Sasanians and Parthians coruled the empire. She writes, "Throughout the Sasanian history there was a dichotomy between the *Pārsīg* (Sasanians) and the *Pahlav*, which forced the Sasanians into a confederate arrangement with the powerful Parthian dynastic families living in their domains" (2017: 3). When the Parthians withdrew their support, the Sasanian dynasty rapidly collapsed in the face of the Arab onslaught. The Parthians negotiated with the Arabs to retain their territorial rights, properties, and wealth for another four centuries at least and manipulated the sources that constitute the *Shah-nameh* (2017: 453–65). Pourshariati herself terms the thesis of her study as an "heretical assessment": "The Sasanian monarchs ruled their realm through a decentralized dynastic system, the backbone of which was the Sasanian-Parthian confederacy" (2017: 2, emphasis in the original). Certainly, for one used to reading about a succession of dynasties, Pourshariat's reading of history is fascinating, but I place it as a footnote because most Iranians would not evaluate their history in this way, largely because this paradigm shift is, as yet, little known.

3

Iran: The Shah's New Dance

A block of sixteen tightly placed dancers, dressed in black suits, white shirts, and a fedora, which became the official men's hat under the sumptuary laws of 1935 (Chehabi 1993: 226), with a white shawl draped across the dancers' shoulders, stand frozen in place in four lines of four dancers each in silhouette, tapping their feet in time, as the six-eight (6/8) drumroll begins. The block formation symbolizes a single, solo dancer who in general performs the improvised figures of this hypermasculine, vernacular, solo male urban dance genre (Shay 2021b). Many of the movements of the dance, known variously as *shāteri* and *jāheli*, choreographically mimic the movements that bakers and their apprentices use in preparing the flat bread (*nān*) that Iranians purchased at the bakeries that were found at the end of most residential streets in Tehran in the 1950s and 1960s. The dancers, manipulating their hats and their shawls in a series of various exaggerated masculine figures, move forward and line-by-line peel off alternately to the right and left until they form a semicircle. They continue performing different steps and movements throughout the original choreography, sometimes punctuated by a soloist contrasted against the chorus performing different movements in the background. This is a choreography created by Jamal, artistic director of the AVAZ International Dance Theatre. Toward the end of the dance, the semicircle forms a straight line, moves to the front of the stage and, as a finale, the dancers end the dance by suddenly raising their hats in the air at the end of their extended arms, revealing that some of the dancers are women, performing what is normally a solo improvised male urban dance.[1] From the first night it premiered in 1994, that dance has received thunderous applause from our mostly Iranian audiences, and numerous emulators, in the diaspora that one can readily locate on YouTube (Figure 6).

In this section, I want to create the links between the creation of professional classical ballet performances, ethno identity folk dance choreographies, and choreographies of an urban solo improvised vernacular origin with additions from classical ballet, which is a recently constructed new genre, known as *raqs-e melli*

FIGURE 6: Iran. Shateri. Choreography: Jamal. Photo: D. Young.

(national dance) that began in the 1930s (Kiann 2016; Meftahi 2016a; Shay 2014b). *Raqs-e melli* constituted a hybrid genre that played a central role in the representational field of Iranian dance until the Iranian Revolution of 1978–79. *Raqs-e melli* was often featured alongside Iranian-themed ballet choreographies, known as "national" ballet, using classical ballet movement vocabulary to the mass movement and spectacle as manifest in the now infamous 2500th-year celebration of the history of royal rule in Iran in October 1971, and the authoritarian state of Pahlavi Iran.

This linkage began in the 1930s with the arrival of three pivotal Armenian ballet-trained teachers (Madame Yelena, Madame Cornelli, Sarkis Djanbazian) and later, in the 1940s, with the American Nilla Cram Cook and her founding of the first small performance group of dance in Iran that received funding to tour in the Middle East with royal support for two extensive tours, a foretelling of state-sponsored dance companies that began in Iran in the 1950s (Kiann 2016). Because of arbitrary decision-making and planning in Iran, the various manifestations of this linkage—the dance ensembles that the Pahlavi regime sponsored and supported—never had the opportunity to mature and reach the levels of professionalism that were attained in most of the other nation-states that are analyzed in this study. A professional dance ensemble requires years to acquire a professional patina.

While sometimes admired by Iranian dancers and other artists for their very existence, the whimsical manner of founding and managing these various dance companies embodies the fragmented and impetuous nature of the existence of these ensembles, largely under the aegis of the Pahlavi family. This mismanagement and sometimes capricious decision-making demonstrate the sultanistic nature, in Chehabi's (1998) terms, of the political situation in which they were founded and ran their courses. Through this arbitrary management and decision-making, Iranian dance ensembles never achieved the maturity, technical proficiency, and professionalism that one found in other dance ensembles, both classical ballet and staged folk dance in other nation-states, such as Yugoslavia, Mexico, Romania, and the Philippines.

Not everyone in Iran accepted dance as a proper field for national representation. For the strict Islamists, the very existence of dance on public stages was damning evidence of *gharbzadegi* (Westoxification, a phrase created by Al-e Ahmad), "a powerful discourse of nativism, rejecting the West and celebrating Iranian authenticity" (Matin-Asgari 2012: 360), that resulted in shuttering all dance activities when Khomeini swept into power in 1980.

Authoritarian Regimes in Iran

No matter the authoritarian hue of the government—competitive or sultanistic—the Pahlavi governments and regimes were all authoritarian from the outset to the end (1924–79).[2] Beginning as competitive authoritarian regimes in Levitsky and Way's (2010) terms, that is, they had the trappings and appearance, such as elections, a constitution, political parties, of constitutional monarchies like Denmark or the Netherlands, which were authentic democratic polities with monarchs, while in Iran the monarchs ruled as well as reigned. "By the late 1960s the four major branches of power and influence were almost entirely subservient to the shah ... It was above all a system driven by loyalty and obedience to the shah and fear of him" (Amanat 2017: 626), all characteristics of sultanic regimes as analyzed by Chehabi (1998).

As Abbas Amanat notes, they derived from "two interconnected personal traits in the shah's personality: a sense of political insecurity and a drive for prestige and glory" (2017: 627).

Unlike the politically correct parliamentary royal regimes with a free press, free elections, and free political campaigns, Iran always had an uneven, politically tilted playing field: The press was strictly controlled and the political parties, except for the Tudeh Party, were largely formed by the government and had no true political meaning. "The Tudeh was the only party with a comprehensive program of social reform, including labor laws, women's full enfranchisement, and land reform. Moreover, it was the only organization that joined together two modern social classes in a strategic political alliance": the workers and the intellectuals (Matin-Asgari 2012: 354).

Both Pahlavi regimes (1925–41; 1941–79) ended as sultanistic regimes, as defined by Chehabi and Linz (1998). In general terms, a sultanistic regime is "based on personal rulership" that stays in place, motivated "not by any charismatic qualities but by a mixture of fear and rewards to his collaborators" (1998: 7), and by historian Homa Katouzian (1998) in its own specific Iranian terms, in "which all genuine opposition had been effectively been banned since 1953. But the Shah became increasingly intolerant of any advice" (1998: 202). Above all, "The ruler exercises his power without restraint, at his own discretion and above all unencumbered by rules" (Chehabi and Linz 1998: 7). Such sultanistic rule is, in a word, arbitrary. Most of the decisions taken by the Shah, his family, and others, especially regarding the arts and spectacle, which I use to make my points, were arbitrary decisions, which becomes clear when reading the reminiscences of the participants (see Ahmadzadeh 2008; De Warren 2009; Ramazani 2002).

The CIA put an end to the Mosaddeq government, the only freely elected government in Iranian history, in 1953. "The shah's authoritarian rule, evident shortly after the coup, further convinced his opponents of the United States' malicious designs to impose on Iran a dictator subservient to its strategic interests" (Amanat 2017: 560). They also founded and initially directed the truly evil security force, SAVAK, in 1957. By 1958, when I arrived as a young student at the University of Tehran, SAVAK, Iran's former notorious security and intelligence service, had yet to make the impact that they later had. SAVAK became pervasive and, through the period of the 1960s until the end of the regime, I heard scores of stories of systematic torture that became a feature of the Pahlavi regime. Almost everyone knew someone who had been jailed and tortured. They even ventured into the arts: "The presence of SAVAK, which, according to opponents of the Shah's regime, abused its mandate, and in some cases resorted to enhanced interrogation techniques was severe everywhere—even at an artistic institution such as Roudaki [sic] Hall Opera" (Kiann 2016: 130. See also the video *Iran's Magnificent Party*). They learned well from their CIA mentors. As in Hollywood melodramas, spies were everywhere; my fellow students at UCLA knew that certain students had been recruited by SAVAK and, as a result, drove expensive cars and lived in good housing.

"The rise and fall of Mosaddeq is generally seen as the crucial turning point where Anglo-American intervention destroyed modern Iran's chances for charting an independent course under a secular nationalist regime" (Matin-Asgari 2012: 355). And, of course, the reason for engineering the coup d'état was to ensure Anglo-American control of Iran's oil.

For the individual living in such authoritarian societies, one frequently feels frustrated and besmirched:

> Corruption reigns supreme at all levels of society. The staff of such a ruler is constituted not by an establishment with distinctive career lines, like a bureaucratic army or a civil service, recruited based on more or less universal criteria, but largely by people chosen directly by the ruler. Among them we very often find members of his family, friends, business associates, or individuals directly involved in using violence to sustain the regime.
>
> (Chehabi and Linz 1998: 7)

And, while one might be tempted to observe that Iran did have something of a bloated civil service, with all of the protocol and inefficiency such an organization brings with it, Katouzian notes:

> Empirically, the Pahlavi state presented a unique experience. Yet its basic features were firmly rooted in thousands of years of Iranian history. In normal periods Iran's social and economic system had been one of arbitrary rule based on the absence of property *rights;* therefore in abnormal periods (the collapse of arbitrary regimes caused by domestic or external forces) it has been visited for relatively long stretches by chaos, confusion, plunder, and the absence of proper central authority before the next arbitrary regime has eventually been established.
>
> (1998: 182, emphasis in the original)

As we will see, in comparing the two regimes, Katouzian's observations will be seen to characterize the regimes of both the father, Reza Shah, and the son, Mohammad Reza Pahlavi. The Pahlavi governments of both shahs fit into my discussion of not only authoritarianism, per se, but also ethnicity and nationalism, and these national and ethnic ideals could be located in dance performances: "The Pahlavi state, on the other hand, was not a traditional system of arbitrary rule, but one that was strongly identified with certain notions of nationalism and modernism" (Katouzian 1998: 189). So powerful was the drive to modernism by the Pahlavi monarchs that Reza Shah enacted sumptuary laws that included unveiling and forcing men to adopt Western clothing. To drive Iran to modernity by force, and at great social cost, the government was involved in a massacre in Mashhad in 1935 that required mass graves to bury the victims (Chehabi 1993). Chehabi concludes:

> While it would be churlish to deny Reza Shah credit for the economic progress accomplished during his reign—a progress whose significance grows as we benefit from greater hindsight—the "catastrophic dislocation" of people's lives was simply commensurate with the socioeconomic progress achieved under his rule. (1993: 228)

And the sumptuary laws touched most individuals in intrusive ways since how we dress is an intimate matter as Chehabi's penetrating article describes and analyzes. Seeing that the sumptuary laws did not work, as they rarely do, by the time I arrived in Iran in the late 1950s, dress was largely a matter of personal choice. However, if Reza Shah had not enforced unveiling in the mid-1930s, it is possible that women would not have had the choice to veil or not, as is currently the case of the hejab that women are required to wear in public spaces.

Reza Shah's sumptuary edicts were a crucial aspect of his drive to make Iran a modern state, and they involved men as well as women: "Making Iranians look like Europeans inevitably meant differentiating them from their immediate neighbors (Turks excepted), which suited the glorifiers of pre-Islamic Iran" (Chehabi 1993: 226–27). Symbolically, this meant that Iran was recovering its ancient pre-Islamic European Aryan roots. Sumptuary laws are always about rigid state control over people's lives.

Iran cannot seem to shake its heritage of authoritarian governments, although one may argue which historic regime, including that of the Islamic Republic, is the most despotic and authoritarian: "The Iranian regime is one of the most repressive in the Middle East, but it is also the only authoritarian regime in the region that presently faces a viable alternative alliance of elites and constituents" (Brownlee 2007: 179). Political scientist Jason Brownlee notes that the Islamic Republic has been a battleground between the traditionalists and the leftist clergy: "No single political trend enjoys hegemony ... In contrast to the durable dictatorships of Egypt and Malaysia, Iran's regime has been both more contested and more repressive—politically more vulnerable to its opponents" (ibid.). The Iranian regime has always sought total control over a human, typical of theocracies, including what one may wear, what kind of music one is permitted to hear, and whether one may dance, even in the privacy of your own home. One of the characteristics of the Iranian government is that authority is both little-known and contested; except for Khamenei, no one is quite sure who makes decisions. The Islamic Republic, its ban on dance, and the twists and turns it utilizes to remain in power are beyond the scope of this study.

> What the Green Movement [of 2009] proved beyond a shadow of a doubt was that the Islamic Republic had failed to manufacture a *Homo Islamicus*, and

> that the defiant spirit of Iran's cosmopolitan political culture ... had resurfaced in triumph.
>
> (Dabashi 2016: 6)

This assessment is reflected in Middle East Studies scholar Narges Bajoghli's study of the power brokers in Iranian media, all supporters of the regime, where she stated

> "Yes, and we need to stop framing our story as one that's just about the Islamic Republic," he said, "It needs to be about Iran. Our young people may not defend the regime because they don't feel a part of it, but they will rise up to defend Iran because they are nationalistic".
>
> (2019: 5)

Thus, just as Stalin turned to Russian folklore to revive and vitalize Russian nationalism in order to face the threat of Hitler's forces because he knew that the population would not defend communism or the communist state, so, too, many in the Islamic Republic understand that Iranian nationalism trumps support of an authoritarian regime, which has largely alienated large swaths of the population, as seen in the Green Movement protests of 2009.

Iranian Nationalism

Iranian nationalism, which I first noticed among my Iranian classmates in the 1950s because it was so different from my own weak sense of nationalist sentiment, was rooted thousands of years in the past, while the United States had not yet reached 200 years. Their nationalistic feelings seemed far closer to the surface than mine. A description and analysis of Iranian nationalism is successfully encapsulated by Katouzian, who characterizes Iranian nationalism:

> There was an intellectual undercurrent of nationalism in the proper European sense of the term, that is, not merely anti-imperialism and aspirations toward complete sovereignty and independence, but an aggressive belief in ancient glories and a romantic desire to turn Iran into a Europeanized—if not European—society.
>
> (1998: 190)

Iranians frequently expressed frustration at not achieving this fully politically independent state in terms of maligning the English and, later, increasingly after 1953, American plots designed to prevent the goal of complete independence for Iran that one can still hear today. Iranian studies scholar Hamid Dabashi states,

> Iranians are a particularly proud people, their confidence about their past compensating for a sense of grievance about their modern history—always thinking they have been given less credit than they deserve, that modernity has handed them the short end of the historical stick. (2016: 23)

Historian Mohamad Tavakoli-Targhi characterizes Iranian nationalism much in the same way that I did in the Introduction:

> The formation of a modern Iranian national identity was linked intimately to the configuration of its national history and restyling of the Persian language. Informed by *dasatiri* texts and inspired by the *Shahnamah* of Firdawsi, modern historical writings harnessed the Iranian homeland (*vatan*) to an immemorial past beginning with Mahabad and Kayumars and pointing toward a future unison with Europe. (2001: 96)

This union with Europe proceeds from the well-known position of Persian among the Indo-European languages, and the fact that many Iranians bought into the pernicious mythology created by the Nazi regime to connect Iranian "Aryan" identity, alongside the modern Germans, placing them as desirable European brethren. "To catch up with the 'civilized world' the architects of Iranian nationalism sought to 'reawaken' the nation to self-consciousness by reactivating and inventing memories of the country's pre-Islamic past" (ibid.). The Pahlavi government promoted these notions through their self-presentation as a continuation of the pre-Islamic Achaemenian and Sasanian dynasties and through school texts and teaching. As I have stated elsewhere (Shay 1999), Iranian identity is often held in tension with an Islamic identity for many Iranian individuals. Dabashi, however, avers: "The idea of the 'nation' in Iran is today trapped within its manufactured postcolonial borders" (2016: 23). Unfortunately, the idea of Persianate culture, expanding over the vast area in which Iranian culture and languages, the *Shahnameh*, and other aspects of Iranian/Persian culture and artistic expression, like dance, remains largely confined within academic circles. As Dabashi notes above, most contemporary Iranians think of their identity as contained within the borders of the Iranian state.

Both Pahlavi regimes quickly attained sultanistic status, characterized by rampant corruption, arbitrary decision-making, and xenophobia. However, Katouzian discerns differences between the father and son:

> Reza Shah's own attitude toward official corruption was peculiar, at least compared with that of his son. He took extreme exception to it and would not tolerate the

> slightest public corruption when ever it was found. But at the same time he himself amassed a great fortune by systematic encroachments on public and private property. (1998: 198)

Reza Shah famously appropriated anyone's property that caught his eye, and that was on a massive scale that included a significant percentage of Iran's arable land. During Mohammad Reza Pahlavi's rule the entire royal family was implicated in corruption. For example, Princess Ashraf, the twin sister of Mohammad Reza Pahlavi, stood out among them and became a byword for corruption and theft, even drug-running, and she caused several international scandals with her unseemly and avaricious behavior that frequently proved to be a diplomatic embarrassment to the Iranian government (Katouzian 1998: 200; Kinzer 2008: 7–8, 200).

Whereas Reza Shah wanted to create a modern, European-style state, which to some degree he set in motion, his son Mohammad Reza Pahlavi wanted to "transform Iran into a major pro-Western regional power with aspirations to eventual world power status" (Saikal 2008: xiii), a goal that his successors, minus the pro-Western part, continue to strive for. The Iranian nationalism promoted by the Pahlavis involved their Arab neighbors: "The shah followed in his father's footsteps to promote a brand of Iranian cultural nationalism that held 'Arabs' as the ultimate 'Other' " (Amanat 2017: 634).

In the case of the ill-fated 2500th Year of the Monarchy celebration, designed to celebrate that national, anti-Arab, anti-Islamic identity, the Shah decided to hold his celebration too early; it signaled the end rather than foretold the future of his grand and magnificent return to pre-Islamic Iranian glory.

The 2500th Year of the Monarchy Celebration, October 1971

The celebration of the 2500th year of monarchy demonstrates how sultanistic authoritarian regimes arbitrarily function in the creation of spectacle to glorify and fortify themselves. "The second Pahlavi era [that of Mohammad Reza Pahlavi] was marked by royal politics of self-aggrandizement, especially in the 1970s" (Amanat 2017: 562). This celebration consisted of one misstep after the other, through which the October 1971 celebration came to symbolize for many Iranians and non-Iranians alike, everything that was dysfunctional and wrong with the Pahlavi regime, "a demonstration of the excesses that eventually brought down the Pahlavi regime" (Amanat 2017: 665). It exposed all of the weaknesses of the government and domestically, through its sultanistic, arbitrary mismanagement and planning, while fatally wounding the regime domestically. For the first time, it gave voice to the exiled Ayatollah Ruhollah Khomeini to call for the violent overthrow of the Pahlavi regime (see *Iran's Magnificent Party*).

Ultimately, it was an unnecessary waste of money, especially since the official and opulent coronation had been successfully held only a few years before (1967), but the Shah and his advisors wanted to prove that Iran was ready to take its place among the leading Western nations—that Iran had caught up with the West and to the promise that had been planted by the glorious Achaemenid and Sasanian dynasties.

> "After 25 centuries Iranian soldiers once again march past the upright pillars on this vast plain, this monument to the age-old grandeur and glory of Persia," the Shah declared. He wanted all the world leaders assembled to understand that the honor of Iran had been restored and that after centuries of slumber the Iranian people were back on the world stage and ready to assume a leadership role.
> (Cooper 2016: 173)

What everyone understood was that the event was a useless waste of money, and even the fact that it was part of a plan to expand education, health, transportation, and tourist facilities was lost in the opulent façade of the three-day celebration—"all choreographed no less spectacularly than a Hollywood epic, and with taste and expertise drawn from Hollywood studios" (Amanat 2017: 665). The major problem was that the Shah and his government did not trust the Iranian people, not only for security purposes but to carry out the culinary and aesthetic aspects of the celebration. Except for a few servants, parade participants from the military forces, and security forces, the Iranian people were largely barred from participating in the event. As historian Andrew Scott Cooper noted,

> Four years earlier, on the eve of his lavish coronation, he had been lauded abroad as a benevolent and progressive king. Now he was criticized for indulging in a Bourbon-style extravaganza while international aid agencies still supplied eighty thousand Iranian mothers and children with powdered milk.
> (2016: 164)

As an example from the same period, everyone from the Shah down were attempting to prove their worth as Iranians and bona fide members of the first world:

> During a stroll through the University of Tehran's new central library, which housed more than six hundred thousand volumes, and a collection of priceless Persian manuscripts, he asked a university official, "What status does this library, as one of the world's institutions of this kind, give us?" His escort replied

> that the university was now one of the best-equipped of its kind. "We've given them a good hiding, haven't we?" the Shah said, beaming. As ever, he was determined to show *them*—the Europeans and the Americans who had once dominated Iran—that this people were catching up.
>
> (Cooper 2016: 159–60, emphasis in the original)

Nevertheless, Iran, at that time, could not shake its status as a third-world nation due to low literacy rates, health issues, and its authoritarian political status.

The Shah's original intention for holding the 2500th-year celebration, announced in 1970, when Iran was flush with petro dollars, was to host " 'the most wonderful thing the world has ever seen'" (Cooper 2016: 163). This need to stage spectacle, as I have mentioned elsewhere (2019), constitutes an important aspect of authoritarianism. The celebration, for all of its pomp and showy theatrical effects, made Iran look like a third-world country attempting to masquerade as a first-world country, due to the officials in charge making often arbitrary and haphazard planning that had made aesthetic and artistic overreach in the parade and other displays of pomp and show, with nothing substantial to show for their efforts.

Empress Farah, who *did* know how to plan such events from her educational experiences in Paris as an artist, was appalled at many of the decisions that had been taken without her knowledge: "But it was only after Queen Farah accepted patronage of the Celebrations Council that she learned that the design and construction of the Tent City had already been outsourced to French Companies" (Cooper 2016: 163). At enormous cost, Maxim's of Paris was going to victual the event, and Jansen's would build and decorate the elaborate tents to house the guests for the event.

The celebration became a diplomatic nightmare with every crown head in the world, plus assorted premiers, presidents, vice presidents, and other dignitaries and their entourages from more than 60 countries attending a hastily put together mishmash. What stood out was lack of Iranian food, decoration, or participation (see *Iran's Magnificent Party* 1974). Queen Farah stated: "The idea that Iranians would pay foreigners to plan their own national event 'went against my Iranian sensibility' " (Cooper 2016: 163). The Queen, who understood the urgency of promoting Iranian talents and products, frequently wore Iranian-made and designed clothes that showed off native talent.

> Farah doubted [court minister] Alam's excuse that Iran lacked the expertise to stage the event in one year. This older generation of Iranians, she believed, had an inferiority complex when it came to their own culture, having been raised to assume that "whatever was European was good, noble, beautiful and

FIGURE 7: Iran. Avaz International Dance Theatre. Dastmali, a dance from Azerbaijan. Choreography: Anthony Shay. Photo: D. Young. From the author's collection.

> praiseworthy." They thought that Iranian things were ugly, mean and open to condemnation.
>
> (Ibid.)

Had the Shah and the government followed her advice and served Persian foods, one of the world's peerless royal cuisines, they could have saved themselves the excessive costs and inevitable bad press they received for the event, while showing Iranian superiority in its ancient cuisine. The increasing petro dollars allowed the Shah and his government to plan an international event that showed more of its inept reliance on European sources than the faith in their own Iranian resources and talent that the people had earned, and at a fraction of the cost to realize the event.

The event featured a three-day round of diplomatic events and meals provided by Maxim's, light and sound shows, fireworks, and an elaborately choreographed parade and event in which members of the armed forces donned what purported to be elaborately researched and reconstructed costumes from the period of Cyrus and Darius to the present, accompanied by period music. In order to accomplish this bold feat and build suitable viewing stands in the shadow of the ruins of Persepolis (they forgot to provide protection from the blazing sun), thirty square miles had to be cleared of hundreds of thousands of poisonous snakes, scorpions, and lizards in a desert space that was host to 70-mile-per-hour storms in order to make it suitable to invite "Princess Grace and her husband, Prince Rainier to join ... more than sixty heads of state in attendance at the 'party of parties,' the biggest gathering of world leaders in recent history" (Cooper 2016: 169).[3] As a fitting last observation Queen Farah stated, "I want our names to be utterly disassociated from those ghastly celebrations" (Cooper 2016: 174).

In this 2500th-year celebration, we find the type of choreographed, spectacular event in which authoritarian regimes indulge in order to symbolically demonstrate mass support for the government. The National Folk Song and Dance Ensemble and the Mahalli Dancers, both ensembles which contributed to the Iranian state's need for spectacle, also participated (de Warren 2009: 243–45; Gholami 2016: 80).

Choreophobia

Unlike Croatia, Spain, and the Dominican Republic, all of which are countries in which the populations have a rich tradition of dancing across the spectrum of the population and in which festivals were held all over those states that featured local dancing, Iran remained choreophobic and dance remained a marginal activity (Shay 1999, 2014b).[4] By contrast, during the socialist period, Yugoslavia, Romania, Bulgaria, and other states of Eastern Europe supported widespread urban youth participation in folk dance groups and they supported elaborate folk dance festivals. These amateur activities greatly added to the technical proficiency that made the establishment of professional state folk ensembles possible. Iran did not have such popular activities. Since the Islamic Revolution, even the use of the term "*raqs*" (dance) is discouraged. Such choreophobic attitudes cast obstacles in the way of research into dance, which I found in my early study (1999) and which dance historian Ida Meftahi discovered in her later study:

> A primary problem was a lack of documents on the subject as well as the understudied status of dance and other forms of performance that involved the dancing body. These prevented a more precise periodization of the genres and trends explored in the ninety-year span this book covers.
>
> (2016a: 5)

This lack of documentation caused me to largely use ethnographic methods and rely on my forty-year experience of dancing and observing dancing among

Iranians, and their attitudes toward dancing and those who danced, in both Iran and the United States (Figure 8).

Nevertheless, a rich tradition of both folk and urban dance genres has always existed there since prehistoric times, prior to the arrival of the first Iranians in the second millennium BCE, as attested by ancient pottery decorations and figurines in various ceramic and metal media. These do not, however, tell us anything about the actual movements that were performed by these dancing figures (Shay 1999; Zoka' 1978). This lack of documentation is due to the phenomenon I term "choreophobia" (1999). Historically throughout the Middle East itinerant and

FIGURE 8: Iran. Avaz International Dance Theatre performs Savaran, a classical Iranian dance. Lynette Houston, soloist. Photo: D. Young. From the author's collection.

urban-based bands of public entertainers existed, and they, especially dancers of both sexes, were generally held by the population to be associated with prostitution. However, I have argued elsewhere that the roots of these strong, negative, and ambiguous feelings toward the public performance of dance, professional dancers, and entertainment, in general, originated in the antique Mediterranean world and were inherited by the Islamic world, as were many social and aesthetic attitudes in Islamic life (Morony 2005; Shay 2014).

As a result of choreophobia, to this day many families discourage their members from dancing in any public context, especially after puberty, or even learning how to dance, by which they echoed the attitudes of the ancient Roman elite of Republican and Imperial Rome (Shay 1999, 2014). Among zealously religious Muslims all forms of music, dance, and theatre were, and are, held to be tempting and evil, and improper for observant Muslims. (Choudhury 1957 provides the hadith that supports this avoidance.) One of the first acts of the Islamic Regime was to ban all forms of music and dance. Slowly the authorities permitted various forms of music, and later dance to be performed, but with heavy restrictions: Folk dance, folk music, and some forms of popular music can now be performed, although the authorities in Iran do not permit any music in 6/8, because of its associations with solo improvised dance, to be performed in public spaces, nor is it permitted to show musical instruments on television (Siamdoust 2017). Women may not appear as vocal soloists in front of mixed audiences. (See the documentary *Avaz-e bi sarzamin* [Song without a country]). Instead of dance, a clunky form of choreographed movement known as *harekāt-e mowzun* (harmonious movements), costumed in featureless garments that cover the body in the most unattractive fashion, which largely feature revolutionary or Islamic thematic inspiration, is permitted, but the authorities oversee and censor every performance for any hint of sexuality (Gholami 2016; Kiann 2016; Meftahi 2016). Thus, in such a restrictive environment, dance as an art form has had a tortured, and relatively brief, trajectory.

A final, but important word: In spite of every attempt, especially by Empress Farah, Iranians, except those who were educated in the West, or those who were otherwise exposed, never developed the habit of attending Western-style, formal performances of dance and music. "The Annual Cultural Reports published by Muhammad Reza Pahlavi's Ministry of Culture and Arts proves the limitedness of the audiences of the performances given by the dance sectors dependent on that ministry" (Meftahi 2016: 45 n.43). My own anecdotal experiences in the late 1950s of playing concerts in the Farhang Auditorium in the Tehran Symphony Orchestra reflects the same results: Most of the attendees were Westerners and a few Western-oriented Iranians; the small hall was never full. However, I attended many enjoyable and satisfying private events in which Iranians played music and recited poetry.

Currently, many Iranians feel the wrath of the government in domestic space for dancing at parties, rather than in public spaces. Dancing "was seen as the worst possible behavior of an undisciplined body in public, and symbol of all vice" (Stellar 2011: 235). Paramilitary and purity forces could force their way into domestic spaces where they believed music and dance were occurring; however, such occurrences have diminished. Life under the Islamic Republic government has a schizophrenic aspect: The government maintains a series of draconian laws against music and dance, even in private. However, the government over the past few years has relaxed its enforcement of those laws in order to contain popular unrest and confine it to private spaces. *New York Times* reporter Thomas Erdbrink has recently observed that in the beginning, "There were lashings, hangings, amputations and mass imprisonment. Thousands of people died and hundreds of thousands left the country, some fleeing for their lives, never to return" (2019: A4). In contrast to this violent beginning, the relaxation of the enforcement of these and sumptuary laws regarding veiling has allowed people to feel normal: "Those changes have been enormous, and Iran today is closer than most outsiders generally appreciate to being that 'normal' country Iranians want" (ibid.). Once activities like dancing that Iranians dared perform only in the privacy of their homes now sometimes take place (according to YouTube recordings) outside as well.

Dancing, once a shameful act in public, has become an act of public defiance. Erdbrink notes that the "walls that long divided the private and public in Iran have been broken down, with Iranians using the streets in the way they like" (ibid.). However, "Iran's leaders face the dilemma of whether to start translating the social changes into new laws and customs or try to hang on to the 40-year old ideals of the revolution" (ibid.). It is in this questionable and shaky environment that the future of dance in Iran hangs.

Dance in Iran and Its Political Uses

Let us now turn to Iran's variegated dance scene and its several strands, many of which were created during the Pahlavi era. First, let us begin with authentic dance traditions that are an organic part of people's lives. Iran is a multilingual, multiethnic nation-state, of which Persian speakers make up just over half of the population. There exists rich village and tribal dance traditions that are performed mostly in groups, but also some solo dances, especially around the perimeter of Iran, outside of the Persian language areas, for which there can also be found analog choreographic genres among the ethnic brethren that dwell across the borders of Azerbaijan, Iraq, the Persian Gulf, Baluchistan, Afghanistan, and

Turkmenistan. For the interested reader these dances are best and most extensively described by Robyn Friend, for which she has provided detailed linguistic and ethnic maps (2016).[5]

For the political and diplomatic purposes to which the government put these dances, the Iranian government under the Pahlavis from the 1950s brought several elaborate regional exhibits, from Khorasan, Gilan, Kurdistan, Baluchistan, among other regions, which, alongside crafts and folk industries, included authentic folk music and dance performances, to Tehran and other provincial cities to acquaint Iranians with people and their traditions from different regional provinces. These dances, while authentic, featured only male dancers and musicians, another sign of choreophobia. Through repeated performances and rehearsals, these village groups became semi-professionalized, able to command performance spaces in front of large audiences for purposes of national and regional representation.

> There was also another group, which was made up of male folk dancers who had been called together from various villages. They would dance and play their traditional instruments in festivities such as weddings and celebrations in their villages. These genuine villagers used to execute the folk dances in a manner that was much more natural and strong when compared to the other group [those professional folk dance ensembles of the government such as the Mahalli Dancers under the direction of Robert DeWarren and the Iranian National and Folk Music, Song, and Dance Ensemble under the direction of Nejad and Haideh Ahmadzadeh, all of whom had received extensive ballet training, rehearsed daily, and toured extensively].
>
> (Gholami 2016: 70–71)[6]

It is in the promotion of regional folk dances in public spaces that one sees one of two strands of official attitudes toward ethnicity. They permitted its performance in the form of dance and music, regarded as politically “innocent” by so many government officials in Iran and elsewhere. Second, the use of local languages and dialects, outside of folk song lyrics, was strongly discouraged or outright banned.

> The Pahlavi state had a dualistic attitude towards cultures of different ethnicities in Iran: even though some aspects of folk cultures such as folk dance and music were promoted, the state had an oppressive approach to many aspects of ethnic identities, language in particular ... I believe this difference in policy can be attributed to the lack of seriousness in accepting dance and music as modes of political communication, whereas a non-Persian language could have seemed directly harmful to the Pahlavi policy of “one nation/one language/one country.”
>
> (Meftahi 2016: 46–47 n.66)

The threat over the secession of certain parts of the country, such as Kurdistan, Azerbaijan, and Gilan, was threatening, and the Soviet Union's occupation of those regions, including the establishment of Soviet Republic-style separatist governments that stressed ethnic independence during World War II, made such a possibility very real (Matin-Asgari 2012; Asgharzadeh 2007) (Figure 9).

Alongside these rich rural dance traditions, there also exists a second, urban, vernacular traditional dance genre that largely consists of solo improvised dances which had, and still has, both domestic and professional forms (see Ameri 2006; Shay 1999). Among the latter genre, dances like *majlesi* (solo improvised dancing that occurs in a social event, *majles*), *raqs-e ā'ineh* (the mirror dance, a competitive dance in which two dancers mirror one another's movements as exactly as possible), *raqs-e mojassameh* (the statue dance in which the dancers stop suddenly and take a pose when the music stops), *jāheli/shāteri* (male urban dances with exaggerated hypermasculine movements, see especially Ameri 2006) enrich this latter tradition, which I described in the opening paragraph of this chapter. These dances form the basis from which ethno identity, that is, staged folk and vernacular dances, are created for purposes of representation of Iran by the state-supported

FIGURE 9: Iran. *Bandari*, dance from the Persian Gulf Region. Avaz International Dance Theatre. Choreography: Anthony Shay. Photo: D. Young. From the author's collection.

dance ensembles that were created during the Pahlavi period. This practice continues in the diaspora (Kiann 2016).

There are two strands of professional urban dances that dominated the professional dance scene in Iran. The first descended from the indigenous *motreb* (public entertainers who could dance, act, perform acrobatics, sing, and play musical instruments) scene that extended far back into Iranian history, at least to the Safavid period (1501–1725) (Breyley and Fatemi 2016; Diba and Ekhtiar 1998; Falk 1972; Fatemi 2005; Gholami 2016; Khaleqi 1974). These performers were very common during the Qajar period when separate groups of male and female motrebs, the latter less numerous, plied their trade, and attractive, sexually available young dancers of both sexes were a feature of the troupes. Public attitudes toward their sexuality are made clear in this passage, which articulates popular attitudes and their disdain toward dancers:

> That night 'Abdi jan's troupe had been called so that the harem occupants could watch the show. Of course, you remember 'Abdi well. Let me, nonetheless, give you a description of his looks. He was a lad of about twelve or thirteen, with large, black eyes, languid and incredibly beautiful and attractive. His face was tanned and good-looking, his lips crimson, and his hair black and thick. Renowned throughout the town, the boy had a thousand adoring lovers. Being a dancer, however, he was unworthy of being anyone's beloved.
>
> (Al-Saltana 1993: 163)[7]

It was from these performances that women in the women's quarters learned to perform new movements in their domestic space, just as young girls would learn dance movements from cabaret dancers that were the feature of both the cabarets and the Iranian film industry in the twentieth century. Many of the movements and figures performed by the motrebs could be found in the movement vocabularies of the two professional dance ensembles that I mentioned above, albeit desexualized and made acceptable to middle-class audiences and the government officials as acceptable to represent in diplomatic occasions.[8]

One of the most striking aspects of the *motreb* dancers, both male and female, absent from both contemporary strands, *raqs-e melli* and cabaret dancing, is the enormous amount of athleticism and gymnastics, described by Khaleqi (1974) and depicted in the numerous paintings of the Qajar period (Diba and Ekhtiar 1998; Falk 1972; Gholami 2016). Motreb dancers each had specialty movements and figures such as backbends, balancing on knives, and somersaults, which they needed to navigate the competitive world of motrebs and survive professionally. Although motreb performances continued during the Pahlavi period in the more traditional parts of cities and towns, the loss of its former elite and royal patronage doomed it to a slow death. The advent of the Islamic Revolution (1979) caused the final demise of the motreb tradition because of clerical hostility toward these forms of entertainment. Both Imam Khomeini and Ayatollah Khamenei'i pronounced in their fatwas that "Motreb music is illicit" (which of course includes dance) (Fatemi 2005: 19).

As the tradition of the male *motreb* dancer, especially, faded due to modernization beginning as early as the late Qajar period, and the seeking of more modern forms and venues of dance, especially among the Westernized elite, female cabaret dancers, with their solo improvised movements, took their places in the private film industry, known as *filmāarsi*, in which the cabaret dancer, as a woman of slack moral character, became a stock role in these films and in the burgeoning cabaret scene spreading throughout Tehran. The government, however, rejected these performers as a political and social embarrassment, in favor of the newly founded state-supported dance ensembles that required Western technique and discipline and, in fact, a new and modern appearance. For these new dancers the government pursued what dance historian Ida Meftahi calls "the invention of the ideal female national dancer" (2016). The government officials in the arts began with the second strand of professional dancing in order to pursue their goal of the appearance of modernity.

The second strand of professional dance originated outside of Iran. Meftahi provides a detailed account of the first troupes of dancers, mostly Armenian and Azerbaijani, who, after the First World War, toured more sophisticated cities like Tehran and Tabriz, in which they gave performances of operettas and musicals featuring dances, mostly of Caucasian origin (see Gholami 2016; Kiann 2016; Meftahi 2016a, 2016b).

In the 1930s, three major figures arrived in Iran—Madame Yelena, Madame Cornelli, and Sarkis Djanbazian—and later Lily Lazarian, non-Iranian professional dance instructor who had ballet training. By 1940, they had all opened studios in which they gave lessons, largely to provide this service to the minority groups because of widespread choreophobia among Iranian Muslims, and for the children of a few Muslim families that had exposure to Western arts traditions (Shay 1999). As part of their curriculum, they provided annual recitals or concerts to celebrate special holidays, like the Shah's birthday. The Pahlavi government began to provide some financial support for these activities (see Gholami 2016; Kiann 2016). The main objective of these figures was to provide community activity and cultural enrichment. Nevertheless, almost every professional dancer in Iran had begun their career with these teachers or with dance teachers, such as Nejad and Haideh Ahmadzadeh, who had studied with them.

These instructors began the use of a style or genre of dance that eventually became known as *raqs-e melli* (national dance). It consists of the use of Armenian and Iranian choreographic movements, especially graceful movements of the hands and arms, the upright and graceful carriage of the torso and head, without *qeir*, a sharp and/or sensual movement of the torso and pelvis, which made this new dance genre acceptable to the upper and middle classes of Iran. The term *raqs-e melli* (national dance) is unfortunate and a misnomer, for it is not a national dance in the same sense as a national anthem, a national football team, or a national costume, but in the Iranian case it is rather a dance tradition begun and first developed by non-Iranians, designed to attract royal, upper-, and middle-class patronage, that became part of the teaching methods of those early instructors and the basis for the new genre of ethno identity dance that became part of the state-supported state folk dance ensembles.[9]

> Iranian National Dance [*Raqs-e melli-ye irani*] is a term used incorrectly by a few post-revolutionary Iranian writers to describe dance and choreographies (particularly solo improvised dance for the purposes of stage performances in an academic context. A specific dance or dance genre can be academized and officially designated by a government as the "national dance" ... The academization of any specific dance or dance genre, which is possible if put into effect by a board of academic dance experts under governmental supervision and conduct, requires development and codification of technique and pedagogical method, creation of terminology, and de-vulgarization and adaptation movements, such as the typical Iranian chest and hip [qer] moves. This academization has never happened in Iran.
> (Kiann 2016: 99–100 n.11)

These choreographer/ballet masters further added to the notion of a "national dance" by creating what they called "national ballets," that is, using nationalistic themes such as dances based on the flag or historical royal themes: *Iranian Flag Ballet* (*Bāleh-ye beyrāq-e Irān*) or the Crown Glory Ballet (*Baleh-ye tāj-e eftekāar*), among others, but utilizing a classical ballet movement vocabulary rather than movements from *raqs-e melli* (national dance) (Kiann 2016: 99). "[Following] the popular concept of 'national dance' in Europe [the Armenians, and later the American Nilla Cram Cook] adapted some movements from Iranian dance in their performances and re-crafted their own classical dances with Iranian movements" (Meftahi 2007: 149).[10]

Above all, what these figures and, even more, the American Nilla Cram Cook realized was that, if they could attach their potentially disreputable dance practices to poetry, the most important of all Iranian forms of aesthetic expression, they would have the opportunity to succeed in their choreographic endeavors. Thus, Ferdowsi's *Shāhnāmeh* and the lyric poems of the most famous national poets, Rumi, Nezami, Sa'adi, and Hafez, provided themes for the dance that these first choreographers created for the stage. Poetry themes in choreography became an "open sesame" to the beginnings of acceptance of staged dance by the more educated elements of the Iranian public. Throughout the Pahlavi period, and later in the diaspora, choreographers created dances based on poetry, patriotic themes, and Iranian miniatures, in order to give respectability to their work.

The third source of inspiration for these choreographers was real or, more often, imagined folk dances and folk scenes, in which young maidens would go to the well for water and engage in play with young village lads. Virtually all of the dances had folklore themes, national themes, and poetic images, a practice that continues into the present in the diaspora (Figure 10).

In these choreographies, the creators did not hesitate to utilize orientalist images that were popular with both domestic and foreign viewers. Nesta Ramazani, one of the first participants in these choreographic activities, states: "My longings and desires found expression through music and dance teacher, Mme. Cornelli, in whose choreography the Orient was represented as a magical land filled with flimsily clad dancing girls" (Ramazani 2002: 75).

It is at this moment, 1946, that the enigmatic figure of the American, Nilla Cram Cook, appears, establishing the first dance group especially designed to

FIGURE 10: Iran. Dance from the Caspian Sea province of Gilan depicting the rice harvest. Choreography: Jamal. Photo: D. Young. From the author's collection.

exclusively represent Iranian traditional ethno identity dances for purposes of representation, both in Iran and abroad. She has been variously portrayed as an intimate follower of Mahatma Gandhi, the cultural attaché in the American embassy in Tehran, a prominent figure in the Iranian Ministry of Culture, and a film censor for the Iranian government (Kiann 2016; Meftahi 2016a, 2016b; Ramazani 2002). What is known is that she founded a group supported variously by different individuals, including members of the royal family, under the title of "The Revival of Ancient Iranian Arts." But, in fact, she created an entirely new group of choreographies that inspired a generation of artists to emulate her work. With the financial aid that she garnered, she was able to tour with her company throughout India, Turkey, Greece, Pakistan, Lebanon, and Egypt during the period 1948–53.

Reflecting the use of the three themes—poetic imagery, nationalist themes, and folkloric dance and village themes—the following passage by one of the first dancers in these performances illustrates their awareness of these choreographic strategies: "I moved easily from performing a Zoroastrian temple dance to interpreting mystical Sufi poetry and to portraying the love of a rose and a nightingale" (Ramazani 2002: xv). She recounts the way in which folk dances were performed, and which I learned among my first experiences of Iranian dance.

> Through pantomime we conveyed such activities as sifting flour, kneading bread, washing clothes, and playfully splashing each other with water. Our work finished, we beautified ourselves, preening while coquettishly swinging one hip. Picking up our chiffon handkerchiefs, we coyly twirled them overhead or from side to side, occasionally flipping them into the air, while spinning rapidly around and around. Unlike the dress of real village girls, our bodices were brief, revealing a bare midriff and garnished with baubles and bangles that glinted in the stage lights.
>
> (Ramazani 2002: 5)

One might think that there were significant breaks between the appearances of motrebs, the classes and recitals of the Armenian teachers, the performances of Cram Cook's Revival of Ancient Iranian Arts (1948–53), Mehrdad Pahlbod, the head of the Fine Arts Administration directing Nejad Ahmadzadeh to open the first government-supported ballet school (1955), the founding of the Iranian National Ballet (1956) by Ahmadzadeh, the Iranian National Folk Music, Song and Dance Ensemble (1958), which was the first folkloric ensemble founded by Nejad and Haideh Ahmadzadeh, and the Mahalli Dancers (1966) founded by Robert DeWarren. But it all happened within a couple of decades, sometimes overlapping, along with activities beginning in the decade in the seedling diaspora, in which I participated. The existence of two state-supported folk dance companies has created a great deal of confusion among researchers.[11] I consulted Iranian dance historian Nima Kiann:

> "The Iranian National and Folk Music, Song and Dance Ensemble" and "The Mahalli Dancers of Iran" were two completely different dance ensembles. The first one was founded by the Ahmadzadehs in 1958 alongside the "The National Ballet Academy of Iran." The ensemble became apparently a sister company of the "Iranian National Ballet Company" meaning that members of the ballet company (particularly Iranian dancers) performed even in the productions of "The Iranian National and Folk Music, Song and Dance Ensemble."
>
> "The Mahalli Dancers of Iran" founded by de Warren in 1966 by the initiative of the Minister of Culture, Mehrdad Pahlbod, was a body of the "National Folklore Society of Iran." The two companies were somehow competing with each other and each of them claimed to be more original. "The Mahalli Dancers of Iran" came to be more known and successful due to the support that de Warren received from the Imperial Court and the friendship he developed with Empress Farah."
>
> (Personal communication, February 14, 2019)[12]

The breaks were not only temporary but there were also cultural and historical links between these performance groups and their founding figures. For example, Nejad and Haideh Ahmadzadeh were among the first members of Nilla Cram Cook's Revival of Ancient Iranian Arts group. Throughout her autobiography, Haideh Ahmadzadeh expresses her gratitude, personal and aesthetic, to Nilla Cram Cook. Thus, when Nima Kiann relates that the Iranian National Ballet not only performed classical works, it should not surprise readers that the Ahmadzadehs also restaged various choreographies that were included in Nilla Cram Cook's Revival of the Iranian Ancient Arts, such as the ballet *Godāfrid*, thus establishing a firm link with the past.[13]

The Iranian State Folk Dance Ensembles

More than any other country, Iran mixed its ballet and folk dance programs. In 1955, Nejad and Haideh Ahmadzadeh, who always seemed to work as a couple, opened the first government-sponsored ballet studio. The next year they were chosen to found the

> School of National Ballet (Honarestān-e Melli-ye Irān), later the National Ballet Academy of Iran (Bāle-ye Melli-ye Irān). The Ahmadzadehs established this

> ballet school on a professional basis, training both Iranian male and female dancers. William Dollar was the first ballet master invited to and employed in September 1956 at the Ahmadzadehs' newly established ballet school. This event was the birth of classical ballet in Iran.
>
> (Gholami 2016: 69)

Dance historian Kiann adds that ballet had been taught in a manner

> that did not necessarily follow the conventional pedagogical system of classical ballet in the West ... So, the engagement of the American ballet master, William Dollar, in the opening of the National Ballet Academy of Iran marked the start of a new era for Iranian classical ballet, both in terms of training and performance.
>
> (2016: 106–107)

The reason that I describe the establishment of the classical ballet company is to avoid the confusion that its founding, and that of the Iranian National Folk Music, Song and Dance Ensemble two years later, caused because they both engaged the same personnel: "In reality, both companies consisted of the same dancers who were doing both types of dance" (Kiann 2016: 108). Two years later, in 1958,

> the first official and government Iranian group of national and folk music and dance was formed for the first time in the history of dance in Iran. The productions of this group were based on materials that were collected and recorded by film cameras in fieldwork trips to the different towns and villages. These dances included mostly simple and repetitive steps, and figures were reworked and choreographed again for the state.
>
> (Gholami 2016: 69)

As with so many other state-sponsored folk dance ensembles, much was made of their field work to gather original sources for their choreographies. A 1969 leaflet of the company furnishes the reader with the company's background:

> The Iranian Group of National Folk Music, Songs and Dances was formed in 1958 by the Ministry of Culture and Art under the direction of Nejad Ahmadzadeh. The aim was to revive, restore and develop all the national and folk music, songs and dances. Groups were sent to villages and far-fetched [sic] provinces of Iran to gather material ... . It gave week of performances at the Iranian Pavilion in Montreal at Expo 67.
>
> (Quoted in Gholami 2016: 69)

One of the major problems that the Iranian government did not always confront forthrightly was that it wanted results from projects they undertook too quickly, as we saw in the example of the 2500th-year celebration. In the arts there are no shortcuts to achieve results. All art traditions require hours of practice, performers as well as performing companies require time to mature and acquire a professional patina through the expenditure of long hours of rehearsal, without which there cannot exist a professional level of performance (Gladwell 2008). They made a better decision in 1958, the year of the group's founding.

> Our big break came in 1958 at the time of the International Expo in Brussels, Belgium as The Fine Arts Department wanted to send the young folk dance group to represent Iran on its special day at the exhibition. Nejad was dispatched to Brussels for a month in advance to arrange everything and help prepare the Iranian pavilion. The dancers, on the other hand, worked and rehearsed like crazy through the hot weather, while mother's atelier was busy making the costumes. We did our best but the officials did not think we would be able to compete with the large companies from Russia, America, etc. and in the end vetoed our trip! They did not have faith in us.
>
> (Haideh Ahmadzadeh. Quoted in Gholami 2016: 70)

The officials were quite right not to give permission for the company to perform in Brussels, despite a supportive letter from Chief of the Fine Arts Administration Mehrdad Pahlbod. In 1958, I saw the Igor Moiseyev Dance Company in both the United States and at the Brussels World Fair, as I was traveling to Iran to attend the university. Having recently been appointed principal flutist to the Tehran Symphony Orchestra, I regularly saw the folk dance group, which rehearsed in a nearby space and, to be kind, they were not yet ready for prime time. The spectacular, polished, highly professional performances of the Igor Moiseyev Dance Company, not to mention those of other Eastern European nations, would have made the recently founded Iranian folk dance company look like an amateur project. And, even though Ahmadzadeh states, "We had no intention of competing with anyone, just a chance to take part and show our artistic enterprise to the other nations that would be performing there" (2008: 136), in fact, at the level they were performing, they would have proved an embarrassment to the sensitive officials of the Iranian government. The Iranian government of the Pahlavis sought and craved spectacle for purposes of representation of their modernity. Historian Saloumeh Gholami captures the Iranian government's intentions exactly:

> The function of the performing arts and especially dance in politics, particularly with regard to foreign policy and international relations was obvious, and the artistic groups employed by 'the Ministry of Culture' played the role of a kind of cultural ambassador.
>
> (2016: 70)

Thus, the Iranian folk dance ensembles, as with other state-supported ensembles, fulfilled the authoritarian desire for spectacle and national representation.[14]

Music and Dance

Music and dance have always been treated differently in Iran. Dancing in public, particularly professionally, has always been a shameful act; by contrast, the finest musicians historically often held important positions at court, although never as high as that of the poet (Shay 2014). While Iranians can identify particular dances as Iranian, it does not, like Polish or Ukrainian folk and ethno identity dance, constitute an important element of their identity. Music, however, does constitute an important aspect of Iranian identity, but not of Islamic identity; music constitutes an ambiguous element for many devout Muslims. As I have stated earlier, for many Iranians, a Muslim identity is held in tension with an Iranian identity.

When negative aspects of music are expressed, for example, when music is banned or denigrated by Islamic authorities, dance is automatically subsumed under it because dance requires music for its performance. "Although music has long played a central role in Iranian national identity, its status within Islam has long been highly ambiguous" (Nooshin 2005: 237). This is because classical music is connected to poetry, prized as a form of spirituality in Sufi ceremonies, and one of the most important forms of cultural expression throughout Iranian history, giving music respectability. Also, most of the performers of dance were young boys or women and their sexualized bodies and sexual availability placed them beyond social respectability, whereas music tends to be performed by older men, although historically many of them had been dancers in their youth (Shay 2014).

In addition, as a separate genre, folk music and dance are performed in celebratory events in villages and tribal settings; Iranian government officials, as urban individuals who are under the influence of nineteenth-century romantic nationalism, tend to view peasants and their music and dances as the essence of Iranian national identity, possessing a kind of apolitical kind of innocence. Village and tribal music, and dance, were among the first musical forms readmitted into public life, although only village men were allowed to perform in front of all-male audiences. It probably did not hurt their case that village musicians sometimes valorized Khomeini by including his name in their verses.

Classical music is performed in various urban settings—sacred Sufi contexts, men's convivial gatherings, and concerts—while popular music, both indigenous and Westernized, is performed in a wide variety of entertainment venues. As one of the most famous musicians in Iran phrased it: "Describing the resurgence of interest in *musiqi-e assil* [classical music], [Hosein] Alizadeh explains how much music making went underground during the period" (quoted in Nooshin 2005: 241). He adds: " 'Playing and teaching music itself became a kind of resistance and a way of maintaining identity' " (ibid.). Denied music on the radio and television, many individuals, craving music in their lives, began to learn musical instruments. Today, an unprecedented number of female instrumentalists, unlike the Pahlavi period when women rarely played musical instruments in public spaces, can be seen and heard in almost equal numbers in scores of performances on YouTube. It can be said that making music has become a widespread activity.

It is for this reason that, while music and dance were both immediately prohibited in Iran as one of the first acts of the Islamic Republic, dance remains forbidden. "Any music that suggested dance movement or included solo female singing was prohibited" (Nooshin 2005: 238). Music, but not dance, has been slowly and increasingly readmitted to public life. The entire popular music industry relocated to Los Angeles and provided banned recordings to a wide Iranian audience via bootlegged recordings that were reportedly widely available in Tehran and other cities (Hemmasi 2020).

Nevertheless, the Iranian Republic with its remarkably young population is faced with a political problem because young people in Iran want popular music to feel "hooked up" with other young people around the world.

> Pop music as entertainment, as aesthetic experience, as commodity or as social behavior, the latter particularly relevant in the context of an emerging youth culture. In failing to take account (or control), the government was later unable to stop them being used to subvert the dominant discourses.
>
> (Nooshin 2005: 239)

I took part in the first symposium on Persian Popular Music at Yale University, January 18–19, 2018, in which several musicians described the skirmishes and negotiations they experienced with the government authorities in order to perform, which the government frequently denied them the right to do.

Aspects of music remain prohibited: Female vocalists, like Qamar ol-Moluk Vaziri, Marzieh, Delkash, and Mahvash, who were extremely popular during the Pahlavi period, may no longer sing solo (see Chehabi 2000; the film *Avaz-e bi sarzamin* 2016); the Islamic establishment deems their voices too sexually tempting to male audiences; 6/8 rhythms, strongly associated with dance, cannot be played; and television and film cameras may not show musical instruments.

In Iran, with the election of Khatami, especially through the younger generations, restrictions on certain forms of popular music have begun to reappear, especially sugary ballads deemed to be politically harmless. "The New pop was generally performed at a moderate speed and never fast enough to imply dance (or any erotically suggestive) movement. Indeed, when broadcast on television, singers [only male] are required to use minimal body movement" (Nooshin 2005: 247). But, so desperate are the younger generations for any kind of popular music that they reportedly embrace this new phenomenon. "As one of the most prominent signifiers of modernity, the reemergence of pop music into public domain has sparked a complex and highly emotive debate over Iran's future in an increasingly global world" (Nooshin 2005: 231). This debate continues, and indeed I hear of continuing skirmishes between performers of popular music and the authorities in the Ministry of Culture and Enlightenment (see *Avaz-e bi sarzamin* 2016).

Unlike most musicians, dancers still practice underground or go out into Iran's endless deserts to perform and experience the freedom to dance, as can be seen by numerous YouTube recordings and e-mail reports I receive on a regular basis, in which young people now practice dance as a form of resistance to the regime, and for the right of people to practice movement as an individual right (Rastovac-Akhbarzadeh 2016, 2020; Shay 2008b).

NOTES

1. Cabaret/filmfarsi women dancers, such as Jamileh, used the hat and scarf props from this dance, variously called *shāteri* or *jāheli*, in their nightclub routines in the 1960s and the 1970s. However, as far as I know, Jamal was the first to create a group choreography from these solo dances in 1994. This staged version was an elaborate choreography of a dance he created for his fellow soldiers in Lashgarak barracks, Tehran, during his stint in the Iranian army in 1972. Four years later, in 1998, Avaz performed the dance in a command performance for Empress Farah Pahlavi in Queens, New York.
2. The Islamic Republic is clearly also an authoritarian regime, on some levels as intrusive, if not more so, in the personal lives of Iranians as the two Pahlavi regimes were. Since dance, other than the so-called *harekāt-e mowzun* (harmonious movement) genre, which are also used for religious and political purposes, does not exist in public spaces, it is beyond the scope of this study. I also have not had personal experience of the Islamic Republic regime, as I did under that of Mohammad Reza Pahlavi (see Gholami 2016; Meftahi 2016a, 2016b).
3. The interested reader can find dozens of documentaries of the event on You Tube in a wide variety of languages. The viewer can see the difficulties facing the planners and what went right and wrong, even without the commentaries.

4. So widespread is choreophobia among Iranians that none of the Iranian professors at UCLA, whom I invited to serve on my Ph.D. committee, would participate. They wanted to have no professional connection to dance studies. Only two brief writings about dance were available during the period that I wrote my dissertation (Rezvani 1962; Shay 1999; Zoka' 1978).
5. Currently, the best survey of Iranian regional folk dances is Friend 2016. In addition, one can view a wide selection of authentic Iranian regional folk and tribal dances on YouTube.
6. The competition between de Warren and the Ahmadzadehs must have been fierce, and the partial cause for the confusion concerning how many dance companies existed, for which they both claimed credit. For example, both claim credit for the mass movements of the military and dancers in the 2500th year of Monarchy celebration in Persepolis (de Warren 2009: 242–47; Ahmadzadeh 2008: 248–50). Ahmadzadeh adds, "He [Robert de Warren] came in the capacity of ballet master and choreographer and was never director or our company as wrongly mentioned in some dance dictionaries and ballet programmes" (2008: 176).
7. In a return visit to Iran, I noticed a strong feeling of nostalgia for all things Qajar, viewed as authentically Iranian, and several nightclubs catered to this new trend, which according to Khosrow Jamali began in the early 1970s (personal communication, February 16, 2019). I saw a dancer in his sixties who had been a motreb dancer as a young boy, in such a nightclub near the grand bazaar called the Ābanbār, he demonstrated many of the movements and styling that he had performed as a young man. It was enthralling to see these performances.
8. In addition to the issues surrounding dance and music, the figure of the male dancer caused embarrassment to the modernizing establishment, which sought to establish heteronormativity in all aspects of Iranian life. (See Najmabadi 2005 for the process in which the Iranian elite sought to establish heteronormativity to become modern in the European sense.)
9. As I think back upon the beginnings of learning and performing dance from Nasrin Farrokh Hekmat in 1954, the year after the final performances of Nilla Cram Cook, I realize that it is probable that Nasrin studied with one or the other of these figures that I mention (Shay 2014b, 2021).
10. For a history of ballet and *raqs-e melli* (national dance) in Iran, see Kiann 2016; Meftahi 2016a, 2016b.
11. Keeping the threads of these companies and their choreographies separate is extremely taxing because the information on the two companies has been hopelessly intermingled. Hayedeh Ahmadzadeh, who together with her husband, Nejad, directed the Iranian National Folk Dance, Song and Music Ensemble, writes: "He [Robert DeWarren] came in the capacity of ballet master and choreographer and was never director of our company as wrongly mentioned in some dance dictionaries and ballet programmes" (n.d.: 176).
12. Historian Ida Meftahi wrote in answer to my inquiry:

> I think the ballet company started by performing both folk and national dances, then at some point they both had a national dance [Iranian national themes using classical ballet movements] repertoire. Later it was fully the responsibility of the Mahalli Dancers to perform the Iranian dance of folk, etc. I don't recall who the last head of the ballet company was; maybe he didn't like the non ballet repertoire.
> (Personal communication, February 13, 2019)

My recollection is that the two folk dance companies continued as Nima Kiann indicated.

13. The cover jacket for Haideh Ahmadzadeh's autobiography shows a photograph of her in the lead role.
14. In 1976, musicians and dancers of these regions traveled to the United States on tour with the Mahalli Dancers under Robert de Warren's direction. As I watched the Turkmen dance suite at the Bovard Auditorium on the campus of the University of Southern California in Los Angeles, I remember thinking that mixing the ballet-trained Mahalli Dancers with the authentic Turkmen was an aesthetic misstep. Even though they were mixed together, the two groups were in every way technically mismatched. The authentic villagers were powerful and made the ballet-trained Mahalli dancers appear effete, and made the overall effect weak.

    De Warren mistakenly cites the scene at Bovary Auditorium at UCLA, which was in fact Bovard Auditorium at USC. I attended the event and had brunch with him and his wife Jacqueline at their hotel right across the street the next day.

4

Croatia: Lado—"Light of Croatian Culture"

In November 1999, six young women whirl rapidly in a circle in silence under a single spotlight, their skirts and pigtails horizontally suspended in space, wearing the iconic red-and-white costumes of Posavina in Central Croatia. The audience immediately understands the iconic vision and breaks into thunderous applause. It is the opening of the 50th anniversary jubilee concert in the National Theatre commemorating the 1949 founding of Lado, the Ensemble of Folk Dances and Songs of Croatia (Figure 11). The ensemble, today's most iconic representation of the Croatian nation, has performed and endured through the historical vicissitudes that, under a variety of regimes, both authoritarian and democratic, has ruled the nation since World War II. Today, Lado has just celebrated its 70th anniversary but, through history, from at least the late Middle Ages, dance has served as a visual representation of a variety of Croatian identities in various ways until the present (Ivančan 1996; Lado 2019; Shay 2016c; Sremac 2001; Vitez and Vučić 2009).[1]

Croatian dance historian Stjepan Sremac writes:

> I noted very early that Croatians, in comparison to neighboring ethnic groups and other people (in Europe), paid more attention to and honored their choreographic and musical traditions, including their staged presentations ... they began immediately to seriously pursue their staged presentations, which continues right down to today.
>
> (2001: 5)

Therefore, as I elaborate throughout the text, I note the periods in which new forms of presentational, ethno identity dances appear. It is important, despite Sremac's quotation above, to issue a caveat that while the dances represent Croatian identity, the dances that were created for public performance had different fields of representation, and the term "Croatian" referred to limited groups of individuals. Before a contemporary Croatian ethnic identity developed that referred

FIGURE 11: Croatia. Dances of Posavina. Avaz International Dance Theatre. Choreography: Anthony Shay. Photo: D. Young. From the author's collection.

to the entire nation, the term "Croatian" did not apply to everyone; these dances represented regional, communal, and class identities rather than a pan-Croatian identity as we know it today. For example, the early *moreška* sword dancers most likely represented the guild or guilds from which the performers were drawn and were used for church and civic calendar celebrations (as were Moorish dances all over Europe). Ultimately, the dances and their dancers represented the specific towns in which they were performed. This would have been the most common form of representation throughout the Middle Ages and Early Modern Europe when most identities were local and national identities did not exist.

In the second instance I describe below, the nineteenth-century choreographed ballroom dances (*dvoransko* or *salonsko kolo*), they were created and performed to represent elite populations of noble and wealthy bourgeois individuals who identified themselves exclusively as Croatian. At that time peasants all over Europe, as in Croatia, had regional and local identities, not national identities.[2] At the end of the nineteenth century, as national and ethnic identities began to be applied to entire populations, the Croatian Seljačka Sloga (Peasant Harmony) created a festival system that enabled the peasants to perform their songs and dances on public stages in order to express not only their regional and local identity but their "Croatian" identity as well (Žganec and Sremec 1950).

Urban youth, increasingly imbued with strong feelings of Croatian nationalism, began to stage peasant dances in the interwar period in the 1930s. After World War II, the government sponsored and encouraged an amateur youth movement that later spread to towns and villages, known as KUD, Cultural Artistic Societies (*Kulturno Umjetničko Društva*), which proliferated throughout Croatia and Yugoslavia. When, in emulation of the Soviet model set by the Moiseyev Dance Company (Shay 2019), Yugoslavia began to establish official professional dance ensembles, the KUD model had already created the model of staging folk dances that dance companies in Yugoslavia adopted (Maners 1995; Shay 2016c; Sremac 2001). Lado is the result of this long history of staging folk dances for public performances and now represents Croatia on the global stage.

Balkanism

I believe that, in all good conscience, it would not be appropriate to discuss Croatia in a study that describes and analyzes specifically the intersection of dance and music with the various authoritarian regimes of Balkan states like Croatia without briefly addressing the topic of Balkanism. I want to establish Balkanism as a conceptual framework in which Western observers have too often viewed the intersection of dance, music, and authoritarianism not only in Croatia but also throughout the entire Balkans of which Croatia furnishes an example. Balkanism, like orientalism, is a lens that enables the viewer to dismiss the behavior of essentialized Others as inevitable, wild, and primitive and deprives them of individual human agency; it is in their "nature" to be violent. How could it be otherwise when prominent writers like Rebecca West forcefully state: "Violence was indeed all I ever knew of the Balkans; all I knew of the South Slavs" (1966: 21). But historian Mark Mazower argues, "Yet for centuries, life in the Balkans was no more violent than elsewhere" (2002: 147). And because, in general, nation-states in the Balkans tend to be small, it is easier to dismiss them as unimportant and not worthy of serious notice.

Yearning to be part of the West, Croatians have never liked their role as a Balkan state: "Now that EU and NATO membership have confirmed Croatia's 'Western' identity, Croats feel less need to do so themselves. But a marked resistance to being included in 'the Balkan,' still a term of odium, remains" (Tanner

2019: xiii). My own experience was that the Balkans was south and east of wherever I was at any given moment.

"Understanding the role and significance of ethnic identities in Southeastern Europe requires us to see them in their historical and political contexts, or else we are in danger of falling into Orientalising or even more properly defined 'Balkanising' discourse" (Dzino 2010: 14). This is the manner, as Said (1978) has shown, in which many individuals from ancient Greece to the present treat the unknown and the Other: "In the historical and literary imagination, the Balkans loom large as a frightening but ill-defined space" (Wachtel 2008: 1; see also Shay 2008c). In other words, the Balkans, like the orient, became an empty space in which to create new, imaginary personal and national identities for many individuals, but especially for amateur dancers and musicians from the West, for whom the Balkans was a wondrous and exotic place (Laušević 2007; Shay 2008c; Todorova 1997). For these reasons, it is crucial to give a detailed, if necessarily brief, history of Croatia to contextualize Lado's existence and the role of dance in that history.

For the reader for whom the term "Balkanism" is unfamiliar, in short, Balkanism is a variety of orientalism, that is, a way of viewing the "Other," which establishes the viewer in a place of power over the object, diminishing it in the process.

> A persistent paradox infuses most of the negative stereotypes entertained in the self-styled West: the Other is hopelessly diverse, fragmented, and internally divided—so much so that in the end all such peoples seem radically alike. Who can make sense of so much difference? It is easier to dismiss it as all the same.
>
> (Bjelić 2002: ix)

Balkanism means regarding a complex geographic area as more or less the same, much as my friends and I regarded homogenized "Balkan" dances:

> The problem is not the Balkans but so-called Balkanism. I think we should say it loud and clear: The real problem is not the indecision about the geographic locations of the Balkans, but the stubborn persistence in overwhelming the term "Balkan" with more stereotypes than it can actually accommodate ... This place is merely a product of constant construction and reconstruction, in which process clichés are at least as important as concrete facts.
>
> (Cioroianu 2002: 211)

How can either Orientalism or Balkanism be possible and why is it important? First, because Westerners "were (and are) little aware and even less interested in the thoughts and sensibilities of their objects" (Todorova 1997: 61). Historian

Larry Wolff noted, "One might describe the invention of Eastern Europe as an intellectual project of demi-Orientalization" (1994: 7). In other words many individuals in those societies, especially scholars, understand that they are scrutinized as the Other and are no longer a Serb or a Greek, but reduced to being a person from the Balkans with the many clichéd characteristics that such an identity bears.

There are, of course, differences between Balkanism and Orientalism, and I will lay those out later in this section but, au fond, they carry deep seeds of disrespect and dismissal, and ultimately they lump into indistinguishable masses of groups of people who show tendencies toward inerasable wildness, primitiveness, and tribalism through which lens journalists and analysts largely reported the wars that marked the disintegration of the former Yugoslavia.

Lord Byron's poems were the introduction to the Balkans, or at least the Greek part, for nineteenth-century elites. His poems echoed and promoted the popular philhellenic cause for freeing the Greeks, whom he imagined as the direct descendants of Plato and Socrates, from the Ottoman yoke, which attracted hundreds of young Englishmen as volunteers to the cause.

> Byron's international fame, which rested on his lifestyle—in particular on his legendary support for the cause of Greek independence and his death at Missolonghi—as on his work, made him by far the most important figure in the Romantic discovery of the Balkans in English literature.
>
> (Goldsworthy 1998: 16)[3]

Byron's high-flown poetry descended to dime-novel entertainment prose within a few generations after the founding of a series of small principalities and kingdoms—Serbia, Romania, Bulgaria, Montenegro—which quickly became the stuff of romance and mystery novels, a space of incognito princes, swordplay, and secret societies, a new fairy-tale playground for novelists and composers of operettas. "The emergence of new kingdoms in the south-eastern corner of Europe drew attention to far-away lands of which the British public hitherto knew little" (Goldsworthy 1998: 43). In these novels Balkan courts and royalty paraded about in silly comic opera costumes in front of fairy-tale castles and carried out bloody vendettas, loosely based on the sensationalized newspaper reports of the goings-on of the Serbian and Romanian royal families and the fertile imaginations of the authors. (See, for example, Agatha Christie, *The Secret of Chimneys* [1925].) Thus, Balkanism took several paths in the popular Western imagination: noble (savage) primitive Montenegrin mountaineers, comic-opera kingdoms, and spy nests.

Later, for folk dance and music enthusiasts, the Balkans became a never-ending source for rapturous musical harmonies and rhythms and fascinating dances (Laušević 2007; Rice 1994; Shay 2008c; Todorova 1997). In the middle of the dance floor of the local coffee house, I, too, donned my balkanist glasses, seeing an idealized festive life in which I could take part. To this day most participants refer to our activities as "Balkan" dancing and "Balkan" music.

It is within this context of the popularity and intense interest in Balkan music and dance in the 1950s, 1960s, and 1970s that many young Americans first encountered the various societies that comprise the area that we knew only as "the Balkans." These young Americans, and other Western individuals, demonstrated and exhibited a deep interest in these music and dance genres, coupled with a profound lack of knowledge and ignorance of the peoples, their histories, and the lives of those who actually performed them in Balkan villages. We permitted Balkanism to shape our perceptions of the various societies of the Balkans whose music and dances we admired so much. Why, if we were so enthusiastic, could we have been so dismissive as to descend into these balkanist attitudes? In short, it was ignorance.[4]

However, Balkanism was not only a fault of ignorant and eager teenagers and young adults; in the eyes of some scholars and politicians from Western countries one can also find Balkanism in their writings. And many people in nation-states in the Balkans are not unaware of this: "In contemporary scholarship, Balkanism is interpreted as the dominant Western strategy for representing the East European periphery" (Kiossev 2002: 179). While scholars in the West are attuned to the dangerous shoals of Orientalist attitudes of othering, they appear to be nearly oblivious to Balkanism. A scholar from Serbia, in an e-mail to me, wrote "it hurts."

Following historian Maria Todorova (1997), I would point out that while the orient, in Said's terms (1978), is a feminine place, timeless and spiritual, sensual and colorful, largely created as a place in the Western imagination of promising fecund, readily available sexuality provided by sensuous dancing girls as described in erotic detail by writers such as Gustave Flaubert (Karayanni 2005; Shay 2014a), the Balkans constitutes a masculine space, peopled in Byronian verses with brave, disheveled, hypermasculine warriors in colorful mountaineer garb. It is perhaps a place in which males are foregrounded due to the fact that some of the earliest and most important travel writings were produced largely by women writers, Rebecca West, Olivia Manning, and Edith Durham, who regarded the Balkans with what we may characterize as "the feminine gaze." What *does* draw together and unite the phenomena of Orientalism and Balkanism is the element of exoticism they both share. It is because of Balkanism, and the ignorance of the history of the region, that I present a relatively long background of Croatian history and identity formation in order to understand the role that Lado, and dance in general, has played in both democratic and authoritarian regimes.

Ethnogenesis of the Croats

The ethnogenesis of many European states remains murky and opaque due to the long period of folk wanderings, Roman and Byzantine wars of aggression, Turkic and Iranian nomad invasions from Central Asia to Eastern Europe, and lack of historical writing that occurred after the gradual fading of Rome, and later Byzantium, from the fifth century. Eager nationalists frequently seek early dates when their people, whom they often regard as a single mass, not unlike themselves, occupied a particular territory:

> The imaginary constructs of the past are transformed into realities of the present, influencing the ways in which modern ethnicities in the region relate to themselves and perceive others around them ... these views of the past are easily manipulated in the present, and ... the present has too frequently determined the way in which the past has been seen.
>
> (Dzino 2010: 15)

Several important prehistoric sites have been uncovered in Croatian territory and, even from those earliest settlements, archaeological and ethnographic investigators have shown how the earliest inhabitants began to exploit the environment in ways that would echo down to the present time (Bakarić et al. 2005). Material culture and daily activities before the appearance of the Croats, such as designs found on pottery, exploitation of plants, methods of hunting, use of dyes, embroidery patterns, clothing construction, herding, fishing, and other elements, began with the earliest inhabitants and succeeding historical periods are reflected in peasant lifestyles (see Gušić 1955). If these early inhabitants had an ethnicity, it remains unknown. They were certainly not Croatians.

The Coming of the Slavs to the Balkans

The Croats are a Slavic people. The term "Slavic" today is understood to have a linguistic connotation that refers to individuals and groups who speak one of the Slavic languages; it does not refer to a genetic or racial group. Through time, many scholars have written on the topic of the origins of the Slavs. One of the most enduring theories claims that the early Slavs came from the Pripet marshes in today's Ukraine and from there left in large, peaceful migrations to the west to become Poles, Slovaks, and Czechs; to the east to become Russians, Ukrainians, and Belarusians; and to the south to become Croats, Slovenes, Serbs, Macedonians, and Bulgarians. These historical reconstructions frequently relied on arcane and problematic linguistic evidence and were frequently marred by political partisanship. "The 'Croat-Slavic' discourse ... showed the Croats as a distinctive Slav group that migrated into post-Roman Illyricum. It emphasized the separate nature of Croat identity" (Dzino 2010: 19). This view was depicted in romantic paintings produced throughout the twentieth century (see Dzino 2010: 24–28).

Some of these reconstructions of Croatian identity and ethnogenesis were used to political ends to prove the ancient origins of a specific ethnic group in order to give them the right to inhabit a particular geographic location.

> We might even say that in essence the view which separated the arrival of the Slav Croats from the other Slavs remained prominent in Communist times, as it reflected Croatian sameness and separateness from other South Slavs. This was encouraged by Tito's "brotherhood-and-unity" ideology of the Yugoslav socialist federation as a commonwealth of "brotherly" South Slavs, different peoples but the same "kin," after 1945.
>
> (Dzino 2010: 20)

This "brotherhood-and-unity" symbol largely informed the repertoires at the beginnings of the formation of the national folk dance companies. Theories and speculation about the arrival and identities of the Slavs and Croats abound, in Danjiel Dzino's terms "becoming Slav, becoming Croat," and nearly all of them carry considerable political baggage (Dzino 2010).

In this section, I wish to look briefly at the ethnic origins of the Croats within a greater Slavic identity: Both came later than is often thought, and even when located in historical annals, those identities were not modern identities. "The Slavs are referred to as Sclavi or Slavi in Roman writings and the earliest legal documents" (Ćirković 2004: 10). Thus,

> Linguistically, the "early Slavs" were speakers of early forms of Slavic language, such as Common Slavic. Historically, they were people described as "Slavs" by outside, foreign sources (Byzantine, Frankish, Arab) and there is no decisive evidence for the self-identification of "Slavs" as Slavs until at least the 12th century.
>
> (Dzino 2010: 93)

However, the "groups labeled 'Slavs' share certain elements of a common habitus" (Dzino 2010: 94) that allowed outsiders to identify them as a distinct group. Much of this transformation of becoming Slav took place in the context of the presence of the Avar Khaganate, in which Slavic became the lingua franca of that polity, indicating the important presence of the Slavs within the Avar Horde (Dzino 2010; Pohl 2018).

The picturesque image of wholesome hordes of virile blond Slavs, or even more unbelievably, Croats or Serbs, arriving on the shores of the Danube River and the Adriatic Sea needs to be put to rest. However, the image continues to live as "many individuals imagined that the songs and dances were those performed by the original Slavic settlers, who began to arrive in the Balkans in the mid-6th century, and this constituted a dream world" (Dubinskas quoted in Shay 2016c: 265). Recent scholarship, through the extensive use of archaeology and contemporary written sources such as Byzantine and Latin chronicles, has effectively challenged these widely held assumptions of Slavic origins that originated in the Romantic movement of nationalism of the nineteenth century and continued well into the twentieth century in academic circles.

The Slavs first appeared in the light of history in the mid-sixth century in Byzantine sources such as those by Jordanes and Procopius who called these new warrior groups Sclavenes. The term "Sclavene" was applied to these new groups and was a term that the Byzantines created. "It might be that 'Sclavene' was initially the self-designation of a particular ethnic group. In its most strictly defined sense, however, the 'Sclavene ethnicity' is a Byzantine invention" (Curta 2001: 119). That designation was applied to all of those who were perceived by the Byzantines to be Slavic speakers, or peoples who were associated with them. Early Slavic identity (not yet differentiated as Slovene, Croatian, or Bulgarian) in the mid-sixth century had not developed into a clear ethnic identity in the modern sense.

The "Great Migration," or the "Great Movement of Nations," terms frequently found in scholarly works such as that of Marijana Gušić (1955: 19, 20), to describe the movement of Slavs out of the Pripet marshes, the supposed *Urheimat* of the Slavs, into the Balkan Peninsula, never occurred in the manner that many people imagine. The Slavs were frequently depicted as peaceful, blond agriculturalists moving in large family or clan groupings into the Balkans to settle and take up a bucolic lifestyle that remained unchanged until the early twentieth century.[5]

Contemporary scholars have completely rejected this earlier image of peaceful Slavic migration. Archaeologist Paul Barford notes of the Slavic migrations:

> The rate of reproduction involved to fill the new territories with descendants of a small original population, no matter how the figures are calculated, is biologically impossible. It may also be stated that there is no evidence that there was wholesale depopulation of any of the territories claimed as the homeland of the Slavs in this period to reflect large-scale folk movements.
>
> (2001: 46)

On the north bank of the Danube a stewpot of peoples formed and reformed into various collectives, few of which had coalesced into what would be described as an ethnic group in today's terms. Medieval historian Patrick J. Geary notes: "Gradually, across the seventh century, Slavic warrior-settlers moved across the Danube and into the Balkans. The chronology is unclear and necessarily so: The process was so decentralized and fluid that it could hardly be dated or documented" (2002: 146).

The Slavs were often associated in Byzantine texts beginning with the first mention of the Slavs in 518 with two other groups: the Antes and, later, in the 560s with the Turkic-speaking Avars. The Avars and associated groups of Slavs became a major threat to the Byzantines. "In a wide area south of the Carpathians (Moravia and Slovakia) the archaeological evidence demonstrates the emergence of a mixed Slav-Avar material culture, suggesting symbiotic coexistence" (Barford 2001: 57). Later, the Slavs assisted Charlemagne's Franks to destroy the Avar Empire. It was at this point that a Croat identity emerged, which some scholars consider to be a self-appellation of the elite who appeared in the Carolingian Empire:

> New elites were neither "Slavic" nor indigenous, although they could appear as "Slavic" to outside observers. They were the result of the earlier process of acculturation and social transition during the period of Avar domination ... Croat identity was the self-identification of the ruling group and "Slav" identity was a perception by the outside observer.
>
> (Dzino 2010: 217)

The Slavic-Croat identity was the result of the amalgamation of Slavic speakers and the pre-Slavic populations. The appellation "Croat" does not appear until the end of the ninth century. On the Dalmatian coast, "The indigenous population transformed by acquiring a different language, Slavic *lingua franca*, which enabled easier communication in the same way that Latin was adopted by their ancestors" (Dzino 2010: 216). Most importantly, " 'becoming Slav' and 'becoming Croat' does show a significant degree of heterogeneity and the absence of linear developments" (ibid.). The process required a long period of time.

That migrations occurred is not disputed, but we know little of their mechanism, but "The Slavic 'migrations' were chaotic population movements of smaller groups, not a Slavic flood, or an organized colonization of the Balkan Peninsula" (Dzino 2010: 212).

Slavs into Croats: The Early Middle Ages

The term "Croat" is generally agreed by most scholars not to be of Slavic origin. Barford notes that,

> Here we should also note a number of modern theories which, on the basis of the ethno and certain linguistic data, hold that the original name "Croats" did

> not in fact refer to Slavs at all but was of Iranian Sarmatian origin and later adopted by their Slav subjects.
>
> (2001: 75)

Barford adds: "The evidence for this suggestion is not very convincing" (ibid.: 295, n.20).[6] Ivo Goldstein notes that the first mention of Croats is carved in stone and dates to the end of the ninth century, 888 AD: "Branimir, Duke of the Croats" (1999: 17).

Christianity

The most momentous event that marks the period after the ninth century is the conversion of the Croats to Christianity, which was a part of an aggressive campaign, initiated by Charlemagne throughout the eastern and northern reaches of his expanding empire. The conversion process was often fraught with great difficulties and did not always flow smoothly. Many individuals and populations resisted accepting the new religion.

> Modern historiography, looking at these processes with hindsight as progress, has rarely considered the conversion of pagan early medieval societies to Christianity as a process involving ideological and ethical conflict. One should not however ignore the fact that the introduction of Christianity attacked the very ideological roots of tribal societies, usually characterized by stubbornly looking back towards their ancestral past. The Christian missionaries were dealing not with "secular" peoples but with peoples with clearly defined religious and ideological structures: paganism was a necessary element of the integration of whole communities and the determination of group identity.
>
> (Bradford 2001: 211)

It is acknowledged by most historians that the conversion process usually began with the ruler, who then forced conversion on his elite warriors and court officials.

> In the early decades of the conversion, Christianity was mainly restricted to the social elites, and we should be aware that the decisions and preferences of the socio-political elite were not automatically transmitted to the bulk of the population ... That the pagan beliefs had not lost their hold on the populace is further illustrated by the mass apostasy which is relatively frequently mentioned with horror in the written sources.
>
> (Barford 2001: 223)

In Croatia, the conversion process occurred largely outside of history. On the Dalmatian coast, interaction between the already long-Christianized Roman population and the newly settled Croats may have led to some of the earliest conversions. "Conversion on a large scale did not begin till the ninth century, when the first missionaries from Byzantium, Italy and the Frankish state reached Croatian territory" (Goldstein 1999: 16). The Pope and the Byzantine Emperor tacitly left Croatia within the orbit of Rome and the Frankish Empire. The clear result of the conversion was that Croatia at the farthest eastern reaches of the Roman Catholic world was clearly in the embrace of Western Europe.

The First Independent Croatian Kingdom

It was the geographic position of Croatia at the fringes of Byzantium, the Frankish Empire, and the rising Bulgarian state that allowed the increasing consolidation of Central Croatia, Slavonia (Eastern Croatia), and Dalmatia, which became the Triune Kingdom. This same geographical position was to be the curse of the soon-to-be frequently divided Croatian kingdom until the 1990s. It is important to again stress how fragile and unstable medieval kingdoms in Europe were. We do not know the actual power and administrative authority controlled by Tomislav and his descendants, but the most powerful European state, that of Charlemagne, is characterized by Fletcher as

> Charlemagne was incontestably the greatest ruler of early medieval Europe ... He expanded his kingdom by means of war and diplomacy in every direction, amassing untold quantities of land and plunder and tribute for judicious distribution to grateful and loyal followers. The Frankish empire was a ramshackle structure in which power lay, as it had always done, with local landed aristocratic families.
> (1998: 194)

We can see that the Christianization of Croatia followed the general western European process of conversion and aided in the development of the first Croatian state. Tomislav, the first Croatian ruler to bear the title of king, gained the fruits of this process for he was "crowned by a papal legate as the first king in 924/5" (Barford 2001: 230).

Croatia under Foreign Rule 1100–1800

Croatia, until after World War II, was a peasant nation throughout its history. Thus, it is important to understand under what conditions they existed. Three broad social, political, and economic movements form themes that underpin the main historical events of this long period. First, the establishment of feudalism created a system of rigorous control over the peasant population that constituted well over 95 per cent of the population of Croatia, and indeed all of Eastern Europe, until the late nineteenth century. The dismemberment of Croatia into three parts, and four if we count Dubrovnik as a separate republic, which characterized Croatia until the nineteenth century, had far-reaching results in the development of the modern state, finally established in 1992. Until the end of the nineteenth century, the peasants were regarded as tools for the familial enrichment of the landowning nobles. Feudalism and the accompanying enserfment of the peasantry was a direct result of interaction with the Franks.

> In what may more properly be called Central Europe—Hungary, Croatia, Bohemia, and Poland—the foundations of feudal society were laid by the foreign, mainly German feudal aristocracy that had spread Christianity and become the military base of the ruling families ... Still the feudal system did not develop here in as complicated a form as in France and Germany.
>
> (Gunst 1989: 60)

Ultimately, this powerful class impeded the economic and political growth that characterized the West.

The lot of peasants under feudalism was unenviable. While there were some distinctions between different groups of peasants such as freedmen and serfdom, these distinctions made little difference in the hard lives they led. Indeed, the peasantry were regarded by the landed classes almost as enemies, aliens, and despicable:

> As early as Merovingian times, some descriptions portray the peasant as wicked, dangerous, and uneducated, likening him more to an animal than as a human being ... Peasant labor was seen as a result of sin—Cain was considered the first peasant.
>
> (Goetz 1996: 133)[7]

As the largest and lowest of social classes, they were hedged in by laws and rules and subject to abuse of every sort, especially their lords who had life-and-death authority over them. They were required to dress in specific ways under strict sumptuary laws and, above all, were not allowed to carry weapons or ride horses, a right reserved for the nobles. They were required to surrender as much as one-fourth of their produce to the landlord, in addition to state and church taxes, and had to perform corvée labor, that is, to work without payment for the lord two days a week.

The English-speaking world hails the Magna Carta as a milestone in the development of contemporary democracy and human rights. So powerful is the image of this fundamental document that it has become a general noun, indicating a foundational document that guarantees "rights, privileges, or liberties" (*Microsoft Encarta College Dictionary* 2001: 864). As such the original intent of the Magna Carta is largely misunderstood. It can in no way be interpreted as anything other than a document which, in 1215, the barons of England forced King John (Lackland, younger brother and heir of the childless Richard II Lionheart) to sign in order to guarantee their rights and privileges at the expense of those of the crown. Neither the barons nor their document referred to the common people. In fact, the document did much to ensure that the common people would remain serfs within their feudal power, since the income of their serfs' labor constituted the basis of their wealth and political power. It was, in fact, simply another skirmish between the aristocracy and the king for power that characterized the entire medieval period.

What is less known in the West is that the Croatian nobility framed a similar document more than a century in advance of the British nobles. Upon the death of Zvonimir, the last native Croatian king who left no heir, the Hungarian princes claimed the Croatian throne through their sister, who was Zvonimir's widow. In the years that followed, the Hungarian pretender, Koloman, defeated the Croatian claimant. The Croatian nobles gathered together to draft a document, the *Pacta Conventa*, the result of a formal meeting between the Croatian nobility and Koloman, the Hungarian king of the Arpad dynasty, which ruled in Croatia until the fourteenth century.

In return for being recognized as the King of Croatia in 1102, under the *Pacta Conventa*, Koloman agreed to confirm the privileges, rights, and properties of the Croatian nobility. This document and its contents were the impetus for the formation of the Sabor, the Croatian Estates, and the major basis upon which the Croatian nobles, and centuries later Croatian members of other classes, managed to retain their positions vis-à-vis the Hungarian state and crown. The *Pacta Conventa* and the Sabor became primary symbols in the formation of modern Croatian identity.

The Hungarian Arpad dynasty ruled Croatia for the next two centuries (1102–1301). It was at this time that the position of the king's paladin, the *ban*, was established and future kings, including the Hapsburgs, ruled through this individual. Unlike the Croatian kings for whom Dalmatia was an important focus, Arpad interests were centered to the north, in Hungary, their dynastic center. This permitted the avaricious Venetians, during the dynastic rule of the Arpads, to seize the Dalmatian coast and islands as part of their territorial expansion, large parts of which they kept under their rule for the most part until the destruction of the Venetian empire in 1797 by Napoleon Bonaparte's forces.

> Dalmatia, because of its urban character and the small size of its land plots, did not lend itself to feudalism and, thus, the peasants of this area rarely worked on the large estates that characterized Slavonia: "Peasants were tenants who enjoyed personal liberty, colons who could lease land at will and who by contract had the right to part of the harvest" (Goldstein 1999: 23). As part of the larger Mediterranean world, Dalmatia, unlike the other regions of Croatia, had several small urban centers that partook of the Renaissance and it was here that Croatian literature first flourished.

In this urban atmosphere the first genre of dance, the *moreška*, an athletic sword dance requiring hours of rehearsals for its performance, appeared. Members of the various guilds in several towns along the Dalmatian coast performed it, and while the first mention of it appears only in 1784 (Sremac 2001: 8), it must have existed for centuries before (see Zebec 2001: 448). One of the most famous variants is still performed in the town of Korčula not only as a tourist attraction but also as a major part of the town's annual ritual calendar and a symbol of local pride.

Ottoman Domination

The single most important event that dominates Europe, and particularly the Balkans during the period from 1389 until 1699 and beyond, was the titanic struggle between the Ottoman Empire, which ruled large sections of the Balkans until the end of the First World War, and the Christian states of Eastern and Central Europe. Large tracts of Croatian land were devastated by the many battles fought in many regions of Croatia prior to 1526, the Battle of Mohacs, after which Slavonia and parts of Northern Croatia were occupied until 1699 when the Treaty of Karlovac (Karlowicz) was signed.

The most lasting mark of Ottoman domination on the Croatian state was the establishment of the Military Frontier (*Vojna Krajina*), whose effects still reverberate as the scene of much of the fighting that occurred during World War II and later the War of Succession with Serbia (1992–95). This area, which stretched along the southern border between Bosnia and Croatia, also marked the border between Hapsburg and Ottoman lands until 1876, when the Hapsburgs occupied and later annexed Bosnia. The Military Frontier was established as a no-man's land, a semi-autonomous buffer region under direct Austrian, rather than Hungarian or Croatian, rule throughout its existence. The configuration of the Military Frontier divided Slavonia from Croatia. The Hapsburgs offered land to settlers in exchange for fighting the Ottoman armies and irregulars who attempted to raid across the borders for hundreds of years. The area was quickly settled by Serbs and Vlachs of the Orthodox faith as well as Croats escaping from Bosnia, forever altering the ethnic composition of the region.

Frustration and Growth, 1797–1918

The major trends in Croatia during the period that began near the end of the eighteenth century and continued until the end of the First World War were characterized by continuing political frustration contrasted with small economic gains and considerable cultural growth. The major intractable problem continued to be the relationship with both Austria and Hungary; the Sabor was engaged in a constant struggle with both Hungary and Austria to maintain the concept of Croatia as a separate political entity through the constant claim of the historical symbols of Croatia's separate status.

The Croatian position, since 1102, had always been that the only link to Hungary that was legally binding was that of a shared king—a king who was crowned separately for each of the kingdoms—who would recognize Croatia's political, legal, and economic uniqueness and separate identity apart from Hungary. Thus, there existed a constant struggle to maintain Croatia as a unique kingdom, with unique laws—the principal theme of Croatian history throughout the nineteenth century.

Throughout this period, Hungary was wracked by its own powerful nationalistic forces, finally gaining equal status with Austria during the middle of the century. Thus politically, Hungary was able to function almost as an independent nation. For Croatia, the consequences of the agreement between the Austrian and Hungarian halves of the Austro-Hungarian Empire were dire. The Hungarians constantly attempted to politically, economically, and culturally dominate, absorb, and assimilate Croatia and Slavonia through linguistic and political means, that is, the process of Magyarization, while Austria ruled directly over Istria and Dalmatia, frustrating Croatian desires to reunify the Triune Kingdom. The culmination of the struggle with Hungary resulted in the *Nagodba* (agreement) in 1868. "Although the *nagodba* included some indisputable benefits (recognition of territorial integrity), it made Croatia completely dependent in financial matters on Hungary, and subordinated the Croatian ban [an elite administrative position] to the Hungarian prime minister" (Goldstein 1999: 83). The Croatians also sought to have the Military Frontier, which was directly ruled by Austria and at its widest extent took up almost half of the national territory and divided Slavonia from Croatia, brought under its control. The Military Frontier, after many delays, was finally integrated into Croatia in 1888. However, Croatian desires to unite the whole of Croatia were never fully realized until a century later.

The Beginnings of Croatian Nationalism

One of the basic elements in the forging of national consciousness is the establishment of a national language. In Croatia, Latin was the official language. In 1829, Ljuedvit Gaj founded the Illyrian Movement, which later became the foundation of the National Party and the Croatian National Revival. Gaj and his associates succeeded in standardizing the language, selecting štokavski as the standard variant. Also, there was improvement in the status of the peasants in Croatia and Slavonia. In 1848, a year that was characterized by revolutions throughout Europe, the Hapsburgs announced what was perhaps the most far-reaching and important event of the century: the emancipation of the serfs. Agricultural production increased because the peasants were able to keep the fruits of their labor.

During this period of high nationalism throughout Central and Eastern Europe, dance masters created "national dances" for the urban elites, who were the first to be influenced by nationalist emotions, based loosely on, or inspired by, peasant dancing as the source of all that was purely "of the nation" (Garafola 1997). As music scholar Frank Dubinskas notes about the period: "The imagery of the folk dance, the *kolo*, and the medium of folk song pervaded the tropes of the cultural renaissance [*prepored*] ... Its central image for unity is a giant *kolo*" (1983: 33; see also March 1983). And however much the elite claimed to have interest in peasant folkloric forms, they had no interest in performing actual peasant dances, in actual peasant costumes, to actual peasant music. They required the services of a dance master to mediate between the authentic peasant dance and the elite ballroom dances they performed at their nationalist-themed social events (Figure 12).

The first instance of the use of a folk-inspired social dance for national representation in Croatia occurred during the visit of Emperor Franz Josef II in 1818.

> The real center-piece of the celebration, however, was a huge *kolo* dance held in front of the bishop's palace. Dancers and singers dressed in folk costumes were led in a circle by Count Janko Drašković. But these were no villagers singing "folk" songs in the Sunday kolo. Drašković and the ersatz "peasants" were nobles and bourgeois of Zagreb, bedecked in "artistic" stylizations of village garb and singing a poem penned by the Count himself.
>
> (Dubinskas 1983: 28–29)

Dance masters created other "national" dances under a number of different names, *hrvatsko*, *dvoransko* or *salonsko* kolo (Croatian or ballroom dance), which were figure dances based on the steps and figures of the quadrille, that held sway as a Croatian national symbol up to World War II in both social and theatrical representations:

FIGURE 12: Croatia. Podravina wedding. Avaz International Dance Theatre. Choreography: Anthony Shay. Scene from the National Public Television special AMAN. 1977.

> And so hrvatsko and slavonsko kolo, in a period of less than five years of its conception in its more or less final form, became part of the repertoire of every dance event not only in Zagreb, but in every part of Croatia. It is truly unusual how these two relatively complex figure dances were able to spread so quickly. Its critical role came about because of its symbolic national meaning, which nevertheless was typically urban, these specifically urban dances raised to the position of overall national dances.
>
> (Sremac 2001: 44. See also Ruyter 2008; Shay 2016c)

In the 1880s the leading figure in the Yugoslav movement was Bishop Josip Strossmayer (1815–1905), who was largely responsible for the founding of the leading cultural foundations of Croatia such as the University in Zagreb and the Yugoslav Academy of Arts and Sciences. He was a passionate believer, like other Illyrian and South Slav unifiers, that the only possible survival for the Croatian nation as a weak state lay in throwing their lot in with the Serbs, and other South

Slavs. The Croat–Serb differences would create a shadow over the two Yugoslav states (1918–41; 1945–92). These differences—religious, ethnic, linguistic, political, economic, and cultural—came to be known as what historian Jill A. Levine termed "The Croat Question" (1993).

> In contrast to the Yugoslavism of Strossmayer and the Illyrian Movement, the enthusiasm for South Slav unification, which swept Croat politics before the First World War, was of a more unitarist variety. Enthusiasm for Serbia was high after the recognition of the independent Serbian Kingdom and many Croats as well as Serbs envisioned Serbia as the Piedmont of any larger South Slav state.
> (Levine 1993: 27)

Moreover, the Serbian kingdom emerged from the war as a winner, albeit a battered one, and attracted admiration among many Croats who had long despaired of having a state of their own.

At the end of the First World War, the Hapsburg Empire crumbled with a dizzying rapidity that left Croatia in dire peril. Italy was preparing to invade the entire Dalmatian coast, over which they had both political and cultural hegemony and against which the Croats had no military forces. In addition, as we have seen, Croatian identity was still being shaped, and many in Dalmatia were ready to throw in their lot with Italy because they had lived under Italian rule and many identified with Italy and had been educated in the Italian language. Italy, which had joined the Allied side in 1915, had been secretly promised possession of large swaths of Croatian territory, including Istria and most of the Adriatic coast and islands, all of which they again acquired from Hitler during World War II.

The Struggle to Form the First Yugoslavia (1918–41)

It is important to discuss in detail relations between the Serbs and Croats prior to the formation of the First Yugoslavia because the failure of understanding between the two groups echoes through history to this day. Little fighting took place on Croatian territory during the First World War, in contrast with the terrible toll the war took on the Serbs, both in battle and from disease epidemics through deprivation. The leading Croatian architects in the creation of the first Yugoslavia were Ante Trumbić (1864–1938) and Frano Supilo (1870–1917), two Dalmatians who wanted to avoid the region falling under Italian rule and thus turned to the Serbian Kingdom as the only viable alternative. It was they who worked with the Serbian government as early as 1915 to arrange for the unification of the former Hapsburg South Slav territories with Serbia.

> Croatian politicians seem to have been aware of the games that were being played with Croatian territory, but they were wrong in imagining that they would have any serious say in postwar decision-making. Some of them turned east because they thought that Croatia would have a better future in a common state with Serbia and Montenegro than if it remained part of Austria-Hungary.
> (Goldstein 1999: 109)

There was only one dissenting voice to the proposed union: Stjepan Radić, the leader of the Croatian Peasant Party. The Croats and Slovenes ended up on the losing side of the First World War, with no international protector states on the Allied side and, thus, stood at a great disadvantage to the Serbs, with whom they had begun negotiations for a postwar common state. It was the Croats who had the most to lose. Croatia, threatened by Hungary and Italy, and Slovenia, which both Italy and Austria sought to annex, were fighting for their very existence.

FIGURE 13: Croatia. Dances of Posavina. Avaz International Dance Theatre.

Serbia had other plans—plans of expansion into a Great Serbia, a term first coined by Svetozar Marković in the nineteenth century (Banac 1984: 109)—which meant an expansion to Serbia's medieval empire's borders and embrace. All of the geographic areas in which Serbians lived were to clash with the other nationalities that were to become part of the future Yugoslav state.

> The official Serbian version of South Slavic unification, as advocated by the men gathered round Regent Aleksandar and Prime Minister Pašić, the leader of the governing NRS, was of course, burdened by visions of Serbian expansionism. 'Liberation' and 'unification' of the Serbs, Croats, and Slovenes meant essentially Serb unification, which, as a secondary aim ("great solution"), did not exclude a wider program of "incorporating the Croats and Slovenes within a Great Serbia, should a favorable opportunity present itself after the war" (Banac 1984: 116) Pašić hoped he could transform the idea of *narodno jedinstvo* [national unity] in a way that would ensure Serbian supremacy.
>
> (Banac 1984: 117)

The political situation of Serbia was stronger. The Serbs were a member of the combatant force of the Allies and could thus expect to benefit in the acquisition of territory at the expense of the losing forces, the Ottoman Empire, from which they had just incorporated territory in the south, and the Habsburg Empire. The Serbs had been self-governing for many decades with a ruling dynasty, government apparatus, a military establishment, and all of the other trappings of an independent state.

Croatia and Slovenia, by contrast, had not been independent for more than a millennium and lacked such a governing apparatus and, even more importantly, had no organized armed defense forces. Furthermore, Serbia had no need for Croatia and Slovenia. Prior to the end of the war, Serbia had a highly focused plan to unite all Serbs within one state, which included Macedonians (whom they called South Serbians) and Montenegro, many of whose citizens considered themselves to be Serbs. This Great Serbia project meant the acquisition of the Habsburg provinces of Bosnia and Herzegovina, the Vojvodina, the Military Frontier of Croatia, all of which had large Serbian populations, and some access to the Adriatic Sea.

> The Serbian government, wishing to retain its dominance at every stage in the creation of the new state, never wanted the *Jugoslavenski Odbor* [JO, the Yugoslav Committee] treated as a significant power, nor did it ever treat it as such. It was pursuing a hypocritical policy. On the one hand, the Serbian government stated at the end of 1914 that "Serbia's fight was a struggle for the liberation and unification of all our enslaved bothers, the Serbs, Croats and Slovenes." It later issued similar proclamations. On the other hand, the Serbian prime minister

> Nikola Pašić (1845–1926) did all he could to annex for Serbia only lands whose annexation would not endanger the emergence of a Serbian majority in the future state. In April 1916 he recognized Italy's right to the eastern Adriatic coast in some Russian papers, saying that Serbia would be content with an outlet to the sea and some parts of Croatia.
>
> (Goldstein 1999: 109)

The major issue that arose between the Serb and Croat negotiators turned on the status of Croatia and Slovenia within the new Yugoslav state. This issue of whether the new state would be a centralized one, totally dominated by Serbia, or a federalized state in which the Serbs, Croats, and Slovenes would be equal partners was never sufficiently addressed prior to the foundation of the new state. Supilo and Trumbić fought strongly for Croatian and Slovenian states within the new Yugoslav state, while "Pašić saw any such action as involving little more than the extension of the Serbian administrative system over a wider territory" (Jelavich 1983: 144).

As the entire Habsburg South Slav domains descended into inevitable chaos due to the withdrawal of military and police forces, the National Committee made its way to Belgrade and presented the formal petition to the regent, Prince Aleksandar (king after 1921). He accepted it on December 1, 1918, and, thus, was born the Kingdom of Serbs, Croats, and Slovenes. (The name was changed to the Kingdom of Yugoslavia in 1929.) From the beginning of this fatally flawed marriage there existed irreconcilable differences. But the weaker parties, Croatia and Slovenia, had no other options than dismemberment of their territories by stronger powers.

The First Yugoslavia: 1918–41

Even though the Corfu Declaration between the Croats of the Yugoslav Committee (Supilo and Trumbić) and the Serbian government proclaimed the determination of Serbs, Croats, and Slovenes to form a united and independent state that would be a "constitutional, democratic, and parliamentary monarchy headed by the Karadjordjević dynasty," in fact, the reality was different. The first Yugoslavia was characterized by an increasingly repressive political state, run at first by the parliament with strong influence by the regent Prince Aleksandar. And, more importantly, it was in essence a Serb state with all the power concentrated in Belgrade. The military and administration were almost exclusively in Serbian hands because they had functioned in the former Kingdom of Serbia and simply extended their domains.

> Serbian centralism had thus triumphed, but at a tremendous cost. A major proportion of the Yugoslav population simply never accepted this arrangement.

> Although the fiercest opposition was to come from Zagreb and the Croatian Peasant Party, many Slovenian, Muslim, Montenegrin, Macedonian, and Albanian groups were similarly unhappy with the unitary structure. Unfortunately, the Serbian leadership, in defending its position, tended to treat any criticism of the constitution as "treason," even when it was aimed at the restructuring and not the destruction of the state.
>
> (Jelavich 1983: 151)

After the assassination of the dictator-king Aleksandar, his successor Paul attempted to bridge the gap between the Serbs and Croats. After several weeks of tough negotiations, a Croatian state within Yugoslavia, with wide internal powers, was agreed upon, albeit with strong opposition from the Serbian parties. But by this time it was too late, and the agreement never had the opportunity to come to true fruition before World War II destroyed the first Yugoslavia within a few days.

During the period from the end of the nineteenth century into the mid-twentieth century, the leading peasant cultural organization, the *Seljačka Sloga* (Peasant Harmony), a branch of the Croatian Peasant Party, the leading political party of Croatia in the interwar years, created a festival system to showcase peasant music and dance, and from the 1930s, the organizers established stringent rules of authenticity (Shay 2016c). "This was the time of the powerful politicization of folklore music and dance among Croatians ... confirming and preserving cultural and national identity and national awareness" (Sremac 2009: 95. See also Žganec and Sremec 1950). These performances inspired Zvonimir Ljevaković, the founding artistic director and choreographer of the Croatian state folk dance ensemble, Lado, to create his first choreographies. They were the first folk choreographies to use actual peasant dance steps and movements and were shown in Berlin in 1936, for which Croatia was awarded first place in the Dance Olympics that accompanied the Olympic Games (Shay 2016c; Sremac 2001). These performances and choreographies created the path for the KUD movement of amateur dance groups and, ultimately, for the establishment of a professional national dance ensemble, founded a decade later in 1949 (Shay 2016c). Those first choreographies, perhaps in altered form, constituted the first dances that were performed first by the amateur (KUD) ensemble Joža Vlahović dance company, and then by the Croatian State Ensemble of Folk Dances and Songs, the new name of Joža Vlahović when it was professionalized in 1949 (Lado 1949–79, Trideset Godina).

World War II and the Great Civil War

The Yugoslav Army, composed mostly of Serbs, capitulated within so few days that even the Germans and Italians, who rapidly occupied the country in ten days, were surprised. The Axis quickly reorganized the territory of Yugoslavia. Germany established a puppet regime in Serbia, took over Bačka, and ceded other parts of the country to their allies—Italy, Bulgaria, and Hungary. Hitler created the Independent State of Croatia, the NDH (*Nezavisna Džzava Hrvatska*) under the leadership of Ante Pavelić.

The Ustaša—The Croatian Fascist State

It is at this point necessary to again emphasize that the Croats are a politically diverse group of people. By all accounts, many Croats who were politically, economically, and culturally frustrated by their position in the first Yugoslavia welcomed the Germans as liberators at first and the establishment of an independent state. But the murderous and genocidal nature of the Ustaša state rapidly disillusioned them.[8] This included many major religious and political figures, like Archbishop Alojzije Stepinac and Vlado Maček, the leader of the Croatian Peasants' Party, who were deeply suspicious of the Communists. Neither publicly repudiated the NDH as a political state, but rather, privately expressed their reservations, especially Stepinac, who attempted to save many Jews and wrote letters of admonition to Pavelić expressing his horror at the reports he received from clergy throughout Croatia regarding the massacres of Serbs.[9]

Pavelic's first priority was to ethnically cleanse the NDH, especially of Serbs, a Herculean task when one considers his small armed forces, but one that he entered with great enthusiasm.

> On June 22 [1941], in Gospić, in the center of the Krajina killing fields, Pavelić's education minister, Mile Budak, openly announced that one-third of the new state's 1.9 million Serbs would be deported to Serbia and another third converted to the Catholic faith and thereby Croatianized (or reconverted given the wild Ustaša claim that 200,000 Croats had been forced into Orthodoxy under interwar Serb pressure). The other third, he added, would simply be killed.
>
> (Lampe 2000: 209)

Lampe observes that "From this regime sprang the most savage intolerance seen anywhere in Europe during World War II, outside of the Nazi regime itself" (2000, 208–209). As the regime turned bloodier, increasing numbers of Croats joined the ranks of the Partisans, especially after 1943. By the end of the war, the Partisans in Croatia numbered more than one hundred and fifty thousand. Adding to the unpopularity of the Ustaša regime, with all of its focus on the murder of many of its citizens, it is little wonder that the Croatian economy fell completely apart. "By the year's end [1941] industrial production had dropped to 20 percent of its prewar level ... The economic incompetence and corruption of the Ustaša derailed Nazi plans to include Croatia in the greater German economy" (Lampe 2000: 223). Food became scarce and many among the urban population went hungry, which further fueled the hostility of the Croatian population toward the Ustaša government.

The Partisans

The Partisans were the fighting forces organized by the small Communist Party of Yugoslavia. The Partisans constituted the third force that participated in the three-way civil war that ensued following the German and Italian occupation of the country. Unlike the other two forces, the Ustaša and the Četniks (the Serbian resistance), the Partisans were highly organized, and most importantly, they were multiethnic. The Communist Party was the only party that had members who came from all ethnic backgrounds and in all areas of the country. In addition, women participated actively in all aspects of the antifascist movement, even as combatants. Technically, the Partisans welcomed all of the various peoples of Yugoslavia to participate in the Antifascist War, as it became known.

The ferocity and speed with which the Ustaša fanned out over the districts in the Croatian Krajina (the Military Border lands) and Bosnia, where they began to massacre thousands of Serbs in the villages there, drove thousands of Serbs into the mountains where the Partisans quickly organized them into an effective fighting force. As a result of the preponderance of Serbs in the first two years of the war, attracting Croats into the Partisans proved difficult.

> In the atmosphere of hatred generated by Ustaša massacres and Četnik reprisals, it was extremely difficult to unite Serbs and Croats in the same resistance movement. This difficulty was exacerbated by Serb Partisans' tendency during the first two years of the war to behave as if they were members of an exclusively Serb organization.
>
> (Levine 1993: 115)

The Communist Party was greatly aware that they needed the participation of the Croats if they were to succeed in defeating the Ustaša and the Germans and Italians. As the situation in Croatia deteriorated, the Croats overcame their reluctance. "In 1942 it was already clear that Ustaša rule and the NDH were in crisis. The Partisans held much of the agricultural land and forests, and many mines and sawmills, and blocked road railway traffic in most of the country" (Goldstein 1999: 146). Goldstein also notes that many famous actors, artists, and literary figures, such as the poets Vladimir Nazor (1876–1949) and Ivan Goran Kovačić (1913–1943), joined the Partisans in 1942, which encouraged a rising tide of Croats to join as well.

The Partisans began with a small force at the beginning of the war. The Communist Party of Yugoslavia, which formed the nucleus of the Partisans, and the later Yugoslav government leadership consisted of only six thousand to eight thousand members, with perhaps ten thousand sympathizers, "one-third of whom formed the Croatian Party" (Goldstein 1999: 140). The small numbers should not surprise anyone since Croatia was a conservative, Catholic, and overwhelmingly peasant state. Peasants did not welcome the idea of collectivization of land anywhere in the Balkans, where "the ideal everywhere was the establishment of small individual family farms" (Jelavich 1983: 19).

Thus, the members of the tiny Communist Party largely consisted of idealistic intellectuals and a few urban workers, like the chairman of the Party, Josip Broz, later taking his nom de guerre, Tito. "The communist movement benefited from having a talented and energetic multiethnic leadership team, an effective clandestine organizational network throughout the country, and the support of enthusiastic young activists" (Cohen 1995: 23).

The biggest windfall to the Partisans came in 1943 when the Italians withdrew from the war, leaving their weapons to the Partisans and greatly raising the morale of the latter. Increased numbers of individuals from the former Italian-occupied regions joined the Partisans in the War of Liberation, including many Italian soldiers. The Partisans convened meetings in Bihač, and more importantly in Jajce, both in Bosnia, in which the future division of Yugoslavia was largely decided. These meetings were held under the organization, AVNOJ, the Antifascist Council of the People's Liberation, which soon after the war was recognized as the official government of Yugoslavia. The core members of the Communist Party of Yugoslavia were probably the only truly committed Yugoslavs in the entire country, in which religion defined the nationality and ethnicity of each individual's identity.

Adding complexity to this political activity was the formation of the Croatian Communist Party which, under its head, Andrija Hebrang, began to act increasingly independently and constructed a parallel organization to AVNOJ, known as ZAVNOH (The Antifascist Council of the People's Liberation of Croatia). Hebrang and the other leaders of the Croatian Communist Party understood that, in order to attract Croats to the Party and detach them from their traditional allegiance to the Croatian Peasants' Party, "they needed to convince them that Communists would protect Croatian national interests" (Levine 1993: 135). It was inevitable that Hebrang and Tito would clash over the role of the Croatian Republic and the Croatian Communist Party within the new Yugoslav Federation.

> As the war drew to a close the two sovereign wills—one Croatian, the other Yugoslav—came into increasing conflict in Croatia. Tito thus condemned ZAVNOH's unilateral proclamation of the incorporation of Istria and other alienated Croatian territories, on the grounds that only AVNOJ was competent to do that; this act was in his view a sign of Croatian separatism.
>
> (Magaš 2007: 603)

The Partisans greatly extended their sphere of influence throughout the country, converging on the Yugoslav capital, Belgrade, in October 1944, accompanying the Red Army to engage the Germans in a direct final battle for the control of the country. After liberating Belgrade, the Soviet Army turned north to Budapest in their pursuit of the German Army. The Yugoslav Partisan Army turned westward toward Zagreb. The last act of World War II was about to unfold. In May 1945, it was apparent that the approaching Partisans constituted a formidable force. Panic enveloped Zagreb and many individuals prepared to flee, including those who

> had been compromised by their activities during the war, such as membership in the Ustaša or the Home Guard [*domobran*], or because they opposed the Partisan political stand. More than 100,000 of these people, with their families and other refugees, decided to flee northward and surrender to the British Army.
>
> (Jelavich 1983: 272)

They were stopped by the British Army at the village of Bleiburg on the Austrian border, put on trains without telling the refugees their destination, and were turned over to the Partisans.

Tito was most concerned that the Ustaša and their supporters should be eliminated, not only for their war crimes but, more importantly, so that they could not form a future threat to Yugoslavia. Thus he gave orders to destroy those who were fleeing. Many were shot out of hand, while the vast majority were marched back into Yugoslavia in what came to be known as "The Way of the Cross" (*Povijest Hrvata* 2007: 261). It is estimated that forty thousand to hundred thousand persons perished (see Winland 2007: 47).[10]

The Partisans were the major victors in the former Yugoslavia after World War II. As the victors they dictated the form and political borders within the second Yugoslavia, which, in turn, dictated the contours of the new states that ultimately emerged from that failed state and failed political experiment. The Partisan war effort became a primary theme in Yugoslav life for the first decade after the war "from the partisans" shared belief in communist ideals and the fact that they worked under the overall ideological umbrella of Tito's party. The story of the war in this interpretation was, one might say, the postwar Yugoslav creation myth" (Wachtel 1998: 133). Lado and other folk ensembles celebrated that founding myth in song and dance, especially in its beginning years, as was the case with many other professional, amateur, and peasant groups.

One cannot but admit the truly heroic aspect of the way in which the Partisans overcame all odds to defeat the enemies they faced on all sides. They now faced the daunting task of governing a nation that had lost about a million individuals in horrifying episodes of interethnic violence, a completely destroyed infrastructure, and severe food shortages.

The New Yugoslavia—1945–66

Yugoslavia emerged from the war in the strongest political position of any of the other Eastern European states, primarily because the Red Army departed after the liberation of Belgrade. Despite widespread destruction, a huge population loss, and an economy in tatters, the Partisans, eight hundred thousand strong by war's end, were, as historian Barbara Jelavich notes, "in full military control" (1983b: 295). In the immediate aftermath of World War II, as the City of Zagreb fell silent following the panic of the fleeing members of the NDH, hardly anyone knew what to expect. Few people knew who Tito was:

> The Zagrebians' curiosity about their new master was soon to be satisfied. Tito arrived in the city on 21 May and delivered a speech to an enormous crowd at St. Mark's Square … If they expected a harangue, they were mistaken. Tito was at his most conciliatory and flattering. He spoke of his joy at being back in "our beloved Zagreb" and said he was speaking "as a Croat."
>
> (Tanner 2001: 172)

It was one of the few times that he publicly mentioned his Croat identity.

Nevertheless, many of those who participated in the war, no matter their ethnic or political status, harbored deep feelings of revenge. The result was anger against social class and whole ethnic groups. "Post war revenge swept through all of Croatia, just as it did all of Yugoslavia … which resulted in equating all Croats with the Ustaše" (Radelić et al. 2006: 16).

However, Tito achieved a major milestone: The first creation of the Republic of Croatia was made territorially whole in the Second Yugoslavia, even though it was a struggle to achieve. The Yugoslavs and Italians clashed over Croatian territories along the Adriatic coast, especially on the Istrian peninsula, until an international peace accord was achieved.[11]

Looking back, the greatest mistake that Tito made, in his otherwise successful stewardship of post-World War II Yugoslavia, was not to have had a major and public reconciliation and airing of differences between the various ethnic groups, especially the two largest groups, the Croats and Serbs, but also with such groups as the Kosovar Albanians and Bosnian Muslims, in order to clear the air and make an authentic new beginning for the new state. In addition, he swept all of the hatreds under the rug as if the ethnic hatred had been wiped out by the exemplary behavior of the Partisans. Instead, he and his closest associates relied on a recovering economy and his slogan, "Brotherhood and Unity" (*bratstvo i jedinstvo*), to do the job of reconciliation and cleansing.[12]

The Yugoslav leaders launched a program of Yugoslavism (*jugoslavenstvo*) that they hoped would replace old ethnic and local identities with a new pan-Yugoslav identity. Few individuals opted for this new identity, including many party leaders. Josip Broz Tito was the consummate Yugoslav and only rarely identified himself as a Croat, having a Croat father and a Slovene mother. He was born in the poverty-stricken Zagorje region of Croatia, just north of Zagreb, in the village of Kumrovec, one of fifteen children. As a youth, he was apprenticed as a locksmith and worked in Croatia, Austria, and Germany. Wounded in the First World War, he was taken to Russia as a prisoner and observed the Communist Revolution. He was a committed Communist from an early age.

The Yugoslavism program Tito espoused was accompanied by what is known in Yugoslav politics as a unitarist, centralizing approach to the state, in which the central role of the Yugoslav federal government was emphasized, while the role of the republics was deemphasized until the end of the period under consideration. In the period 1946–66, he discouraged displays of nationalism and ethnic identity, except under the "innocent" guise of costumed dancers, and believed that only if everyone adopted a Yugoslav identity could the nation overcome its fractured ethnic history.

> This was the only time in Yugoslav history that the government was centrally involved in cultural policy making; in the first fifteen postwar years party authorities played a central role in defining a new Yugoslav culture. The separate national cultures were allowed to exist at the harmless level of folk culture.
>
> (Wachtel 1998: 9)

And, in this period the national dance ensembles, the widespread amateur dance ensembles that emulated them (KUD), and the popular festival system played a role. The many festivals sponsored by the government, in which dancers in regional folk costumes embodied "brotherhood-and-unity," also became fierce competitions.

In 1947, Joža Vlahović journeyed to Prague to the Communist Youth Festival, in which competitions of ethno identity folk dance were a major feature, and won second prize, right after Moiseyev. Back in Yugoslavia, this was counted as a major political coup. Miša Šokčić, one of the dancers, remembered:

> Of course, it was almost a law that the first prize would go to Moiseyev. First, they were a professional company, but more than that, the Russians had to win everything. Still, for us to take home the coveted second prize, over all the other 34 professional ensembles from eighteen different nations participating in that massive festival was a great thing.
>
> (Personal interview, October 15, 1999)[13]

This triumph was followed by winning first prize in a huge all-Yugoslav festival in Belgrade. That recognition impelled the Croatian Republican government to establish the State Professional Ensemble of Croatia, with Zvonko Ljevaković as artistic director on November 11, 1949. Three months later they gave their first performance in the National Theatre with the same program they had given as Joža Vlahović three months earlier, but under their new name: The State Ensemble of Folk Dance Songs of Croatia (*Državni zbor Narodnih plesova I pjesama Hrvatske*) (Figure 14).[14]

In the founding of professional and amateur dance ensembles, Tito and his associates were following the model established by the Soviet Union, that is to say, the Moiseyev model. Ljevaković, a Croatian nationalist, resisted this and established, instead, an authenticity-based model that featured authentic steps and movements, vocal and instrumental production, and the wearing of authentic costumes that came to be known "in professional circles within Croatia and outside its borders as the Zagreb School" (Sremac 2009: 104).

To emphasize the political aspects of what sounds like benign support of the arts, one of the founding members of Lado, who transitioned from Joža Vlahović, is illuminating:

> The first years were both wonderful and difficult. The wonderful part was that we were treated like movie stars. We had special rehearsal outfits and when we wore them, we had free access to public transportation and everyone admired us. The difficulties came from the [Communist] Party. The Party was everywhere. The party frequently dismissed good dancers. I remember one excellent dancer was thrown out because a relative had been a member of the Ustasha and another because he sang a patriotic song of that period when he was a little drunk.
>
> Life was difficult after the war. Food was scarce, the economy was in a shambles. We were to travel to London and Western Europe in 1950. The Party ordered special fabrics from Switzerland to make us suitable clothes, and we were fed

FIGURE 14: Croatia. Dances from Pokuplje. Avaz International Dance Theatre. Choreography: Anthony Shay. Photo: D. Young. From the author's collection.

> three square meals a day in the best hotel in Zagreb so that we would not appear emaciated and poor. In those early years when we traveled abroad the Party sent agents to watch over us and report everything. In the beginning they were very diligent and reported everything. After that, those agents, who received far more money than we did, landed with us, went shopping, and never saw us again until we returned. In spite of those efforts, defections occurred on every tour.
>
> (Nena Šokčić, personal interview, October 16, 1999)

In an authoritarian state, no one escapes scrutiny, and folk dancers were no exception.

Political Conditions

Tito and his colleagues inaugurated a "Red Terror," similar to regimes in the other Eastern Bloc countries, under Stalin's direction. As Milovan Djilas famously put it: "We communists did not want any opposition, none whatsoever" (quoted in Tanner 2001: 168). And, indeed, the Communists rigged elections, intimidated noncommunist political figures, and used every tactic they could to prevent free elections right after the war. In this they were successful.

The "shock and awe" tactics the Party employed included show trials, such as those of Draža Mihailović and the Archbishop Alojzije Stepinac; individuals were murdered in the streets by the security forces and thousands were sent to prisons. In 1947, there were so many men in camps or prisons that the penal system started to buckle under the strain. Croatian historian Branka Magaš notes: "The consolidation of the Communist government in Croatia was accompanied by widespread terror, which did not abate for three years" (2007: 606).

Tito placed Aleksandar Ranković, a Serb, who as head of the secret security forces staffed the ranks of the secret police with Serbs and Montenegrins, to oversee the planning and execution of the terror, until his spectacular fall from power in 1966. Lampe observes that, due to the real threat of invasion by Stalin, "at the time both the regime and its supporters saw these measures as means to preserve Yugoslavia's independence and Communist power and not as devices to gain ethnic advantage" (2000: 254).

Stalin's plans for Yugoslavia, as with the other Eastern European nations, were founded on the idea that they were to serve as a source of raw goods for the industrial building and growth of the USSR. However, the main reason for the break between the two countries was "the independent Yugoslav attitude and the failure to consult the Soviet government on every action" (Jelavich 1983: 324). The break in 1948 was not over political ideals but a naked power struggle.

Stalin launched a vicious personal attack against Tito and his close colleagues, echoed obediently by the leaders in the satellite states. This included several border clashes and diplomatic incidents with neighboring states. In addition, Stalin nakedly encouraged other fervent Yugoslav Communist Party members to get rid of their leadership. Tito and the other Party leaders decided to resist the Soviet machinations and find a new road for Yugoslav Communism. This they did through a series of constitutions and reinterpretation of Marxism, each marked by an increasing departure from Soviet practices.

Yugoslav authority Dennison Rusinow called workers' self-management "the most famous legislative act of the postwar era in Yugoslavia" (1977: 57–58). In theory it "took away from the state the ownership of the means of production, which were declared 'social' property. The workers were now considered trustees for the management of the individual enterprises" (Jelavich 1983: 386). Yet, as Croatian historian Branka Magaš notes, "Nevertheless, for many years the federal government still decided what was to be built, where, and how" (Magaš 2007: 615). Theoretically, the Communist Party, renaming itself the League of

Communists of Yugoslavia (LCY) in 1952, withdrew to an advisory position, letting the workers, in concert with the managers of state enterprises, make the crucial economic decisions about their institutions. This included artistic collectives like Lado. But, in fact, political power remained with the Party. Even more, the ultimate power in the state, backed by the Yugoslav Army (JNA), resided with Tito until his death in 1980 at age 87.

It was throughout this period that two major opposing forces within the Communist Party emerged. The first, the unitarist or centralizing group, wanted to keep all power concentrated in Belgrade, which, because Belgrade was both the capital of Serbia and Yugoslavia, also meant in Serbian hands. This group constituted the conservative group of Yugoslavia and was spearheaded by Aleksandar Ranković, the head of the Serbian Communist Party and the secret police. The second group, the federalists, attempted to obtain more power and decision-making authority. Tito used the struggle for power between these two groups to divide and rule. Nevertheless, as early as 1964, Tito was becoming convinced that centralization, and the denial of ethnic and national identity, had become unproductive. At the Eighth Congress of the League of Communists of Yugoslavia (LCY) Tito "rejected the idea held previously that it was possible to create a single Yugoslav nation. According to him, this policy of *jugoslavenstvo* was tantamount to 'assimilation and bureaucratic centralism, to unitarism and hegemony' " (Levine 1993: 255). It was at this Eighth Congress that, for the first time, "party leaders were identified by nationality. The fact that Tito was identified as a Croat rather than a Yugoslav came as a shock to some of those present" (Magaš 2007: 617).

Life in Croatia

After the first three years, and beginning in 1950, the general situation, politically and economically, improved and in the second decade improvement accelerated. Tito had to address two specific problems in Croatia: Archbishop Alojzije Stepinac and Andrija Hebrang, who showed dangerous separatist tendencies. For many individuals, these two early Croatian figures became martyrs. First, Tito turned to the problem of the most influential figures in Croatian public life, Archbishop Alojzije Stepinac, who outspokenly opposed the new communist regime. Tito attempted to hint Stepinac out of the country, but the archbishop was adamantly opposed to leaving. Stepinac eloquently defended his behavior during the war; he had personally saved many Jews and had several times privately expressed his reservations about the excesses of the Ustaša against the Serbs and Jews to both Pavelić and Artuković. However, he had not publicly opposed the NDH and the Ustaša, which gave the Yugoslav leadership a pretext to prosecute him.

In spite of the eloquence of Stepinac's defense, Tito was determined to take Stepinac out of the public eye.

> The Catholic Church and the Archbishop himself were powerful national symbols ... Stepinac's role as defender of Croat national aims, as much as his religious authority, made him a potential threat to the political goals of the CPY [Communist Party of Yugoslavia].
>
> (Levine 1993: 236–37)[15]

After serving a short time in the Lepoglava prison, he was, in 1951, placed under house arrest on the grounds of his home parish. He died in 1960, after a long illness, and Tito allowed him a funeral with "all the honors due a prince of the church" (Tanner 2001: 186).

Immediately after the war, Tito also turned his attention to Andrija Hebrang. Hebrang served as the leader of the Croatian Communist Party, in which role he made several independent decisions regarding the role of Croatia in the second Yugoslavia that alarmed Tito and his lieutenants. Hebrang was accused of spying for the Soviets and sent to prison where he was secretly executed. In his place, Tito appointed Vladimir Bakarić, a colorless functionary who was completely obedient to him as head of the Croatian Communist Party, and Bakarić held this position until his death in 1983.

Croatia remained politically quiet throughout the period 1950–66. The fear of charges of nationalism and separatism were too strong. The economic situation, too, clearly stronger than that of the other states in Eastern Europe, produced some satisfaction. The rise of new, energetic, well-educated Croat politicians changed the situation and gave hopeful young Croats a new voice: Maspok, the Croatian Spring.

Maspok, the Croatian Spring

The first volley announcing Maspok, the Croatian Spring, fast on the heels of the fall of Ranković in 1966, came in 1967, centered on the position of the Croatian language. Maspok is an abbreviation for *masovni pokret*, mass movement, which describes both the popularity of the cultural, economic, and political movement and the reason for its ultimate demise in 1972. Totalitarian governments only like crowds and masses if they can totally control them. Thus, the Croatian Spring lasted for four and one-half years, amid mounting excitement in Croatia, and corresponding alarm in the other republics, and ultimately, it was the specter of mass political movement that caused Tito to quash it, the memory of which survived to the establishment of the Independent Croatian Republic two decades later.

Economic Issues

The Croatian Spring began with an acrimonious national linguistic debate in the late 1960s and early 1970s. From there, Savka Dabčević-Kučar, Miko Tripalo, and Pero Pirker aggressively advanced into the realm of the economy because they saw that Belgrade was impeding Croatia's economic growth.

> Even four years after the reform, Belgrade's banks had a stranglehold on the Yugoslav economy, controlling more than half of total credits and some 81.5 percent of foreign credits ... Belgrade's foreign trade companies, moreover, were said to enjoy a virtual monopoly garnering 77.1 percent of Yugoslav income in this sector, with Ljubljana accounting for most of the rest (19.4 percent), and Zagreb for a mere 2.4 percent.
>
> (Ramet 1984: 104)

While for many the language issue was important, the economy was even more of a persistent thorn in the side of the Croatian body politic. As we saw above, Belgrade hoarded a lion's share of foreign currencies, trade agreements, and other lucrative income, including siphoning off much of the 40 per cent of foreign currency garnered by the Croatian tourist industry. "Led by Miko Tripalo and Savka Dabčević-Kučar, this group called for a further political decentralization of the government and a reform of the banking and currency regulations" in order to adjust the economic and political balance between the republics (Jelavich 1983: 396). This group of Croatian party leaders began to seek widespread changes: "LCC [League of Communists of Croatia] reformers emphasized the primacy of Croatian statehood and the importance of placing Croatian political interests above the interests of the Yugoslav state as a whole" (Levine 1993: 256–57).

As demands spiraled, Matica Hrvatska called for

> a change in the distribution of power in the Yugoslav federation. Croatia would have a separate monetary policy and complete control over its tax revenues. Croatian would be the sole official language. Perhaps the most striking aspect of this proposed constitution was its call for the formation of an independent defense force in Croatia.
>
> (Levine 1993: 266)

Clearly, events were veering out of the control of Dabčević-Kučar, Tripalo, and Pirker, who either from a genuine democratic impulse to allow the Croatian public to have a comprehensive dialogue or an inability to control events were heading toward a clash with Tito and the other republics as well as the federal government and the Yugoslav Army, with their demands. "Ultimately, the nationalist group gathered around Matica Hrvatska explicitly raised the cry for complete Croatian independence: Secession was fast becoming mainstream political sentiment in Croatia" (Ramet 1984: 135).

Tito observed these events, which he had at first supported, with increasing alarm. He warned the liberal leaders in Croatia that nationalism was running wild "in some villages because of nervousness the Serbs are drilling and arming themselves ... Do you want to have 1941 again?" (quoted in Jelavich 1983: 397). Tito summoned the Croatian leadership to the old royal hunting lodge at Karadjordjevo in Vojvodina, on December 1, 1971, and remonstrated with them in the strongest terms. On December 12, under pressure, they resigned. "In the aftermath of the crisis, literally tens of thousands of members, were expelled from the party" (Ramet 1984: 138–39). Others, like Franjo Tuđman, were sentenced to long prison terms. Liberalism was over but, to appease the general public, Tito granted many of the nationalist demands made during the Croatian Spring, particularly in the field of economics. In the political arena, however, old obedient conservatives, like Edvard Kardelj and Vladimir Bakarić, always subservient to Tito, replaced the young, democratically oriented liberal politicians. Springtime was over and Croatia again became the silent republic for the next two decades.[16]

The Yugoslav Economy until 1989

Throughout the 1950s industry was developed, not always efficiently, but the economy grew steadily, far surpassing the surrounding Communist states. "The Yugoslav leaders were concerned with adopting institutions that worked in practice, and they were thus willing to modify or discard practices that proved unsuccessful, no matter what their ideological basis" (Jelavich 1983: 388). This economic development was accompanied by a liberalization in many other areas of national life, shown particularly by the freedom given to Yugoslav citizens to travel and work abroad, which greatly aided the economy through remittances, as well as encouraging tourists to come to Yugoslavia, particularly to Croatia, the republic that possessed the most important tourist destinations.

It was economic conditions, in which economic and political power was based in Belgrade, that brought about the political challenges and discontent that led to the "Croatian Spring."

> Serbia had gained 89 per cent of federal investment in the 1965–1970 five-year plan ... Belgrade banks and foreign-trade firms, which were under Serbian management, thus held the bulk (over 70 per cent) of the Yugoslav financial capital.

> The concentration of foreign-trade firms in Belgrade gave Serbia 56 percent of Yugoslav foreign trade, compared with Croatia's 18 per cent.
>
> (Magaš 2007: 623–24)

Still the economy grew at a rapid pace, especially in Slovenia and Croatia, until Tito's death in 1980. One major element of the economy of Yugoslavia stood out so dramatically that even a casual observer would notice: the disparity between the economic prosperity of the north and south. The annual average income of Slovenia was seven times the average income in Kosovo or Macedonia, and Croatia only slightly under that figure.

In sum,

> In its initial stages, the Titoist reform model also proved quite successful in advancing Yugoslav economic development ... Growth rates in terms of gross domestic product, labor productivity, and real personal incomes were the highest in the country's history and compared very favorably with other developing countries. In only two decades, Yugoslavia had been transformed from an underdeveloped agrarian society into a "moderately developed industrial country."
>
> (Cohen 1995: 30)

The Croatian Economy

The Croatian economy grew, especially during the period of the 1960s and 1970s. Tourism became a major factor in the Croatian economy because of the famous, stunningly beautiful coastline. In the 1960s the Jadranska Magistrala highway that linked the entire coastline from Italy to Dubrovnik, was completed, creating a further spur to the economy since Europeans and Yugoslavs from other republics could drive there by automobile. Lado became part of the burgeoning tourist economy, performing night after night for the entire season in luxury hotels and outdoor concert stages up and down the coast.

Throughout those years, Lado, other amateur Croatian dance ensembles, and the festival system thrived and prospered. Recalling my major point—that these dance ensembles reflect the political terrain—they quietly dropped Partisan-themed numbers like "*Opšaj diri*" from the repertoire. Lado's unique style of presentation led *New York Times* reviewer Anna Kisselgoff to observe in 1992, "History, strife and politics are resonant in the name change, but Lado itself remains what it has always been: one of the world's great folk companies" (*New York Times*, November 4, 1992).

Yugoslavia 1980–90: Descent into Madness

Franjo Tuđman. Among the most enigmatic figures during the Wars of Secession (known in Croatia as the War for the Homeland or the Patriotic War) was Franjo Tuđman, president of Croatia from 1991 to 1999. His role is less well understood to the general public than that of Slobodan Milošević, the more flamboyant and rough-edged of the two major leaders. But it seems from several accounts that, in his somewhat more quiet fashion, he had been equally sinister. "Complex shifting alliances, communicated to the public in a bizarre hybrid language, obscured the intentions of Milošević and Tuđman, whose antagonism in turn obscured a more sinister mutual respect" (Glenny 2001: 630). At the height of the tension between Croatia and Serbia,

> it is well documented that Milošević and Tuđman held a meeting in March 1991 at Karadjordjevo in Vojvodina, which included a discussion on the partition of Bosnia-Hercegovina between Croatia and Serbia ... Under this scheme, a Greater Croatia and a Greater Serbia would be carved out of what was formerly known as Bosnia-Hercegovina.
>
> (Finlan 2004: 37)

In fact, his ultimate aim was to work with Milošević to divide Bosnia between them, and Tuđman "hoped even in 1999 to divide Bosnia with Milošević" (Ramet 2006: 584).

Born in 1922, he fought with the Partisans and became an officer in the JNA, leaving the organization at the rank of major general. He became a historian, teaching at the University of Zagreb, and was jailed for his nationalist writings during the Croatian Spring, in the early 1970s and again in the 1980s. In 1989, he founded one of the first parties in the 1989–90 multiparty system, the HDZ (Croatian Democratic Union), of which the "Croatian" part of the description was accurate. The party garnered 42 percent of the vote, but due to the peculiarities of the electoral system, the HDZ was entitled to the majority of the seats, and Tuđman became the first president of Croatia until his death in 1999. "In fact, the HDZ had never won more than 50 percent of the vote in any parliamentary election" (Soberg 2007: 36).

On a personal level, Tuđman often came across as autocratic, stiff, and formal. He had a considerable taste for the dramatic:

> In the weeks following the [1990] election Tudjman busied himself with the writing of a new constitution, and indulged his historical tastes with the renaming of streets and squares ... A ceremonial guard of honor for the President in Ruritanian fancy dress was soon strutting up and down outside the Ban's Palace in the Upper Town.
>
> (Tanner 2001: 229)

Ivo Goldstein adds: "There is practically no field of life in Croatia in which President Tudjman does not have an influence if he wants it. He arbitrates in cultural matters—e.g., over which films are shown—and in sport" (1999: 259). Tuđman was moving from competitive to sultanistic. Historian Marcus Tanner noted that "Tudjman's era had been marked by an increasing trend toward authoritarianism, xenophobia and economic and diplomatic incompetence" (2019: 308).

Despite the term "democratic" in his party's title, historian Sabrina P. Ramet describes Tudjman and the politics of the HDZ:

> Tudjman's rule has been compared with old-fashioned caudillo politics in Latin America. Tudjman used the levers of power to aggrandize himself and his family, his cronies, and his party, used computers to falsify election returns, and used the security and intelligence services to carry out a secret war against the liberal faction within the HDZ, and also against opposition parties, non-governmental organizations, and similar [organizations].
>
> (2006: 584)

Early on, in the 1980s, he took intolerant stances vis-à-vis the Serbs and attempted to rehabilitate the Ustaša in order to attract the considerable funding available in the ultra-right-wing part of the émigré communities, especially those of the United States and Canada, ultimately placing a major fundraiser, Gojko Šušak, a Canadian Croatian, as defense minister, "who had been able to deliver millions of dollars to the HDZ campaign and worked as a point of contact with the generally right-wing Diaspora" (Soberg 2007: 40). The émigrés did not contribute this merely for the homeland: Many were awarded state properties that helped to skew the Croatian economy so that the European organization, Transparency International, considered Croatia "to be the 15th ranked country in terms of corruption among 99 countries" (Ramet 2006: 586). "Over time, Tudjman purged all members of the opposition from the government, the army, the judiciary, and public enterprises" (Soberg 2007: 48). Thus the appellation "democratic" became increasingly ludicrous when applied to the HDZ throughout the 1990s.

As tensions rose between the Croats and the Croatian Serbs, beginning in 1989, Tuđman would frequently, in words at least, attempt to pacify Serbian fears of a revival of the NDH: "Tudjman's supporters noted that he was always careful to mention that the Serbs in Croatia would be granted democratic rights" (Cohen 1995: 97). But, Tuđman's words were cynical. "During the summer of 1989, extremist followers of the HDZ in Dalmatia mounted enough physical attacks on local Serbs to make the new party's nationalist rhetoric seem truly threatening" (Lampe 2000: 354). Of course, these actions were matched and ratcheted up by the Krajina Serbs, led by Slobodan Milošević. The HDZ's "media campaign exulted in 'a Croatia for Croatians only.' Such slogans encouraged the excesses of local supporters and returning émigrés" (Lampe 2000: 360). Along with forcing the Serbs out of positions in the police, various enterprises, and administrative positions, all of the actions spearheaded by Tuđman and the HDZ brought Croat–Serb relations to the boiling point.

Tuđman also relied on Milošević's covert messages to him that Milošević had no interest in the Croatian Serbs, even though he posed as the savior of the Serbs outside of Serbia. Stjepan Mesić, who succeeded Tudjman to the presidency of Croatia in 2000, and quit the HDZ in 1994 because he perceived Tuđman's behavior to be unethical and bordering on the criminal, especially, as we will see in Tuđman's role in the war in Bosnia, recalled a meeting, in which he, Mesić, met with Borisav Jović, then president of Yugoslavia and later Serbia, prior to a meeting between Tuđman and Miloševic. Mesić appeared to be shocked by the cynicism displayed by Milošević and Jović:

> He [Jović] replied that Serbs in Croatia were of no interest to Serbia. They are your citizens, do whatever you want with them, impale them, it's no business of ours. "Are you interested in Croatian territory?" I asked him. He replied that they were not interested in Croatian territory either, and he meant it: during and after Operations Flash and Storm [the 1995 Croatian military offensives to regain Serb-occupied Croatian territory] Milošević did not lift a finger to help these Serbs, but left them to their fate ... "We are interested in 66 percent of the territory of Bosnia and Hercegovina, and this we shall take. It was Serb, it is Serb and it will remain Serb."
>
> (Mesić 2001: 11–12)

Lenard J. Cohen, regarding Franjo Tuđman, notes: "some of his more prescient Yugoslav critics unflatteringly referred to Tudjman as the 'Croatian Milošević.' " (Cohen 1995: 98). In assessing the characters of Tudjman and Milosevic, there did not appear much to choose from between them. And, "to the outside world, the two men seemed poles apart" (Glenny 2001: 633).

> One of the things that emerges most strongly is the degree of President Tudjman's co-responsibility for the war in Bosnia—which, while it may not reach full equivalence with the responsibility of Milošević, must now be seen as approaching it more closely than previous evidence had suggested.
>
> (Malcolm 2001: xix)

However much individuals' attempt to exonerate Tudjman's undemocratic behavior as necessary to the war effort, that he was uninvolved in any criminal activities, that he did not know about the atrocities occurring in Bosnia, in the end he incriminated himself:

> Within a year, secret tape recordings made by Tudjman, recording conversations at the Pantov presidential palace, had been released, proving that Tudjman had masterminded Croatia's intervention in the war in Bosnia, had known about atrocities, and ... Carla Del Ponte [head of the International War Crimes Tribunal in the Hague] admitted that, but for his death in late 1999, Tudjman would have found his name on the list of persons indicted for war crimes by the International War Crimes Tribunal in The Hague.
>
> (Ramet 2006: 584)

The War of Succession

The first step Croatia and Slovenia took on the road to independence was to establish a multiparty system for the 1990 elections, held first in Slovenia in April of that year, supported by Germany, and in Croatia a month later. This move shocked the communists, and especially the leadership of the JNA, which regarded itself as "the last bastion of Yugoslavism and state unity" (Cohen 1995: 182). In August, the Serbs blockaded roads in their area and, on December 21, 1990, the Serbs declared the Republic of Krajina, supported by the JNA. Belgrade directed all the activity of the Krajina Serbs.

The second step, taken early in 1991, was for the Slovenian Assembly and the Croatian *Sabor* to declare that laws passed in the parliaments of their respective republics took precedence over federal Yugoslav laws. Both republics held referenda in which they asked the public if they wanted to remain in Yugoslavia or have independent states; not surprisingly, the overwhelming majority voted for independence. "The creation of the Croatian Army (HV) began with the change of government on 30 May 1990" (Tus 2001: 47). In February 1991, Martin Špegelj, minister of defense, actively began to build a national army and secretly amass weapons. At the end of that month he "learned of the existence of a plan to intervene in Slovenia and Croatia" (2001: 25).

The third step, taken by both republics on June 25, 1991, was to declare independence. This formal announcement, rejected by the Yugoslav (by this time almost entirely Serbian) leadership, set the path for war, which broke out almost immediately.

The distinction between the two republics was that Slovenia had no sizeable minority living in its borders but, of Croatia's nearly five million population in 1990 about 12 percent was Serbian, of which three-quarters lived in Krajina and parts of Slavonia. As the Croatian government showed signs of increasing independence, the Serbs, driven by the lies broadcast from Belgrade and memories of the Ustaša reign of terror, responded by declaring an independent Republic of Krajina, which the JNA supported through weapons.

The JNA secretly attempted to take the Territorial Defense force's (TO) arms in 1990. "Our greatest error was that after the successful nonviolent blockade of the garrisons in summer 1991 we did not go on in September and October to occupy all the JNA garrisons and depots in Croatia" (Tus 2001: 50). Tuđman let it happen, which infuriated Špegelj and General Anton Tus, but the Slovenes were cagier and stopped the JNA early enough that they were able to prevent the TO arms from being seized. The Croats would rue Tudjman's decision.

War in Croatia

While the war in Slovenia ended in ten days with the Slovenes victorious, Croatia was not so fortunate.[17] While Slovenia possesses a compact geographic territory, Croatia's horseshoe-shaped boundary, with its long borders, made its territory difficult to defend. The war had two major zones, Krajina along the Bosnian border in the south and east, and the eastern theater in Slavonia, the eastern-most part of the country. Both had sizeable Serbian populations, especially the former.

The war in the former Yugoslavia might be said to have begun on August 17, 1990, when the JNA armed and supported the Serb insurrection in the Krajina, in Knin, the so-called "*balvan*" revolution (log revolution, because the Serbian insurrectionists closed the roads by barricading them with logs) (Tus 2001: 42). Milan Babić, the leader of the Serbs of Krajina, announced the formation of the Autonomous Province of Serbian Krajina on August 25, 1990.

Martin Špegelj and his staff were not idle. They built the military forces to meet the inevitable aggression of the Serbs. This they had to do secretly due to interference by Tuđman and his entourage. The period was characterized by political meddling by Tuđman and his cohorts that prolonged the war, creating a series of missed opportunities that would have allowed Croatia to regain its lost territories, and resulted in large loss of life and destruction of property (see Špegelj 2001).

It was only on "3 August 1991 that the government decided to form the Croatian Army general staff" (Tus 2001: 47). This was very late indeed. The JNA harbored the same pernicious ethnic stereotype of the Croats that they did of the Slovenes: that they were timid and not ready to fight.

> In contrast to the mobilization of reservists which was ordered in Serbia and Montenegro, the Croatian government found little if any resistance to its mobilization ... Not only were the Croats willing to fight, they fought exceptionally bravely and for the most part effectively destroying a myth rooted in the Second

> World War that Croats are cowards who cannot recognize one end of a gun from the other.
>
> (Glenny 1996: 116–17)

As in the Slovenian case, that myth was to cost the Yugoslav Army dearly.

The JNA, Serbian paramilitary groups, and the Krajina Serbs took advantage of the Croat political leadership's inaction described in bitter detail by Martin Spegelj and Anton Tus (see Špegelj 2001; Tus 2001).

> Thus, between July and December 1991, JNA and Serbian paramilitary forces, working in close cooperation, consolidated their control over almost one-third of the Croatian state's territory in bitter warfare that resulted in high military and civilian casualties (over 10,000 people killed and approximately 30,000 wounded), savage atrocities, the dislocation of hundreds of thousands of people, and the widespread destruction of property and historic monuments.
>
> (Cohen 1995: 229)

The intense portion of the war was relatively short, compared to the nearly four-year war in Bosnia. At the time that the JNA attacked, the first instances of ethnic cleansing occurred: "The JNA and the local Serbs expelled all non-Serbs from the territories they conquered, and by the end of the year [1991] the number of displaced persons and refugees in Croatia was almost 500,000" (Goldstein 1999: 233). This amounted to nearly one-tenth of the entire population, with the economic consequences that accompanied it.

Serbs attacked from the east (Baranja-Srijem) and laid siege to the beautiful Baroque city of Vukovar. The Serbs began intensive shelling of the city on August 24, 1991, especially aiming at the hospital and other civilian targets. The Serbian paramilitary groups, Arkan's Tigers included, attacked villages throughout the region, committing many atrocities, and joined the JNA in surrounding Vukovar. The suffering of the people in Vukovar was intense. And yet, ironically, it was the JNA's decision to take Vukovar at all costs that allowed the Croat army, now built up to over two hundred thousand men, to retake much of the territory that had been seized.

> Sixty per cent of western Slavonia was liberated in this operation by 25 December 1991, and it was realistically estimated that all of it could have been liberated by 5 January; but the operation was halted by Tuđman's intervention, about which no one in the military command was notified in advance.
>
> (Špegelj 2001: 38)

In order to distract the Croatian Army's successful activities in the east, in December the JNA savagely attacked Dubrovnik; this turned out to be a miscalculation. International public opinion was outraged at the attempted destruction of one of the world's most beautiful cities that was clearly a tourist destination of no strategic importance, and this attack focused a high degree of international public attention on the war in the former Yugoslavia.

Both Tus and Špegelj claimed that the Croatian Army, militarily and morale-wise, had become superior to the JNA, which, although it had more arms, was deteriorating. In large part, this was due to the fact that non-Serbs were leaving the army and young Serbian men in Serbia did not want to fight in Croatia and Bosnia, viewing the war as both immoral and not possible to win, reminiscent of young middle-class Americans during the Vietnam War. More than two hundred thousand left Serbia and thousands of others went into hiding to avoid the army muster. In Belgrade, the rate of avoiding the army's call-up was about 85 percent. What is less known is that nine thousand Serbs served as volunteers in the Croatian Army (Tus 2001: 48 n.6).

Both Špegelj and Tus estimate that, in Slavonia, they needed only one more week to take back everything the JNA had occupied in Croatia when, again, Tuđman gave secret orders to underlings to cease all fighting.

> The 2 January 1992 truce found us with an army of 230,000 armed soldiers in 65 brigades, and many independent units in all three branches of the armed forces, as well as around 40,000 police from the Ministry of the Interior, of whom one third were deployed in war positions.
>
> (Tus 2001: 51)

Croatia signed the Vance agreement on January 2, 1992. The war in Croatia ceased until 1995 with Operations Flash and Storm; the Serbs would hold much of Eastern Croatia and Kajina, nearly one-third of Croatian territory, for the next three years.

Sociologist Ozren Žunec, who studied the war in detail, notes: "In many discussions with Croatian military experts and generals, the theme always comes up that during the war, politics, at least in Croatia, always halted operations just when the Croatian Army was in the most favourable situation" (2001: 68). Špegelj and Tus could only fume as they watched the politicians in Zagreb tie their hands for the next three years.

Croats and the War in Bosnia

A complete history and analysis of the War in Bosnia is beyond the scope of this book (see Cohen 1995; Glenny 1996, 2001; Magaš and Žanić 2001; Ramet 2006). In this section, I will only address the involvement of Croatia in Bosnia, which became a terrible misstep for the Croats. The two wars, that of Croatia and that of Bosnia, are inextricably bound together because of the hubristic ambitions of Milošević and Tuđman to divide Bosnia and Herzegovina. Misha Glenny claims that the not-so-secret meetings between Milošević and Tuđman resulted in their agreement to divide Bosnia in half "along the lines envisaged in the Cvetković-Maček *sporazum* of 1939—half going to Croatia, half to Serbia" (2001: 633). Croatia's reputation suffered internationally as a result of the behavior of the Croatian Army and the paramilitaries that operated, especially in western Herzegovina. With less than 20% of the population of Bosnia and Herzegovina as ethnic Croatian, it is difficult to see how Croatia could have controlled half of that territory.

Brigadier General of the Bosnian Army Jovan Divjak notes: "Sadly, more Croatian soldiers were killed in battles against the ARBiH [Army of Bosnia and Hercegovina] than fighting in Croatia itself, against either the JNA or the Serb Krajina forces" (Magaš and Žanić 2001: 102). Martin Špegelj adds: "Generals involved in it say that more than 13,000 Croat soldiers were killed ... there are graves of soldiers and officers killed in Bosnia-Herzegovina—and many were never brought home at all" (2001: 107–108).

Historian Vladimir Bilandžić offers this harsh assessment of Croatia's involvement in Bosnia-Herzegovina:

> The stain left on the Croatian nation by the crimes committed in the war cannot be removed, and, especially as regards Bosnia-Herzegovina, will remain a national stigma for a very long time. It can be alleviated by humanism, tolerance, liberal democracy, but it can never be wiped clean.
>
> (2001: 91)

In early 1994, the Americans and Germans twisted arms on both the Muslim and Croat sides and managed to create a working relationship between the two. President Bill Clinton, heeding increasingly stronger calls in the United States for intervention, decided to act. Although the Clinton administration continued to shy away from direct unilateral American intervention in the Bosnian conflict there were signs that behind the scenes Washington was gradually expanding its military support for the Moslems and Croats. Finally, he gave tacit permission for the Croats to move.

Operations Flash (Bljesak) and Storm (Oluja)—The Phoenix Rises

The end of the war in Croatia began in May 1995 with Operation Flash (*Blijesak*) when one hundred and fifty thousand soldiers attacked the JNA and Serb militias in western Slavonia along a 500-mile line and in a few hours retook all of western Slavonia. Along with thousands of Serb soldiers, about one hundred thousand Serb civilians, many living in Croatian houses, fled across the border into Bosnia and Serbia. The Croatian Army liberated all of western Slavonia and part of eastern Slavonia in a day and a half. This successful military operation proved to be a rehearsal for the larger Operation Storm (*Oluja*).

On August 4, 1995, two hundred thousand Croatian troops carried out the blitzkrieg Operation Storm that, like Operation Flash, employed "shock and awe" tactics. On August 4, they attacked in full force, and the Serb Krajina Republic forces crumbled (Glenny 1996; Magaš and Žamoć 2001; Tanner 2001).

Tellingly, neither the JNA nor the Serb Republic of Bosnia's Army helped the Krajina Serbs; they had been abandoned. The entire area fell to the Croats within a week. Predictably, one hundred thousand to two hundred thousand Serb civilians fled in panic. The Muslim-Croat Army in Bosnia and Herzegovina regained a huge amount of territory, forcing the Serbs of Bosnia, now abandoned by Milošević, to come to terms with the Dayton agreement.

Croatia was made whole again, but at a cost of more than ten thousand casualties and enormous damage to the infrastructure:

> the interior of Croatia was a wasteland—mile upon mile of burned-out houses and ruined churches. What had not been burned down by the Serbs in 1991 because it was Croatian had been burned down in 1995 because it was Serbian.
> (Tanner 2001: 301)[18]

During this period, Lado dropped its all-Yugoslav program and, as in its beginnings, became an exclusively Croatian ensemble.

Tuđman's Croatia 1991–99

Most observers, both inside and outside of Croatia, characterize the Franjo Tuđman period as one of autocratic decision-making, intolerance, and an almost total lack of democracy and, above all, a political swing to the far right. Many feared that fascism would make a triumphal return to Croatia.

In the early 1990s, as V. P. Gagnon, Jr., notes: "Deranged men marched menacingly through downtown Zagreb sporting fascist insignia; kiosks and stands sold Ustaša relics; foreigners were treated with great suspicion" (2004: xiii). Historian Sabrina Ramet adds:

> In touring Croatia in 1997, two years after the war had ended, I was struck by the occurrence of "U" (for Ustaša, plural Ustaša) in graffiti in Zagreb and other towns ... the appearance of such graffiti was a clear sign that, at least for some Croats, to love Croatia meant to embrace those who had murdered large numbers of Serbs. And while Ustaša nationalism is not the only kind of nationalism that exists in the world, this phenomenon *in Croatia* raises the question as to the role that nationalism can play in Croatia. Again, to belabor the point, Ustaša nationalism is not the only form of nationalism in Croatia, but again, where the Tudjman regime is concerned, Vjeko Perica is probably not alone in thinking that Tudjman's effort to reintegrate the Ustaša quisling state into Croatian history often came across as rehabilitating fascism.
>
> (2007: 3, emphasis in the original)

More seriously, émigrés with radical fascist ideology carried undue influence in the government during the war, especially given their small numbers, which only began to diminish after 1995, following the failure of their hopes for acquiring territory in Bosnia-Herzegovina. Many homeland Croats deeply resented their influence:

> Propaganda from the army [JNA] and Serbian leadership also harped on about an Ustasha revival in Croatia and said that the events of 1941 were repeating themselves, which unfortunately was partly true. The Ustaša ideology was imported from abroad with the return of extremist émigrés–not those who had not really been NDH officials, but those who thought they could use this ideology for their own benefit now that a new order was being established in Croatia. And they did indeed benefit and acquire power; because of them, because of their presence in politics, the structures of power have remained shaky and there are major problems to this day.
>
> (Špegelj 2001: 31)

Thuggish pressure was mounted against liberal writers in the form of death threats so that many of them felt compelled to emigrate (see Drakulić 1999; Ugrešić 1998). By 2000, the liberal newspaper *Nacional* "described the system as a 'gangster state' " (Ramet 2006: 586).

Tuđman had a tiger by the tail when he engaged the far-right elements of the HDZ Party. "While Tudjman tried to 'square the circle,' simultaneously emulating Tito, rehabilitating Pavelić, dancing around NDH atrocities, praising Croats as anti-fascists, and celebrating an exclusivist, expansionist nationalism, many of his supporters embraced Ustaša mythology openly and without qualification" (Ramet 2006: 586).

Perhaps the most egregious and long-lasting legacy of the HDZ, and the one resented the most by the electorate, was the disastrous state of the economy. This consisted of two elements: corruption and cronyism. "Indeed, the HDZ elite had used their control over the state to shift state assets into the hands of its own loyalists and allies in ways that enabled them to gain control of capital at virtually no cost to themselves" (Gagnon 2004: 175). In other words, the transfer of state property to the most corrupt elements of the population followed the same road as that which has envenomed the politics of post-communist Russia. "Croatia's gross national product had shrunk 50 percent from 1990 to 1993, and that production capacity had slipped 40 percent in the same period" (Cohen 1995: 348).

Political scientist Vladimir Bilandžić notes of the period 1990–99:

> The Croatian regime insists that the country is in good standing economically, politically, psychologically and in every other way, but I have to say that in these past nine years it has sharply declined in civilizational terms. Here are some indicators. First, what may be called de-industrialization: ten years ago Croatia had 1,690,000 people in employment, now there are about 1 million: 700,000 jobs have been lost, mostly in industry. Second, there is an ongoing degradation of the nation's intellectual and spiritual life.
>
> (2001: 90)

President Stjepan Mesić, Tudjman's successor, who broke with the HDZ in 1994, shares Bilandzic's opinion:

> If, as Professor Bilandzic has said, Croatia has become deindustrialized … if whole areas of Croatia have become depopulated, then that is a loss for the whole of Croatia … Croatia has reverted to being a peasant society. A country whose standards were close to those of Europe is now down to the level of the most backward.
>
> (2001: 103)

In the eyes of many, Tuđman's Croatia, because of its role in Bosnia, had become a pariah state. In that sense, Mesić, to a large degree, redeemed Croatia: "The West greeted Mesic's victory with almost indecent enthusiasm" (Tanner 2019: 310).

Croatia in the Twenty-First Century

Close observers of Croatia—despite the terrible decade of the 1990s and the superficial, but real, signs of incipient fascism—realized that most Croats wanted democracy and to observe the standards of political and ethical conduct of Western Europe. What the radical-right members of the HDZ and Paraga's Party of the Right failed to realize was that, while they attempted to resurrect an Ustaša state, the vast majority of Croats had undergone a very different experience. The Croats who had remained in Croatia had the advantages of excellent education, book

FIGURE 15: Croatia. Dance from Valpovo, Slavonia. Avaz International Dance Theatre. Choreography: Anthony Shay. Photo: D. Young. From the author's collection.

publishing, the thirst for reading, and the sophisticated literary and artistic scene that characterized urban life; this had the effect of creating an audience as sophisticated as any in Europe. Once the war ended, during which the country pulled together, the homeland Croats had no interest in participating in an intolerant state (Figure 15). Rather, economic woes and issues dominated the Croatian political scene of the next two decades (Tanner 2019).

In the 2000 elections, Stjepan Mesić won an overwhelming victory that was greeted by Western Europe and the United States eagerly. "The base or core of the HDZ's support had been reduced to the poorest parts of Croatia and the oldest voters and those with the least education" (Gagnon 2004: 171). In a very important study edited by Sabrina P. Ramet and Davorka Matić—*Democratic Transition in Croatia* (2007), a wide variety of scholars in the fields of history, social science, anthropology, and political science demonstrate conclusively that, as one of the contributors, Marius Soberg, states, "The period after Tuđman has seen a revitalization of Croatian society and politics" (2007: 34).

As a result of much hard work to burnish its democratic image, Mesić's regime has joined NATO and is next in line to join the European Union, the world's largest trading bloc, thus fulfilling the dreams of the vast majority of Croats to take their proper place in Europe.

Lado reflected the optimism of the new Croatia. They toured widely, especially since 2000, and gave concerts throughout the world, as well as increasing its domestic appearances (see Lado's annual reports, Godišnjak, for each year). Their popularity at home grew with each year, especially with the addition of Christmas and Easter concerts.

Following Mesić diplomatically reaching out to the Serbian regime in a gesture of reconciliation, Lado and Kolo, the Serbian State Folk Dance Ensemble, began in 2015 to give joint concerts and hold joint conferences with scholars and artists looking at the issues facing state-supported folk dance companies. They acted as "bridges of culture" (Lado 2019: 40). The two ensembles serve as a harbinger to a new period of constructive political relations.

NOTES

1. For an in-depth, highly detailed history of Croatia in English, I recommend Branka Magaš's *Croatia Through History* (2007). For those who can read Croatian, I recommend the authoritative three-volume work *Povijest Hrvata*, Franjo Sanjek, general editor (volume 1, 2003; volume 2, 2005; volume 3, 2007). Ivo Goldstein has written a fine one-volume work, *Hrvatska Povijest* (2003). Goldstein also has an abridged version, *Croatia, A History*, in English (1999).

2. Croatians began arriving in the United States in the 1850s. Immigrant John Filcic, who was born in Istria, remembers: "Dalmatians frequently did not know they were Croatians. They always called themselves Slavs or Slavonians, never Croatians" (personal interview, March 2, 2003) (see also Shay 2006, chapter 8).
3. Byron was "Mad, Bad, and Dangerous to Know." This characterization of Byron was famously made by Lady Caroline Lamb, who was madly in love with the bisexual Byron. As his biographer Louis Crompton remarked (1995: 197), it actually applied more to Lamb because of her relentless pursuit of Byron. She exposed his unorthodox sexual activities and he was forced to flee England and return to Greece where he died while attempting to organize the Greeks to fight the Ottoman army.
4. Americans still remain largely ignorant of geography: A recent survey by the National Geographic Education Foundation and Roper Public Affairs found that half of the population could not locate the state of Mississippi on a map. "Three quarters of young Americans polled could not find Indonesia on a map. And half or fewer could pick out New York or Ohio on a map of the United States" (Stall 2006: B19). Imagine, then the chances of Americans, even many Balkan enthusiasts, locating Croatia, Serbia, or Montenegro in their atlases.
5. See especially Barford (2001) and Curta (2001) for detailed discussions of the problems with studies coming from these regions as well as the "Great Migration" theory that Mirjana Gušić (1955) references. Croatian historian Ivo Goldstein follows the "Great Migration" theory in his more recent work in which he describes the migration process as slow because "most Slavs were farmers and shepherds" (1999: 13), a claim that Curta disputes through the evidence of Slavs among the warriors that repeatedly attacked the Byzantine Empire for the entire second half of the sixth century.
6. See especially Banac (1995) for the theory of the Iranian and Saramatian origins of Croatians.
7. See Goetz for a detailed discussion of the distinctions and differences between various categories of peasants.
8. The reader will encounter two spellings of Ustasha or Ustaša in Croatian. The first "Ustasha" is the singular form and refers to the government and regime 1941–45, while "Ustashe" is the plural form and used to cover groups of individuals who were associated with the organization. Different authors use one or the other of the forms, while others use both.
9. It is important to note that, outside of the scope of this study, other ethnic violence occurred on the former Yugoslav territories: Serbs and Albanians, Serbs and Muslims, and so on.
10. Andrija Artukovic, the NDH Minister of the Interior, and therefore in charge of the death camps, also escaped where he lived in California, protected by the Croatian immigrant community with ultraright American politicians who, in a twist of logic, felt it important to protect a known mass murderer because he was anticommunist.

11. The Istrian peninsula was eventually divided into the Allied occupied Zone A, which included the city of Trieste (Trst), and the Yugoslav Zone B. Ultimately, Zone A was given to Italy, while Zone B was awarded to Yugoslavia and added territory to the new republics of Croatia and Slovenia. Tito's claims to the heavily Slovenian areas of Carinthia, in Austria failed. A plebiscite was held and the majority of the population voted to remain in Austria.
12. As an example of touting the new Yugoslavia and its friendly interethnic relations and the forgetting of the past, Tito named the newly constructed highway, built by "volunteer" labor of the nation's youth, the Highway of Brotherhood and Unity. In view of the disintegration of Yugoslavia following his death, it might have been more auspicious had he simply named it Highway One as my UCLA political science professor suggested.
13. Igor Moiseyev agreed. In his autobiography he wrote:

> To me it was amazing why did we make such efforts to win in competitions that we organized, and drew in other countries? On the contrary, as organizers, it was necessary for us to be more modes ... But the Komsomols always fiercely battled to win first place, it had to be ours.
>
> (1996: 82. Quoted in Shay 2019: 129–30)

14. The first program performed by Lado is reprinted in Vitez and Vučić (2009: 98). The name Lado was adopted in 1950.
15. To Tito's fury, the Vatican made Stepinac a cardinal in 1952, bringing Stepinac into the public eye once again.
16. Branka Magaš notes: "He [Tito] would later tell Savka that he had been given no choice, that the army was putting great pressure on him to yield them up, and that it was either him or them" (2007: 646).
17. One of the most fascinating, full accounts of the war is *The War in Croatia and Bosnia-Herzegovina, 1991–1995*, edited by Branka Magaš and Ivo Žanić (2001), an edited volume that includes testimony of many of the leading participants on the Croat side: Stjepan Mesic, the second president of Yugoslavia, Martin Špegelj, minister of defense, a former general in the Yugoslav Army, and Anton Tus, the head of the Croatian Army General Staff.
18. One of the reasons that there were so many houses set on fire during the War of Succession was to prevent the former owners returning to claim them, thus ensuring that ethnic cleansing lasted.

5

Spain: Women's Work—Franco's Sección Femenina and Spanish Folk Dance

Any discussion of the use of folk dance or, in my parlance, ethno identity dance, that is, dances that have been spectacularized, theatricalized, or otherwise augmented and adjusted for use on stages for purposes of representation, must be seen in the context of those regimes which use it as a tool. Authoritarian regimes have a special obsession with their use (Shay 2002, 2019). For purposes of this chapter that would be Franco's Falange Party in Spain, which came to power as a result of the Spanish Civil War (1936–39). In the Spanish case, Franco's government utilized *esquela bolera*, a theatrical form that mixes ballet and folk dance as a form of ethno identity dance for the representation of Spanishness:

> The Choruses and Dances have influenced and been influenced by the *esquela bolera*, and have used its repertory, with steps and dances from the *escuela bolera* described as "typical" steps and folk dances from Madrid and Andalusia in existing documents about them. These went on to be danced at folk festivals as "traditional" Spanish dances.
>
> (Monés et al. 2000: 153)

As we will see, the Choruses and Dances (coros y danzas) became a propagandistic tool for Franco's Spanish government, which had become a political pariah state, to reenter the diplomatic world after World War II, when all of the other major fascist powers had collapsed. Thus, the use of ballet-informed movements in ethno identity dances can add an element of spectacularized and virtuosic movements—higher kicks, faster turns, pointed toes—that do not exist in the authentic versions of a folk or vernacular dance, in order to create a more spectacular effect in performances that have come to characterize these staged folk dances from their use in the romantic ballet of the nineteenth century.

Francisco Franco and the Spanish Civil War

"The civil war was the most destructive experience in modern Spanish history, rivaled only by the French [Napoleonic] invasion of 1808" (Payne 2012: 245). Most observers saw the cruel conflict as a rehearsal for World War II, and Nazi Germany and the Soviet Union both provided aid and comfort to the two sides. Many Americans from the political left also participated and gave their lives for the Republican side, especially the heavily decimated Abraham Lincoln Brigade. Professor of Spanish John A. Crow characterized the struggle as "one of the cruelest struggles in history ... a full-fledged blood bath of the most horrible kind" (1985: 319). Crow lays the fault at the feet of the extreme left and the extreme right: "Both groups were so egocentric that they did not see, or were unwilling to work for, the common good" (1985: 285). However, the left was a democratically elected government; the right were illegal insurgents who essentially destroyed Spain, its social structure and economy, which did not recover until after the death of Franco. Franco and his generals, on the extreme right, hated the Republic, which they regarded as weak.

> The military uprising, wrongly termed "nationalist uprising" by Franco and his supporters, for it was certainly far from being national, was mainly inspired by the old-line conservative tradition of absolutism. The generals who were Franco's companions-in-arms all hated the Republic because it was liberal and because it was weak, too weak to prevent disorder. These generals had no political or social program to offer. Everything they stood for was purely negative.
> (Crow 1985: 320, emphasis in the original)

Franco was no Abraham Lincoln: He did not seek to reconcile the nation; he merely sought bloody revenge and complete repression, which were practiced to the end. This was especially true toward separatist groups such as the Catalans and Basques. He banned the use of their languages, and any expression of ethnic or national identity, other than the most folkloric. Clearly, although Franco and his regime had the trappings of a fascist regime, unlike Hitler, Franco had no particular political philosophy, he wanted the security of an absolutist state with support of the Catholic Church (Balfour 2000; Crow 1985; Payne 2012).

The old saying concerning power corrupting was certainly true of Francisco Franco: "Franco had developed a fascist-type state with a single party and an elaborate apparatus, although combined with a vigorous Catholicism and a stress on traditional culture" in which Spanish ethno identity dance played a key role, crucially opening otherwise diplomatically closed doors. The means to maintain the pseudo-fascist state were "mass executions, imprisonment, redemption through penal labor, and the inculcation of the regime's values through education, psychological programming, and media propaganda" (Balfour 2000: 266). In other words, this state was a child of Nazi Germany, including the Nazi salute (see Balfour 2000: 267, illustration).

As to Franco, he became a self-important monster, which characterized his behavior until his death in 1975: "In the process he had grown arrogant and overweening, convinced that his victory was a miracle and that he had been designated by divine providence the legitimate ruler of Spain" (Payne 2012: 247). The actual miracle was that he was one of the few dictators who died in bed, with his boots on, of natural causes, and with the restoration of the Spanish throne, democracy ensued relatively quickly, in many ways perhaps too easily since many guilty Falangist sadists were pardoned (Balfour 2000).

In my earlier study of professional state-supported folk dance ensembles (2002), I focused on the most successful and visible form of how the rural folk, the peasants, who were thought to be the basis of the nation, were to be shown in public arenas, both to home audiences and to the world at large, using what I call ethno identity dances, that is, dances that are specifically prepared for national and ethnic representation in staged performances (Shay 2016). These appearances frequently consisted of "Folk expressions, either resuscitated or reinvented" (Martínez del Fresno 2013: 106), which became the currency of ethno identity repertoires in folk dance ensembles, amateur and professional, across the political spectrum. "The Women's Section co-opted the folk repertoires and transferred them from a rural to an urban milieu, from the village plaza and the local, festive *romería* pilgrimage to the theatre stage" (Martínez del Fresno 2013: 106). I have described similar patterns in the former Yugoslavia, and even in the United States in the 1950s–1990s when I was active in that context (Shay 2002, 2008, 2016, 2019).

Folk and vernacular dance have had and continue to have a particular attraction for authoritarian regimes—fascist, communist, and personal, which deeply rely on ethnic and national identities as a source of legitimation for their regimes and their political priorities. Franco's Spain was among them (Martínez del Fresno 2013, 2014, 2017; Pérez Zalduondo 2017; Sánchez Ekizia 2017). This is because folklore and folk dance, specifically, were considered a "safe outlet to express regional loyalties" (Richmond 2003: 75), in Spain as well as the former Soviet Union. In Spain,

> in the period following the war, folk songs and dances acquired a strong symbolic power as official expressions of the people and the fatherland ... folk songs and dances were invoked in numerous propaganda events and played an ever-present role in the ceremonies held in city streets and squares.
>
> (Martínez del Fresno 2013: 101)

"The Francoist state was essentially a conservative and authoritarian regime. Its totalitarian tendencies, represented by the Falange, were displayed in the pageantry of the state" (Balfour 2000: 265). And Spanish ethno identity dance was central to that pageantry.

The politics of representation constitutes a particular method in which a government, nation-state, or ethnic group negotiates how it represents itself, both to itself and to the world at-large. The type of staging to be pursued requires organization and a philosophy to underpin the decisions.

Sánchez Ekezia makes clear that one of the motivations for staging Basque dances during the Franco regime "was the search for the spectacular" (2017: 45). In all cases, unlike folk dance, which is an organic part of people's lives, ethno identity dance allows the producer and presenter to show a group in its Sunday clothes, well-rehearsed, at its best. Instead of a range of ages, sizes, and shapes of performers found in a village context, one views dancers who are young, athletic, slim, and attractive to project an image of the nation that is young and vigorous.

When staging folklore, no matter in which genre but particularly in dance and music, the question of authenticity raises its head. Competition, like the competitions and festivals held by the Franco regime in the field of presenting staged folk dance, as in so many other competitions in dance from Hawaii to Ireland to Turkey, produces various groups attempting to win (Shay 2016a). This means that "inauthentic" elements, even if as miniscule as borrowing a movement from a neighboring village or ethnic group, are introduced into the performances in order to win. Nevertheless, the stated reason that governments and individuals frequently express for holding such competitions and festivals is to "preserve the authenticity of the dances" (Sánchez Ekezia 2017: 43). Claims for authenticity abound, but the very context of these performances turns folk dances into ethno identity dances: performances are timed, costumes are altered [in the case of Spain for purposes of fascist-Catholic female modesty (Sánchez Ekezia 2017; see also Casero 2000: 65)], all-male dances become all-female dances or female dancers take the place of male dancers (Martínez del Fresno 2014: 264, Casero 2000: 65), only attractive young dancers appear on stage (note poster Martínez del Fresno 2014: 251), they are highlighted in the publicity for state-supported folk dance groups, orchestras replace solo instruments, modern instruments replace traditional ones, harmony is introduced in vocal music, and so on.

Dance in Franco's Spain was women's work. The Sección Femenina (sometimes "SF") promoted the use of Spanish folk dance and music and served as the umbrella for a widespread system of festivals to demonstrate symbolic support for Franco's regime (see Escudero 1984 and Echagüe 1963).

> After the Civil War, the Sección Femenina of the one political party that existed under Franco's dictatorship (the Spanish Falange) decided to commission the women of the Coros y Danzas (a department of the Music Division) to compile information about folk dance.
>
> (Monés et al. 2000: 152)

The model of staging folk dance followed by the Franco regime was the use of highly rehearsed performances by local performers, guided by rules established by the conservative, fascist, pro-modesty, Catholic-Fascist Falange Party's Sección Femenina (Women's Section) (see Casero 2000). They sought a means of pure, in the sense of morally decent, and morally uplifting expression of Spanish national identity, to override the image of "decadent" flamenco and, more explicitly, to cover up potential ethnic and regional fissures, and, of course, that would be through the use of regional folk dances and music, prepared for the stage by local performers, known as *Coros y Danzas*. "The 'pure' and 'joyful' image of young women who had appropriated traditional dance and performed them in a mass format were called to function as an effective collective icon of the [Franco's] New Spain" (Martínez del Fresno 2014: 246). The vehicle for showing these dances domestically, emphasizing the purity and modesty of folk dance, was the competition and festival system established by the Franco regime through the Sección Femenina, as well as in numerous propaganda events of all kinds (Casero 2000; *Spanish Songs and Folk Dances* 1957; Pérez Zalduondo 2017).

Ethno identity dances always refer to a specific regional folk or vernacular dance genre, no matter how tenuous a relationship the staged version has to the original folk or vernacular form. The Women's Section print materials stressed time after time the need to resuscitate the authentic folklore "performing only the authentic, executing in authentic costumes, and using only the traditional instruments" (Martínez del Fresno 2013: 111), but many of their so-called folklorists were not trained and could not evaluate true folklore from folklorism or fakelore. These women were not trained dance ethnologists, but amateur enthusiasts, but their compilations proved valuable for the study of Spanish folk dance. Coros y Danzas altered many aspects of their performances for purposes of the stage, perhaps the most common one was the use of all-female dance teams until 1961, when male dancers were permitted to appear.

> Until that moment, this truly aberrant anomaly was produced in the total distortion of Spanish folk dances, the majority of which are in couples. In order to overcome this "small inconvenience," they were danced with two women dressed as such, or one dressed as a woman and the other as a man.
>
> (Casero 2000: 65)[1]

The most successful model of ethno dance presentation was that which characterized the former Soviet Union and Eastern Bloc: the formation of the professional state-supported folk dance ensemble. By contrast, Spain followed a different model: *coros y danzas*, which was founded by the Sección Femenina, the Women's Section of Franco's Falange Party, which relied on local "experts," using amateur young urban women. At first they used only young women in their teen years and early twenties, to create ethno identity dances from each of Spain's 50 regions (later provinces) for domestic propaganda. In the beginning, the only male performers were instrumentalists, and later they added male dancers for more spectacular effects. Eventually, beginning in 1948, it was used as a successful diplomatic vehicle of Spanish identity, designed, as was the Igor Moiseyev Dance Company (and many other ensembles), to represent the idea of "unity in diversity," to mask the reality that several Spanish regions wished to create various degrees of separatism from Spain, ranging from internal autonomy to outright national independence (Catalonia, Galicia, the Basque Country).[2] Pilar Primo de Rivera, the founder of the Seccíon Femenina, famously proclaimed:

> When Catalans can sing the songs of Castile; when in Castile they know what *sardanas* are ... when the songs of Galicia are known in the Levant; when fifty or sixty thousand voices join in the same song, then we shall have achieved unity among the people and the lands of Spain.
>
> (Quoted in Richmond 2003: 75)

Music historian Beatriz Martínez del Fresno notes, "Franco's New Spain was, though, a nationalist country which did not ... contemplate any territorial fracture, or make it possible to split the central power" (2013: 109).

"The hidden intention behind this recuperation of folk culture was to promote an idea of unity in a politically and socially divided country, through such nationalist acts as the recuperation of traditions involving music and dance" (Monés et al. 2000: 152). In Spain, "The Feminine Division's Choruses and Dances worked on this project [documenting regional folk dances] under Franco's regime for forty years (1937–1977)" (Monés et al. 2000: 152).

Here we find "unity in diversity" idealized in song, but the same rules did not apply to dance in which

> those responsible for the summer camp [where these dances were taught] were threatened of being punished if, for instance, the girls practiced dances from outside their home province ... [and] instructors ... were required to prevent the spontaneous exchange of dances among girls from different places.
>
> (Martínez del Fresno 2013: 120)

This was a gendered activity: the posters announcing the arrival of coros y danzas stress an all-girl show (no mention of the all-male musicians who accompanied them), which characterized the visit as "The Spiritual Embassy of 150 Girls" (Martínez del Fresno 2014: 251). It may seem politically incorrect, but only unmarried girls, rather than women, participated in these dance performances because of the implied purity of "girls." Was it sexist? Yes, from the perspective of the twenty-first century. But such views were not limited to Franco's Spain; one need only view Hollywood films and sitcoms to see to what degree the word "girls" was used to cover even mature women. Underscoring my observation, prominently featured on the poster of the Spanish coros y danzas group is a photograph of a young woman who closely resembles Lana Turner, a glamorous movie star of the period, rather than any peasant girl.

"In the 1950s SF regulations became stricter and shunn[ed] the concept of region, identity was narrowed down to province" (Martínez del Fresno 2013: 120), and this regional division is clearly shown in the souvenir program of 1957 (*Spanish Songs and Folk Dances* 1957). Unlike the Soviet Union, which utilized professionally trained dancers to carry out their mission, Spain chose to utilize local amateurs although, like the Igor Moiseyev Dance Company, they were urban girls, and later boys especially after 1961, who were trained and rehearsed to perform regional folk dances, not native to them, only those dances from their home province, under the then prevalent (but not yet dead) notion that "Instructors would never be able to perform well alien dances 'since each region has its temperament and its own characteristics, which are very different and clearly marked' " (Martínez del Fresno 2013: 121). This is what I call the "it's in the blood" syndrome, that is, only people from a particular place carry the particular genetic codes that permit them to expertly perform specific songs and dances (see for flamenco Machin-Autenrieth 2017: 70). In the Spanish case, "The rules clearly specified that both provincial and local dance groups had to abide by the prohibition to [not] perform dances from other provinces, except in special cases authorized by the Central Council of Culture" (ibid.). This meant that, in Spain, the founding of a Moiseyev-like dance company would not have been possible since, in Moiseyev, all of the dancers are expected to perform in every number and, thus, a single dancer would represent Russia, Ukraine, Uzbekistan, Greece, Spain, Argentina, Serbia, Latvia, among many others. The Spanish model was in direct opposition to that established by Moiseyev. Aside from the versatility of the dancers in the Moiseyev company, in contrast to the province-specific Spanish dancer, the professional Moiseyev dancer, and the amateur dancer of Spain, the economic model of the Spanish ensembles was much more expensive, requiring many dancers and musicians to represent a viable number of Spanish regions (Shay 2019).

All of these folk dance ensembles, professional and amateur, depicted an idealized, bucolic period, some "Golden Age" of peasant happiness that never existed: "The new [Franco] regime retrieved archaic and timeless expressions that bid a return to the austerity of the Castilian peasant life, to simplicity, and to a romanticized vision of the rural world" (Martínez del Fresno 2013: 107) that were dreamed of by and aimed at urban populations, who dominated national life and had no connection to the poverty and hardships of village life. All of the nation-states that used ethno identity dance for purposes of representation utilized that "Golden Age" image of an idealized peasant or court population dancing idealized dances in an ahistorical never-never land.

The Moiseyev model was created by Igor Moiseyev beginning in 1937, developing a dance ensemble of more than 100 performers, a new dance genre created from a number of sources with which he was familiar—classical ballet, folk dance, character dance, and gymnastics—a highly athletic and spectacularized repertoire of choreographies that were designed to represent the rainbow of ethnic diversity of the former Soviet Union and a new type of dancer: the professional folk dancer, who conveyed the political message that the Soviet Union and Russia were young, energetic, athletic, and united (Shay 2019). Spain, through coros y danzas, was also sending a political message: that life in Spain was good, pure, united, and happy. "The assertions of former members that there was no political motive in their encouragement of songs in Catalan, Basque and Galician cannot be taken seriously" (Richmond 2003: 75).

The Igor Moiseyev Dance Company, officially named the State Academic Ensemble of Folk Dances of the Peoples of the Soviet Union, carried out a series of highly successful tours, first within the Soviet Union itself, especially entertaining the troops, followed in the late 1940s and early 1950s in Eastern Europe and China, in 1955 in England and France, and in 1958 in the United States. Several nonsocialist states, many with suppressive regimes, which saw the success of these performances, such as Iran, Egypt, Turkey, Greece, the Philippines, Ghana, and Senegal, and many other nation-states also founded ensembles based on the Moiseyev model for purposes that closely aligned with those of the Igor Moiseyev Dance Company. In particular, their ensembles showed an ethnic rainbow population living together in harmony and, thereby, created positive diplomatic appearances. Unlike the Moiseyev model, to my knowledge, the coros y danzas model of using dancers who came from a specific region was not followed outside of Spain.

And in Spain, "The propaganda triumph of 1948, the performance of its choir and dance teams (coros y danzas) to foreign audiences, was scheduled to continue with further trips approved by central government" (Richmond 2003: 85). However, in Spain the model of sending a collection of various regional groups had to be expensive if it followed the 1948 model in which, "The tour was financed through SF existing budgets" (Richmond 2003: 75) because Spain was extremely poor in that era.

Let me be clear: Founding and maintaining such dance ensembles is expensive because, in order to be effective, they must be spectacular, with large casts, requiring huge outlays of money for dancers' and musicians' salaries and benefits, as well as those of the supporting staff, technicians, costumes, stage sets, maintenance of rehearsal halls, and, sometimes, performance spaces. In addition, these companies require advertising, marketing, and other forms of publicity and promotion in order for the ensemble to create sources of income and performance opportunities. These ensembles have been created specifically for performances. Their success in the fields of diplomacy, tourist development, and economy is necessary for continued economic and political support from their respective sponsoring nation-states.

Prior to the founding of the Igor Moiseyev Dance Company, several states experimented with other methods of presenting folk dance. This point is most important because various states experimented with the activity of producing folk dance for political reasons. At the height of the popularity of state-supported ethno identity performances, the period 1930–80, before settling on the Moiseyev model as the least expensive and most effective one, various states wanted to capitalize on the vision of masses of peasants dancing in huge public spaces to give the impression that masses of people supported the regime. One of the earliest methods, used by the Nazis in Germany and the Metaxas regime in Greece (1936–40), was to bus hundreds and even thousands of peasants into the capital city or to a city like Nuremberg, to a large public stadium and have them perform throughout a period of several days (Von Bibra 1987; Loutzaki 2008). This method had the advantage of making it appear as if these mass performances represented mass support for unpopular regimes. But these performances were expensive—the performers had to be fed, housed, and transported to the performance spaces—and were often chaotic, producing uneven results in quality of performance that were not always successful. This is because the peasants were frequently given few or no directions in what and how to perform—just wear colorful costumes and dance to traditional music the way your grandparents did—often with minimal preparation and rehearsal. Most of the governments that sponsored these performances wanted a professional level of performance that these peasants were unable to provide.

Prior to the founding of the Igor Moiseyev Dance Company, the Soviet Union attempted another model that was more curated and prepared in advance: the *dekady* (ten days), in which the central authorities in Moscow brought in not only performers but also workers, peasants, visual artists, literary figures, and others to show off the cultural and economic resources of a specific republic and introduce them to audiences in the capital, Moscow. The dance and music performers were carefully overseen by Russian artists, like Igor Moiseyev, who oversaw these performances so that they appeared professional and smooth—the communist regime was obsessed with perfection and also monumentality in the politics of representation. This model of presentation continued into the 1960s but was never sent on tour.

Yugoslavia, in 1949–52, attempted a loosely similar model in which they sent 150 performers: the Serbian professional ensemble Kolo, the Croatian amateur ensemble Jožo Vlahović from Zagreb (later to become the professional ensemble Lado), and the village dancers of Lazaropolje in Macedonia, a group that had performed frequently in the festival circuit to Llangollen, Wales (as did coros y danzas), Switzerland, and Greece. They quickly abandoned this model as too expensive and requiring immense preparation and security. They professionalized the three ensembles and instead of performing dances only from their own republic, the three ensembles, by the early 1950s, were touring with "all Yugoslav" repertoires, often under the generic title of "The Yugoslav Folk Ballet".

Spain, Franco's Fascist Falange Party, and the Seccíon Femenina

Franco seized the Falange Party when its founder, José Antonio Primo de Rivera, was executed in 1937 by the Republican forces. Pilar Primo de Rivera, his sister, founded the Seccíon Femenina in 1934 to carry out her brother's fascist values in determining the role of women in Franco Spain; throughout her life, she never lost sight of those founding fascist values. "It meant contributing to the regime's acceptance and stability by a ceremonial and propaganda role in Spain and abroad" (Richmond 2003: 11). The Sección Femenina promoted the use of Spanish folk dance and music and served as the umbrella for a widespread system of festivals to demonstrate symbolic support for Franco's regime (see Escudero 1984; Echagüe 1963; *Spanish Songs and Dances* 1957).

It is important to recall that SF cast a wide net and the coros y danzas movement was only one of the many programs that SF carried out, and not even its major program. "Underpinning all fascist regimes is a core belief in the power of the nation as a higher entity and quasi spiritual ideal," an ideal Pilar Primo de Rivera followed, largely with Franco's acquiescence, throughout her life (Richmond 2003: 1). In short, the Sección Femenina involved itself in every aspect of women's lives throughout its organizational life, which was so successful that it lasted beyond the Franco regime, until 1977.[3] Nevertheless, coros y danzas was probably the SF program that lasted the longest and had the most impact. Coros y danzas was regarded as "wholly positive" by the public (Richmond 2003: 76). In the eyes of the conservative Spanish elite, there existed the hope that these regional folk dances would replace the lure and popularity of flamenco and replace it as the image of Spain with wholesome, innocent, modest folk dances instead of sexually charged flamenco performances.

To the chagrin of the Spanish elites, the development of the theatricalized genre of music, song, and dance known by the nineteenth century as flamenco, and the popularity of its despised Gitano performers, had seized the public imagination as a fiery, sexy dance and music genre (see Fauser 2005; Machin-Autenrieth 2017). Flamenco was very popular outside of Spain, as a "sexy" dance. "For the French, Spain was the most exotic of Europeans cultures" (Fauser 2005: 263). Spain became the first in a series of tourist destinations that had, through the appearances of flamenco performances at World's Fairs, targeted Spain as a place of primitiveness, over-the-top sexuality, and exoticism. The female flamenco dancer, even to this day, became the image of Spain and drew tourists, mostly male, to the fleshpots of Andalusia, Madrid, and Barcelona. This was the beginning of sexual tourism in the late eighteenth and early nineteenth centuries. Later, other genres, such as belly dance and tango (Savigliano 1995), would draw increasing numbers of tourists seeking the exotic and the sexy, but flamenco was the first; to this day, flamenco remains one of the major tourist draws to Spain.

Sandie Holguín and other scholars have called attention to the degree to which many members of the Spanish elite fought the symbolic relation between Spanish identity and flamenco performances. Like Hitler and Metaxas of Greece, Francisco Franco and the Falange Party sought Spanish folk dance to be the true symbolic form of ethno identity dance to represent Spain as opposed to flamenco, and the coros y danzas became the traveling diplomats to represent Spain from 1948 to 1965.

> A study of dance in Spain also illuminates the question of nationalism ... The Franco era promoted a centralized Spanish nationalism that smothered other forms of expression in culture, art, language and history—a nationalism exemplified in the dance world by the Coros y Danzas (Chorus and Dance) Division of the Sección Femenina.
>
> (Monés et al. 2000: 144)

Part of this program was to deflect attention from the flamenco genre as a popular symbol of Spanish national identity.

> The Catholic Church and the leaders of the Spanish Falange thoroughly discouraged flamenco and other forms of musical entertainment for purposes of the representation of Spain. Instead, the female contingent of the fascist Falange Party, the Sección Femenina, established folk singing and dancing groups as a way to counteract the dangers of flamenco and solidify a new kind of national identity after the civil war that was predicated on "unity in difference."
>
> (Holguín 2019: 23)

By "unity in difference" we can see such a popular manner in many state-supported folk dance ensembles, like those of the former Yugoslavia, the Philippines, and Mexico, of showing rainbow ethnic and regional dances to demonstrate national unity (Shay 2002).

The women who carried out the research into these dances were not trained dance ethnologists, but amateur enthusiasts, but their compilations proved valuable for the study of Spanish folk dance. The result of all of this decades-long and extensive activity in folk dance had a huge impact on dance performance to this day:

> Since its presence was spread out across the whole of the national area (in 1960 it comprised 24,000 members in 1,600 groups), most dance professionals in Spain at present have had some form of direct or indirect contact with the Choruses and Dances.
>
> (Ibid.)

Nevertheless, like the Moiseyev and other ensembles, Franco Spain craved monumentality and the spectacular. The SF utilized *esquela bolera*, a theatrical form that mixes ballet and folk dance as a form of ethno identity dance:

> The Choruses and Dances have influenced and been influenced by the *esquela bolera*, and have used its repertory, with steps and dances from the *escuela bolera* described as "typical" steps and folk dances from Madrid and Andalusia in existing documents about them. These went on to be danced at folk festivals as "traditional" Spanish dances.
>
> (Monés et al. 2000: 153)

Thus, the use of ballet-informed movements can add an element of spectacularized and virtuosic movements that do not exist in the authentic versions of a folk or vernacular dance, in order to create a more spectacular effect in performances that have become an integral part of ethno identity dances, dances created for public representation, that has come to characterize these staged folk dances since the establishment of the Igor Moiseyev Dance Company in 1937 (Shay 2019). Essentially the creators of this ethno identity dance tradition in Spain, by adding elements of other dance genres to spectacularize it, follow the same trajectory that Igor Moiseyev, and the creators of other ethno identity dance genres I describe for Iran and Uzbekistan, did. In fact, most national dance companies seem to add these elements in the creation of new dance genres suitable for stage.

Thus, like all other political regimes, Franco's Falange Party claimed to save pure, unadulterated Spanish folk dance, while making profound changes to it in the form of ethno identity dance. Like other regimes across the political spectrum,

Franco's Spain found folk dance to be a useful propaganda tool but, unlike most other regimes, the Sección Femenina chose to organize regional dance teams to represent Spain, rather than form a national dance ensemble, making its form of representation unique. During that process they changed many aspects, especially adding men after 1961, to what had been an exclusively female activity because, only with the addition of male dancers could the coros y danzas become fully spectacularized and an even more valuable propaganda tool projecting a vision of Spain as young, vigorous, and athletic.

It appears that folk dance as a spectacularized performance phenomenon gave way to flamenco, which under brilliant performers like Antonio Gades, became a worldwide sensation. Also, flamenco became an international success spawning world famous American performers like José Greco, unlike Spanish folk dance, which remained a Spanish performance art. Nevertheless, the coros y danzas movement touched everyone in the dance world in Spain, so the impression they made with their stylized performances continues to influence the staging of folk dance in Spain, but without the state support that it received during Franco's era.

NOTES

1. A lavish souvenir program of the Coros y Danzas (*Spanish Songs and Folk Dances* 1957, 10th edition) shows the transition state of bringing men into the performances. Of the various represented regions, Andalusia, Old Castile, Santander, and Murica had all women groups. Asturias had a photograph showing the backs of the figures in male costume that could have been either women in men's clothes or men. Valencia had several men, Catalonia, Navarre, New Castile, the Basque Country, and the Canary Islands showed one or two men only. Four years later, in 1961, men became a regular feature of folk dance performances. The Yugoslav government produced a similar, souvenir program with many photographs. Both the Yugoslav and the Spanish groups appeared in Llangollen Festival in Wales where both groups received prizes.
2. A strong, unified regionalist movement in Andalusia did not really appear until the late 1970s … Unlike the historically-rooted regionalist identities that were fostered in regions such as the Basque County and Catalonia, a regional consciousness in Andalusia has not been part of the day-to-day life until relatively recently (Machlin-Autenreith 2017: 5).
3. See Casero (2000, plate 21) for a schematic organization plan of Sección Femenina.

6

Dominican Republic: The Dictator's Fancy Dance—Trujillo, Merengue, and Nationalism

The history of merengue in astounding ways furnishes the reader with an ideal case study in the manner in which dance and politics intersect, almost containing the full ingredients for a television drama, along the lines of *Game of Thrones*. The plot of the story of the Dominican Republic provides us with five hundred years of tumultuous history: a lowly regional folk dance becomes famous, constituting a popular social dance, and its music becomes the ultimate national symbol of the Dominican Republic and then goes on to become a cosmopolitan dance craze around the world in its urban big-band form; add to that, a fancy-dancing dictator, Rafael Leónidas Trujillo Molina (r. 1930–1961), referred to simply as Trujillo, who, using powders and creams to whiten his face, begins his career as a petty criminal and graduates to mass murderer, lurid sexual predator, and kleptocratic megalomaniac and ends his life in a hail of bullets in a plot sponsored and abetted by the CIA; and finally, mix in torture, humiliation, and assassination, complex issues of race, a long and chaotic history of a nation beginning with Columbus, the one who sailed the ocean blue in 1492, the disappearance of more than a million native island dwellers shortly thereafter (population estimates vary), Spanish and French colonialism, the importation of thousands of Africans and slavery, slave revolts, two ugly American military invasions and occupations to "save democracy," more racial issues, including the American brand of racism used against the local populace, and profound identity confusion. The only survivor of all of this tumult? the merengue itself.[1]

In order to understand the complex embeddedness of the merengue in Dominican society, it is first important to untangle certain key elements of history in the country's formation. This presents the readers with various racial and ethnic strands that make up both Dominican identity and the place of the merengue in its pattern. We will see how the two American invasions of the Dominican Republic helped become an impetus for Dominicans, even the elite, to embrace it. As dictator

Trujillo elevates a rural folk dance to a symbol of national Dominican identity, we will see merengue's characteristics and history and, finally, its assent to a world famous ballroom dance.

I also want to enlarge the lens through which I examine the use to which Trujillo utilized the merengue, demonstrating how we can consider the reign of Trujillo as a sultanistic regime, in Hartlyn, Chehabi, and Linz's terms (1998). Hartlyn states, "Of all the cases considered ... the Trujillo regime may well be the closest approximation to the ideal type of a regime with high levels of sultanistic tendencies" (1998: 87). While I outlined what constitutes sultanistic regimes in the Introduction, Hartlyn synthesizes the specific ways in which they apply to Trujillo:

> The regime was based on personal rule, with loyalty grounded in a mixture of fear and rewards. Trujillo exercised power without restraint within his small republic, acting at his own discretion, unencumbered by ideology or bureaucratic norms. During his reign, as he accumulated fabulous wealth and power, the country experienced large-scale but centralized and controlled corruption, arbitrary and capricious decisions combined with scrupulous attention to legal forms, and ruthless violence.
>
> (Hartlyn 1998: 87)

Of all of the regimes with sultanistic tendencies in the Caribbean and Latin America, Trujillo's regime was probably the most sultanistic of them all. And, taking in sum all that others and I write, especially focusing issues of megalomania and arbitrariness, Trujillo's rule had the essence of a surreal work of fiction like *Game of Thrones*.

Dance and Nationalism, Dance and Race, Dance and Sex

In all discussions of New World dances, especially those that developed using elements of African, Native American, and European origin, questions surrounding race, sex, and gender present themselves. This is most true of dance because it is embodied. It is gratifying to see how many scholars outside of the field of dance studies recognize the role of dance in the creation of various New World identities. Anthropologist Peter Wade notes that

> With blacks in Latin America (and elsewhere), just as important are the intertwined images of sexual, musical and dancing power. This is an underlying element in the literary trends of *negrismo* that emerged in the 1920s ... The

> ambivalent sexual attraction felt by whites for blacks is also a recurrent theme in colonial contexts. Sex and music often fit together.
>
> (2010: 110)

This is especially observed in the context of "slumming," a phenomenon in which wealthy white people, usually men, go to the poorer areas of town to experience hotter music and hotter dance than can be experienced in the more decorous parts of town. As a well-known example, whites in Central Manhattan traveled to Harlem to hear the best jazz in nightclubs, which often catered their performances to attract this lucrative trade. This type of slumming was also true for tango as upper-class men went to classy brothels to experience it (Shay 2014).[2]

As Wade points out: "The reasons for the rise of this music are complex, but one element was the 'modern', liberated sexuality it was held to embody" (2010: 110). Illicit sex was an important aspect of slumming. And although Wade is discussing Colombian music, his observation is true of tango, merengue, and other forms of "hot" music. "Styles of music associated with blacks, or as danced to by blacks, are still seen as sexually immoral and/or exciting by many people in Colombia" (Wade 2010: 110).

But, like the tango and the merengue, the beat, the movements, the music become irresistible, and the formerly immoral dance triumphs. And though he is describing the scene in Colombia, it is equally valid in the Dominican Republic:

> The rise of musical styles associated with blackness did not only occur in Colombia, but was characteristic of "for example, Cuba and Brazil at slightly earlier dates ... The point is that, within the cultural space of the nation, images of racialized powers—indigenous magic, black sexuality, white civilization—are symbols competing for room, for legitimacy, in defining what the nation is and can become.
>
> (Wade 2010: 110)

This struggle for cultural and national legitimacy is still playing out in the Dominican Republic, and a dance with undeniable Africanist elements was, and is, playing a role in the ongoing struggle.

Wade observes,

> A black woman has to cope with the weight of the particular history of white male sexual relations with black women ... This imaginary can shape black women's movements themselves: some Afro-Latin women's organisations in Honduras, the Dominican Republic and Brazil promote and celebrate black culture in ways which cast black women as dancers, singers, performers, providers of food, often quite sexualized.
>
> (2010: 136) (See Mayes 2014)

As the reader can see, the question of racial identity is central to a person's identity and highly contested in the Dominican context, as in other areas of Latin America. "One of the legacies of the country's chaotic history and fragile sovereignty has been the failure to develop a strong and coherent sense of ethnic or national identity" (Manuel 2006: 117). Trujillo, like more recent political figures, understood this fragility and national identity confusion and played on its themes to tighten his authoritarian rule. I now turn to the specific racial and ethnic history of the Dominican Republic.

The Native American Element

When Christopher Columbus arrived in the "New World" (at least to Europeans), he first "discovered" the island that he dubbed *La Española* (Hispaniola, in English), later founding Santo Domingo de Guzmán (later Santo Domingo), the first permanent European settlement in the New World. Prior to the Spanish arrival, the island contained a large native population estimated to be about a million native inhabitants known as Taíno, belonging to the Arawak language and cultural group, where they had migrated from the Amazon basin prior to the arrival of Columbus. "The native population of Hispaniola—at least a million persons—was so rapidly reduced by warfare, disease, and suicide that its replacement by an African work force [i.e. slaves] began as early as 1502" (Davis 1998: 850), barely a decade after the Spanish arrival. Within a few years, only five hundred Taíno remained and, ultimately all were gone within fifty years after the Spanish arrival—in Agatha Christie's terms, "And then there were none"—all decimated through extermination and disease, a pattern that was to be repeated throughout the Americas over the following centuries with similar dreary statistics of millions dead through colonial contact.

Today the Taíno are important only to the discourse of race and racism in the Dominican Republic and a kind of nostalgia, for they left little cultural imprint on Dominican life, in spite of a nostalgic concept of them as part of Dominican identity, known as *indigenismo*. This concept formed part of Dominican literature, which Romance Languages and Literature scholar Lorgia García-Peña characterizes as a "mythical exaltation of Native heroes" (2016: 34). To this day,

> the middle and upper classes traditionally identified with Spain, and even the black and mulatto lower classes euphemistically refer to themselves as *indios* or *indios oscuros* (dark-skinned Indians) on their identification cards ... Dominican nationalism developed in opposition not to Spain but to Haiti and has traditionally been animated by fear and denial of Afro-Caribbean culture.
>
> (Manuel 2006: 117).

A true *mestizaje*, that is, a mixing of native American populations with Europeans, such as that which occurred in Mexico, never happened in Hispaniola, and the native population was soon replaced with African slave laborers, who formed the majority of the population. The result was that, through the mixture of white and African blood lines, the Dominican Republic became a mulatto society. "Although *indigenismo* may have represented a genuine anticolonial posture in countries whose populations consisted largely of Native Americans and mestizos, in the Dominican Republic it served largely as a strategy for rejecting African heritage" (Austerlitz 1997: 20). To admit to having African heritage would have been looked upon as unpatriotic.

"The Taíno Indians were exterminated in the first fifty years of colonial rule, yet Dominicans place great import upon the indigenous culture as a marker of identity," even though one finds few traces of the Taíno culture mostly in food preparation (Douglas 2005: 182. See also Dunay 1994: 69). In addition to claiming a Taíno identity for themselves, some Dominicans will claim Taíno provenance for certain musical instruments or other musical elements, or dance elements, but ethnomusicologist Martha Ellen Davis, the foremost expert on Dominican music, tells us there is no Taíno element in the music of the Dominican Republic. "Taíno musical culture is represented by little material evidence, since much of it was vocal" (1998: 845), as was that of the early Spanish musical contribution. She adds elsewhere,

> The Native American component (Taíno, a subgroup of the Arawak) is now virtually absent due to the early demise of the native population. Consequently, contemporary Dominican culture is "creole," *criollo* or *criolla* traditionally defined as "born in the New World." It is a fusion of Old-World elements of Hispanic and African provenance, tempered by New World circumstance and creativity. (2007: 189)

We would certainly not know if there were any trace of Taíno dance in the dance traditions of the Dominican Republic because they were gone long before the current dance traditions evolved, and dance leaves even fewer traces than music. That said, the descriptions left by the friars like Bartolomé de Las Casas, who accompanied Columbus, describes large-scale communal dances in lines and circles, accompanied by singing, a far cry from the couple dances that are accompanied by instrumental music with vocal soloists that dominate the contemporary big-band dance scene, and even the historic nineteenth-century dance scene of Dominican creole social life and culture. Thus, it is only surrounding the discourse of race, which constantly crops up in a number of ways in the Dominican experience, that the Taíinos appear. So, aside from mentioning the unfortunate demise of so many human beings, the Taíinos will, similarly, disappear from this narrative.

The Spanish Element

The Spaniards soon depleted whatever mineral wealth existed on Santo Domingo, which was the Spanish crown's sole interest, and they set their sights on more lucrative locations such as Peru and Mexico, leaving Santo Domingo to languish. The Spanish ceded to the French the western portion of the island as part of a European peace treaty (The Peace of Ryswick, 1697), creating the space for the future political entities of Haiti and the Dominican Republic.

> The Spanish colony remained Santo Domingo, and the French settlement became Saint-Domingue. While the French possession was soon home to a large population, mostly enslaved Africans, inhabitants of the sparsely settled Spanish were for the most part a rich racial mix.
>
> (Austerlitz 1997: 8)

As in other parts of the Spanish colonial world, Spaniards from all parts of Spain, looking for economic and social advancement, came to the New World, as well as Sephardic Jews and Muslims escaping persecution, especially with the fall of Granada one month before Columbus set sail, so already there was an ethnic mix that did not favor the performance of any particular regional Spanish folk tradition. As is often the case when immigrants come to the New World, an individual does not have access to the specific regional dances and musics that they performed in their native villages and towns because that individual might be the sole person from a particular place. Rather, they turn to the performances of music and dance genres that they have in common or they learn the popular music and dance of the new location in which they settle, which is often a creole creation combing elements from many dances and musical forms. Martha Ellen Davis notes that the first music sung by the crew on Columbus's ships was a religious work common to all Spaniards of the time, *Salve Regina*, a religious hymn (1998). Spain itself was already an amalgam of Arab, Iberian, Celtic, and Sephardic Jewish elements, and "the first Africans (*ladinos*) were Spanish-speaking Christians from Spain, present there in servitude for a century before 1492" (Davis 1998: 850). Certain dances, with many regional variations, like the *jota* and *fandango*, which underwent new development and significant change, creolization, in the New World became popular throughout Spanish-dominated Latin America as far north as Early California (Shay 2015).

A similar process occurred when Dominicans moved to New York where "regional and class boundaries are transcended by a national-as-ethnic minority identity, which serves as a common denominator" (Davis 2002: 128), and the big-band merengue serves as an ethnic marker for all Dominican expatriates in their new environment, although merengue típico survives in pockets of the Dominican diaspora.

The African Element

The mountainous and wild terrain of Hispaniola lent itself to refuge areas in which runaway slaves established Maroon societies, as they did in many areas of Latin America, that in Haiti ultimately led to the ousting of the French plantation owners in 1804. "The first slave insurrection took place in 1522 . . . Slave revolts in the colony were well documented and so widespread, 'many did not dare venture into the countryside unless it were in groups of up to 20 armed men' " (Moya Pons 2010: 36. Quoted in Douglas 2005: 68). After numerous slave revolts that wracked the island of Hispaniola from the late eighteenth century, the rebellious slave population of Saint-Domingue successfully expelled the French.

> The Haitian Revolution sent thousands of French slave owners, slaves, and free people of color to eastern Cuba, to Puerto Rico, and to Louisiana and New Orleans, among other places, with lasting influence on cultural practices and the dance and music of these areas.
>
> (Gerstin 2010: 30)

In 1804, the successful rebels created the second independent state in the New World, Haiti, which, declaring itself a black republic, had repercussions in other slave-holding areas, including in the American South, which tightened vigilance and laws regarding their own slave population. This included the famous ban on slaves dancing and playing music on Congo Square in New Orleans in the early nineteenth century (Gerstin 2010); above all, the whites feared the drumming that, to them, signaled the beginning of a slave revolt.

As a part of the Atlantic slave trade, the so-called Middle Passage, Africans, too, came from various parts of Central and West Africa, which meant that their musical and dance tradition also underwent a form of creolization, incorporating elements that were common to large swaths of Africa from which the newly introduced Africans came. Music scholar Julian Gerstin cautions, however, that "Certain dance styles and musical practices appear Congolese/Angolan in nature, yet few if any unambiguous cases of direct ancestry exist" (2010: 32). Certain choreographic elements such as

> pelvic isolation and sexy couple dancing occur in many places in Africa including the stretch from Liberia through Nigeria that sent large numbers of enslaved

> people to the Caribbean. I have spoken of challenge dances as Congolese, yet dance and music competitions exist in many places.
>
> (2010: 32–33)

Untangling origins and adaptations, as many dance scholars know, frequently results in speculation. Dance names also present problems to the researcher: The same dance can have different names in different locations; conversely, while many dances may share a name, they may have no historical connection.

Martha Ellen Davis states,

> The millions of Africans brought by the French into Saint-Domingue [later Haiti] and their ethnic origins led to the development of society more densely populated than and culturally different from neighboring Santo Domingo [later Dominican Republic] ... The racial and cultural contrast between these neighbors lies at the core of Dominican national cultural policy.
>
> (1998: 845)

I will argue that the anti-Black, anti-African, anti-Haitian core of that policy solidified under Trujillo, resulting in a mass genocide of Haitians living along the Haitian–Dominican Republic border, which he ordered in 1937. Scholar of Dominican Studies Richard Lee Turits states,

> But by far Trujillo's most extensive act of state terror occurred ... in 1937 [when] the Dominican military massacred some fifteen thousand ethnic Haitians whose families had been living peacefully for generations in the northern frontier region near the border that the Dominican Republic shares with Haiti. The following year Trujillo ordered the deportation to Haiti of thousands of ethnic Haitians from the southern frontier zones, many of whom were killed in this military action.
>
> (2003: 6)

The number of victims of the massacre is contested and may never be known: "Since there were no mass graves and many bodies were thrown to the sharks, it is impossible to establish an accurate body count for those killed" (Derby 2009: 208 n.11). Different sources give different numbers: "Estimates of the number of victims range from 12,000 to 40,000; Trujillo's own unofficial estimate was 18,000 ... Trujillo considered the 'Dominicanization of the border' a significant event in the development of Dominican identity" (Austerlitz 1997: 65). Trujillo enshrined this anti-Haitian attitude even though his own grandmother was of Haitian background, and she came from a distinguished background. He powdered his skin to make it appear whiter, a not infrequent phenomenon in Latin American countries in which racial identities are crucial (Shay 2002). Needless to say, his crime went unpunished. Such is the advantage when you are in charge. From 2013 to 2015 hundreds of Haitians were expelled from the Dominican Republic, thus continuing the ethnic and racial tensions between the two nations.

This denial of the mulatto rather than mestizo identity of three-quarters or more of the population has contributed to the current confusion over national identity. To this I would add that Dominican identity is nuanced beyond race. It is also influenced by class, urban or rural, region to region, and, like the rest of Latin America, the Dominican Republic is actually culturally heterogeneous. However, the creole culture has resulted in a combination of African and European elements, rather than Native American and European, despite the references to Taíno identity.

Haunted by fears of the French returning slavery to the island, the Haitians, in 1822, occupied the entire island until 1844, when the Dominicans rebelled, expelled the Haitians, and established the Dominican Republic as an independent nation. The memory of the Haitian occupation gave many Dominicans a feeling of anti-Haitian sentiment and, by extension, anti-Black and anti-African that characterizes the ways in which Dominican national identity was established and continues to dominate Dominican national and racial discourse to the present (Austerlitz 1997; García-Peña 2016; Mayes 2014).

> The Haitian occupation of Santo Domingo (1822–1844) is used by the twentieth-century Dominican elite as justification for the official affirmation of *hispanidad* (Hispanic racial and cultural purity) and the repulsion of all that is black, African, or Haitian. This policy, promoted by dictator Rafael Leónidas Trujillo Molina (1930–1961), has continued under successive governments.
>
> (Davis 1998: 845)

What that means for this study is that Dominican scholars have attempted to deny African elements their music and dances that non-Dominican music and dance scholars can clearly detect. However, as Davis predicts, “Eventually, Dominican scholars, musicians, and the public will probably arrive at a realistic view of Dominican culture as essentially a creole composite, born in the New World of the fusion and evolution of multiple cultural components” (1998: 845). But that is because, under the influence of non-Dominican ethnomusicology and dance scholars, the Dominican scholars have had to give way to the evidence of the research findings that the non-Dominicans have presented to them.

The First American Invasion

While it may appear odd, the American military invasions and attempts to colonize the Dominican Republic have contributed significantly to the growth of Dominican national identity.

> The long and unequal relationship between the United States and the Dominican Republic has been relegated to the often unread margins of the U.S. archive ... This omission exists despite the fact that the United States attempted to purchase Dominican territories between 1824 and 1884 and established unofficial military bases in the Dominican southwest region during the U.S. occupations of 1916–1924.
> (García-Peña 2016: 2–3)

I would argue that the attempted occupation allowed Dominicans of all classes to drop whatever it was that divided them in order to come together in the face of the foreign invaders. A common Dominican activity in the face of invasion was to dance the merengue. The popularity of merengue as a symbol of that identity grew during the first American invasion. The merengue constituted one of the potent and subtle weapons in the cultural arsenal to reject American imperialism, especially since most of the American troops were notoriously poor at dancing it.

Its occupation "marked the beginning of an eight-year military occupation that Dominicans countered with both armed struggle and a cultural movement that celebrated all things Dominican, including merengue cibaeño" (Austerlitz 1997: 30). The Americans seized all reigns of power, displacing all of the Dominican ministers and replacing them with U.S. Marine officers, including taking charge of the economy, and as one can imagine with all of the testosterone flowing among the young invaders, these invading forces sometimes abused their authority. They punished the Dominicans with a weapon ban. "Indeed, the disarmament methods, which included arbitrary arrests, imprisonment, and torture, were applied so thoroughly that very few people wished to run the risk of keeping revolvers, rifles, shotguns, and munitions in their houses" (Moya Pons 2010: 322). Injected into the invasion was the rampant racism that existed at that time when the invading troops would all have been white. "U.S. foreign policy elites emphasized racial inferiority to justify U.S. intervention throughout the region. As early as the 1850s, debates about Dominicans' race influenced U.S. interactions with the country" (Mayes 2014: 19). Carrying out their duties amidst a population that had a high degree of mulattos, where most of the American Marines had been reared in an environment in which they believed that one drop of African blood made you black, one can imagine the kinds of interpersonal engagements that would have ensued.

> In other plantation societies of the New World that have not known the American "one-drop rule," the location boundaries on the somatic continuum varies even more ... As Hoetink noticed some time ago, "one and the same person may be considered white in the Dominican Republic or Puerto Rico ... 'Colored' in Jamaica, Martinique or Curaçao ... [and] may be called a 'Negro' in Georgia'."
> (Hoetink 1967: xii, quoted in Wimmer 2013: 83)

Still, the Dominicans were privileged by the occupying forces, over Haitians and other darker Caribbean peoples:

> As a mixed-race people, Dominicans fared better in the struggle for racial improvement because, according to the theories of the time, their European blood bequeathed them the capacity for intellectual growth through apprenticeship to U.S. military officials and foreign policy elites.
> (Mayes 2014: 109)

Still, Dominicans of all classes and racial mixtures resented the invasion and turned to symbols of Dominican identity as well as outright physical rebellion to reject the American occupation.

"An equally violent, though not yet studied effect of the occupation is the criminalization of Afro-religious [religious and musical] practices and practitioners through official and unofficial channels" (García-Peña 2016: 60). Such violent behavior included

> the public desecration of Afro-religious articles, particularly sacred drums; raids of religious celebrations, including birth blessings and funerals in the borderland towns; the imprisonment of *santeros* [the believers in santería religious practices] under vagrancy laws; and the branding of the Afro-religious as savage or bandit.
> (2016: 60)

I would argue that the echoes of the overthrow of the white plantation owners by the Haitian slave rebellion continued and created a fear of all African-influenced cultural expression. García-Peña adds, "The confiscation and desecration of Alcántara's sacred drums epitomized the marines' racism and intolerance toward cultural and religious practices" (2016: 61). Just as the banning of gatherings of slaves who danced and played drums in the South,

> some Marines even complained that the drumming was driving them mad. The confiscation of drums and the imprisoning of drummers became a common

> practice of occupying marines in their efforts to "civilize" Hispaniola and as a response to their fear of blackness.
>
> (Ibid.)

Shunned at high-society dances before the U.S. invasion, native music became popular in ballrooms as the nationalist cultural movement took shape ... High society's about-face regarding merengue, from violent scorn before the invasion to enthusiastic acceptance during the occupation, illustrates the link between neocolonial domination and the rise of cultural nationalism. (Austerlitz 1997: 46–47)

As Austerlitz details, Dominican composers also created art music compositions using the merengue. The Dominicans utilized the merengue as one of the symbols of their identity and dancing it, among all classes, came to symbolize opposition to that American invasion. The Dominicans created a new variant of the merengue called "*pambiche* (from the English Palm Beach), the latter supposedly an imitation of U.S. soldiers trying to dance the folk merengue during the First Occupation (1916–1924)" (Davis 2007: 211). American racial attitudes soured any possibility of cooperation between Dominicans and Americans. "For the most part, U.S. hegemony was explained as having derived from the racial superiority of Anglo Saxons over Latin Americans" (Mayes 2014: 21). One need only read Edgar Rice Burroughs's very popular *Tarzan* novels, written at the turn of the century, valorizing Tarzan's exalted Anglo-Saxon nobility, a fact stressed throughout the novels, to comprehend the deep-seated racism of the period. It constituted the cultural furniture in turn-of-the-century America under the widespread belief in social Darwinism, which placed Anglo-Saxon men at the apex of civilization (Shay 2006).

Ultimately, the protest was successful and they forced the American invaders to leave. Although departed, however, they left behind an ambitious young military figure, admired by the American officers for his fastidious grooming who, by all accounts, rose rapidly through the ranks, and shortly after the Americans left the country, and with their blessing, seized power: Trujillo.

Rafael Leónidas Trujillo Molina and the Trujillo Regime

We turn now to the figure of Rafael Leónidas Trujillo Molina, who is central to the story of how authoritarian regimes can seize upon a particular genre of dance or music and use it as a vehicle for building national identity and strong feelings of national pride.

> Taking full advantage of the authority, opportunities for pillage, and visibility that his position as head of state afforded him, Trujillo was known for his lasciviousness, vanity, and larger-than-life theatricality. This was evidenced in his

> penchant for grandiose costumes, his immaculate grooming, and the prodigious consumption of food, drink, and women for which he and his inner circle were notorious, and for which he earned the sobriquet "the goat."
>
> (Derby 2009: 1)

Derby's pithy introduction of Trujillo and his character are echoed throughout every description of him and his rule. When he was assassinated many merengue composers created new songs which feature, *el chivo*, the goat, in the new lyrics, still sung today. Had he not been a mass murderer, as we will see below, his life would have veered between grand opera and soap opera. He even named his two sons Ramfis and Rhadamés, two characters in Verdi's dramatic opera, *Aïda*. His 30-year reign also featured his much-married and equally notorious sometime son-in-law Porfirio Rubirosa, whose sexual exploits around the world, and marriages to some of the world's richest women, vied with Trujillo's life in the tabloids of the period (see Moats 1977; Levy 2005).

It is important to note "that the U.S. Occupation provoked a crisis of masculinity among political elites, and General Trujillo appealed to the majority of Dominican men because he embodied the dangerous masculinity of the street-wise male—tíguere" (Mayes 2014: 11), a trait that is also valued in both male, merenguero, and female, merenguera, performers in the merengue scene (see Hutchinson 2016). Trujillo used that trait to gain power:

> Trujillo's rise to power and initial consolidation built upon historical patterns of caudillo (local strongman) rule within the country, combined with structural changes including the establishment of more professional armed forces and improved transportation and communication services in the country that were a consequence of the U.S. occupation, as well as the U.S. shift to a policy of nonintervention that promoted the success of his plotting.
>
> (Hartlyn 1998: 93)

Despite all of his excesses, the United States more or less supported him because he was *their* dictator, a role he cultivated until the end, when he was no longer regarded as biddable by the American government and the CIA.

> In light of Trujillo's record as one of the most ruthless and long-reigning dictators of the history of the Americas, his populist rhetoric comes across today as empty propaganda. Yet for Dominican peasants in 1932, it was indeed noteworthy to hear the president of the country celebrate at mass rallies and to call those who labored in the field his "best friends."
>
> (2003: 1)

Thus, for the crucial first two decades of his reign, Trujillo valorized the peasant, carried out land distribution plans, rationalized agriculture, and concentrated a great deal of the state's resources to improve peasant life. Turits concludes, "The legacy of peasant loyalty to Trujillo, an adherence that impelled peasants to defend the regime against revolutionary exiles, would endure even for decades after Trujillo's assassination" (2003: 2–3).

The brutality of Trujillo's rule cannot be denied: "Ultimately, Trujillo consolidated power only by ordering the assassination of hundreds of his opponents during his first year in office" (Turits 2003: 2). Killing almost all sources of opposition, attracting the positive support of the peasantry with his populist rhetoric and, in general, aiding the peasantry in a very public way, he cleared the way for a rule with little opposition for more than 30 years. Nevertheless, he was clearly an unsavory person. First, there were his financial predations: "By the close of his regime, the Trujillo's' holdings were estimated at $500 million, a sum close to the Dominican national income" (Turits 2003: 5). In addition, Trujillo confiscated nearly 10% of Dominican lands for himself and his family. The sources that write about his wealth vary as to the amount of money, business, and property he acquired during his reign, but it was undoubtedly enormous.

Trujillo exhibited clear signs of megalomania using surreal means to glorify his personal image. "In some realms, moreover, Trujillo was indeed capable of exercising seemingly unconstrained power and discretion. This included glorifying himself and his family in extreme and even surreal fashion" (Turits 2003: 5). He named the capital city after himself, Ciudad Trujillo, following the hurricane that flattened it in 1930, perhaps following Stalin's example of naming cities like Stalingrad and Stalinabad, the former capital of the Tajik SSR, after himself. He also named the highest mountain in the Antilles after himself. In addition,

> Approximately eighteen hundred sculptures of the dictator dotted the nation's public spaces, some of enormous proportions, perhaps more than any other ruler in the world. The press heaped seemingly limitless praise on Trujillo that bordered on apotheosis, more effusive even than the Soviet press's glorification of its leaders … And signs were erected throughout the country glorifying the dictator, one of the most droll being "We Owe It All to Trujillo," posted on the front door of a mental hospital near the capital. Another infamous sign, "God and Trujillo," greeted ships entering the port of Ciudad Trujillo as well as Dominicans in other locations.
>
> (Turits 2003: 6–7)

His picture, likely, adorned almost every wall in every public building and private home in the Dominican Republic.

He loved titles and styled himself as a true sultan: "He was officially referred to as His Excellency, the Genralissimo, Doctor Rafael Leónidas Trujillo Molina, Honorable President of the Republic, Benefactor of the Nation, Restorer of the Financial Independence of the Country, and Commander-in-Chief of the Armed Forces" (Hartlyn 1998: 94). He had uniforms and boots to match.

He was excessively careful in his grooming. His uniforms, replete with a good deal of gold braid and ostrich feathers attached to his helmet, appear to have been made for a Gilbert and Sullivan opera (see Derby 2009: 198). He was fixated on military medals and awards. With his efforts to appear white, through the use of powder and makeup,

> he had his photos retouched to make him appear lighter-skinned—he frequently sought to frame himself as white by ensuring that the elite military (such as the Guardia Blanca) surrounding him on presidential visits were white (and kept their heads covered) and sported crisp uniforms made in Miami.
>
> (Derby 2009: 197)

He admired the dressing skills of his daughter, and her notorious philandering first husband Porfirio Rubirosa, who like Trujillo exhibited the admired characteristics of el tíguere (see Levy 2005; Derby 2009).

And while this all sounds like Looney Tunes and buffoonery, on a more serious note, Trujillo was a sexual predator whose "tyranny was marked by extraordinary violence and abuse" (Turits 2003: 6). Elite families hid their daughters and wives from him.

One might ask how, with such destructive behavior, he was able to sustain his brutal reign for so long. It lies in part because of the fact that the people he abused the most were those who were closest to him and, therefore, potential threats who were easy to target; he apparently did not show that side of himself to the peasantry as he toured the countryside with his musical bands to entertain the peasants with music and flattery. The list of his ugly and abusive behavior is too long to be useful here and, instead, I will focus on the dancing dictator (see Derby 2009; Turits 2003).

The Second American Invasion

The Americans invaded and occupied the Dominican Republic again in 1965.

> Pro-[Juan] Bosch, pro-Constitution military men competed with a rightist wing of the military, while thousands of unarmed demonstrators took to the streets of Santo Domingo in support of the Constitutionalists ... The pro-Bosch faction

> was on the verge of victory when President Lyndon Johnson of the United States ordered an invasion of the Dominican Republic.
>
> (Austerlitz 1997: 88)

Johnson, a product of the Cold War, thought he was saving democracy from the liberal forces, which he equated with Communists, "to prevent the emergence of another Cuba." The well-publicized event had another important aspect:

> The U.S. military actions served to distract the attention from the first military escalation of the United States in Vietnam. In April 1965, there were only 17,000 U.S. Marines in Indochina while in December that number had risen to 245,000.
>
> (Moya Pons 2010: 289)

Johnson also included

> troops from Brazil, Honduras, Paraguay and Costa Rica. After U.S. manipulation of the OAS, these countries formed a so-called Inter-American Peace Force to make the unilateral intervention of the United States appear legal, although the action was in violation of the OAS charter, as well as that of the United Nations.
>
> (Moya Pons 2010: 389)

By sending Bosch into exile, and installing a government more in line with American interests, Johnson condemned the Dominican Republic to another three decades of brutal dictatorship under Joaquín Balaguer who, once again, employed death squads to eliminate any competition for power.

And again, the Dominicans turned to the merengue that "[Johnny] Ventura, whose musical style was so influenced by North American rock, enlisted that music [merengue] to oppose U.S. hegemony" (Austerlitz 1997: 89). Merengue to the rescue! Only this time people did not need to be convinced of its value as a national symbol, which had already been established by Trujillo.

The only difference between the Trujillo and Balaguer dictatorships was that Trujillo rarely granted permission to travel, while Balaguer did. This resulted in the emigration of at least 15% of the population, thousands of Dominicans, particularly to New York City, to escape the impoverished standard of living that the two dictators caused through their frightful and personal authoritarian mismanagement. The mass migration launched the popularity of merengue on a transnational scale.

Dance and Music of the Dominican Republic

As we have seen, the history of Hispaniola contains many ethnic and racial elements. This is reflected in the wide variety of regional folk songs and dances found in the Dominican Republic, which the interested reader can find in the rich research and writing of Martha Ellen Davis (1998, 2002, 2007, 2010). I will only cite Davis's interesting comment:

> Nonetheless, Haiti is actually more European than commonly thought to be, and the Dominican Republic is more African ... At the same time, the African presence in Dominican dance is not circumscribed to the dance with the most African-influenced music, that of the semisacred palos. On the contrary, it is subtly or overtly present in the movement of many dances.
>
> (2002: 132–33)

Those dances are beyond this chapter, which focuses on the merengue and its role in the construction and maintenance of Dominican identity.

I do not wish to give the impression that the Dominican people only dance merengue. Like all of the people in the Caribbean and Latin America, they dance urban ballroom dances like salsa, waltz, polka, one-step, two-step, and mazurka. All of these regions have various regional folk dances, some specific to a particular region, others more widespread (see Davis 2007). The Dominican Republic had one of the first documented ballet folklorico groups in Latin America.

> The first documented fieldwork-based folk-dance troupe was founded in Miches about 1941 by René Carrasco, a self-made folklorist, and the next was established in the capital by Edna Garrido (1913–2010) at the public university about 1945. Later groups, though essentially derivatives of Carrasco's, lack fieldwork-based authenticity and exhibit the accelerated tempi, the uniform costumery, the synchronized movements, and the entertainment and national-identity agenda typical of this genre throughout Latin America.
>
> (Davis 1998: 861)

These groups were founded a decade prior to the famous Ballet Folklórico de México that Amalia Hernández founded in 1952.

The current Ballet Folklórico Nacional Dominicano was founded in 1973 by Fradique Lizardo; it is a professional company under the Ministry of Culture, with a home in the Bellas Artes (Fine Arts). Its current artistic director, Elizabeth Crooke, stated that one of the purposes was to portray the richness of Dominican dance and culture and to show that the Dominican Republic is "*más que merengue i bachata* (more than merengue and bachata)" (YouTube Ballet Folklórico Nacional Dominicano. Viewed September 2, 2018). In performance the company appears to be a tropical version of Ballet Folklórico de México.

But it was the merengue cibaeño that became the dominant dance symbol of the Dominican Republic under Trujillo.

Merengue

> Merengue, I discovered, was inescapable. It blared from huge speakers on street corners where cassette vendors displayed their wares. It enveloped passengers crammed sardine-style in inner-city buses and conchos, the tiny cars used for public transportation. It poured out of shops and small grocery stores (bodegas), and songs jumbled in the streets and patios of the countless houses where the music was played on cassettes, TVs and radios. And not only was the merengue played, it was danced as—anywhere and at any time: waiting for conchos; in the aisles of buses; on the beach; by women doing housework; by preschool children at recess. It was everywhere at once.
>
> (Sellers 2004: 1–2)

The colorful passage that writer Julie Sellers related above gives the reader the sense of the overwhelming place in Dominican life that merengue holds, in spite of the rich heritage of music and dance that Davis (1998, 2007) and other authors describe. Dominicans will tell you that merengue is "in their blood." Almost every writer, no matter what their academic discipline, notes the ubiquitous presence of merengue in Dominican life, as I noted above in Douglas's study (2005): It has become one of the principal symbols of Dominican identity, both at home in the Dominican Republic and in the diaspora populations of Puerto Rico and New York City, which has the largest Dominican population outside of Santo Domingo.

Thus, it was satisfying to find that García-Peña underscores many of the points that I make: "Merengue became a tool for Trujillo's totalizing nationalization project. The dictator owned merengue orchestras and promoted the genre as a 'high-class' national dance" (2016: 182). The perception of merengue's importance in Dominicans' lives, both now and historically, is obvious to many careful observers:

> The early history of the merengue is obscure, although as reconstructed by Dominican writers and by ethnomusicologist Paul Austerlitz, it seems clear that one strain of the genre developed in the mid-1800s as a creole variant of the family of interrelated, syncopated couple dances variously called contredanse, contradanza, danza, and merengue in Cuba, Hispaniola, and Puerto Rico ...

> This early salon, like its counterparts elsewhere, may have been predominantly European in origin, but outside the ballrooms very different forms of merengue flourished, most with a marked Afro-Caribbean flavor in their lively rhythms and call-and-response final section.
>
> (Manuel 2006: 118–19)

Moreover, although it is interesting to speculate on the origins of these dance and musical forms, and we can see and experience the connections between mambo, cha-cha, and salsa, it is difficult to untangle all of the elements that comprise other dance and musical forms like merengue, like the earlier *tumba*. And, clearly, Trujillo did not understand or ignored the African element of the merengue, but he knew that it resonated with many campesinos.

> The Dominican Republic is popularly known as the "land of merengue" (*la tierra del merengue*) because the merengue is the dance genre that has come to symbolize Dominican national identity. However, the merengue is but one dance genre from one region—the Cibao or northern region—that has become ubiquitous throughout the country and now the expatriate communities as well as internationally commercialized. Today the traditional form of this merengue, called *merengue tipico* or *perico repiao*, which appears to have changed little in the past hundred years, coexists alongside an orchestrated merengue that is constantly evolving.
>
> (Davis 2002: 127)

Thus, this is the story of multiple merengues, urban big-band merengue, and the countryside where merengue típico takes on a folkloric aspect. And this seems to be recognized by Dominicans as well: "Many Dominicans relate to the dual symbolism represented by the two coexisting subspecies of merengue: the one of bucolic rusticity and the other of world-class cachet" (Davis 2002: 128). Like many forms of dance and music, merengue began its life as a regional folk dance. Social scientist Jorge Dunay asks a most important question: "Why did a rural folk dance become a symbol of national identity?" (1994: 65). It is important to note that it has both an urban and a rural form that is still performed. "Until several decades ago, the Dominican elite condemned merengue as undignified music because of its association with poor uneducated peasants" (Dunay 1994: 71). As we saw above, Trujillo's choice to raise this choreographic and musical idiom as a national symbol demonstrated his cleverness in identifying with the peasants, even as he lived in multiple palaces. This phenomenon of a folk origin becoming popular is a common denominator of genres of folk music and dance that ultimately becomes popular in a variety of societies. It should be noted that both the big-band version and the folk version, típico, continue to coexist in New York in the largest Dominican diaspora community:

> Within the New York merengue world, horn-based orquesta merengue tends to be preferred in upper Manhattan's Washington Heights Community, many of whose constituents hail from urban Santo Domingo. But in Queens, where immigrants tend to be more recent and from the Cibao hinterland, it is merengue típico that rules, with several small clubs featuring live music.
>
> (Manuel 2006: 129)

The orchestras that accompany each genre, and especially between elite, modern urban classes and rural forms, vary, especially in the instruments they use.

> At its most basic level, merengue típico is defined by its instruments and principal rhythms, as well as by contrast to related styles like *orquesta* or big-band merengue. The two-headed tambora drum, the metal güira scraper, and the diatonic button accordion are required components and no típico group is without this basic trio.
>
> (Hutchinson 2016: 15)

However, what both folk and popular music contain, as Dunay responds to the question posed above, is that "Popular music articulates the dominant themes and concerns of a national culture" (ibid.).

Many of us are familiar with the allure of the hip-swinging, two-step social and vernacular couple dance. The dancers can move one step to the right on the right foot, draw the left foot parallel to the right, and repeat, moving side to side, forward and back, or swaying in place. During the dance the couple can assume ballroom dance position facing one another and mirroring one another, or move away from each other and perform independent and improvised figures. The dancer moves his or her hip side to side, in a figure eight, or in a circle, among other choices. One can perform slow turns under the partner's arm in place or circling the partner.

Because its hip motion, probably a little more decorous in the nineteenth century, shocked the elite classes, it was declared lascivious, like so many dances before it, the tango being a case in point. Ethnomusicologist Paul Austerlitz comments, "In spite of references to hip motion in nineteenth-century merengue, evidence suggests that dancing merengue cibaeño involved little or no such motion in the early twentieth century ... early merengue cibaeño was performed rather slowly" (Austerlitz 1997: 35). However, that might have been the rather restrained style that characterized the upper-class ballrooms. The situation in the less elegant parts of town may have been much more earthy. Rich men went to the red light district in Santo

Domingo and Santiago de los Caballeros, the capital city of the Cibao region. This process of the rich, men generally because sex is often involved, escaping his staid environment to the poorer areas where the music is hot and the dances hotter, is known as "slumming." This same process took place in the history and development of other sensual dances and music like jazz, flamenco, and tango Shay (2016a). Frequently, the site of the development of these popular and seductive dances is the red-light district. These dances and musical idioms often also pass through a sanitizing or whitening process to make them "safe" for the middle classes and elites, by ironing out or downplaying the hip movements, increasing the distance the partners are from one another, especially with the stance known as polishing belt buckles, and other means of cleaning up a clearly erotic dance genre.

> Although merengue had once been performed in elite ballrooms, by the beginning of the twentieth century it was entrenched as típico (typical, authentic, or folk) form played only by campesinos and those who dwelled in the barrios ... The Cibao's largest city, Santiago de los Caballeros, became a focal point for the development of merengue típico cibaeño, or Cibao folk merengue.
>
> (Austerlitz 1997: 31)

Thus, one must remember that although the big band is the most popular and well-known form of the dance to the world at large, many regional and folk versions coexist with it. The folk musical idiom has a constellation of instruments featuring the accordion and, later, in the 1920s, the alto saxophone was introduced as the melody instrument, with the *tambora*, a drum held on the lap and played with a drum stick in one hand and the use of the palm of the hand on the other, and calabash güiro, later replaced by a metal one in the twentieth century, as the rhythm instrument (Austerlitz 1997: 32, who also gives several musical examples; see also Davis 2010). Adding to the pleasure of the dance and instrumental music, vocalists sang about political topics, gossip, witty songs, and downright erotic ones to amuse the listeners. Trujillo, as we have seen, hired composers of merengue to praise him in the lyrics.

Although we know the merengue as a symbol of Dominican identity, it is a more widespread dance genre, including the Haitian *mereng*:

> Merengue was a pan-Caribbean genre already in the nineteenth century. Haiti, Venezuela, Colombia, and Puerto Rico each developed local forms of the music; with the exception of the Puerto Rican version, all are still played today. Like another pan-Caribbean form, the *danza*, the Caribbean merengues fused the European contredanse with local, African-derived elements.
>
> (Austerlitz 1997: 15)

The merengue often opens with a part known as *paseo*, which is "an eight-measure marchlike instrumental introduction that serves as a signal for couples to take the dance floor" (1997: 38). The middle section is the merengue that "features an eight-measure European-influenced melody sung and played instrumentally several times ... The final and longest section, the jaleo, consists of a two-measure repeating pattern ... and exhibits a highly African-influenced aesthetic" (ibid.).

> The later introductions of blacks were directly from Africa from increasingly southerly points of origin: first from Senegambia, starting in the early seventeenth century from Guinea, and starting in the mid-eighteenth century from the Bantu (Congo and Angolan) region. Those aspects of musical culture considered "typically" Dominican may well be of an older, more extended and established origin, from the early Senegambia or Guinea influence; the folk merengue should be examined in this light.
>
> (Davis 1994: 124)

Trujillo created the merengue as a national symbol, but he chose the variant found in Cibao, the whitest part of the Dominican Republic, in keeping with his official Hispanidad project: "The dictator and his allies hailed merengue as a Creole version of Hispanic folklore, with its preference for traditional Spanish poetry such as the *copla* and *decima*" (Dunay 1994: 73). I suggest that the Spanish lyrics conformed to his notion of hispanidad, rather than any music or choreographic elements in the genre. Above all, he loved it when the lyrics, and he paid for many, celebrated him.

The popular big-band merengue as characterized by ethnomusicologist Sydney Hutchinson characterizes it:

> Merengue de orquesta (orquesta or big-band merengue) often functions as típico's binary opposite, standing for modernity, the Dominican nation, and the urban context. Orquesta was born more or less with the regime of dictator Rafael Trujillo (1930–1961): while efforts to play merengue with higher-class, urban dance bands predate this period, it was Trujillo and his associates who mandated the transformation and thus were able to turn the formerly reviled, lower-class music into a national symbol.
>
> (2016: 222)

But this music was only reviled by the small elite in the capital. The peasants loved it, and they loved that Trujillo loved it. It was clever of him to realize that he had knowingly chosen the beloved dance of the campesinos to stand as the Dominican national symbol, and crisscrossed the land with a merengue band in tow. To this day, the people still love the merengue.

Some Sociological Aspects of Merengue

People practice merengue, and those involved in the scene are known as merengueros and merengueras. They hold a special place in Dominican society, in which they play out their highly gendered roles as they enact Dominicanness. It is a place in which men play out their machismo. Recently, as documented by ethnomusicologist Sydney Hutchinson, women too have broken into the scene, some of them, like the famous Fefita la Grande, very successfully. "Fefita la Grande (Fefita the Great, born Manuela Josefa Cabrera Taveras) the woman with the longest career in merengue típico, and one of the most beloved figures in the Dominican Republic" (Hutchinson 2016: 83), embodies both the tiguere and the successful merengueras. The merengueros enact the role, for which Trujillo was famous, that of the ubermasculine *tiguere* (tiger). But, Hutchinson notes that women, too, can become tigrures. "I analyze feminine *tigueraje*, a forceful, even aggressive role that somewhat resembles what Judith Halberstam (1998) has described as 'female masculinities,' or construction of maleness that can also be performed by women" (2016: 15). She notes that gay men and women, although playing different gender roles than those found in the United States, have also entered on the scene.

As we have seen, historically different genres of merengue have been associated with different classes:

> On another level, típico can be defined by its social relations. Outsiders tend to see it as the music of peasants, urban lower classes, or return migrants, all groups with a low status. For insiders, however, it can be associated with upward mobility, as its consumers adapt to urban living and work situations, reacclimate themselves to Dominican life after amassing financial resources abroad, or use musical patronage to demonstrate economic success.
>
> (Hutchinson 2016: 16)

Echoing the practice that Trujillo began, "businessmen commission *homenajes* or praise songs" (ibid.).

Following the assassination of Trujillo, the peasantry continued to dance *merengue típico*, but many members of the urban classes, particularly the youth, who associated big-band merengue, with Trujillo, ceased dancing it. Johnny Ventura, a major vocalist in the big-band merengue states,

> During those years, soon after Trujillo died, it was evident that traditional was identified with the tyranny and had been pushed aside by the enormous enthusiasm that 'rock and roll' had awakened in the Dominican youth. Because during that epoch I was an adolescent, and after many, many gyrations to the rhythms

> of "rock," and later the twist, there arose in me the spirit and the vocation of the merenguero. It was merengue I loved the most, and I remember that I was very mortified when I came to recognize that merengue could disappear ... While original merengue remained the interpretive responsibility of our folklore groups, and of the museums of history and popular art, the merengue of the modern orchestras and bands has to march shoulder to shoulder with the progress of popular music worldwide.
>
> (2014: 435)

Nonetheless, Johnny Ventura went on to take merengue to new heights of worldwide popularity through his original style of performance.

Trujillo and the Merengue

Trujillo's valorization of the peasant paid off in their support for him during his rule and beyond and, even though in the 1950s he dispossessed many of them to create large sugar plantations that would enrich him and his family, as Turits noted, he largely kept the peasants' loyalty through the projection of a populist image that included his elevation of the merengue into a national dance that lasts to the present day. Martha Ellen Davis states,

> In light of this policy, Trujillo's support of the merengue as the dance symbol of national identity is interesting, since this genre, like many other social dances, is not Hispanic. Rather, in style and instrumentation it is creole, born in the New World of various cultural components, European and African.
>
> (2002: 129)

But I do not believe that Trujillo or, indeed, many Dominicans were able to discern Africanist elements in music and dance, especially since the lyrics were sung in Spanish, and he chose the genre of local merengue that came from the Cibao, merengue cibaeño, one of the whitest, most Spanish regions of the Dominican Republic. Perhaps he thought its place of origin made it suitable as a national symbol.

Ethnomusicologist Peter Manuel notes that

> Of particular significance was Trujillo's influence on merengue ... Trujillo promoted the Cibao-style merengue, of which he was an enthusiast, as a populist symbol. Merengue groups accompanied him on his campaigns and tours, and hundreds of songs were commissioned to sing the praises of his policies and activities. At parties at his palaces, he liked to dance merengue, shouting "Viva

> Trujillo!" as he turned his partner, and occasionally imprisoning any musician who made a mistake.
>
> (2006: 122)

And through the American occupation and Trujillo's sponsorship, the merengue did indeed become a notable element of Dominican national identity. It was acts like this that ensured his popularity. Trujillo biographer Richard Lee Turits notes that Trujillo's popularity was authentic, at least to the rural population whose champion he became:

> The Trujillo regime may be unique among dictatorships in twentieth-century Latin America for the extent to which elderly peasants have nostalgically recalled its support of the peasantry ... And they suggest that Trujillo's hegemony in the countryside was founded not only on material support ... but also on cultural factors, and specifically on the ways that the regime appeared to fashion state projects to reflect and reinforce peasants' own evolving cultural norms.
>
> (2003: 206)

Surely his performance and support for a dance of the people reinforced, in the most public way, his understanding of Dominican peasant psyche, when other public figures would have avoided being associated with peasants. In her study of the ethnogenesis of Dominican national identity, Cynthia Marie Douglas identified the merengue as one of the core markers of Dominican identity: "Dominicans have an embedded identity in merengue" (2005: 119).

The valorization of the Spanish over the African characterized Trujillo's personal conflict over all things Africanist or Haitian, especially since he was part Haitian. Like Sammy Sosa, the famous baseball star of the Chicago Cubs, Trujillo, "although a much lighter-skinned man than Sosa, like Sosa he faithfully applied powder to his face to whiten his appearance" (Mayes 2014: 2). He raised Spanish identity and cultural heritage and the Catholic Church, which unquestioningly supported him, no matter how vile his behavior, as twin pillars of his rule. Historian April Mayes states,

> It is also the case that twentieth-century iterations of this national identity—hispanidad—achieved their most brutal expression during General Trujillo's dictatorship. The architects of anti-black, and anti-Haitian *hispanidad* in the 1930s and 1940s in effect transformed a racist conceptualization of the Dominican nation—as a collective unified by its rejection of blackness, vodoun, and Kreyol—held by a small group of intellectual and bureaucratic elites into an ideology that has since permeated Dominican society and culture.
>
> (Mayes 2014: 2)

She adds that it was not only whites who created and supported this official policy: "Dominicans of color also participated in this process" (Mayes 2014: 13). Because of this valorization of a European over an African identity, his choice of merengue, with its African elements, constitutes a paradox but, as I argued above, the Spanish lyrics may have led him to believe in its Spanish origins.

Trujillo was snubbed by polite society, and he never forgave them. Merengue, a dance that polite society in the capital did not accept, became a means of revenge. According to Crassweiler, Trujillo's sense of rejection was " 'one of the most formative of all the influences playing upon him' " (quoted in Austerlitz 1997: 68).

> His talent as a merengue dancer perhaps brought some small solace. Arístides Incháusteghui believes: "Trujillo had a problem with high society. Since society originally did not accept merengue, he imposed it in these places [salons] in order to harass the upper class. And he danced better than any of them, since he knew how to dance this. So people talked a lot about how well Trujillo danced."
>
> (interview, ibid.)

But, if it did not endear him to the elite, the country folk and urban lower classes ate it up.

Trujillo's role in raising the merengue to a national symbol was considerable and he "played a special role in the development of the merengue. Like the European totalitarian leaders, the Dominican dictator understood that rural expressive forms could serve as effective symbols of national identity" (Austerlitz 1997: 52). Whenever Trujillo toured, he took a dance band with him to play merengue music, and merengue became a symbol of his regime, but far outlasted it.

> In 1936, the dictator brought Luis Alberti's group to the capital to work as his personal dance band. Renamed Orquesta Presidente Trujillo, the band was required to specialize in merengue. Merengue cibaeño had never been performed in elite ballrooms outside of the Cibao, and upper-class *capitaleños* (residents of the capital) were shocked to hear it at their functions.
>
> (Austerlitz 1997: 54)

But who was going to question the boss who had the power to have you beaten in public? The elite classes must have understood that Trujillo was having revenge for their rejection of him.

> The regime required all of the country's dance bands to feature the merengue in their repertoires, and accordion-based merengue cibaeño groups performed

> throughout the country … Trujillo's iron will thus transformed a regional music, merengue cibaeño into a state symbol recognized throughout the country.
>
> (Austerlitz 1997: 54–55)

It is at this point that the local accordion-based rural orchestra fused with jazz and big-band elements and the results were: "The fusion of the essence of merengue cibaeño—jaleos—with jazz was at the heart of the national music's link with both típico and cosmopolitan culture" (Austerlitz 1997: 56). It was this potent and spicy mix that launched this local folk dance onto the ballroom floors of Latin America and the world. "The development of merengue reflects the history of the Dominican Republic" (Dunay 1994: 80).

Trujillo's Charisma

Clearly, at least for the rural majority, Trujillo had some kind of charisma and, like a good choreographer, he had, "a sure grasp of those sensitive areas of the national psychology" (Crassweiler 1966: 78). But that last idea raises a question that one must ask when dealing with authoritarian regimes: To what extent did the dictator, king, or other authoritarian figure have charisma?

> Trujillo's charisma—his superhuman aura of *fucú* as it might be termed in popular Dominican parlance—was the product of a complex series of negotiations and symbolic exchanges between leaders, followers, and these interstitial brokers, who played a key role in concealing as well as at times revealing Trujillo's trickery.
>
> (Derby 2009: 9)

They revealed his trickery because, as all students of anthropology know, in Africanist lore and African-based societies, the trickster figure is paramount and admired.

Trujillo certainly knew how to use the media to publicize his deeds, beginning with hurricane San Zenón, which struck Santo Domingo, a small city at the time, killing several thousand people in 1930, just eighteen days after he seized power and the government through fraudulent elections. Trujillo seized the moment, making certain that he and members of his family were seen everywhere, taking charge, handing out food baskets and cash, and pitching in to help where needed.

> Trujillo's retinue of press sycophants wrote daily of his seemingly "superhuman" efforts, "at all hours, at dawn, in the daytime, at night, untiring vigilant, energetic," "challenging death face-to-face." This ready chorus of servile griots was

> prompted to weave these actions into a charismatic narrative of Trujillo's one-to-one identification with the people.
>
> (Derby 2009: 81)

This event, and his taking masterful charge of the narrative, demonstrates his shrewd ability to create a populist image. He made certain that, to all appearances, he was everywhere at once, and he converted the provincial backwater town into a city. The hurricane gave Trujillo many opportunities. "In response to the cyclone, Trujillo was granted sweeping emergency powers, which he used to consolidate his control ..." (Hartlyn 1998: 93).

Nevertheless, one has to question his personal charisma. Derby notes,

> Trujillo had little personal charisma to speak of; portly in his later years, he was fiery, enigmatic, and had a notoriously squeaky voice. But he gained personal prestige in the Dominican Republic through his ability to achieve absolute power and wealth from a socially marginal, mulatto, provincial background.
>
> (Derby 2009: 184)

Because he made no distinction between the Dominican treasury and his own wallet, he became one of the richest men in the world, which did not leave much for the rest of the Dominican polity to share. Derby sums up, "Trujillo's charisma made him not as much a divine king but a state fetish, the diabolical product of a conjuring trick" (2009: 9).

Unlike other dictators, like the Shah of Iran and Ferdinand Marcos of the Philippines, whose wives made attractive consorts and, through their beauty and philanthropic activities, softened the edges of these harsh regimes, Trujillo's three wives were often dowdy and stay-at-home women, or helped themselves to the available wealth. Thus, unlike the first lady of the Philippines and the Empress of Iran, both of whom supported dance in very public ways, in the Dominican case, it was the dancing dictator himself who popularized the merengue and built it into a national symbol. This did not mean that women did not figure in the Trujillo narrative: they figured as victims of his well-known lust and sexual predation.

One sensitive area of Trujillo's political regime revolved around the discourse of race and Dominican identity. Historian April Mayes states,

> Although *hispanicismo* had been, since the 1880s, a key element in intellectual conversations about *dominicanidad* (Dominicanness), its significance became more pronounced ... while the path from *hispanicismo* toward official *hispanidad* was never linear, a patriarchal, racist, and authoritarian

> representation of the Dominican nation became viable and acceptable among modernizing elites by the 1920s.
>
> (2014: 2)

Hispanidad was the belief that everything Spanish, and therefore white and European, was different from and superior to the African cultural elements that informed Haitian culture and that Dominicans were part of this culture.

> In this century it has been a central feature of the ideology and cultural policy of Rafael Leónidas Trujillo, dictator from 1930–61, and of his mastermind and heir, Joaquín Balaguer, president in 1966–76 and from 1982 to the present.
>
> (Davis 1994: 120)

However, one must remember that, in many Latin American and Caribbean societies, "class can trump race when, for example, brown Dominicans are reclassed as virtually white because they are educated and hold a white-collar job" (Derby 2009: 202). I have noted that phenomenon in colonial Mexico, in which a seemingly rigid racial classification made life seem rigid but, in fact, many people managed to get themselves and family members reclassified for one's *casta* determined where one could live, one's profession, one's right to bear a weapon, the clothes one was allowed to wear, and whether one could ride a horse or had to walk. There existed over a dozen official, named classifications, depending on the amount of European, African, or Native American blood that ran through one's veins, all of which appeared in visual depictions of the various seventeenth-century *casta* paintings, of which more than a thousand survive. They show a man and his wife, each of the various classifications and their children. The ability to surmount racial classifications was much more fluid in the Caribbean and Latin America than in the American South, with its notorious one-drop rule.

This racist doctrine became official and enforced in a number of ways under Trujillo when, for example, "It is only since the death of the dictator Trujillo in 1961 and a trend toward free and democratic expression that Vodú [extra-official folk-Catholic practices, reflecting an increasing African influence], still legally proscribed, can be practiced openly" (Davis 2010: 193). Mayes believes that "Trujillo-era nationalism was an ideological invention unique to the dictatorship that drew on long-held ideas that national unity derived from Dominicans' culturally pure Hispanic tradition" (2014: 2). But it was an "invention" that had staying power long after Trujillo's unlamented demise, at least among members of the upper and middle classes of the country.

But, in the end, his rule was ended in a hail of bullets; his days of usefulness to the United States had ended.

> A critical factor in explaining Trujillo's fall, however—if not the central one—was the shift in attitude of the United States ... In May 1961, when Trujillo was assassinated, the Central Intelligence Agency was intimately involved in the plots leading up to his death, and the United States interfered extensively to ensure that Trujillo's family would not retain power. The change in attitude of the United States is explained by one fact: the Cuban revolution.
> (Hartlyn 1998: 104)

The withdrawal of American political patronage of dictators reverberates like a theme song in our story of merengue and its greatest champion.

NOTES

1. For a thorough history of the merengue see Paul Austerlitz's valuable history *Merengue* (1997). He provides samples of the music, rhythm patterns, and lyrics of merengues of all types. He also gives details of the lives and careers of important *merengueros* (those who play the music) and traces its transnational progress, all of which are beyond the scope of this study.
2. The phenomenon of slumming was and is really global. The foundation of "hot" music and dance occurred in the beginnings of Japanese kabuki, when samurai fought over the original young male performers, in India during the Mughal period and the early Raj, in the beginnings of flamenco, and in the Greek tavernas after the population exchange following the First World War as upper-class men sought the excitement of new, lower-class music and dance forms that also often included the promise of sexual adventures.

7

Uzbekistan: Old Lamps for New—The Creation of Uzbek Classical Dance

Agar ān tork-e shirāzi
Be dast ārad del-e mārā
Be khāl-e henduyash bakhsham
Samarqand o Bokhārārā
If that Shirazi Turk
Would possess my heart
For the mole on his cheek
I would give him as a gift, Samarqand and Bukhara

(Hafez)

Introduction

In choosing Uzbekistan for the final case study for this volume on the links between dance and authoritarianism, ethnicity and nationalism, I harked back to my original quest for going there. Contemporary Uzbekistan is the location of two of the historical, fabled, and legendary Persian/Iranian silk road cities of Central Asia: Samarqand and Bokhārā (to use the contemporary Iranian pronunciation, however, I will use the more common spelling of Bukhara), cited in the above poetic lines, which I had sung in scores of public performances. Before my multiple journeys, I had been in correspondence with the Committee for Friendship and Cultural Relations with Foreign Countries since the 1960s. They had sent me multiple books, phonograph records, scholarly publications on dance, music, folklore, and costumes for many years. And, they kindly arranged for me to see the Bahor Dance Company on my three trips to Tashkent. Each time, I spent three happy days, viewing, filming, and learning dances and dance traditions I was later able to stage for my own dance company, the Avaz International Dance Theatre (Figure 16).

I encountered references to these cities again in my readings in the literature faculty as a student of Persian language and literature at the University of Tehran in other Persian poems such as the famous one by the Bukharan poet, Rudaki (ca. 858–940): *Ey, Bokhārā, ey, Bokhārā, shād bāsh o dir zi* (O, Bokhārā, live long and be happy) from the tenth century AD. "Indeed the fame of Iran as a center of arts has persisted down the ages, and Bukhara was part of the world of Iran" (Frye 1997: 84). Therefore the question I posed to myself was, did Samarqand and Bukhara retain any of the Persian historical, linguistic, and cultural heritage that Richard N. Frye describes in great detail? Are those cities, as they had been for centuries in the past, still aesthetically and culturally a part of the Persianate world? The answer, after three journeys there (1976, 1986, and 1989) in which I was attempting to determine links to Iranian dance traditions with those that I found in those cities, was a resounding "yes"[1] (see Frye 1996).

The majority populations of both cities still speak Persian (or Tajik as the Soviets had renamed it, before 1924 it was Farsi), and their social form of the

FIGURE 16: Avaz International Dance Theatre performs a classical dance from the old Silk Road city of Samarqand. Choreography: Anthony Shay. Music: Jamal. Photo: D. Young. From the author's collection.

solo improvised dance tradition was the same as what I found throughout urban Iran, although, as I will argue later in this chapter, the creation of the Uzbek "classical" dance tradition during the Soviet period, as an ethno identity dance genre, an invented tradition, followed a parallel, but different trajectory than the creation of a similarly invented tradition, the so-called *raqs-e melli* of Iran, and I will compare and contrast these two dance genres later in the chapter. It also followed a similar track as that which I describe and analyze for the Igor Moiseyev Dance Company. (See Doi 2002; Meftahi 2016a; Shay 1999, 2014a, 2014b, 2019 and the chapter on Iran in this volume.)[2]

"In cities like Bukhara there continued down to the nineteenth century a prevalence of Iranian racial types—descendants of the ancient inhabitants of the oases reinforced by generations of captives from Iran, prisoners-of-war or the victims of slave-raids" (Hambly 1969: 173). During the wars between the Uzbek Shaybanids and Iranian Safavids in the eighteenth century, the Uzbeks destroyed the entire area around the Iranian city of Marv, including the elaborate irrigation system, followed by "the systematic deportation of its Iranian inhabitants, who so glutted the slave-markets of Bukhara that prices fell to a level unknown in living memory" (Hambly 1969: 181).

These slaves from Iran and their Shia background, as well as local orphans, were the principal source of dancing boys, who as sexually available individuals constituted a despised, but highly desired, class of performers. They came from the most socially powerless backgrounds, slaves and orphans (Levin 2016; Shay 2014a). These professional dancing boys, despite early Russian and later Soviet attempts, still exist and their steps, figures, and gestures were one of the sources of the current Uzbek classical dance.[3]

Themes

The first theme in this final case study about Uzbekistan is a study of old and new, ancient and modern; the old justifies the new, the ancient secures acceptance of the modern. Everywhere in Central Asia, one encounters the old, the new, and the ancient. Old and new, ancient and modern will be woven throughout the description and analysis of the role of dance and music in Uzbekistan, and through all aspects of Uzbek life and society, during the pre-Soviet, Soviet, and post-Soviet periods.

Currently, music and dance, created and arranged during the Soviet period, formed centerpieces for the national celebrations of the former Uzbek dictator, Islam Karimov, and after his death in 2016; as the position is currently held by Shavkat Mirizaev (also Mirziyoyev), ethno identity Uzbek dance continues to be even more elaborate and central to the *nav ruz* (now ruz) celebrations than ever before, as they were for the emir of Bukhara before him, to demonstrate the splendor and generosity of their respective regimes in providing the performances for the public.[4] Thus, we can observe the old private, family holiday, dressed in new holiday clothes in its new context as a publicly celebrated national holiday, designed to celebrate Uzbek national identity. In dance we find the solo social dance form and the newly invented professional dance tradition (Doi 2002; Shay 1999).

In their study of modern Central Asia and the unsavory regimes that now dominate the region, political scientists Alexander Cooley and John Heathershaw state,

> *Dictators Without Borders* tells this very modern story of Central Asia. It thus differs from many other books on the region you might have read, with their tales of the Orient, the ancient silk routes and fractious clans, or warnings of Islamism and ethnic conflicts. We avoid discussion of these pre-modern themes as they are frankly far less important to the true nature of Central Asia than the high-tech finance and low-tech politics detailed here.
>
> (2017: xi)

In contrast, I will argue that without that historical background that they denigrate, one cannot understand the new Uzbekistan. After all, how different are these new dictators than Timur and Genghis Khan? Stalin and Lenin?

I will look at the ethnogenesis of Uzbek and Tajik identities and the historic attempts to create new ethnic and national identities that occurred in Central Asia during the Soviet period, which historically and politically anchor the contemporary regimes and their artificial borders. Without such reference to the past, Cooley and Heathershaw's study of modern authoritarianism will lack its full meaning.

Another theme that will pervade this case study is the ethnic distinctions between Turk and Iranian, Uzbek and Tajik, Turkic and Persian, which have on various levels dominated Central Asian history for more than two millennia, and the contemporary political scene (Frye 1991, 1996). Most scholars cite this contestation—linguistic, historical, political—as a major theme that continues to dominate the current political scene. Central Asian specialist Alexandre Bennigsen argues that "the traditional distinction was not linguistic (Turks versus Iranians), but between nomads and settled people" (1971: 174–75). I will argue that both of these constitute important themes, especially prior to the Soviet Union and the creation of the Central Asian republics. "In Khiva [a city in Uzbekistan], the traditional tension between nomads and cultivators and between Uzbeks and Tajiks, was further complicated by the presence of the Turkomans" (Hambly 1969: 183), who were nomads, showing that both the Turkish–Iranian and nomadic–sedentary themes appear repeatedly.

I consider the linguistic issue to be the more salient one because the Soviet authorities focused more on linguistic issues as a determinant of political status, that is, which group received a republic, which group received an autonomous area, and which received no recognition. "Stalin's linguistic policy was to give each delimited Union republic or Autonomous republic its own language. This led the policy makers in Moscow to exaggerate the differences between several Central Asian languages [that] ... were rooted mainly in Turkic" (Hiro 2011: 46). These distinctions between Turkic dialects resulted in the formation of an official language for Turkmenistan, Kyrgyzstan, Kazakhstan, and Uzbekistan. Dialects of Turkic languages were divided and made "official" because the Soviets opposed "the ideal of adhering to a unique, pan-Turkic or pan-Muslim nation [which] existed among the pre-revolutionary Muslim intelligentsia" (Bennigsen 1971: 176). And today, the nomadic–sedentary distinction has all but disappeared, but the Uzbek–Tajik ethnic-linguistic divide remains. Prior to the Soviet period

> The Central Asians themselves were an undistinguished mass of various self-identifying tribes or city-states [like Samarqand and Bukhara], which were differentiated from one another, first by the nature of the economies—whether the populations were nomadic or sedentary—and second, by the languages they spoke, whether their primary language was Turkic or Persian in origin.
>
> (Olcott 1994: 211–12)

This may be an oversimplification. "In more recent times the Iranian people inside the oases were different in language, culture, and customs from those outside who, in most general terms, might be called Turkic-speaking nomads" (Frye 1996: 36). For those looking beneath the surface of identity politics in Central Asia, the presence of Turkic and Persian speakers, and their differences and commonalities, requires our attention, and therefore Turkish and Iranian identities merit closer scrutiny because they now have new identities, Uzbek and Tajik, respectively, that replicate the past ones and have increasing political consequences. Political scientist Graham E. Fuller states, "Overall Uzbek-Tajik frictions are potentially the most serious of all in Central Asia" (1994: 30).

Sedentary and nomadic differences, my third theme, constitute another major point of difference that determined the current borders for the other major Central Asian Turkic-speaking nations, the Kyrghyz, Kazakhs, and Turkmen republics. "Similarly, sedenites [sic] who farmed in essentially the same way but spoke Turkic or Persian dialects at home now became 'Uzbeks' and 'Tajiks,' respectively" (Olcott 1994: 212). Therefore, unlike Cooley and Heathershaw, I will not avoid looking into the past because the Soviet policies on nationalities, based on sometimes questionable criteria, have determined the political realities of today.

> Certainly the ruling elites of Central Asia held no illusions that the five republics of the region [Central Asia] were anything but artificial creations of the Stalinist period, drawn up in large part to dilute and divide existing populations in order to facilitate political control by Moscow.
>
> (Olcott 1994: 211)[5]

Both of our studies, that of Cooley and Heathershaw and mine, address authoritarianism, but through very different lenses, theirs through political power and money and the corruption of everyday life, mine through nonverbal forms of expression, music and dance, and how they serve as vehicles through which authoritarian regimes express their power and authority.[6]

A Brief History of Central Asia

The history of Central Asia is ancient, with some of the earliest human fossil finds, due to its arid climate, and the subsequent source of human movements and city building. Because Central Asian history is so long and storied, I will, therefore, emphasize those aspects and periods of that long history that have an impact on contemporary Uzbek identity. The history of Central Asia is one of steppe and oasis, in which one nomadic group after another in search of pasturage for their herds moved into the steppe area in waves, often driven there by stronger groups moving into the rich grasslands north of China. Many of them, like the Bulgars, Huns, and Avars, eventually ended up in Europe on the Pannonian plains in today's Hungary and Croatia, part of a vast human movement, in the search for pasturage and water, that lasted for millennia. But earlier Iranian nomads also settled and built cities, like Panjikent in today's Tajikistan, only a vast ruin today, and like other urban centers played a role in the creation of the silk road that was the sedentary aspect of Central Asian life. Thus, the theme of nomad and sedentary human groups appears from the earliest times.

The earliest groups were linguistically Iranian and the later ones were Turkic and Mongol speakers, not only in Central Asia but in Iran itself. "Although the expansion of the Iranians over this vast area began in the second millennium BC ... Our information is very sparse until the foundation of the Achaemenid Empire in the sixth century BC" (Frye 1991, 37). Frye adds,

> The domination of the Iranians, culturally and ethnically rather than politically, lasted down to the close of the first millennium AD when Turks gradually

> replaced the Iranians, first as political masters of Central Asia and then as the dominant linguistic group.
>
> (Ibid.)

Frye is referring to the Samanids (818–999), the last ethnically Persian dynasty, extinguished in 999 by newly arrived Turkish nomads, until the twentieth century, with the Pahlavis (1925–79) of Iran.

The city of Bukhara under the Samanids has left architectural monuments, awe-inspiring to this day, but its greatest influence was the revival and nurturing of the Persian language in its contemporary form. As historian Richard N. Frye notes, "Perhaps more than anything else which gave Bukhara fame was the sheer number of savants gathered there" (1996: 93). Rudaki, one of the earliest poets, has written in a lucid Persian style that contemporary Iranians can comfortably read. However, in spite of Turkic-language speakers' dominant numbers, Persian remained the language of court and culture until the fall of the emirates of Bukhara and Khiva in 1920. The court literati and clerks were Iranian while the Turks dominated the political and military scene. This latter pattern has been noted by most historians of Iran and Central Asia, "that the Turks were meant to be soldiers and rulers, whereas the Persians were relegated to the arts, crafts, manners, and literature, all of which were called *adab* in Arabic" (Frye 1997: 121).

Characteristic of many medieval courts of Central Asia and Iran:

> The Timurid dynasty, like the Mongols before them, used a dual administration; Chaghatays held most military commands and many of the highest court positions, while Persians were almost exclusively in bureaucratic positions dealing with financial administration or official correspondence.
>
> (Manz 1992: 39)

I have mentioned this pattern elsewhere, because this courtly arrangement was common from the courts of the Mongols, the Mughals, the Ghaznavids, the Seljuqs, and other centers of power and culture in the region. In this Turco-Persian mix, it is important to remember that the Turks often constituted a minority who conquered areas of Central Asia by superior military tactics. That changed:

> From the sixteenth century onwards Turks probably formed a majority in the racial composition of the population of Mawarannahr [Central Asia north of the Amu-Darya River] and it seems likely that there was also an increase in the proportion of nomads to sedentary cultivators or towns-folk.
>
> (Hambly 1966: 172)

Muhammad Shaybani, the leader of "formidable Uzbek clans" (Hamby 1969: 156), by the end of the first decade of the sixteenth century had taken control of most of Khorasan but, facing Shah Ismael of Iran who killed him in battle, the Uzbeks lost Khorasan; however, after a number of battles, they kept control of Mawarannahr, which contained the cities of Samarqand and Bukhara. While seemingly just a depressing list of battles, their significance for Central Asian history has been crucial, because they marked the decline of the region into intellectual and economic provincialism. The Safavids (1501–1725) officially changed Iran in 1501 into a Shia state that effectively cut Central Asia off from the rest of the Islamic world, "an isolation which was to blight her intellectual and cultural life down to the close of the nineteenth century" (Hambly 1969: 164). Thus, the Uzbek Shaybanids retained control over Mawarannahr and oversaw its slow disintegration over the next three centuries, until the arrival of the Russians in 1865.

The Persian Language and Its Legacy

The importance of the Persian language lasted well into the twentieth century in Central Asia, as well as Afghanistan and Iran:

> The fact remains that Persian was the cultural language of sedentary Central Asia into the beginning of this century. Despite the efforts of that grand man of letters, Mir Ali Shir Nawa'i, "Turki" [as sedentary Central Asian Turkic was called until the 1920s] did not overtake Persian as the cultural language, though it incorporated a prodigious number of Persian words and phrases.
>
> (Naby 1994: 40)

I should add that the division between Safavid Shia Persia and Shaybanid Sunni Mawarannahr did not alter the superior status of the Persian language. "This language usage was not a reflection of ethnicity but a reflection of the prestige and cultural wealth of Persian" (Naby 1994: 40). This prestige may have been somewhat diminished by the establishment of Central Asian republics and may well have been the reason that the two largest Tajik cities—Samarqand and Bukhara—were awarded to Uzbekistan by the Soviets in order to place these cities and their populations outside of the future possibility of Iranian political influence.

One of the major reasons for this was that Persian was the prestige language of literature and administration in all of these court settings. This pattern continued into the twentieth century. In 1920, "The flight of the emir and the installation of the Young Bukharans sealed the fate of the city's [Bukhara] traditional Persian-writing cultural elite and the court-centered culture it reproduced" (Khalid 2015: 135).

Young Muslim intellectuals from Central Asia wrote and communicated in Persian: "Up until the revolution [Abdurauf] Fitrat [probably the leading intellectual figure in the Jadids] wrote almost exclusively in Persian. In 1917, he switched to Uzbek, which he also sought to reform and reshape" (Khalid 2015: 54). Khalid adds,

> The turn to Turkism was among other things a revolt against the Persianate tradition, a form of de-Persianization of identity. In the Chaghatayist view, Central Asians who spoke Persian did so under the cultural influence of morally corrupt royal courts.
>
> (2015: 258)

From then, the use of Uzbek began to grow.

The Uzbek Language

In discussing the appearance of the Uzbeks and their history, because it constitutes an important element in contemporary Uzbek identity, I will address the Chaghatay (also Chaghatai) Turkish language, which the Soviet authorities called "Old Uzbek" because it is central to Uzbek identity. The supreme figure in Chaghatay Turkic was the above-mentioned Amir Alishir Nava'i.

> Amir Alishir Nava'i was instrumental and not just in promoting Persian literary humanism but in laying the foundation of Chagatai Turkic literature. He is rightly considered to have done what Geoffrey Chaucer (ca. 1343–1400) did for English or Dante Alighieri (ca. 1265–1321) did for Italian. His voluminous work in Chagatai may in fact be considered as the inaugural moment of Turkish literary humanism.
>
> (Dabashi 2012: 174, emphasis in the original)

The model for this new Turkic literature and grammar was Persian. As Uzbek intellectuals constructed a new identity, one of the sources to which they turned was Chaghatay Turkish. Historian Beatrice Forbes Manz states:

> The Chaghatays originated as the ruling group first in the Ulus Chaghatay, a nomad tribal confederation controlling Transoxiana, named after Ghingis [sic] Khan's son Chaghatay. It was here that the great conqueror Tamerlane (1370–1405) rose to power ... During the rule of Tamerlane and his successors, they became a defined and self-conscious group of people. They were distinct not only from the members of their subject population, largely Persian speaking and

> agricultural ... The name Chaghatay was used for this group both by its own members and by outside people, including the Ottoman, Byzantines, and *Uzbeks* ... The use of the term Chaghatay to designate the ruling group descended from the tribes of the Ulus Chaghatay continued through the Timurid period.
>
> (1992: 27, 37, emphasis added)

It is important to quote Manz at length to convey crucial aspects of Chaghatay identity, since the Uzbeks were given a separate identity at that time, according to Manz's statement above. This is interesting since contemporary Uzbeks claim Chaghatay identity as their own. Manz adds that "It is not entirely clear what defined Chaghatay identity" (1992: 41). However, it is most likely that Chaghatay Turkish language was one of the major elements of that identity.

Chaghatay Turkish was promoted and developed as a literary language by the nobleman, Ali Shir Navā'i, who complained that while most Turks knew Persian, hardly any Persians knew Turkish. Nevertheless, Navā'i constructed Chaghatay as a literary language based closely on the Persian language during the long reign of Shāhrokh (r. 1405–47), Timur's youngest son. Shāhrokh was arguably more important than Timur himself in the history of Central Asia and the development of a stable center of art, literature, and culture: "A devout Muslim and a passionate admirer of Iranian culture, Shah Rukh [sic] transformed Timur's Central Asian empire into an orthodox Islamic sultanate with its centre in Khurasan. Herat replaced Samarqand as the capital of the empire" (Hambly 1969: 154).

It was important to the Soviet authorities that each republic have an official language to justify its existence. "The Uzbeks, unlike some other peoples of Central Asia, already had their own literary language, Chagatai [sic] (also known as Old Uzbek). However, it was a refined, learned medium, far removed from the spoken dialects of the region" (1996: 336). In this way Chaghatay resembled Ottoman Turkish. As a courtly language the pro-Russian group rejected it, as Ataturk and his followers had rejected Ottoman Turkish, turning to Anatolian Turkish as more relevant to modern Turkey.

> The pro-Russian [Central Asian Turkish] group, who were in favour of developing a new literary form based on the dialects of Tashkent and Ferghana. These were the dialects of the economic and political centres of the new republic, and also of the burgeoning print language. They were untypical of the main body of Uzbek dialects in that they were highly Iranised [sic] and had lost much of their vowel harmony, the most distinctive feature of the Turkic languages. Nevertheless, they were adopted as the base for the national language.
>
> (Akiner 1996: 336–37)

During the Timurid period Chaghatai Turkish had developed rapidly as a language of polite learning ... had become by Shaybanid times a mature vehicle for literary expression and complementary to Persian which, however, it failed to replace as the language of the cultural elite. (Hambly 1969: 171)

Thus, once again, we encounter the interaction between Persian and Turkish culture, a theme of this chapter. Eventually, the Shaybanid holdings devolved into three emirates, Bukhara, Khiva, and Kokand, that endured into the Russian/Soviet period until the five new republics—Uzbekistan, Tajikistan, Kyrgyzstan, Turkmenistan, and Kazakhstan—came into being in the ashes of the Shaybanid emirates.

Modern Uzbeks did not simply embrace Chaghatay Turkish, which had become "the cast-off language of the few literate Uzbeks," but rather, "Chaghatay, thus came to assume the role of a dead language that could be of interest only to a small group [of] orientalists and philologists" (Landau and Kellner-Heinkele (2001: 155–56). They add, "Modern Uzbek itself, however, emerged in [the] late 1980s, as a vehicle for opposition to linguistic russification" (ibid.), indicating how modern the current Uzbek identity is. "With time, Uzbekistan's new literary and state language became far removed—both in vocabulary and in grammar—from the idiom that had formed the literary *lingua franca* of Turkestan area and beyond" (Landau and Kellner-Heinkele 2001: 155). One should note that the Uzbek language, during the Soviet period, became so neglected, other than as a colloquial spoken language, that most literate and university-educated Uzbeks, like individuals in many other Central Asians, functioned and communicated in a more sophisticated fashion and more easily in Russian than in their native language. "Uzbek has not been nurtured by a strong and stable intelligentsia. It is thus more fluid and there is an obvious need to define and strengthen 'genuine Uzbek'" (Dollerup 1998: 147). "The replacement of Russian vocabulary with a revitalized pre-Soviet Uzbek one, usually termed Chaghatay and consisting predominantly of Persian and Arabic words, can be observed, as well as the parallel existence of modern Uzbek and traditional vocabulary" (Landau and Kellner-Hienkele 2001: 158).

From the very beginning of the establishment of the Uzbek Republic, the language issue remained a major problem. The Uzbek intelligentsia

> had Uzbekistan; now they had to make Uzbeks. The sedentary turcophone population of Central Asia was far from being a speech community. It retained an enormous variety of dialects. The language planners' task of creating a single language of this variety reflected the broader problem of building a single nation out of the disparate sedentary groups that had found themselves classified as

> Uzbek ... The fundamental question was whether Soviet Uzbek national culture should be rooted in the masses or in the high traditions of the past.
> (Khalid 2015: 281–82)

Ultimately, they chose the latter in the figure of Timur and the Chaghatay language.

In Uzbekistan today, efforts are being made to create a functional Uzbek language that can be used in administrative and academic activities. "The classical language of Central Asia, Chaghatay or, in Soviet terms, 'Old Uzbek'" (Landau and Heinkele 2001: 135) has become a dead language, even though it serves as a source of old Turkish vocabulary for constructors of modern Uzbek to replace Russian. Thus, language building in Uzbekistan indicates that "Uzbekistan is currently engaged in a nationalizing project" (Koroteyeva and Makarova 1998: 137), one that has continued into the twenty-first century (Figure 17).

FIGURE 17: Avaz International Dance Theatre performs an Uzbek dance from the Ferghana Valley region of Uzbekistan. Choreography: Ixchel Dimetral-Maerker. Photo: D. Young. From the author's collection.

Islam

One cannot address Central Asia without at least a brief discussion of Islam. Since the seventh century, Islam has been the dominant religious and cultural factor in the lives of the peoples of Central Asia. To whatever degree people were believers or not, Islam and Islamic celebrations marked the lives of the inhabitants of this vast region, even through the Soviet period that supported atheism. "Traditional Islamic ritual such as circumcision funerals, or the observance of Ramadan are important cultural expressions of Muslim identity" (1992: 7).

But the reader must keep in mind, as anthropologist Dale Eickelman reminds us, that Islam is hardly a unifying factor: One would better conceptualize the Islamic world as multiple "Islams." "The political principles of the Muslim world are highly varied—there are vigorous debates over just which principles are 'Islamic'—and not all advocates of Islamic conduct place equal stress on political participation" (1993: 13). In Central Asia one finds an unusual number of Sufi orders, and it was they who spread a popular version of Islam among the nomadic population: "Thus it was the dervish rather than the town- or village-based *mulla* who moulded the shape of Islam as a popular faith in Central Asia" (Hambly 1969: 171). These Sufi leaders, "deriving their support, therefore from the most turbulent and indeed barbarous elements in the population" (ibid.) held considerable political power and influence. Islam spread in Central Asia through the Little Tradition rather than the Greater Tradition.

There also exists the notion that since communism dominated the Islamic lands of Central Asia, Islamic belief was eradicated there, and after the fall of the Soviet Union, Islam was reimported from forces outside of Central Asia. That would be an error. "Central Asian religious activism was, however, homegrown, although influenced by other parts of the Islamic world" (Abduvakhitov 1993: 79). The most important fact that the reader can take away about the various ethnic, national, and religious identities found in Central Asia is that "Islam has been and continues to be a major source of identity among the Muslims of Central Asia" (Gross 1992: 16). Current dictators, following Soviet practice in that region, frequently justify their brutality as repressing radical Islam.

Most readers are aware of the differences between Shia and Sunni Islam, not perhaps on a doctrinal level but a political one as it played out in Central Asia. "Raiding Persian territories to the south had religious merit (since people there were of the heretical Shii denomination) and brought material rewards in the form of captives for the slave markets of Khiva and Bukhara" (Souchek 2000: 182). This schism has had an impact on the ethnic composition of Central Asia. Making slaves of fellow Muslims was an anathema in the Islamic world; however, since the Shias and Sunnis were considered to be heretics to one another, they provided fair game for enslavement. And, of course, it was profitable.

A modernizing element entered the Islamic scene in various European, and later Central Asian, societies in the second half of the nineteenth century whose members made up the region's tiny intellectual class. "Most were educated men (and a few women), often trained in Russian and European institutions as well as Islamic, and frequently well traveled both inside Russia and abroad" (Lazzerini 1992: 151). These individuals sought to modernize Islam so that it could better fit the modern world and confront the Russian culture and influence that was engulfing their societies (Lazzerini 1992; Khalid 2015). Although small in number, they were to have a major impact on the creation of the current nation-states of Central Asia. Most were destroyed and executed by the Soviet government in the 1930s.

Islam played a prominent role in the development of dance in Central Asia. The extremely powerful Islamic clergy banned women from dancing in public and, therefore, from an early period only young boys dressed in ambiguous clothing, neither male nor female, were permitted to dance in public settings (Doi 2002; Levin 2016; Shay 2014a). These dancing boys, with their widespread popularity and high levels of performance, were the basis of Uzbek classical dance.

The Appearance of the Russians

In the middle of the nineteenth century European powers were still vying for territories in Africa and Asia. Fearing British influence in India, Russia looked to Central Asia as a space for Russian expansion.

> It [Central Asia] was conquered very much in the context of imperial competition with other European powers at a time when imperial rule over "uncivilized" peoples was clearly seen as a hallmark of civilization ... there was no question that the Russian advance into Central Asia was part of the European conquest of non-European lands in the age of empire.
>
> (Khalid 2015: 29)

However, we should not overlook the other aspect of colonialism, that is, material gain: "The prime motivation of the Russian conquest had been economic self-interest, and the evolution of the colony between 1868–1917 amply met that goal" (Souchek 2000: 203). The principal material gain was provided by "white gold," or cotton, as anyone who has ever been to Central Asia knows, both during and after the Russian conquest until the present day. Growing cotton in Central Asia has had devastating effects on the environment that have nearly destroyed the health of hundreds of thousands of individuals, and the near disappearance of the Aral Sea.

Kazakhstan suffered the indignity of having its arable land seized by the millions of Russian and Ukrainian settlers who practiced European-style agriculture and who today make up more than half of the population of Kazakhstan. The other Central Asian republics, however, did not have land resources that lent themselves to European-style agriculture in what was essentially a desert climate.

The Bolsheviks, for all of their purported belief in the equality of men and the workers, did not want to give up this prime piece of real estate. In spite of the confusion and turmoil of the revolution, they moved into the region and took over from the Tsarist forces. While the Tsarist Russians made attempts not to cause antagonism among the Muslim population, keeping Russian peasants out of the area, for example, Communist Party adherents were intent on utterly changing every aspect of life for the native peoples. Nevertheless, the Russians under both regimes had a disdain for the native population, which I frequently saw in evidence in my trips there.

In 1865, the Russians made Tashkent the seat of their colonial administration.

> The Russians built a quarter of their own alongside the native city, establishing a pattern that they would follow in a number of other places: a European city developed through a rational system of urban planning, presenting a sharp contrast to the traditional native quarters.
>
> (Souchek 2000: 203)

One could see this pattern throughout Central Asia. The Russians gathered together in their own neighborhoods as rulers under both regimes.

The Creation of the Soviet Union and the Uzbek Soviet Socialist Republic

Lest anyone think that the Uzbek population remained passive during the process of creating the republic, historian Dilip Hiro writes,

> Between 1914 and 1923, Central Asia underwent turmoil of extraordinary severity: conventional warfare, revolution, civil strife, periodic shifting of the borders of its constituents, administrative reforms, founding of an all-powerful political party, the purging of chauvinist Russian settlers from the region, and sweeping land reform which uprooted centuries-old property relations.
>
> (2011: 31)

In short, life was hell.

Muslim intellectuals first fought for a pan-Turkic entity, a Republic of Turkistan, which would include all of the Muslims of Central Asia. "At the First Conference of the Muslim Organizations in Tashkent in May 1919, the representatives of the 108 bodies demanded the establishment of the Soviet Republic of United Turkistan to include the Turks of Russia and the Caucasus" (Hiro 2011: 39). However, one should remember that "'Turkestan,' of course, was the creation of Russian rule" (Khalid 2015: 42), rather than a political concept created by the native intelligentsia.

The Russians who dominated the former Tsarist colonial holdings encountered the 1917 Revolution and the Bolsheviks, who came out as the winners, were faced with a basic problem: how to reorganize the new state and, in the process, keep hold of the former Russian colonial empire. Marx and Engels were little interested in issues of national state formation, but "After 1917, Lenin's position on federation underwent a complete change: from regarding 'the right to federation' as 'meaningless,' to an acceptance of it as the most suitable form of organisation for a multiethnic state" (Smith 1996: 5). Thus, the answer the Bolsheviks decided upon was to create the Union of Soviet Socialist Republics that was based on

> geographical borders [that] were artificially created on the basis of macroethnic identities. The Soviet Union, in an effort to deal with its non-Russian populations in a newly created Soviet Communist state, created a Union of Socialist Republics, defined primarily in terms of nationalities [based on language and local tradition].
> (Gross 1992: 3)

The many legacies of the Soviet Union include the Soviet theory and practice of 'the nationality question.' Not only did the late Soviet regime create its own economic, ideological, and political system, but over the years, to a large extent, it defined ethnicity itself within its territory. It virtually created nations and nationalities following criteria and purposes that were its own (Szporluk 1994: 4)

And those invented entities, Uzbekistan among them, have a large degree of artificiality because "The Soviets did not intend to create nations and 'their' corresponding states as entities capable of independent or autonomous existence" (Szporluk 1994: 5). Political scientist Martha Brill Olcott adds, "These territorial divisions were drawn to impede the exercise of statehood rather than encourage it" (1994: 209). It is crucial that we understand how Uzbekistan, as a totally new political entity based on an artificial foundation, turned to historical symbols to create a new nation and genuine Uzbeks out of their still unformed citizens. "In Central Asia it is political artifice and social engineering that have produced the sociocultural mix we see today" (1994: 34). After considerable research, historian and political scientist Adeeb Khalid argues, to the contrary, that "Muslim intellectuals, not Soviet ethnographers or party functionaries, were the true authors of Uzbekistan and the Uzbek nation" (2015: 15). However, as he notes, they were soon excluded from participation in the fledgling political entity: "The first purge of the national intelligentsia in 1929–30, I argue, was a landmark in the exclusion of the intelligentsia from the political process, and the end of an era" (Khalid 2015: 17).

"The Uzbeks are a people of predominantly Turkic origin, with a significant admixture of Iranian and Turkicised Mongol elements. They speak Uzbek, a language that evolved out of Chagatai [sic], the chief literary medium of the eastern Turkic world" (Akiner 1996: 334). And while Akiner's description succinctly describes today's Uzbek population, she importantly notes,

> The ethnonym "Uzbek" was not often used by the local population ... By the early years of the 20th century a handful of intellectuals had begun to raise the question of ethnic identity, but in a vague, tentative way.
>
> (1996: 335)

And therein lie the issues that I raised in the creation of the Republic of Uzbekistan, among which the themes of the Chaghatay-Uzbek language, and Turkic-Iranian linguistic and ethnic relations appear frequently. One of the central elements of Uzbek identity obviously is the Uzbek language. Adeeb Khalid calls this use of Chaghatay "Chaghatayism, to describe this view of the Uzbek nation" (2015: 15), a topic he pursues in depth in his important study.

Few readers know about Uzbekistan today. This is due to Great Power politics, especially contestation between Russia and Great Britain over India and Afghanistan (see Bacon 1994), then its subsequent status as a constituent, and distant, Soviet republic (1924–91) (see Khalid 2015; Olcott 1994), and finally its establishment as an independent republic in 1991 whose authoritarian leader, Islam Karimov (r. 1991–2016), kept Uzbekistan further closed off, even from its nearest neighbors (Starr and Cornell 2018). Its current importance lies in "most obviously, its population of 32 million is equal to that of the other four post-Soviet Central Asian states combined. Geographically, Uzbekistan borders all Central Asian states including Afghanistan, [and] counts substantial ethnic Uzbek populations on the territory of all its neighbors" (Cornell 2018: 6).

In the case of Uzbekistan, it is a newly created geographic and political entity (1924), most of its inhabitants did not know at the founding of the nation that they were Uzbeks, and many of the rural population still do not know their new identity. It was not a nation established through the pressures of the majority of its population wanting a homeland. The knowledge of being an Uzbek lay with a tiny minority of intellectuals who wanted to resurrect an older historical identity in order to create a new identity. This small intellectual circle, many of whom were *jadids* (an intellectual group from the turn of the twentieth century who sought to modernize Islam), searched for old symbols, like the person of Amir of (Tamerlane), the Chaghatay Turkish language and Ali Shir Navā'i, the intellectual nobleman who developed it, and a host of other historical symbols, many of which they shared with the Persian-speaking population, such as a veneration of the *Shahnameh*, in order to underpin their new Uzbek identity from a previous Bukharan identity: old lamps for new. The veneration of the *Shahnameh* and celebration of no-ruz (nav ruz) are among the elements that make Uzbekistan part of what scholars call the Persianate World (see *Journal of Persianate Studies*; Shay 2021).

From the beginning of the newly minted Uzbek republic, the architects of the nation seized upon the historical figure of the Timur (Tamarlane) as the progenitor of the Uzbek nation: "Six centuries later, eager to establish a long-standing Uzbek identity, the post-Communist regime in Uzbekistan would zealously declare him the progenitor of the Uzbek nation" (Hiro 2011: 17). They were very anxious to, in Adeeb Khalid's terms, "Make Uzbeks Uzbek" (2015: 281), even if, in fact, Timur was not an ethnic Uzbek.

Because the borders of today's five Central Asian republics had little meaning less than one hundred years ago, it is important to place Uzbekistan in the larger context of Central Asian history, one that features Iranian and Turkish differences. "The Iranian plateau, comprising the modern states of Iran and Afghanistan, is usually not included in any concept of Central Asia, but it always has been connected with Central Asia" (Frye 1996: 35) through, language, literature, culture, and history. In this section I have shown that the ethnogenesis of the Uzbek nation, which we have seen in less than a century, contrasts with the ethnogenesis of the Croatian nation, and that of Iran.

These identities are new to the majority of the population, *but today they have become real*, as most scholars note. Referring to Tajikistan, international relations scholar John Anderson notes,

> It is far from clear if the residents of this artificial state had any clear sense of personal belonging, for, with the exception of a few intellectuals aware of their Persian heritage, most residents of this predominantly rural country identified themselves in terms of family, communal and regional ties … as late as 1979 Tajiks still made up only 59 per cent of the population, whilst Uzbeks, located largely in the northern and western regions, comprised nearly a quarter.
>
> (1997: 165)

And, more importantly, the Soviet authorities assigned Samarqand and Bukhara, the two largest Persian (Tajik)-speaking cities, to Uzbekistan. And

Tajiks remain furious over this decision, because they know their ethnic and linguistic brethren there have been persecuted for their Tajik identity.[7] Meanwhile, the Uzbeks outside of Uzbekistan, who largely live adjacent to Uzbekistan, "on occasion flirted with the idea or reuniting with their larger neighbor" (Anderson 1997: 177). This plan is not yet off the table and may yet play a role in the future of Uzbekistan and its neighbors.

To enlarge the new ethnic picture of Central Asia, to include Iran and Afghanistan, to remain true to the historical reality of the region, as I will elaborate later in the chapter, "An estimated 350,000 Turkmens, 1.5 million Uzbeks, and 3.5 million Tajiks live in Afghanistan; 650,000 Turkmens live in Iran" (Kaiser 1994: 237), and these figures are now larger two decades later, which show that these populations live, for the most part, adjacent to their titular republics in the former Soviet Union. Thus, Olcott's notion of divide and conquer has come to pass; some clashes along ethnic lines have already occurred and could ignite more strife in the future.

Soviet Uzbekistan

Historian Thomas R. McCray puts it succinctly:

> Uzbekistan has enough farmland, oil, gold, and water to build a prosperous economy, but it is generally poor by Western standards. It is a country surrounded by clouds of warlordism, Islamism, capitalism, authoritarianism, colonialism, and halting democracy. It is a country with a classic strongman leadership, stubbornly corrupt institutions, and serious environmental handicaps.
>
> (2004: 10)

But Uzbekistan as a political entity is new, lying upon the ruins of a series of ancient to old political entities and empires. I argue that Uzbeks are still searching for ways to construct a modern Uzbek identity because there were no ready-made symbols that could be utilized unmediated.

As Khalid details, these political units changed from the period of Genghis (Changiz) Khan, to Timur (Tamerlane) and his descendants, the Shaybanis (who brought together and united the disparate Uzbek tribes), and the founding of the emirates of Bukhara, Khiva, and Kokand (Qoqand), which lasted under the encroachments of the Russian Tsarist government, to be divided into a number of different political configurations under the Bolsheviks, including the short-lived, but important Bukharan Soviet Republic and the Republic of Turkistan. The entire area of Central Asia, including today's Uzbeks, are living in a newly constructed political environment, which, throughout the 1920s, witnessed several border changes and iterations, including the newly established republic of Tajikistan.

Ethnicity in Uzbekistan

The ethnicities of today differ from those of the past. Some ethnicities of the past, like the Sarts, which often referred to sedentary town dwellers, have disappeared while other designations were changed by the Soviet authorities.

> In the 1926 census the "Sarts" were divided into Uzbeks and Tajiks, but there were no doubt some people who had been classified in 1897 as Uygurs, Taranchis, and Kashgaris, and who had been reclassified in 1926 as Uzbeks or were included with other groups.
>
> (Menges 1994: 106)

Thus, during the census taking in the former Soviet Union, one could have whatever ethnic identity classification the census taker thought the authorities would like to hear. "Soviet authorities 'consolidated' local variations of group identities into a single Uzbek nationality. Sart, Muslim, Chaghatay, Xoja, Turk, and other identities faded (but did not disappear) in the wake of what Ingebor Baldauf called 'radical Uzbekism,'" the forcible and rapid development of a Soviet-defined Uzbek national language, literature, and culture. In an attempt to naturalize the idea of the Uzbek nation, the Soviets glossed over these complexities of identity, complexities that persisted in troubling Uzbekistan's contemporary nation-building project in the postindependence period (Adams 2010: 37). The invented ethnicities, like "Tajik" and "Uzbek," took on a life of their own during the Soviet period and continue into the post-Soviet period, and an understanding of these ethnicities is crucial to understanding the identity politics of contemporary Central Asia. Because Uzbek intellectuals, especially the jadids, the pre-Soviet and early Soviet intellectuals, who were brutally destroyed, most of them shot, during the 1930s, sought meaning for their current ethnic identity in past historical events and linguistic practices, much of what they decided to use as symbols has remained in the post-Soviet period. These classificatory divisions have taken on their own reality.

We are dealing with Uzbekistan, a new nation—less than a hundred years old—constructed and created largely from the outside (Moscow). It did not exist, except possibly in the minds of a handful of intellectuals before its inception in 1924 (see Khalid 2015). The geographic borders were cobbled together out of previous emirates and other entities. There is scholarly contestation about who had the ultimate say in its birth and ultimate national limits. However, even then, in the 1920s, further adjustments to its borders were made and parts of the new nation were ceded to an even newer nation, Tajikistan, in 1929. The difficulties that faced the architects of the new Uzbek Republic were enormous: "Defining Uzbekness in the immediate aftermath of the creation of Uzbekistan was a deeply fraught process in which Uzbek intellectuals had to contend with the requirements of the Soviet state and of the Communist Party" (Khalid 2015: 290). Most of them paid for it with their lives.

The contestation between Tajiks and Uzbeks continues to persist today, and I profoundly experienced it in several episodes during my three visits there (1976, 1986, 1989) to study the dance traditions and contexts during the Soviet period, ever more forcefully as the demise of the former Soviet Union approached.

> Many ethnic Tajiks, concentrated in the traditionally Tajik cities of Samarkand [sic] and Bukhara in Uzbekistan fear the rise of pan-Turkism ... Should an opposition seize power that is identified too closely to pan-Turkist ideals, these Tajik cities may well erupt in rebellion.
>
> (Hale 1994: 166)

Adeeb Khalid adds, "Tajik intellectuals, who see themselves as keepers of the Iranian (or 'Aryan') flame in a sea of Tukicness, feel aggrieved that the ancient centers of Persian culture [Samarqand and Bukhara] belong to Uzbekistan" (2015: 291). I do not envision Uzbekistan ceding Samarqand and Bukhara to Tajikistan, and Uzbekistan has a larger population and army.

The Invented Tradition of Uzbek Classical Music and Dance

The Uzbek classic dance tradition that I came to study and observe during the Soviet period in the 1970s and 1980s, which I argue is an invented tradition, continues to be supported by the Uzbek successor state; therefore, it is important to provide a history of its construction and development, which began in the 1930s. The dance genre has continued to be developed and refined for contemporary use in state building and ethnic and nationality construction (Doi 2002). Sociologist Laura Adams notes,

> In Uzbekistan, national dance [which I refer to here as Uzbek classical dance] is the cultural form that the nation is invested in, so the issue of invention and russification in national dance was an especially sensitive one that people discussed with me.
>
> (2010: 83)

Many contemporary Uzbeks regard Uzbek history and language as a precious heritage from antiquity and an authentic symbol of Uzbek national identity.

Therefore, it is important that I unpeel its relatively brief history so that the reader can understand its constructedness and contemporary salience. In the 2019 *Nav ruz* celebration seen on YouTube, this dance genre was the most important ingredient in the spectacular day-long festival which the Uzbek state served up for its people. Its creation began in the decade after the establishment of the Uzbek SSR with the solo dances of Tamara Khanum, Mukarram Turghunbaeva, and other pioneer artists, and its development continued steadily until the 1960s with the establishment of elaborate and spectacular mass choreographies that Mukarram Turghunbaeva created for the Bahor State Academic Ensemble of Uzbek Dance beginning in 1957 (Figure 18), the year of its founding (Doi 2002; Karimova 1979; Shirokaya 1973).

Thus, Uzbekistan belongs firmly in this study of the relationship between dance and music and authoritarianism, for it is a nation-state that, until recently, meted out gruesome death sentences, like being boiled alive, and therefore can be located among the least attractive authoritarian governments in the world, at least during the Karimov period (1991–2016) (see Cooley and Heathershaw 2017). In fact,

FIGURE 18: Avaz International Dance Theatre performs Katta Uyin, a classical Uzbek dance. Choreography: Jamal. Music: Jamal. Photo: D. Young. From the author's collection.

I could have selected any of the Central Asian Republics to illustrate my point since, to some degree, they are all ruled by corrupt and brutal despots that differ from one another only to the degree of megalomania apparent in the golden statues, fairy-tale castles, celebratory festivals, squares, streets and buildings named after them, their photographs in every public space, and the paper money and postage stamps engraved with their faces.

Perhaps more than the other Central Asian states, Uzbekistan has chosen dance as an important representational field, continuing an intense support that began with the former Soviet state. Since I had made three visits there during the Soviet period, and viewed and studied the dance tradition that was created there, I chose to include Uzbekistan among my case studies.

Because these republics are newly minted, they must turn to a glorious historical "golden age" to justify their inglorious present existence, including "folklore" that has always been supported by nationalists. Inherent in these dance performances, through costumes, music, and old miniature paintings, lays the claim to ancient practices. Whenever the *sorna* and *korna* (double-reed instruments) appear with *dairehs* (*doire*) (frame drums), as in Iran, it means the event has taken on ancient traditions and harks to memories of folklore of the past, "the cacophonous karnay and surnay, reedy and bellowing horns played during holiday spectacles ... These traditional instruments were used in spectacles to signal folk, festive, and inviting themes" (Adams 2010: 133). On several YouTube recordings, Uzbek classical dance accompanies the appearance of these instruments; it is not always a comfortable aesthetic fit, any more than it is with the popular song videos that also frequently feature the professional classical Uzbek dancers. Thus, this dance tradition is sought after for valorizing all types of music, perhaps because the dancers are very professional and can adapt their movements and gestures to a wide variety of accompaniment. However, as we will see, the Uzbek classical dance tradition is an invented tradition, not based on folklore, but on urban forms, calling on past practices to suggest ancient origins, but whose origins do not lie in the far past. Mary Masayo Doi remarked, "They seemed curiously encapsulated from change. Several scholars even told me to study Persian miniatures as background for understanding the dress and poses the dancers used" (2002: 137). Doi would have found little information on either the dance movements or the actual clothes people wore in historical periods in the aforementioned Persian miniatures, since they tell us only that dance occurred on festive occasions.

My study is about invented tradition, not only the invented tradition of ethnic groups but also the invented tradition of a new dance genre, and a new musical genre that is only a few decades old, but based on something old, movements and figures from the movement vocabulary of the professional dancing boys combined with a few folk elements, especially in the Khorazmian style, ballet and character dance. In its new iteration this dance genre is different in its historical context, including the gender of its performers, and its ethnic and national identity.

Across Central Asia one finds a range of dance and music that characterizes the Middle East and North Africa as well. There exist multiple forms of regional folk music and dance that is regionally specific and that is beyond the scope of this chapter. There also exist a variety of professional forms, of which the best known is belly dance. I argue that all of these musical and dance forms share a common aesthetic, many of them having a corresponding domestic version that women, but also men, perform in private celebratory events like weddings (Doi 2002; Shay 1997, 1999; Shay and Sellers-Young 2005).

Dance in Uzbekistan

Dance from the Central Asian area known today as Uzbekistan figured in the history of this region as a commodity in Silk Route change. Richard N. Frye notes, "The Chinese, especially at court, sought dancers, acrobats, and especially musicians from the west, for their entertainment. Kucha early became famous as a source of desirable musicians" (1996: 187) and mentions that Samarqand was also a source (ibid.). Whether the dancers were male, female, or both is not mentioned.

The dance genre that I will focus on in this chapter is that of what is sometimes called Uzbek classical dance. Like Uzbek nationality itself, Uzbek classical dance is a socially constructed invented tradition. As I detail in my history of the Moiseyev Dance Company, the State Academic Ensemble of Folk Dances of the Peoples of the Soviet Socialist Republic, Soviet authorities had deemed that "folk dance," in an athletic and spectacularized form created by Igor Moiseyev and approved by the state, was to become a major form of national representation that all national groups were to follow (Shay 2019). The pioneer creators of the new tradition in Uzbekistan followed the Moiseyev model, mixing the elements of professional dance performed by the bachehs, the professional boy dancers, ballet, some folk dance elements, especially in its Khorazmian variation, character dancing, and the Igor Moiseyev method of mass choreography, which did not exist in prerevolutionary Uzbekistan.

Professional dance in Uzbekistan and Tajikistan, commonly performed by dancing boys for the urban elite, too, has commonalities across this vast region as with calligraphy and architectural decoration, which include improvisation, geometry, and the abstract design that flows from it (Al-Faruqi 1987; Shay 1997, 1999). Dance, too, is an abstract form and, with geometry and improvisation, is linked to other Islamic forms of expression (Shay 1999).

We can call it "classic" in that during the period from the 1930s to the 1960s, Uzbek choreographers like Tamara Khanum, Mukarram Turganbaeva, Isahar

Akilov, and Roziya Karimova created a named vocabulary of movements, a cannon, and an institution, all with enormous financial support of the state, that Iran, which had embarked on a similar project, never accomplished (see chapter 3 this volume; Meftahi 2016a, 2016b; Shay 2014). Whereas, historically, this dance genre was largely improvised, when the new, "classical" system was standardized and sponsored and supported by the government, dancers became studio-trained with set choreographic routines. The finest solo dancers, having mastered the art form, often choreographed solos, or large choreographies for ensembles to perform.

Uzbek classical dance is made up of the movements of former professional dancing boys—who are never mentioned as a source in any of the histories (except Doi 2002; Levin 2016) because of the profound homophobia of the Soviets and contemporary Uzbek authorities—along with some folk elements, and ballet and character dance. Following the directives set out in the 1930s in Russia, Ukraine, and other European areas, the state laid out how "folk" dance was to appear in public spaces (Shay 2019). Mary Masayo Doi, in her study of the created nature of this dance tradition, states:

> When the Soviet state put Uzbek dances on the stage, the Soviet State fundamentally changed the nature of the dances. Like raw materials undergoing manufacturing processes, the dances became more elaborate, incorporating Russian ballet and character dance techniques. Once the dances were turned into a finished "product" the Soviet State displayed them to foreigners as tokens of the Uzbek national character. After the close of World War II, "national" dances became aesthetic "commodities" exported from Uzbekistan to Moscow and abroad for the benefit of the Soviet empire.
>
> (2002: 107)

Professional dance genres wherever they are found throughout the Middle East and Central Asia evolve from urban social dance forms and are typically an elaborate version of them, as Najwa Adra describes this phenomenon for belly dancing in the Arab world (2005). Thus, we are not dealing with a folk (*narodny*) dance genre, as Uzbeks often think this is, and use that term. It could only be conceived of a folk form, *narodny*, for the former Soviets and fits that category for the present Uzbek authorities.

The Dancing Boys of Uzbekistan (bacheh, bacha)

While we have many historic and even prehistoric objects and depictions of dance and dancers in the region, created in many media from pictographs to silver vessels and miniatures beginning from the Timurid period, these objects and depictions tell little of historical context, the movements, or the social position of the performers but only that dance existed (Gray 1998: 305). The earliest descriptions we have of dancing, its movements, and its performers are several vivid descriptions of the dancing boys written by European travelers and adventurers who were fascinated by them. We find these descriptions in the memoirs, diaries, and accounts of European travelers, especially from English and Russian upper-class men in the late nineteenth century, who combined adventure with political missions in the region, especially the period of the "Big Game" (ca. 1850–1914). In the best tradition of travel literature that included valuable details, these intrepid men attempted to repress their Victorian prudery regarding the existence of male dancers, and their clearly sexual appeal to the local audiences, but never quite managed.

In Uzbekistan and other parts of urban Central Asia, the powerful Muslim clergy forbade women to dance in public to avoid *fitnah* (social chaos); only boys were permitted to do so. The word *bacheh/bacha* is a nongendered word in Persian (meaning child) and came to also mean male dancers, mainly adolescents, generally orphans or slaves, who were carefully trained in the profession. Much in the manner of deciding that it would be preferable for boys to perform women's roles in Shakespeare, the clergy would have preferred to ban them altogether, but allowing only boys to dance was a choice they made.

One of the best sources and descriptions of the dances comes from Englishman Eugene Schuyler (1885). Having written that women did not dance in public, Schuyler writes of an exception:

> It is not only boys who dance in Central Asia, girls and women do so as well; but their exhibitions are in general confined to the women's court. On one occasion, however Asudullah Bek invited me to see a splendid *tamosha*, or spectacle—a dance of women—a thing looked on with orthodox horror by most Mussulmen [sic]; but Asuddullah Bek, being a Persian and a Shiite, was rather more lax in his notions than the rest, though even he was desirous that the fame of this should not be much noised abroad among his patients ... the dances were very similar to those danced by boys, though less vigorous and less graceful; and there was little variety in style.
>
> (1885: 136–37)

Nevertheless, it was the dancing boys that held audiences enthralled whenever they might perform in public spaces and attracted "vast crowds which they drew together" (Schuyler 1885: 134–35). The viewers paid handsomely to attend. Schuyler describes a performance in rare detail:

> The batcha [sic] begins to throw himself into graceful attitudes, merely keeping time with his feet and hands to the beating of the tambourines and the weird monotonous song of the leader. Soon his movements become wilder, and the spectators all clap their hands in measure; he circles madly about, throwing out his arms, and after turning several summersaults [sis] kneels facing the musicians. After a moment's pause he begins to sing in reply to the leader, playing his arms in graceful movements over his head. Soon he rises, and, with body trembling all over, slowly waltzes about the edge of the carpet, and with still wilder and wilder motions again kneels and bows to us. A thrill and murmur of delight runs through the audience, an extra robe is thrown over him, and a bowl of tea handed to him as he takes his seat. This first dance is called *kaata-uin* (the great play), in contradistinction to the special dances.
>
> (1885: 134)

In Schuyler's colorful prose, we can capture the excitement of the dance, the skill of the dancer, and the reactions of the viewers, and why they would serve as the basis for the new dance genre. He notes that only one dance had two dancers: "I saw for the first time in Karshi, was the Kabuli, a sort of gymnastic game, where two boys armed each with two wands strike them constantly in alternate cadence, while performing complicated figures, twists, and summersaults [sic]" (1885: 135). These stick dances, which can be considered as regional folk dances, are performed throughout Eastern Iran and Afghanistan and require enormous skill, as can be seen on YouTube.

What I will emphasize here is that, in Egypt, the Ottoman Empire, and Iran, both male and female professional dancers were considered sexually available and desirable by their all-male audiences, so boy dancers did not replace female dancers, but coexisted alongside them (Shay 2005, 2008, 2014). The dancers and musicians constituted the lowest social class and they came from sources that were from the most socially powerless elements: slaves, orphans, and religious and ethnic minorities (Shay 2014a). However, since ancient Greece, those who owned the services of public entertainers could turn a "fast buck," as the saying goes. Owning a performer, such as singing slave girls, in medieval Baghdad, was profitable, and all of the accounts note the rapturous reception of their performances by their native audiences in Uzbekistan as well (Shay 2014a).

Because they were so valuable due to their training, they, like their successors to the tradition during the Soviet period, were rigorously trained. Of all of the trades and professions in pre-Soviet Central Asia, that of public entertainers was one of the most tightly organized. Competition was fierce, and to qualify to perform in the highest circles of society required exquisite control of one's craft: the ability to perform gracefully, execute intricate gymnastics, and have charisma. Such star performers commanded the highest fees.

The dancers were often divided by the talents they displayed: Some performed difficult gymnastic and athletic skills, while others, those deemed to have the most sex appeal, usually 12–16 years of age, performed the most sensual dances. Schuyler's account (1888: 132–37) confirms this observation:

> According to Rempel', up to twenty *bachas*—most of them orphans, and around forty musicians (*dâyradast*) were housed in the *ghalibxāna*. These *bachas* not only performed for the emir and his circle but, with permission from the *mirshab*, the chief of the night patrol in the emir's police force, also were loaned out to perform at the toys [festivities] of well-to-do Bukharans. In order to employ musicians or bachas to perform at a *toy*, a host had to have written permission from the head of the *ghalibxāna*, who acted as their booking agent ... The *ghalibxāna* had carts to take musicians and their instruments to toys around the city. Income from the *toys* (which came from money which guests gave to performers who arranged the performance.
>
> (Quoted in Levin 1996: 298 n.13)

I quote from this passage at length to indicate how organized such performances were because, although they were expensive to arrange, they generated considerable amounts of money for the organizers. The public performers, not only dancers but also musicians, actors, and acrobats, belonged to an urban guild called the *mehterlik* (ibid., n.14).

Below is a lengthy description of a performance, after which I will deconstruct aspects of it for the reader.

> The bachehs are young men specially trained to perform a particular set of dances. Barefoot, and dressed like women in long, brightly-coloured silk smocks reaching below their knees and narrow trousers fastened tightly around their ankles, their arms and hands sparkle with rings and bracelets. They wear their hair long, reaching below the shoulders, though the front part of the head is clean shaven [which matches a photograph taken thirty years later (Naumkin 1993: 107)]. The nails of the hands and feet are painted red, the eyebrows are jet black and meet over the bridge of the nose [a mark of beauty at that time]. The dances consist of sensuous contortions of the body and a rhythmical pacing to and fro, with the hands and arms raised in a trembling movement. As the ballet proceeded the number of dancers increased, the circle grew in size, the music waxed shriller and shriller and the eyes of the native onlookers shone with admiration, while the bachehs intoned a piercing melody in time with the ever-growing tempo of the music. The Heir explained that they were chanting of love and the beauty of women. Swifter and swifter moved the dancers till

> they finally sank to the floor, seemingly exhausted and enchanted by love. They were followed by others, but the general theme was usually the same.
>
> In between, we were treated to other types of dances, also accompanied by the orchestra, which were really more like circus turns than anything else. I remember a small boy who was tossed like a ball high into the air by his partners and who never failed to come down on his feet, bowing gracefully to the audience. There were also war dances, with drawn swords glittering in the moonlight. Though I thought the performance very long, my hosts were very excited and seemed to enjoy themselves enormously.
>
> (Pahlen [1875] 1964: 171)

We can see that, according to Pahlen's description, the dancers were divided into their professional dancing abilities. The youngest and oldest performed as acrobats, war dancers, and other roles, while the middle group, as the most sexually attractive, performed the "sensuous" dances. The groups were large, but there is no indication that they performed what would be today termed as choreography, if that concept even existed at that time and place. When the performers danced together, it was in the form of a skit, like quarreling lovers who eventually make up, or a suitor pursuing a beloved.

In discussing the appearance of the dancing boys, various authors, depending upon their acuity in observation, describe the dancers variously as "effeminate," "appearing as women," "dressed as women," etc. While the dancers exhibited a degree of effeminacy to indicate their potential sex role and, thus their attractiveness to their patrons, they always appeared as males because they were attractive as males, not as males dressed as females and, thus, the front of the head was shaved to indicate male identity. All accounts of adolescent boy performers from Japan to Egypt note that, while they utilized certain parts of female garb, hairstyle, makeup, or jewelry, they never hid their male identity. I would rather describe their appearance as ambiguous, with aspects of both male and female dress, hairstyles, makeup, clothing, and so on. It is not unusual to encounter "The dancers looked like women" (Naumkin 1993: 106) and, yet, an accompanying photograph would clearly indicate a male dancer. While a European of the nineteenth century might receive that impression, in fact, their appearance was that of a professional dancer.

Another English observer noted, "Good-looking boys of an effeminate appearance, with long hair streaming down their shoulders, and dressed a little like the women, lounged about, and seemed to have nothing in particular to do" (Burnaby [1876] 1997: 307). Clearly these "good-looking" boys were off-duty dancers; however, he noted that they were boys, not women.

What the description does not indicate, nor can it, is their sexuality; unlike in the West, as orphans they did not choose either their profession or their sex partners. Most of them went on to marry and have children. Frequently, as they aged and were no longer considered attractive for sex, they became teachers of younger dancers or entered the ranks of the musicians.

> The batchas practice their profession from a very early age until sometimes so late as twenty or twenty-five, or at all events until it is impossible to conceal their beards. The life which they have led hardly fits them for independent existence thereafter. So long as they are young and pretty they have their own way in everything; every command is obeyed by their adorers, every purse is at their disposition, and they fall into a life of caprice, extravagance, and dissipation. Rarely do they lay up any money, and more rarely still are they able to profit by it afterwards. Frequently a batcha is set up as a keeper of a teahouse by his admirers, where he will always have a good clientele, and sometimes he is stated as a small merchant. Occasionally one succeeds, and becomes a prosperous man, though the remembrance of his past life will frequently place the then odious affix, batcha, to his name. I have known one or two men, now rich and respected citizens, who began life in this way.
>
> (Schuyler 1885: 135–36)

Dancing boys attracted enormous attention among most townsmen in Central Asia and, paradoxically despite their low social position, were considered very desirable because, as historian Michael Uebel states, "Otherness causes desire" (2003: 231):

> These batchas, or dancing boys, are a recognized institution throughout the whole of the settled portions of Central Asia, though they are most in vogue in Bukhara, and the neighboring Samarkand. Batchas are as much respected as the greatest singers and artistes are with us. Every movement they make is followed and applauded, and I have never seen such breathless interest as they excite, for the whole crowd seems to devour them with their eyes, while their hands beat time to every step … it is as much the custom for a Bokhoriot gentleman to keep one as it was in the Middle Ages for each knight to have his squire. In fact no establishment of a man of rank or position would be complete with one, and men of small means club together to keep one among them to amuse them in their hours of rest and recreation.
>
> (Schuyler 1885: 132)

A decade later, another English traveler, Henry Lansdale, added, "Their appreciation of the batchas was intense. They offered them tea and fruit, and, when the boys sat, they could hardly have been made more of had they been the stars of a London season" (1887 [1978], 304, quoted in Shay 2005: 73).

Having Victorian morals, the Russians when they arrived with a different set of values and mores detested the practice of *bacheh-bāzi*, but for the most part they were in Central Asia to exploit the cotton industry and keep the British out. The colonial Russians did not interfere in native life very often.

The Communists, holding even more prudish views, sought to eradicate the practice, but they were only partially successful: The practice simply went underground. Such disapproval continues into the present. Authorities in Uzbekistan do not wish, any more than the Soviets, to utilize images for purposes of representation that they consider embarrassing.

> Mikhail, a theater director, told me about a stage designer he knew who tried to use the "wrong" heritage when he participated in a fashion festival. His work was based on Oriental themes such as the baccha, the dancing boys who were part of the urban culture of sexual relations between men and boys in prerevolutionary Turkistan. "It is, after all, an authentic part of local historical culture, and there's no denying it was exploited in the past with postcards and the like, before the Soviet period. But the government doesn't want to see bacchas as part of that heritage."
>
> (Adams 2010: 65–66)

"Among sedentary dwellers, female performers have traditionally entertained at women's festivities, and male performers have traditionally entertained at men's festivities" (Levin et al. 2016: 34), a practice that was common in Iran at the same period (Breyley and Fatemi 2016; Fatemi 2005; Shay 2014a). "Performers alive at the end of the twentieth century recounted seeing boy dancers called *bachas* who wore women's dresses and painted their lips and eyebrows. Under Soviet rules, *bachas* were illegal, but while their number diminished their tradition did not end" (Levin et al. 2016: 35). I saw one, more discretely dressed, in Urgench in Uzbekistan, who had been hired to entertain us for an evening. I was especially struck by his ability to play the *charpareh*, a kind of castanet made of metal or stones.

> Other wedding entertainment was provided by a male singer-dancer called *mavrigikhon* (*mavrigi:* from Merv'). Like socially marginalized female entertainers, the typical *mavrigikhon* has belonged to a marginalized social group, in this case, the minority Shi'a population of Bukhara, known as Bukharan Irani or Farsi, who trace their ancestry to slaves captured in Iran by Turkmen and brought via Merv to Bukhara.
>
> (Ibid.)

All of this demonstrates the degree to which public entertainers, from antiquity to the present, have endured ostracism and marginalization for exposing their bodies to the public and carrying the reputation for sexual availability. That was about to change. Moscow had decided in the 1930s that folklore, especially in a spectacularized form, was to characterize and represent each of the constituent republics. The Soviets considered folklore to be innocent and healthy, in contrast to the professional performances of Central Asia.

The Soviets and Uzbek Music

Unlike the Caucasus regions, whose music and dances seemed ready for staging and representational purposes by the Soviet authorities—Armenian and Georgian folk music had provided orientalist musical themes for Russian composers like Tchaikovsky and Borodin for decades—Central Asian music and dance was totally unsuitable for the stage from the Soviet point of view:

> Socialist culture across the Union and Central Asia was simultaneously supposed to be "both national in form and socialist in content," a difficult push-and-pull between old and new, near and far became inevitable, a tug between incompatible places, worldviews, and truths.
>
> (MacFadyen 2006: xiii)

The Soviets were frustrated with the music and dance traditions that they found in Central Asia. First, they hated the Uzbek–Tajik classical music tradition with its microtones, monophony, nontempered maqām intervals, intricate melodic structure, and strained vocal production, which all seemed resistant to Soviet attempts to "civilize" it. Worse, the local population adored it and the musicians resisted the changes that Russian musicians were ready to generously bequeath to them, like tempered scales, bel canto singing styles, and mass orchestral setting. "Under the Soviets, major reorganization was therefore called for in order to make this smallness big" (MacFadyen 2006: 48), embodying my references to spectacle in the Introduction. Based on the belief that if one violin is good, then forty violins must be forty times better, as long as they were playing in the tempered scale, and thus in the 1930s and beyond, the Soviets began to reorganize Central Asian music and dance along Russian lines, especially through spectacularization.

> According to the criticism leveled against them in the Russian press, most Central Asian musicians put up considerable resistance to the innovations brought in via Russia from the West. Such Russian attacks concentrated upon the stubborn preference of Central Asians for traditional music and texts, monophony instead of polyphony and harmony, liking for a throaty manner of singing,

> and microtonal and heterophonic orchestra music ... and accused Uzbeks and others of intentionally avoiding the composition of Western types of operas or performance of Western ballets.
>
> (Spector 1994: 479–80)

It was an avoidance that some Uzbeks, with considerable Russian assistance and pressure, overcame in order to produce some unremarkable operas and ballets to fit in with the Communist Party demands—and to survive. Ethnomusicologist Joanna Spector notes that musicians first gave priority to tuning to achieve a sort of uniformity to meet Russian tastes. "All Central Asian music is now notated in the Western notation of equal temperament" (1994: 483). In the Soviet view Central Asian music was "a carry-over from 'feudal times' " (ibid.) and required drastic attention to bring it in line with Soviet practices.

> Responding to these new dictates, the State Radio Orchestra and the Uzbek Philharmonia both developed active ensembles of Westernized, "reconstructed" folk instruments and by 1948, the Tashkent Conservatory had opened a faculty dedicated to indigenous music. Folk music was no longer to be developed along ethnographic lines but with Western harmonic structures and in more orchestral forms.
>
> (MacFadyen 2006: 49)

Thus, Uzbek music had finally, after a prolonged struggle, arrived to a "civilized" state, ready to represent the Uzbek SSR, as long as they did not perform authentic *shash maqām* music.

Uzbek Classical Dance

As to dance, the Soviets found easier answers. First, from the outset, the Communist Party supported a sexually conservative program for both public and private spaces, and it was the boy dancers to whom they objected. The effeminate dancing boys, and the sexuality that their presence implied, did not fall into their picture of strict heteronormativity. The answer was simpler than the structural requirements that changing musical forms demanded: One needed only to change the sex of the dancers, so that young girls, new, learning their trade, and unable to contest governmental decisions, were the answer.

However, the dancing boys did not totally disappear, as they did not later disappear in Afghanistan when the Soviets, and later the Americans, occupied the country, but went underground. The image they conveyed did not fit into the new

Communist heteronormative image of Central Asia. Soon after the establishment of the Uzbek (and Tajik) Republic, the Bolsheviks came to understand the power of music and dance as a vehicle for expressing state and national power. Music and dance in Uzbekistan were about to undergo a major makeover.

Henceforth, dance was to become largely a female domain. In the beginning, it was a perilous enterprise because, as we saw earlier, Muslims did not find women dancing in public spaces, on a stage, acceptable behavior. A famous story/myth concerns a young woman, Noor Khon, who appeared on the stage with Tamara Khanum in Kari-Yakubov's ensemble, whose brother killed her in 1928 for appearing on the stage as a dancer. Choreophobia was alive and well in Central Asia! (Shay 1999). "This tragedy shows how incendiary public dance performances by women were in the opening decades of the Soviet program ... Her tragic end has become one of the chartering myths of professional dancers" (Doi 2002: 47). Her photo appears in Tamara Khanum's museum as a reminder of how Soviet authorities supported Muslim women in their fight for freedom from religious oppression.

Second, and related to the problem of the image of dancing boys, the Soviets found an exceptional dancer in the person of Tamara Khanum (née Tamara Artyomovna Petrosyan, 1906–91). Tamara Khanum was an Armenian woman who was born in Uzbekistan. She was a largely self-taught performer; not being a Muslim allowed her more freedom than a Muslim woman. Most households allowed the women to watch performances of *bachehs* from spaces created for that purpose when festivities were held in the home, where they were undetectable. Many accounts, and stories that I heard, indicate that women frequently learned how to dance from watching professional dancers, whether they watched from the women's quarters or, later, seeing them in films. Watching professionals became a major method for women to learn new gestures and movements.

Tamara Khanum joined the company of Mukhayiddin Kari-Yakubov, whom she subsequently married. In the beginning she was the only woman in the company, learning dancing and singing from master teachers, all male (Shirokaya 1973: n.pag.). It is entirely possible that her master teachers were formerly bachehs, otherwise, how would they know how to teach eager young female dancers the art of dancing professionally? Most men would have been unable to teach at a professional level. Clearly, Soviet-period publications would not admit that. Isahar Akilov is a name that is mentioned in the genealogy of dance teachers; unless he was a former bacheh, how could he teach this tradition to women?

Importantly, in 1930 in an All-Union art contest in Moscow, and again in 1935, the Kari-Yakubov ensemble traveled to London where Tamara Khanum earned a gold medal in the folk dance competition, earning favorable attention from the Soviet government and for which she was later named as People's Artist of the Uzbek SSR, and then People's Artist of the U.S.S.R. The title of one of her "new" dances, the *Silk Spinner*, indicates that using familiar movements, she was contributing to the creation of what was to become a new genre, Uzbek classical dance. Her biography states, "The young dancer worked tirelessly developing a new dancing style" (Shirokaya 1973: n.pag.). But, participating in the development of a new dance genre, she remained throughout her life a solo dance artist. In addition, as a soloist, she sought to create an international dance repertoire.

I met Tamara Khanum in 1986, when she came to the Intourist Hotel to visit the members of the tour I was leading, exhibiting her impressive charisma, stage presence, and talent in her seventieth year, when she was still vigorous. At that time, she was living in her home, which was already a museum honoring her achievements and artistry. But her arrival at the hotel caused an immense stir among the staff who greeted her like the gracious celebrity that she was.

A second figure, whom I met in 1976 and who added the other aspect sought by the Soviet authorities, mass choreography, was Mukarram Turghunbaeva, who founded the Bahor State Academic Ensemble of Uzbekistan for which she created numerous choreographies that are still performed today. Together with other dancers, she created a new form consisting of the movements and figures of dancing boys, ballet, and character dance, the same mixture that Igor Moiseyev used in creating his new Russian folk dance genre. One can see his influence in her choreographies (Karimova 1979; Shay 2019), but her imprint on the creation of the new dance genre is probably larger. "By the end of the Soviet period, Mukarram Turghunbayeva had become a heroic pioneer. Her biographer praised her for founding Uzbek dance" (Doi 2002: 65).

Roziya Karimova is the third figure in the creation of Uzbek classical dance and, aside from teaching, her contribution to the new genre was the codification project, which she began after World War II (Karimova 1973, 1975, 1977, 1979). Her own training, in addition to learning to play the *doira* (frame drum), included learning to dance, "using 117 movements (*harakat*)" (Doi 2002: 50). Her books, like that of Tkachenko (1954), serve as the syllabus for formal training that each dancer now receives at the *koregrafskii instutut*, now known by its Uzbek term *maktab*. All three of these dancers appeared with the Kari-Yakubov ensemble prior to World War II. That this dance genre is an invented tradition is further emphasized by Doi's observation that "the names of the steps were a recent invention: Karimova named many of the movement motifs when she documented the different regional styles and designated a systematic syllabus" (2002: 104). In this way, Karimova created a "classical" named movement vocabulary that paralleled the named vocabulary of classical ballet.

As they developed this new dance genre, these pioneering figures created three distinct styles to represent the three major oases in Uzbekistan: Ferghana, Bukhara, and Khorazmia. To what degree these styles were actually invented traditions is unknown, although the last—Khorazmian—is the closest style to the regional folk dance from that region that is performed by men and women, young and old, and with extraordinary vigor. The Ferghana style, which appeared similar to the dances that I encountered in Samarqand, exhibited a great deal of lyricism and was the closest to the Iranian solo improvised dance, an invented tradition of *raqs-e melli* (national dance) with which I was most familiar. The Bukharan style required enormous physical strength and was the closest to the bacheh/dancing boy style of dancing for which that region was famous (see above). Doi notes in her experience, "Bukharan dance could also be the most overtly seductive, a quality I found disconcerting" (2002: 52).

Mary Masayo Doi notes,

> Films I saw from the 1940s used a wider variety of motifs, suggesting that innovation declined as the Uzbek dance canon evolved ... Over time each style seems to have become simplified into a stereotype of regional identity. Homogenization occurred more *within* a regional style, rather than across styles.
>
> (2002: 105, emphasis in the original)

Doi adds, "I concluded that Uzbek dance during the early Soviet years reflected the construction of an Uzbek national identity from the three historically important and diverse areas" (2002: 52).

Ballet provided an element of this dance genre that is often overlooked or ignored, but it is a crucial element, and all dancers in training must spend hours in ballet class. Doi notes,

> Some dancers criticized balletic steps as inauthentic. On the other hand, one teacher who had studied in Moscow explained that ballet had been beneficial for Uzbek dance because it led to the development of Uzbek dance technique. The similarities between ballet and professional Uzbek dance techniques are marked ... The structure of the class and many of the exercises were the same as a ballet class.
>
> (2002: 102)

I noticed this in Moiseyev rehearsals as well (personal observation, May 28–June 1, 2016, Shay 2019). Like other styles of dance that I note in this study, such as the Spanish "folk" dances influenced by ballet and *escuela bolera*, or *raqs-e melli* (national dance) in Iran, as well as the invented tradition of Russian folk dance created by Igor Moiseyev (Shay 2019), ballet, with its reputation as a refined and esteemed court dance genre, with its system of training and named vocabulary, became an irresistible element in many government-supported ethno identity dance genres.

Uzbek classical dance is clearly an evolving genre: "When I left in 1994, people had begun adding the Qashqa Daryo and Samarkand provinces to the list of major dance styles" (Doi 2002: 138). These styles become important in political ethnic identity strategies: "Anya Peterson Royce argues that 'style'—clothing, music, dance, literature—can be a 'strategy of ethnicity.' Uzbek national dance companies were one social domain in which music, songs, costumes, and regional themes appeared freely" (Doi 2002: 133). Thus, one can posit that the creation of three national dance styles, from principal oasis centers, symbolically "united" different Uzbek regions and identities, most prominently that of Tajik and Uzbek.

In all three of my visits, I went to the school, which resembles a high school for the performing arts specializing in dance, and I made films of the classes, which I studied for hours. The students at these times (twice in late spring, once in fall) were preparing for their graduation. The best of them would be placed in ensembles in the capital Tashkent, such as Bahor, an all-female dance company, and Shadlik, which featured both male and female dancers. While the female students received a full five-year course of learning the full scope of the dance genre, male students were restricted to a movement vocabulary designed to distance them from the unspoken shame of the *bacheh* and which consisted of a great deal of arm flailing, foot-stamping and posing heroically to contrast to the female dancers (Shay 2008d). At that time, during the Soviet period, the Russian children were placed in an eight-year classical ballet program, while the native children were placed in the five-year Uzbek classical dance course.

In contrast to the example of music, in which the Soviet authorities and Russian musicians kept a running series of skirmishes with old musicians entrenched in their tradition, in dance the Soviet authorities, declining to use dancing boys, found a new cadre of young women, mostly orphans or of socially questionable backgrounds, eager to seize an opportunity to create new lives in an art form that could bring them fame and fortune. As Doi writes, "Dance became a means of upward mobility and financial independence for women who danced during the Soviet period" (2002: 113). I was told that most of the women who eventually married were forced by their husbands to cease dancing for the honor of the family.

In the Soviet period at the height of the Cold War, Bahor, especially, frequently traveled to developing countries in the Islamic world. Bahor was especially useful in Soviet diplomacy to announce that, whereas America was plagued with racism as witnessed by lynchings and Jim Crow laws, by contrast, the Soviet Union was supportive of its Muslim minority nationalities. The Soviets wanted to send a message that, whereas Islam oppressed women, the female dancers in Bahor were emancipated, and the Soviet state supported activities like dance to free Muslim women from their oppression. The Noor Khon story certainly underpinned that message.

In short, during the Soviet period Uzbek classical dance performances formed a suitable vehicle for diplomatic missions, especially to Muslim nations. Like all Soviet dance ensembles, companies like Bahor provided spectacle, an idealized vision of a society that was filled with young, athletic, healthy people, that is, we, too, are a youthful, athletic, and morally strong people. Domestically, the company provided a vision of the emancipated Muslim woman and cemented the newly established notion of a new Uzbek identity, while the regional styles in the repertoire reminded the audiences that there is Uzbek unity in ethnic and regional diversity.

After the Fall

When, in 1991, Uzbekistan became an independent state, two things occurred: the wages of dancers (and practically everyone else) dropped considerably, forcing them to moonlight (Doi 2002; Gray 1998) and the meaning of public performances of Uzbek classical dances changed. I will briefly address both of these issues.

Laurel Victoria Gray, a long-time observer of the Uzbek dance scene, notes that

> economic reforms have forced many companies to reduce their size and some professional dancers and musicians to seek employment outside the arts. Small, privately sponsored dance groups have sprung up to entertain tourists, foreign business people, and night club audiences. Traditional Uzbek dance has become more commercial in nature, abandoning many of the older dances in favor of lively numbers performed to ethno-pop-style music.
>
> (1998, volume 6: 307; see also Doi 2002)

This reaction occurred in several of the former communist states, that is, if the state-supported dance ensembles were too closely connected to an unpopular regime, people sometimes turned their backs on them (see, for example, Nielsen 2008). In other cases, especially when ensembles made strategic changes to make themselves relevant to people's needs as old political entities collapsed, and new ones assumed power, their popularity increased, as was the case for Lado in Croatia (Shay 2016c).

The new, independent Uzbek state has new political priorities, and the state-supported dance ensembles which perform Uzbek classical dance, serve those needs. They currently appear most often in the new Independence Day celebrations, as well as the newly revived nav ruz (now ruz), which celebrate a glorious Uzbek past. They have a new role:

> In independent Uzbekistan, the dancers' status as perennial "girls" and their seemingly timeless quality facilitated yet another role: icons of history. Reviving and reimagining Central Asian history was an important aspect of building a post-Soviet national identity ... With the fall of the Soviet Union, however, Uzbek national dance was a ready-made storehouse filled with a wealth of Central Asian music, costumes, verse, and dance.
>
> (Doi 2002: 137, 138; see also Meftahi 2016b for a similar use of young female dancers in Iran)

There seemed no problem for the state to assign new meaning to these dance companies from the Soviet era.

Doi noted that, in 1994 when she was studying Uzbek dance and conducting research, the need for dancers was greater than ever, and the entire class of the state *maktab* (*koreografskii institut*) was instantly hired by the top dance ensembles in the country. The marriage of this dance tradition and the state appears to be a fruitful union, as seen by the centrality of Uzbek classical dance in the nav ruz celebrations.[8]

NOTES

1. In one surreal scene in 1986, the Committee for Friendship and Cultural Relations with Foreign Countries (a fixture of every Communist government) held a ceremony in their reception rooms and made me an honorary Uzbek. The next day, May 1, for the annual May Day parade, I found myself standing on the reviewing stand, in freezing weather, dressed in my honorary robe (*chapan*) and traditional hat (*döppi*) on the main square in Tashkent between the president and the first general of the Uzbek SSR, both dour and dressed in warmer clothing than I was wearing, to review the parade. I think the event qualified as my fifteen minutes of fame, for individuals pointed to me in public spaces for the next two days because they had seen me on Uzbek national television. The parade itself was charmingly tacky and not at all the frightening military spectacle I expected. It featured happy workers from the local ladies underwear factory and equally engaging and whimsical floats from other industrial organizations.
2. It is important to note that Mary Masayo Doi's excellent study (2002) of Uzbek dance comes to somewhat different, as well as many similar, findings and conclusions as mine because our lenses were different. Doi was in Uzbekistan to learn a dance tradition new to her, which she spent several months in class, without making links to other dance traditions, or even

any deep investigation of the original dance style of professional boy dancers. Rather, she learned and absorbed the contemporary professional dance tradition that is currently performed only by women. I was there to make the connection between the dance traditions of Uzbek and Iranian dance because I viewed the dance tradition as variants of a single dance tradition through movement, literary, linguistic, and historic lenses.

3. I saw the performance of a dancing boy in the city of Urgench (as well as one in Afghanistan in 1976) during our 1986 trip. He was part of a small, local troupe that included musicians, a female dancer, and vocalist. He employed the same movements as female dancers and had a much wider, more athletic range of movements than they or the young men trained in the Koreografski Institut in Tashkent. He did not wear female garments.
4. One can see the various *nav ruz* (Persian New Year) celebrations in Tashkent on YouTube, listed by year. In all of them dance and music constitute a constant presence, the performances oriented directly to the Uzbek president, Shavkat Mirzaev, who sits in the front center of the festive setting, smiling, beaming, and nodding in the most avuncular fashion to all of his subjects. The 2019 celebration held at Homa Arena in Tashkent was perhaps the most spectacular to date, with a cast of thousands, including over one hundred professionally trained Uzbek classical dancers performing a score of elaborate choreographies in an ever-changing array of elaborate costumes. During the two-hour performance, professional dancers dominated the stage, replacing the many amateur performers of earlier years. The constant references to "Uzbekistan" marry the new post-Soviet Republic to the old custom of nav ruz. Anthropologist David Guss notes: "The extensive use of festivals by Hitler and his National Socialists combined folkloric exhumation with new patriotic holidays" (2000: 13). Guss could have inserted Karimov or Mirzaev in place of Hitler. In the celebration of nav ruz, one can see Turkic and Iranian identities.
5. This is a point that historian Adeeb Khalid vigorously opposes.

   > Few episodes in Central Asian history have been more prone to mythmaking than the so-called national-territorial delimitation of 1924 that led to the creation of ethno-territorial republics in place of the old entities of Turkestan, Bukhara, and Khiva. It is all too easy to see the process as a classic case of divide and conquer. Indeed, this judgment remains unshakably in place in Western accounts of the region and has proved immune to current historiography in Central Asia itself. (2015: 13)

   He adds, "No account of delimitation, however, has paid adequate attention to the role of Central Asia's indigenous elites in the process or place the delimitation in context of the rise of national movements in the region" (ibid.: 14).
6. By contrast, in the Baltic Republics, the Soviet Union did not alter borders to mix the Baltic populations but rather encouraged Russians and other Slavs to settle in the three republics to dilute the populations.

7. While leading a tour in the Soviet Union in 1986 in the City of Samarqand, I heard, in Persian, of a concert of music and dance of the five Central Asian republics. Gathering several tour members, we attended the concert (making our Russian guide very unhappy), in which the group from Tajikistan not only appeared but sang a most seditious song demanding that Samarqand, "our blood," be returned to us (May 4, 1986).
8. As a dance historian, one should never be surprised when a dance enthusiast expressers her- or himself in an exuberant manner toward a particular dance genre, but alas, sometimes one encounters such an entry in Wikipedia, which is why one warns students to avoid its use in researching academic subjects. Under the topic heading "Dance in Uzbekistan," I encountered such a startling entry, unsupported by references. So for purposes of this chapter, I need to unpack and address each point, in case my students find it.

   Uzbekistan dance consists of between fifteen and twenty thousand movements by a performer, depending on the complexity of the dance. An Uzbek dance portrays a story told by the flowing movements and rhythms. The lithe and expressive hands of a dancer raise and then interweave like two twigs of an almond tree, then one hand is above the head and the other is making swift movements around the body. A medieval poet wrote: "A dancing women! She is swiftly dancing, spinning like snow carried away by a whirlwind. Restless, she is spinning to the left and to the right" There are three schools of dance in Uzbekistan: Khorezm, Fergana, and Bukhara. Each one has its peculiarities and specific features.

   The anonymous author here refers to one type of dance, an invented tradition that is of great interest to the many points that I make in this volume. To address some of the more egregious assertions that the author posits to make the dance appear more interesting: First, no dance genre contains fifteen to twenty thousand movements, and certainly not this one. Second, Uzbek dance does not tell stories, like all dance in the Middle East and Central Asia, Uzbek classical dance is an abstract art. Unlike Balinese, Javanese, and Indian classical forms, Uzbek dance does not tell a story. Except in feverish imaginations, the "lithe hands" do not create "almond twigs." I am unfamiliar with this poet, or which language he wrote in. Persian and Turkish do not have gender, so unless the poet actually uses the word "woman" we cannot know if the dancer is male or female. As the well-known Persian literature scholar Ehsan Yar-Shater notes, "As a rule the beloved is not a woman, but a young man" (quoted in Shay 2015: 61).
9. The three dance styles (not schools)—Ferghana, Bukhara, Khorazmia—were artificially created at the same time as the dance to indicate the three principal regions of the newly founded Uzbek Republic.

Conclusion

One of the most valuable aspects of dance as a form of nonverbal human behavior is to serve as a lens for scholars to observe, describe, and analyze that behavior. I believe so much in the idea of dance as an invaluable lens and perspective as an analytic tool that part of my scholarly career has been invested, through writings and lectures, in sharing the idea of using dance and other forms of choreographed mass activities as an additional lens in their research of analyzing human behavior, whether it is at the level of social and class behavior, gender roles and issues of sexuality, or representational fields of ethnicity and nationalism.

In this volume I argue that dance and mass choreographed movement is a particularly valuable lens for analyzing political behavior, especially as it is found in various forms of authoritarian regimes. The reason I argue that dance can be an effective tool in political contexts is that the dance performances utilized in authoritarian regimes are among the most public and they are created to be public in order to be of use to the various regimes that sponsor them to symbolically convey national and regime ideals. Dance can convey messages that language cannot. The Igor Moiseyev Dance Company under the regime of the former Soviet Union, in the most diplomatic fashion, sent the choreographed message that the Soviet Union was a place of youth, ethnic harmony, prosperity, and mass power. In 1958, when areas of the United States had Jim Crow laws and racial segregation were the reality, this message was widely received, not only in the United States during its first tour but also worldwide, for example, in Brussels at the 1958 World's Fair. So effective was the appearance of the Igor Moiseyev Dance Company there and at the numerous quadrennial World Youth Festivals that preceded and succeeded it that countries like Egypt, Iran, the Philippines, Ghana, and Mexico established dance companies in emulation throughout the 1950s (Shay 2019). As another example, the message sent by the Chinese government at the opening ceremonies of the 2008 Beijing Olympic Games, in probably one of the most spectacular mass events in human history, as I received it, was: the twentieth century may have been the American century, but the twenty-first will be the Chinese century—only China has the manpower, economic will, youthful masses, and intellectual capacity to produce a spectacle on this level. Government-supported Chinese dance productions continue to fortify this message (NBC 2008; Wilcox 2019).

Using this lens, scholars have recently begun to give attention to dance as a form of activity that is, and historically has been, a vehicle for conveying messages from various political regimes. Perhaps one of the most famous examples of dance serving an authoritarian regime is that of Louis XIV, who starred in court ballets and spectacles that gave the message to the viewer that he was the absolute center of the universe, that all power was vested in him, and that all good flowed from him. It was a symbolic message that the viewers of these court ballets unambiguously received. These court ballets were expensive and time consuming to produce but, although dance activities took up a great deal of the royal expenditure of the French courts, they continued from Early Modern France until the elaborate productions of Louis XIV (Cowart 2008; Nevile 2008).

In an earlier study (2002), I noted how a wide variety of political regimes utilized folk, traditional, and vernacular dance genres, altered in the form of ethno identity dance for the stage, as vehicles of propaganda and diplomacy. In general, as in the case of the Igor Moiseyev Dance Company (The Igor Moiseyev Ballet), these state-supported ensembles achieved great artistic, diplomatic, and financial success. Following the achievements of the Moiseyev, the Soviet government understood the value and political impact the performances of such ensembles had and directed each of the constituent Soviet Republics to establish a similar dance group (Shay 2019). Soon after World War II, as the Soviet grip on Eastern Europe tightened, and as Communist governments formed there, a national dance company, or in some cases more than one, also became an integral part of that reorganization. Thus, some of the better-known ensembles, like the Hungarian State Folk Ensemble, the Filip Koutev Ensemble of Bulgaria, and Mazowsze of Poland, were established. Like the Moiseyev Dance Company, these ensembles began to travel and tour internationally and perform on special national holidays domestically.

I saw and wrote about the political implications of the performances of these state-supported companies, which I had been surprised to find at the time I wrote the book had been little studied by dance scholars, and thus, those performances and the ensembles who performed them went largely unanalyzed. Given the fact that their performances largely dominated concert stages throughout the world for much of the second half of the twentieth century, their performances required analysis on a number of levels (Shay 2002). I also noted the influences that such companies as the Ballet Folklórico de México and the Dora Stratou Greek Dances Theatre had on diaspora populations in the United States. Appearances of the Ballet Folklórico de México were life-changing for thousands of Mexican

Americans who had never witnessed Mexican dance and culture on the level that Ballet Folklórico presented it (Shay 2002).

All of these state-supported national folk dance ensembles served the state in that they embodied ethnic and national identities with a mass of dancers in colorful ethnic and national costumes, which many nation-states politically emphasize in their quest for public support. This is particularly true for authoritarian states, most of which purport to support and protect ethnic and national identities, above all other political issues. Franjo Tuđman's support and emphasis of Croatian identity, like Adolf Hitler's nationalist socialism and its constant manifestations of German identity, the *Volk*, serves as an example of how music and dance embody, in nonverbal fashion, the ethnic and national political priorities of those regimes. Dance played a visible role in those regimes' political agendas. Lado, the State Ensemble of Folk Dances and Songs of Croatia, in its most recent publicity literature, bills itself as "The Light of Croatian Culture" (Lado 2019).

Many of these ensembles also provide considerable tourist revenues and other financial benefits for the state. It is the rare tourist in Mexico City who does not attend a concert of Ballet Folklórico in the old Baroque Fine Arts Theatre. *Riverdance*, with its ancient Celtic references, while not an official state folk dance company of the Irish government, provided a significant portion of the Irish government's revenue during the economic boom of the 1990s.

In my first study of national dance companies (2002), I focused on the dance companies and details of the artistic production—music, costume, choreography, training of dancers—but gave little attention to the regimes that brought them into being and supported them financially. In this study, I have given greater emphasis to the political regimes that support these dance ensembles, especially in the role the dance genre or specific ensemble plays in ethnic and national priorities of a specific regime. In order to better understand the role that ethnicity and nationalism visually play in those political and choreographic agendas, I pay particular attention to the ethnogenesis of each case. In many cases, large portions of viewers, both foreign and domestic, view the dances and costumes as the folk patrimony of the nation-state that stretches back in time to the beginnings of the ethnic group or nation that the dance performance represents.

Ethnogenesis, real and imagined, which I described in detail, plays a role in how the nation is choreographically represented. The case of Iran is illustrative of a nation-state with a long history of nation formation, which features prominently in the historically inspired choreographies and performances of the former state-supported dance companies. By contrast, the formation of Uzbek identity took place in the twentieth century on a territory where it has replaced various historic Iranian and Turkic identities. Their dance companies perform a new genre of dance that is ahistorical in choreography, movement, and costuming, that seem to vaguely refer to medieval Persian miniatures dating from the Timurid period, when the city of Samarqand served as the dynasty's capital city. The Uzbek case supports my notion of how malleable and contingent ethnic and identities can be, and dance has a part in the construction of those identities.

As I delved more deeply into the study of these dance ensembles, in which I had focused on their artistic, ethnic, and nationalistic implications, as well as the political impact they had, I realized two important points, which I have focused on in this study. Most of those ensembles had been established under authoritarian regimes and, even when the regime changed to a democratic regime, as in Croatia, or became another authoritarian state, as occurred in Uzbekistan, the state support for these ensembles continued because of the political and symbolic value they had for their regimes, as well as the viewers of their performances.

First, I realized from my own experience as a director of a large dance company (without state backing) that I had modeled on them, I found that state-supported professional folk dance ensembles are extremely expensive to establish and maintain. Aside from the salaries and benefits of the performers and staff, a place for rehearsals and administrative activities had to be found and maintained; costumes, jewelry, and props must be purchased or made and stored; choreographies created and music arranged; dancers and musicians must rehearse, tours arranged, publicity created, budgets and accounting established. All of this requires a huge financial outlay. Who will finance these activities? Who will approve the financial outlay of this funding?

As I looked from the point of view of a director of such an ensemble, I saw that, for the most part, democratic governments were simply too cumbersome, with too many bureaucratic and political layers to negotiate, to begin such an enterprise. Elsewhere, I have written about why the United States does not have or support a national folk dance ensemble (Shay 2013). Every politician, and his or her constituents, would want a say in what the repertoire contained, who would direct it, what the costumes would look like, and, above all, who would and would not be represented, and in what manner would they be represented.

I realized that almost all of these major dance ensembles were established in political systems in which one man, or a man or woman within his orbit, could, with a wave of his or her hand, remove all of the bureaucratic nightmares and miasma of decision-making processes that would impede such an expensive undertaking. In short, only an authoritarian figure, for example, Josef Stalin, Josip Broz Tito, Francisco Franco, the Shah of Iran, or someone near them, had the power to create these spectacular, state-supported dance companies. Once established and successful, like the Moiseyev Dance Company or Lado, the State Ensemble of Folk Dances and Songs of Croatia, future governments of whatever political stripe almost always see the symbolic national and cultural value of their performances, their use as a political and diplomatic vehicle, and as a source of tourist income, and they continue to include them in their budgets.

Second, these ensembles often served states that veered from democratic to authoritarian, as was the case in Turkey, or as in the case of Croatia, from authoritarian to democratic and back again. Such changes in political circumstances can have profound impacts on the contexts in which the companies appear, the contents of their repertoire, and the ways in which they serve the nation-state that supports and sponsors them. In the case of Croatia, for example, after the war for independence, all non-Croatian repertoire from their former all-Yugoslav programs was dropped, and the costumes put in mothballs. Or by contrast and more rarely, if a government no longer found the national dance company suitable as a field of representation, they abruptly terminated them, as was the case in Iran after the collapse of the Pahlavi regime in 1979 (Meftahi 2016a).

The histories, national political events, and artistic trajectories of these ensembles, to a large degree, show parallel levels of artistic development and professional maturation that led to their ultimate success. For example, the beginnings of each company can prove difficult and requires patience to develop into a full-fledged professional dance company. For example, it takes time and grueling rehearsal hours to create the professional patina the state wants for purposes of representation. Igor Moiseyev ruefully described his first performances and bemoaned the raw enthusiasm but lack of professional veneer that his dancers had and that he desired in the first performances of the Moiseyev Dance Company that can only, like fine wine, come with time (Moiseyev 1996).

As I went through the Lado archives, I could tell from the earliest photographs, with depictions of unsmiling faces and stiff body postures, that they had gone through the same amateur-to-professional experience that I had in the beginnings of the Aman Folk Ensemble (Shay 2016c). It simply takes multiple performances and rehearsals before the members gel and form into a real ensemble ready to perform at a professional level.

Another excellent example of the maturation of a company is provided by the award-winning Polish feature film *Cold War* (2018) directed by Pawel Pawlikowski, which opens with, and later shows, scenes of the founding of Mazowsze, the State Folk Dance and Song Ensemble of Poland (1948), as a back story to the main love-story plot. In the beginning, in a run-down country villa, the ensemble's center, they show the first arrival and tryouts for members of the new company, emphasizing how raw they were, with many peasants having to audition to enter the new, as yet unnamed, state dance company. Later, one of the Party officials wants the company to sing an ode to Stalin, to the disgust of the artistic directors. In the next scene, the ensemble is gathered on a stage singing, as a huge photo of the Soviet dictator lowers behind the company, dwarfing it.

Predictably, one of the Polish officials in a reception following the performance, loftily tells the company directors that the performance was good, "for folk dance." Folk dance and music are clearly beneath the dignity of the elite urban official but he can, nevertheless, see the political value of the performances. To back up my suspicion that the film depicted the founding moments, and a few scenes while the company was on tour in Croatia, and in concert back in Poland, the ending credits reveal that Mazowsze, the Polish State Dance Ensemble, had supplied most of the singing and dancing scenes. The film, for the discerning eye, provides a behind-the-scenes glimpse of the birth pains of founding and developing such an ensemble.

Earlier, I completed a study of Igor Moiseyev Dance Company, in which I follow this trajectory and follow the growth and success of the ensemble and also demonstrate the political role that the company played, especially its spectacular appearances in the United States as the first Soviet participant in the Cultural Cold War (2019). For this study, I chose five lesser-known examples of the use of dance, but not always in the state dance ensemble form, across a variety of authoritarian regimes and nations and across different dance genres. I wanted to trace five lesser-known examples of how dance fulfilled political objectives to underscore the main points that I make in this study. In every case, the government and dictator that used the advantage of dance performances fell under the category of an authoritarian regime. For this reason, while referring to the well-known examples of the Igor Moiseyev Dance Company, and the use of folk dance in the Nuremburg rallies under Adolf Hitler, I turned to the lesser-known examples provided by Iran, Croatia, Spain, the Dominican Republic, and Uzbekistan. The dictators of the Dominican Republic and Spain, Trujillo and Franco, respectively, did not have the Moiseyev Dance Company as a model and created new vehicles in which dance reflected well on their regimes. As yet, the Moiseyev model was unknown in the West. Today, after Trujillo, the Dominican Republic boasts a national dance ensemble.

Authoritarian Regimes

As I began to write this study, one of the first issues that I faced was that there is a large spectrum of regimes that one can identify as authoritarian, and I felt a need to break them down into smaller subtypes. Of the two subtypes that I identified, the first was provided by a study by political science scholars Steven Levitsky and Lucan A. Way, identifying a type of authoritarian government that they called competitive regimes (2010). These regimes pretend to observe the hallmarks of democratic regimes in the form of holding "open elections," having multiple political parties, and permitting a free press to operate. Of course, they do not permit any such thing, or perhaps, they have a state media, to which rival candidates are not given access. The Russian Federation is a good example of a competitive regime. And, these governments can and do rely on violence. It is a ready weapon and part of the repertoire of political tools. Putin has no problem ordering his thugs to beat up or kill opponents who might provide serious competition to his rule. I recall watching Recep Tayyip Erdoğan's "security forces" beat up Turkish and American protesters in Washington D.C., who objected to his increasingly authoritarian behavior and Turkish suppression of Kurds, on CNN on May 16, 2017, as Erdoğan was shown looking on.

Under competitive regimes, the playing field in the election process is not even: The press is not available to the opposition, elections are rigged, voters for the opposition are threatened, and opposition candidates are intimidated. However, occasionally, as in the case of Croatia in 2000, when Stjepan Mesić won an election following Tuđman's authoritarian regime and untimely death, his victory came as a surprise. Mesić launched a new, democratic era in Croatian history that continues today.

Scholars Houchang E. Chehabi and Juan Linz provide the second example, in which they describe and analyze a type of authoritarian regime they identify as "sultanistic" (1998). I found sultanistic regimes were the ones that could most effectively use dance and music as a political weapon, as was the case in Stalin's Soviet Union. The term describes the unfettered rule of individuals like Kim Jong-un of North Korea, who permits no free press or free elections, has one political party, makes no pretense of any competition, and spends his nation's treasure on anything he wants, like a sultan clapping his hands to order what he wishes. North Korea sponsors many mass choreographed dance and movement events glorifying its "dear leader" (Lim 2015).

The government of Leónidas Trujillo of the Dominican Republic epitomized a sultanistic regime: The government treasury served as his wallet. He had gigantic statues of himself erected, and named many towns and cities after himself. The danger of such regimes is clear: They are whimsical and capricious and decisions, including those of life and death, depend on the minute-to-minute state of mind of the ruler. Persian literature is full of examples of the whims and caprices of sultans (see, e.g., Sa'adi *Bustan* or the *Rubbaiyyat* of Omar Khayyam).

Some of these sultanistic regimes were hybrids like that of Iran. They had the trappings of a competitive regime, like having two political parties, both of which the Shah established, and a "free" press, but his regime operated like a sultanistic regime, especially with the presence of a particularly vicious and thuggish security service, SAVAK, and, therefore, constituted a type of hybrid regime, but with mostly sultanistic features. A characteristic of sultanistic regimes is glorification of the ruler, with pictures on stamps, money, and in every office, bank, and shop, while towns, cities, and streets are named after the ruler or his predecessor, as was the case in Iran where, for example, the port of Enzeli became Bandar-e Pahlavi. The Shah crowned himself and the Empress Farah, in his expensive, over-the-top investiture ceremony, and a few years later celebrated 2,500 years of monarchical rule in an ill-judged, Las Vegas-style ceremony, held in the middle of the desert, the cost of which was staggering. The National Dance Companies participated, as well as a historical parade of participants wearing military garb from a variety of glorious Iranian empires performing choreographed movements in front of a panoply of world leaders, reminding the assemblage of Iran's long and glorious history, of which the Pahlavis were the apex.

These are the two types of regimes that can indulge in the financial support of special dance genres, state-supported professional dance ensembles, and other mass choreographed spectacles, like that of the opening of the 2008 Beijing Olympic Games. They serve to remind viewers of the importance of the regimes and the ethnic and national groups that they represent. Choreographed dance and mass movements symbolically suggest mass support.

The Case Studies

Among the examples that I analyze and describe in this study, Trujillo, a truly sultanistic thug, sexual predator, and murderer, turned to merengue, a combination of folk dance and vernacular dance genre, that later became a popular international social dance form that reflected the class, racial and ethnic, regional tensions found in the Dominican Republic during his 30-year rule. Trujillo exploited the music and dance of merengue for his political uses as he elevated it to a national symbol, a role it still occupies. He carried a dance band to play the iconic music, wherever he appeared at political and mass rallies and, in the process, won the hearts of the peasant population whom, as he danced for their enjoyment, he swindled and defrauded on every level.

Francisco Franco turned the project of supporting dance over to Pilar Primo de Rivera, a political figure in her own right through her deceased brother who was one of Franco's early associates in the fascist Falange movement. With Franco's blessing and financial support, she created the feminine image of Spanish folk dance that was to choreographically represent Spain through the Franco era, the *coros y danzas*. She chose the model of the festival, found in fascist states like Hitler's Germany and Metaxas's Greece, and combined dancers, singers, and musicians from a number of regions, each allowed to only perform the folklore of their specific region, into a touring ensemble that permitted the Spanish government, diplomatically a pariah state, to once again return to the company of respectable nations (Loutzaki 2008; Von Bibra 2001). However, she turned dance into women's work by using unmarried girls as the featured performers. The girls who formed the core of the *coros y danzas* movement of Spanish folk dance represented Spanish Catholic purity. The charm and winsomeness of Spanish girls performing regional folk dances proved a far stronger force than the Spanish military. Their tours opened diplomatic doors that had been closed to what had been a pariah regime due to its murderous fascist policies and actions, and its illegal takeover from the democratically elected Spanish Republic.

My three other examples—Iran, Croatia, and Uzbekistan—came in the post-Moiseyev era. The dictators of these three states, or others whom they appointed to manage cultural activities, established state folk dance ensembles in the mode of Igor Moiseyev. In Iran, throughout the latter part of the Pahlavi regime, the Empress Farah and the Shah's brother-in-law, Mehrdad Pahlbod, were both deeply engaged in the cultural activities of the state. They directed and financially supported the establishment of the two Iranian state-sponsored dance companies that were established in emulation of the success of the Moiseyev model and saw to their continuing financial support.

Unfortunately, the ensembles never had the opportunity to mature into professional-level performance groups that one associates with Soviet-era Eastern European dance ensembles, due to the short period of their existence. They performed for important state events and toured internationally (Ahmadzadeh 2008; De Warren 2009). Their repertoires featured choreographies that glorified historical Iranian monarchies, and symbolically the Pahlavi dynasty and ideal of royal figures as political leaders, and even the petroleum industry that brought Iran economic prosperity. Immediately following the Revolution of 1979–80, one of the first acts of the Islamic regime was to ban all dance activity and close down all professional dance companies, which dispersed many of its performers and directors into the diaspora (Kiann 2016; Meftahi 2016a, Stellar 2011).

At various times in different parts of the politically fractured Croatian territories, different types of presentational dance represented important political fields, beginning in the late medieval period (Sremac 2001; Shay 2016c). After World War II, following in the steps of the Soviet Union, Josip Broz Tito oversaw the establishment of several professional dance ensembles, in emulation of the Moiseyev model. Zvonimir Ljevaković, the founding director of Lado, the State Ensemble of Folk Dances and Songs of Croatia, resisted and rejected the Moiseyev model, creating an ensemble that would truly reflect the best of Croatian peasant art through the use of nuanced choreographies using authentic elements of dance movement, music, and costume found in their original village contexts.

In my last example, Uzbekistan, the governments and regimes have always been authoritarian. In fact, Uzbekistan as a nation, a political entity, or even a name did not exist before the twentieth century. Uzbekistan was a name and country that came together from former political units—portions of the emirates of Bukhara and Khiva, the short-lived Turkistan, the Russian Colonial governments—and as the historical end of earlier empires, and dynasties, the Sasanid, Samanid, Timurids, and others. Thus, Uzbekistan as a name and the territory it occupies today only appeared in 1929, when the final borders were drawn, alongside several other Central Asian territories, as a constituent republic of the former Soviet Union. Today, that nation-state and the majority of its population have come to accept their new identity as Uzbeks. Uzbekistan today is a political reality, and Uzbeks now constitute an ethnic group.

As part of the nation-building process, overseen largely from Moscow, the establishment of state-supported dance companies became integral to that process. And, like the Uzbek language and Uzbek identity, individuals like Tamara Khanom, Rozia Karimova, and Mukarram Turghunbaeva, following the example of Igor Moiseyev, created a wholly new ethno identity tradition made up from elements of classical ballet, domestic solo improvised dance, the professional dance tradition of former boy dancers, and folk dance. This new genre acquired a classical form, with three crucial elements that form the basis for classical genres: an institution, today's *maktab* to teach dance in a formal, systematic fashion (formerly koreografskii institute), a named movement vocabulary (see Karimova 1973–79), and a canon of choreographed works, largely by Turghunbaeva, that all professional dancers are taught and must master in order to graduate as professional dancers. This new dance genre has been embraced and is even more popular than ever under a succession of dictatorial regimes that sponsor these dance performances even more than in the past under the Soviets (Adams 2010; Doi 2002).

Thus, within the array of various authoritarian regimes, the ethnogenesis of the peoples they represent, and tumultuous histories that brought them into existence, I have attempted to show how dance and dance performances have played a role in the creation and maintenance of these regimes. Importantly, I have attempted to show how dance can become a useful lens through which to analyze human behavior.

References

Abduvakhitov, Abdujabar (1993), "Islamic revivalism in Uzbekistan," in D. F. Eickelman (ed.), *Russia's Muslim Frontiers: New Directions in Cross-Cultural Analysis*, Bloomington: Indiana University Press, pp. 79–97.

Adams, J. N. (2003), *Bilingualism and the Latin Language*, Cambridge: Cambridge University Press.

Adams, Laurel L. (2010), *The Spectacular State: Culture and National Identity in Uzbekistan*, Durham, NC: Duke University Press.

Adanir, Fikret (1992), "The Macedonians in the Ottoman Empire, 1878–1912," in A. Kaeppler (ed.), in collaboration with F. Adanir and A. O'Day, *The Formation of National Elites: Comparative Studies on Governments and Non-dominant Ethnic Groups in Europe, 1850–1940*, Aldershot: Dartmouth, pp. 161–90.

Adra, Najwa (2005), "Belly dance: An urban folk dance," in A. Shay and B. Sellers-Young (eds), *Belly Dance: Orientalism, Transnationalism & Harem Fantasy*, Costa Mesa: Mazda, pp. 28–50.

Ahmadzadeh, Haideh (2008), *My Life as a Persian Ballerina*, self-published.

Akiner, Shirin (1996), "Uzbekistan and the Uzbeks," in G. Smith (ed.), *The Nationalities Question in the Post-Soviet States*, London and New York: Longman, pp. 334–47.

Alam, Asadollah (2008), *The Shah and I: The Confidential Diary of Iran's Royal Court, 1968–77* (intro. and ed. A. Alikhani), London: I.B. Tauris.

Albright, Ann Cooper (1997), *Choreographing Difference: The Body and Identity in Contemporary Dance*, Middletown, CT: Wesleyan University Press.

Aldrich, Elizabeth (2008), "Plunge not into the mire of worldly folly: Nineteenth-century and early twentieth-century religious objects to social dance in the United States," in N. Jackson and T. Shapiro-Phim (eds), *Dance Human Rights and Social Justice: Dignity in Motion*, London and Lanham, MD: Scarecrow Press, pp. 20–33.

Al-Faruqi, Lois Ibsen (1987), "Dance as an expression of Islamic culture," *Dance Research Journal*, 10:2, pp. 6–17.

Alexander, Ronelle (2006), *Bosnian, Croatian, Serbian: A Grammar with Sociolinguistic Commentary*, Madison: University of Wisconsin Press.

Allahar, Anton L. (2001), "Charisma and populism: Theoretical reflections on leadership and legitimacy," in A. L. Allahar (ed.), *Caribbean Charisma: Reflections on Leadership, Legitmacy and Populist Politics*, Kingston: Ian Randle, pp. 1–31.

Al-Saltana, Taj (1993), *Crowning Anguish: Memoirs of a Persian Princess from the Harem to Modernity* (ed. with notes and intro. A. Amanat; trans. A. Vanzan and A. Neshati), Wasnington, DC: Mage.

Amanat, Abbas (2017), *Iran: A Modern History*, New Haven, CT: Yale University Press.

Ameri, Azardokht (2006), "Iranian urban popular social dance and so-called classical dance: A comparative investigation the district of Tehran," translated from the Persian by Anthony Shay, *Dance Research Journal*, 38:1&2, Summer/Winter, pp. 163–79.

And, Metin (1959), *Dances of Anatolian Turkey*, New York: Dance Perspectives, number 3, Summer.

Anderson, John (1997), *The International Politics of Central Asia*, Manchester: Manchester University Press.

Antonaccio, Carla M. (2001), "Ethnicity and colonization," in I. Malkin (ed.), *Ancient Perceptions of Greek Ethnicity*, Washington, DC: Center for Hellenic Studies, Trustees for Harvard University, pp. 113–57.

Antonaccio, Carla M. (2007), "Colonization: Greece on the move, 900–480," in H. A. Shapiro (ed.), *Archaic Greece*, New York: Cambridge University Press, pp. 201–24.

Arberry, A. J. (1958), *Classical Persian Literature*, London: George Allen & Unwin.

Arkin, Lisa C. and Smith, Marian (1997), "National dance in the romantic ballet," in L. Garafola (ed.), *Rethinking the Sylph: New Perspectives on the Romantic Ballet*, Middletown, CT: Wesleyan University Press, pp. 11–68.

Armstrong, John A. (1982), *Nations Before Nationalism*, Chapel Hill: University of North Carolina Press.

Asgharzadeh, Alireza (2007), *Iran and the Challenge of Diversity: Islamic Fundamentalism, Aryanist Racism, and Democratic Struggles*, New York: Palgrave Macmillan.

Austerlitz, Paul (1997), *Merengue: Dominican Music and Dominican Identity* (forward by Robert Farris Thompson), Philadelphia, PA: Temple University Press.

Bacon, Elizabeth E. (1994), *Central Asians under Russian Rule: A Study in Culture Change* (with an Introduction to the Paperback, ed. M. M. J. Fischer), Ithaca, NY: Cornell University Press.

Bajoghli, Narges (2019), *Iran Reframed: Anxieties of Power in the Islamic Republic*, Stanford, CA: Stanford University Press.

Bakarić, Lidija, Dubravka Belen-Letunic, Jacqueline Balen, and Sanjin Mihelic. (2005), *Vodič Pretpovijesna Zbirka*, Zagreb: Arheološki Muzej.

Bakić-Hayden, Melica (2002), "What's so Byzantine about the Balkans?" in D. I. Bjelić and O. Savić (eds), *Balkan as Metaphor: Between Globalization and Fragmentation*, Cambridge: MIT Press, pp. 61–78.

Balfour, Sebastian (2000), "Spain from 1951 to the present," in R. Carr (ed.), *Spain: A History*, Oxford: Oxford University Press, pp. 243–82.

Bálint, Csanád (1989), "Some ethnospecific features in central and eastern European archeaeology during the early Middle Ages: The case of Avars and Hungarians," in S. J. Shennan (ed.), *Archeological Approaches to Cultural Identity*, London and New York: Routledge, pp. 185–94.

Banac, Ivo (1984), *The National Question in Yugoslavia: Origins, History, Politics*, Ithaca, NY: Cornell University Press.

Barber, Charles, Joan C. Beal, and Philip A. Shaw (2009), *The English Language: A Historical Introduction*, 2nd ed., Cambridge: Cambridge University Press.

Barford, Paul M. (2001), *Early Slavs: Culture and Society in Early Medieval Eastern Europe*, London: British Museum Press.

Barth, Fredrik (1969) (1998 reissue), "Preface 1998," in F. Barth (ed.), *Ethnic Groups and Boundaries: The Social Organization of Cultural Difference*, Long Grove, IL: Waveland Press, pp. 5–7.

Barth, Fredrik (1969) (1998 reissue), "Introduction," in F. Barth (ed.), *Ethnic Groups and Boundaries: The Social Organization of Cultural Difference*, Long Grove, IL: Waveland Press, pp. 9–38.

Barth, Fredrik (1969) (1998 reissue), "Pathan identity and its maintainence," in F. Barth (ed.), *Ethnic Groups and Boundaries: The Social Organization of Cultural Difference*, Long Grove, IL: Waveland Press, pp. 117–34.

Barthes, Roland (1972), *Mythologies*, New York: Noonday Press.

Beiza'i, Bahram (1965), *Namayash dar Iran*, Tehran: Keivan.

Bellwood, Peter (2013a), "Neolithic migrations: food production and population expansion," in P. Bellwood (ed.), *The Global Prehistory of Human Migration*, Oxford: Wiley Blackwell, pp. 79–86.

Bellwood, Peter (2013b), "Human migrations and the histories of major language families," in P. Bellwood (ed.), *The Global Prehistory of Human Migration*, Oxford: Wiley Blackwell, pp. 87–96.

Bennigsen, Alexandre (1971), "Islamic or local consciousness among Soviet nationalities?" in E. Allsworth (ed.), *Soviet Nationality Problems*, New York: Columbia University Press, pp. 168–82.

Bilandžić, Vladimir (2001), "Termination and aftermath of the war in Croatia," in B. Magaš and I. Žanić (eds), *War in Croatia and Bosnia-Herzegovina, 1991–1995*, London: Frank Cass, pp. 84–91.

Billig, Michael (1995), *Banal Nationalism*, Los Angeles: Sage.

Biondich, Mark (2011), *The Balkans: Revolution, War, and Political Violence since 1878*, Oxford: Oxford University Press.

Bjelić, Dušan I. (2002a), "Introduction: Blowing up the bridge," in D. I. Bjelić and O. Savić (eds), *Balkan as Metaphor: Between Globalization and Fragmentation*, Cambridge: MIT Press, pp. 1–22.

Bjelić, Dušan I. (2002b), "Foreword," in D. I. Bjelić and O. Savić (eds), *Balkan as Metaphor: Between Globalization and Fragmentation*, Cambridge: MIT Press, pp. ix–xii.

Bjelić, Dušan I. and Obrad Savić (eds) (2002), *Balkan as Metaphor: Between Globalization and Fragmentation*, Cambridge: MIT Press.

Boardman, John and Eugenio La Rocca (1978), *Eros in Greece*, London: John Murray.

Boatwright, Mary T., Daniel J. Gargola, and Richard J. A. Talbert (2004), *The Romans From Village to Empire: A History of Ancient Rome from Earliest Times to Constantine*, New York and Oxford: Oxford University Press.

Bond, Sarah E. (2016), *Trade and Taboo: Disreputable Professions in the Roman Mediterranean*, Ann Arbor: University of Michigan Press.

Borza, Eugene N. (1990), *In the Shadow of Olympus: The Emergence of Macedon*, Princeton, NJ: Princeton University Press.

Bowlus, Charles R. (2002), "Ethnogenesis: The Tyranny of a Concept," in A. Gillett (ed.), *On Barbarian Identity: Critical Approaches to Ethnicity in the Early Middle Ages*, Turnhout, Belgium: Brepols, pp. 241–56.

Bowman, Glen (1994), "Xenophobia, fantasy after the nation: The logic of ethnic violence in former Yugoslavia," in V. A. Goddard, J. R. Llobera, and C. Shore (eds), *The Anthropology of Europe: Identities and Boundaries in Conflict*, Oxford: Berg, pp. 143–72.

Bown, Matthew Cullerne (1991), *Art Under Stalin*, New York: Homes & Meier.

Bradley, Keith (1994), *Slavery and Society at Rome*, Cambridge: Cambridge University Press.

Breyley, G. J. and Sasan Fatemi (2016), *Iranian Music and Popular Entertainment: From Motrebi to Losanjelesi and Beyond*, London and New York: Routledge.

Brown, Garrett W., Iain McLean, and Alistair McMillan (2018), *Oxford Dictionary of Politics and International Relations*, 4th ed., Oxford: Oxford University Press.

Browne, Edward G. ([1902] 1964), *A Literary History of Persia. Volume I: From the Earliest Times until Firdawsi*, Cambridge: Cambridge University Press.

Browne, Edward G. ([1906] 1964), *A Literary History of Persia. Volume II: From Firdausi to Sa'di*, Cambridge: Cambridge University Press.

Brownlee, Jason (2007), *Authoritarianism in an Age of Democratization*, New York: Cambridge University Press.

Buch, Esteban, Igora Contreras Zubillaga, and Manuel Deniz Silva (eds) (2016), *Composing for the State: Music in Twentieth-Century Dictatorships*, Abingdon: Ashgate.

Buckland, Theresa Jill (2010), "Shifting perspectives on dance ethnography," in A. Carter and J. O'Shea (eds), *Dance Studies Reader*, 2nd ed., London and New York: Routledge, pp. 335–43.

Budak, Neven (2004), "Post-socialist historiography in Croatia," in U. Brunnbauer (ed.), *(Re) Writing History: Historiography in Southeast Europe after Socialism*, Münster: Verlag Münster, pp. 128–64.

Burnaby, Fredrick ([1876] 1997), *A Ride to Khiva: Travels and Adventures in Central Asia* (with a Preface by P. Hopkirk), Oxford: Oxford University Press.

Burrow, Rufus Jr. (1999), *Personalism: A Critical Introduction*, St. Louis: Chalice Press.

Burt, Ramsay (1998), *Alien Bodies: Representations of Modernity, "Race" and Nation in Early Modern Dance*, New York and London: Routledge.

Busse, Heribert (1975), "Iran under the Buyids," in R. N. Frye (ed.), *The Cambridge History of Iran. Volume 4: The Period from the Arab Invasion to the Saljuqs*, Cambridge: Cambridge University Press, pp. 250–304.

Calhoun, Craig (1994a), "Preface," in C. Calhoun (ed.), *Social Theory and the Politics of Identity*, Oxford: Blackwell, pp. 1–7.

Calhoun, Craig (1994b), "Social theory and the politics of identity," in C. Calhoun (ed.), *Social Theory and the Politics of Identity*, Oxford: Blackwell, pp. 9–36.

Calhoun, Craig (1994c), "Nationalism and civil society: Democracy, diversity and self-determination," in C. Calhoun (ed.), *Social Theory and the Politics of Identity*, Oxford: Blackwell, pp. 304–35.

Carr, Raymond (ed.) (2000), *Spain: A History*, London: Oxford University Press, pp. ix–xxiv.

Casero, Estrella (2000), *La España que bailó con Franco: Coros y Danzas de la Sección Femenina*, Madrid: Nuevas Estructuras.

Cefkin, Melissa (1993), "Choreographing culture: Dance, folklore, and the politics of identity in Turkey," unpublished Ph.D. dissertation, Rice University.

Chan, Christine Emi (2016), "Beyond colonization, commodification, and reclamation: Hula and Hawaiian identity," in A. Shay and B. Sellers-Young (eds), *The Oxford Handbook of Dance and Ethnicity*, New York: Oxford University Press, pp. 636–63.

Chauveau, Michel (2000), *Egypt in the Age of Cleopatra* (trans. D. Lorton), Ithaca, NY: Cornell University Press.

Chehabi, H. E. (1993), "Staging the emperor's new clothes: Dress codes and nation-building under Reza Shah," *Iranian Studies*, 26:3–4, Summer/Fall, pp. 209–23.

Chehabi, H. E. (2000), "Voices unveiled: Women singers in Iran," in R. Mathee and B. Baron (eds), *Iran and Beyond: Essay in Middle Eastern History in Honor of Nikki R. Keddie*, Costa Mesa, CA: Mazda, pp. 151–66.

Chehabi, H. E. and Juan J. Linz (1998a), "A theory of Sultanism 1: A type of nondemocratic rule," in H. E. Chehabi and J. J. Linz (eds), *Sutlanistic Regimes*, Baltimore: John Hopkins University Press, pp. 3–25.

Chehabi, H. E. and Juan J. Linz (1998b), "A theory of Sultanism 2: Genesis and demise of Sultanistic regimes," in H. E. Chehabi and J. J. Linz (eds), *Sutlanistic Regimes*, Baltimore: John Hopkins University Press, pp. 26–48.

Chirot, Daniel (ed.) (1989), *The Origins of Backwardness in Eastern Europe: Economics and Politics from the Middle Ages until the Early Twentieth Century*, Berkeley and Los Angeles: University of California Press.

Choudhury, M. L. Roy (1957), "Music in Islam," *Journal of Asiatic Society*, 23:2, pp. 45–102.

Chudnovsky, Mikhael A. (1959), *Folk Dance Company of the U.S.S.R.: Igor Moiseyev, Art Director*, Moscow: Foreign Languages Publishing House.

Chung, Hazel and Mantle Hood (1998), "Asian dance traditions: An overview," in S. J. Cohen (ed.), *International Encyclopedia of Dance*, vol. 1, New York: Oxford University Press, pp. 162–76.

Cioroianu, Adrian (2002), "The impossible escape: Romanians and the Balkans," in D. I. Bjelić and O. Savić (eds), *Balkan as Metaphor: Between Globalization and Fragmentation*, Cambridge: MIT Press, pp. 209–34.

Ćirković, Sima (2004), *The Serbs*, Oxford: Blackwell Publishing.

Coakley, John (2012), *Nationalism, Ethnicity and the State: Making and Breaking a Nation*, London: Sage.

Cohen, Abner (1974), "Introduction: The lesson of ethnicity," in A. Cohen (ed.), *Urban Ethnicity*, London: Tavistock, pp. ix–xxiv.

Cohen, Anthony P. (1994), *Self Consciousness: An Alternative Anthropology of Identity*, London and New York: Routledge.

Cohen, Beth (2001), "Ethnic identity in democratic Athens and the visual vocabulary of male costume," in I. Malkin (ed.), *Ancient Perceptions of Greek Ethnicity*, Washington, DC: Center for Hellenic Studies, Trustees for Harvard University, pp. 235–74.

Cohen, Lenard J. (1995), *Broken Bonds: Yugoslavia's Disintegration and Balkan Politics in Transition*, 2nd ed., Boulder, CO: Westview.

Collard, Anna (1989), "Investigating 'social memory' in a Greek context," in E. Tonkin, M. McDonald, and M. Chapman (eds), *History and Ethnicity*, London: Routledge, pp. 89–103.

Cooley, Alexander and John Heathershaw (2017), *Dictators without Borders: Power and Money in Central Asia*, New Haven, CT: Yale University Press.

Cooper, Andrew Scott (2016), *The Fall of Heaven: The Pahlavis and the Final Days of Imperial Iran*, New York: Henry Holt.

Cornell, Svante E. (2018), "The center of Central Asia: Uzbekistan in regional and international politics," in S. F. Starr and S. E. Cornell (eds), *Uzbekistan's New Face*, Lanham, MD: Rowman and Littlefield, pp. 5–17.

Cottam, Richard W. (1979), *Nationalism in Iran*, Pittsburgh: University of Pittsburgh Press.

Covarrubias, Luis (n.d), *Trajes Regionales de Mexico*, Mexico City: Fischgrund.

Cowan, Jane (1990), *Dance and the Body Politic in Northern Greece*, Princeton, NJ: Princeton University Press.

Cowan, Jane and Brown, K. S. (2000), "Introduction: Macedonian inflections," in Jane Cowan (ed.), *Macedonia: The Politics of Identity and Difference*, London: Pluto Press, pp. 1–27.

Cowart, Georgia L. (2008), *The Triumph of Pleasure: Louis XIV and the Politics of Spectacle*, Chicago: University of Chicago Press.

Crasssweller, Robert D. (1966), *Trujillo: The Life and Times of a Caribbean Dictator*, New York: Macmillan.

Crielaard, Jan Paulb (2009), "The Ionians in the Archaic period: Shift in identities in a changing world," in T. Derks and N. Roymans (eds), *Ethnic Constructs in Antiquity: The Role of Power and Tradition*, Amsterdam: Amsterdam University Press, pp. 37–84.

Crompton, Louis (1985), *Byron and Greek Love: Homophobia in 19th-Century England*, Berkeley: University of California Press.

Crow, John A. (1985), *Spain: The Root and the Flower*, Berkeley: University of California Press.

Crum, Richard (1998), "Yugoslavia: Traditional dance," in S. J. Cohen, G. Dorris, N. Goldner, B. Gordon, N. Reynolds, D. Vaughn, and S. Youngerman (eds), *International Encyclopedia of Dance*, New York and Oxford: Oxford University Press, pp. 426–31.

Cunliffe, Barry (2008), *Europe between the Oceans: 9000 BC-AD 1000*, New Haven, CT: Yale University Press.

Curta, Floriin (2001), *The Making of the Slavs: History and Archaeology of the Lower Danube Region, c. 500–700*, Cambridge: Cambridge University Press.

Curta, Floriin (2006), *Southeastern Europe in the Middle Ages, 500–1250*, Cambridge: Cambridge University Press.

Dabashi, Hamid (2012), *The World of Persian Literary Humanism*, Cambridge, MA: Harvard University Press.

Dabashi, Hamid (2016), *Iran Without Borders: Towards a Critique of the Postcolonial Nation*, London: Verso.

Dabashi, Hamid (2019), *The Shahnameh: The Persian Epic as World Literature*, New York: Columbia University Press.

Davaran, Fereshteh (2010), *Continuity in Iranian Identity: Resilience of a Cultural Heritage*, Abingdon: Routledege.

Davidson, Olga M. (1994), *Poet and Hero in the Persian Book of Kings*, Ithaca, NY: Cornell University Press.

Davis, Dick (2006), *Epic and Sedition: The Case of Ferdowsi's Shahnameh*, Washington, DC: Mage.

Davis, Martha Ellen (1994), "Music and Black ethnicity in the Dominican Republic," in G. H. Béhague (ed.), *Music and Black Ethnicity: The Caribbean and South America*, Miami: University of Miami North-South Press, pp. 119–55.

Davis, Martha Ellen (1998), "The Dominican Republic," in D. A. Olsen and D. E. Sheehy (eds), *The Garland Encyclopedia of World Music: Volume 2. South America, Mexico, Central America and the Caribbean*, New York and London: Garland Publishing, pp. 845–63.

Davis, Martha Ellen (2002), "Dominican folk dance and the shaping of national identity," in S. Sloat (ed.), *Caribbean Dance From Abakuá to Zouk: How Movement Shapes Identity*, Gainsville: University Press of Florida, pp. 127–51.

Davis, Martha Ellen (2007a), "Oral musical traditions of the Dominican Republic," in M. Kuss (ed.), *Music in Latin America and the Caribbean: Volume 2: Performing the Caribbean Experience*, Austin: University of Texas Press, pp. 189–215.

Davis, Martha Ellen (2007b), "The Dominican Republic," in M. Kuss (ed.), *Music in Latin America and the Caribbean: Volume 2: Performing the Caribbean Experience*, Austin: University of Texas Press, pp. 217–36.

Davis, Martha Ellen (2010), "Dance of the Dominican Misterios," in S. Sloat (ed.), *Making Caribbean Dance: Continuity and Creativity in Island Cultures*, Tallahassee: University of Press of Florida, pp. 181–97.

Deagan, Kathleen (2001), "Dynamics of imperial adjustment in Spanish America: Ideology and social integration," in S. E. Alcock, T. N. D'Altroy, K. D. Morrison, and C. M. Sinopoli (eds), *Empires: Perspectives from Archeology and History*, Cambridge: Cambridge University Press, pp. 179–94.

Debord, Guy (2010), *Society of the Spectacle*, Kalamazoo: Black and Red.

Dedijer, Vladimir (1996), "Titoism," in G. Augustinos (ed.), *The National Idea in Eastern Europe: The Politics of Ethnic and Civic Community*, Lexington, MA: D. C. Heath, pp. 81–87.

DeFrantz, Thomas F. (2002), "African American dance: A complex history," in T. F. DeFrantz (ed.), *Dancing Many Drums: Excavations in African American Dance*, Madison: University of Wisconsin Press, pp. 3–35.

Dench, Emma (2018), "Rome the disrupter: Reconsidering race, identity and power in the Roman Empire," Lecture given at Pomona College, Claremont, CA, October 6.

Derby, Lauren (2009), *The Dictator's Seduction: Politics and the Popular Imagination in the Era of Trujillo*, Durham, NC: Duke University Press, 2009.

Derks, Ton (2009), "Ethnic identity in the Roman frontier: The epigraphy of Batavi and other lower Rhine tribes," in T. Derks and N. Roymans (eds), *Ethnic Constructs in Antiquity: The Role of Power and Tradition*, Amsterdam: Amsterdam University Press, pp. 239–82.

Derks, Ton and Roymans, Nico (2009), "Introduction," in T. Derks and N. Roymans (eds), *Ethnic Constructs in Antiquity: The Role of Power and Tradition*, Amsterdam: Amsterdam University Press, pp. 1–9.

Desmond, Jane C. (1997), "Embodying difference: Issues in dance and cultural studies," in C. F. Delgado and J. E. Muñoz (eds), *Everynight Life: Culture and Dance in Latin/o America*, Durham, NC: Duke University Press, pp. 33–64.

Desmond, Jane C. (1999), *Staging Tourism: Bodies on Display from Waikiki to Sea World*, Chicago: Chicago University Press.

Desmond, Jane C. (2001), "Introduction: Making the invisible visible: Staging sexualities through dance," in J. C. Desmond (ed.), *Dancing Desires: Choreographing Sexualities on and off Stage*, Madison: University of Wisconsin Press, pp. 3–32.

De Vos, George A. and Hiroshi Wagatsuma (1995), "Cultural identity and minority status in Japan," in L. Romanucci-Ross and G. DeVos (eds), *Ethnic Identity: Creation, Conflict, and Accommodation*, 3rd ed., Walnut Creek: AltaMira Press, pp. 264–97.

De Warren, Robert (2009), *Destiny's Waltz: In Step with Giants*, New York: Eloquent Books.

De Warren, Robert and Peter Williams (1973), "Discovery in Persia," *Dance and Dancers*, January, pp. 28–32.

Diba, Layla and Maryam Ekhtiar (1998), *Royal Persian Paintings: The Qajar Epoch, 1785–1925*, New York: Brooklyn Museum of Art.

Dietzfelbinger, Eckart (1996), *Faszination und Gewalt: Das Reichsparteitagsgelände in Nürnberg*, Nuremberg: Museen der stadt nürnberg.

Doi, Mary Masayo (2002), *Gesture, Gender, Nation: Dance and Social Change in Uzbekistan*, Westport, CT: Bergin and Garvey.

Dollerup, Cay (1998), "Language and culture in transition in Uzbekistan," in T. Atabaki and J. O'Kane (eds), *Post-Soviet Central Asia*, London and New York: Tauris Academic Studies in Association with The International Institute for Asian Studies, Brill and Amsterdam, pp. 144–56.

Douglas, Cynthia Maria (2005), "Ethnogenesis, identity, and the Dominican Republic, 1844-present," Ph.D. dissertation, Tuscon: University of Arizona.

Drakulić, Slavenka (1999), *Café Europa: Life after Communism*, New York: Penguin Books.

Drieu, Cloé (2018), *Cinema, Nation, and Empire in Uzbekistan, 1919–1937* (trans. A. Morfee), Bloomington: Indiana University Press.

Drinkwater, John and Hugh Elton (1992), *Fifth-Century Gaul: A Crisis of Identity?* Cambridge: Cambridge University Press.

Duany, Jorge (1994), "Ethnicity, identity, and music: An anthropological analysis of the Dominican Merengue," in G. H. Béhague (ed.), *Music and Black Ethnicity: The Caribbean and South America*, Miami: University of Miami North-South Press, pp. 65–82.

Dubinskas, Frank (1983), "Performing Slavonian folklore: The politics of reminiscence and remembering the past," Ph.D. dissertation, Stanford: Stanford University.

Dundović, Hanibal (1999), *Dečki, Fajerunt: Sječanja. Varaždinskke Toplice*, Croatia: Tonimir.

Dundović, Hanibal (2003), "Moj Život s Ladom," in *Godišnjak*, Zagreb: Lado, pp. 5–19.

Dundović, Hanibal (2008), Personal interview, Croatia: Zabreb.

Dzino, Danijel (2010), *Becoming Slav; Becoming Croat: Identity Transformations in Post-Roman and Early Medieval Dalmatia*, Leiden: Brill.

Echagüe, José Ortiz (1963), *España: Tipos y Trajes*, Undécima Edición, Madrid: Publicaciones Ortiz-Echagüe.

Eickelman, Dale F. (1993), "Introduction: The other 'orientalist' crisis," in D. F. Eickelman (ed.), *Russia's Muslim Frontiers: New Directions in Cross-Cultural Analysis*, Bloomington: Indiana University Press, pp. 1–15.

Epstein, A. L. (1978 [2009]), *Ethos and Identity: Three Studies in Ethnicity*, New Brunswick, NJ: Aldine.

Erdbrink, Thomas (2016), "After attacks, many argue against a United Belgium," *New York Times*, April 8, p. A8.

Erdbrink, Thomas (2019), "Revolution at 40: Iranians loosen ideology's grip on daily life," *New York Times*, 11 Februray A4.

Eriksen, Thomas Hylland (2002), *Ethnicity and Nationalism*, 2nd ed., London: Pluto Press.

Escudero, Maria Luisa Herrera (1984), *Trajes y Bailes de España*, León-La Coruña: Editorial Everest, S.A.

Falk, S. J. (1972), *Qajar Painting*, London: Sotheby.

Fatemi, Sasan (2005), "La Musique Legere Urbaine dans La Culture Iranienne: Reflexion sur les notions de classique et populaire," Ph.D. dissertation, Universite Paris X-Nanterre, Paris.

Fauser, Annegret (2005), *Musical Encounters at the 1889 Paris World's Fair*, Rochester: University of Rochester.

Feinberg, Joseph Grim (2018), *The Paradox of Authenticity: Folklore Performance in Post-Communist Slovakia*, Madison: University of Wisconsin Press.

Fenton, Steve (2003), *Ethnicity*, Cambridge: Polity Press.

Filanovskaya, Tatyana Aleksandrovna (2016), *Istoriia Khoreograficheskovo Obrazovaniia v Rossii*, Moskva: Planeta Muzyiki.

Findling, John E. and Kimberly D. Pelle (eds) (2008), *Encyclopedia of World's Fairs and Expositions*, Jefferson, NC: McFarland.

Fine, John V. A., Jr. (1983), *The Early Medieval Balkans: A Critical Survey from the Sixth to the Late Twelfth Century*, Ann Arbor: University of Michigan Press.

Fine, John V. A., Jr. (1994), *The Late Medieval Balkans: A Critical Survey from the Late Twelfth Century to the Ottoman Conquest*, Ann Arbor: University of Michigan Press.

Fine, John V. A., Jr. (2006), *When Ethnicity Did Not Matter in the Balkans: A Study of Identity in Pre-Nationalist Croatia, Dalmatia, and Slavonia in the Medieval and Early-Modern Periods*, Ann Arbor: University of Michigan Press.

Finlan, Alastair (2004), *The Collapse of Yugoslavia, 1991–1999*, London and New York: Osprey.

Fisher, Jennifer (2016), "Ballet and whiteness: Will ballet forever be the kingdom of the pale?" in A. Shay and B. Sellers-Young (eds), *The Oxford Handbook of Dance and Ethnicity*, New York: Oxford University Press, pp. 585–97.

Fisher, Jennifer and Shay, Anthony (eds) (2009), *When Men Dance: Choreographing Masculinities Across Borders*, New York: Oxford University Press.

Fisher, N. R. E. (2001), *Slavery in Classical Greece*, 2nd ed., London: Bristol Classical Press.

Fletcher, Richard (1998), *The Barbarian Conversion: From Paganism to Christianity*, New York: Henry Holt.

Fredrickson, George M. (2002), *Racism: A Short History*, Princeton: Princeton University Press.

Friend, Robyn (2016), "Regional dances of Iran," in S. Gholami (ed.), *Dance in Iran: Past and Present*, Wiesbaden: Reichert Verlag, pp. 9–34.

Frosch, Joan (1999), "Dance ethnography: Tracing the weave of dance in the fabric of culture," in S. Horton Fraleigh and P. Hanstein (eds), *Researching Dance: Evolving Modes of Inquiry*, Pittsburgh: University of Pittsburgh Press, pp. 249–80.

Frye, Richard N. (1991), "Pre-Islamic and early Islamic cultures in Central Asia," in Robert L. Canfield (ed.), *Turko-Persia in Historical Perspective*, Cambridge: Cambridge University Press, pp. 35–77.

Frye, Richard N. (1996), *The Heritage of Central Asia: From Antiquity to Turkish Expansion*, Princeton: Markus Wiener.

Frye, Richard N. (1997), *Bukhara: The Medieval Achievement*, Costa Mesa: Mazda.

Fuchs, Lívia (2000), "Hungary: On Hungarian dance," in A. Grau and S. Jordan (eds), *Europe Dancing: Perspectives on Theatre Dance and Cultural Identity*, London: Routledge, pp. 79–99.

Fuller, Graham E. (1994), "The new geopolitical order," in Ali Banuazizi and Myron Weiner (eds), *The New Geopolitics of Central Asia and Its Borderlands*, Bloomington: Indiana University Press, pp. 19–43.

Gagnon, V. P., Jr. (2004), *The Myth of Ethnic War: Serbia and Croatia in the 1990s*, Ithaca, NY: Cornell University Press.

Garafola, Lynn (1997), "Introduction," in L. Garafola (ed.), *Rethinking the Sylph: New Perspectives on Romantic Ballet*, Hanover and London: Wesleyan University Press, pp. 1–10.

García-Peña, Lorgia (2016), *The Borders of Dominicanidad: Race, Nation, and Archives of Contradiction*, Durham, NC: Duke University Press, 2016.

Gardet, Louis (1970), "Religion and culture," in P. M. Holt, A. K. S. Lambton, and B. Lewis (eds), *The Cambridge History of Islam. Volume II, The Further Islamic Lands, Islamic Society and Civilization*, Cambridge: Cambridge University Press, pp. 569–603.

Gat, Azar (2013), *Nations: The Long History and Deep Roots of Political Ethnicity and Nationalism*, Cambridge: Cambridge University Press.

Geary, Patrick J. (2002), *The Myth of Nations: The Medieval Origins of Europe*, Princeton and New York: Princeton University Press.

Gehrke, Hans-Joachim (2009), "From Athenian identity to European ethnicity—the cultural biography of the myth of marathon," in T. Derks and N. Roymans (eds), *Ethnic Constructs in Antiquity: The Role of Power and Tradition*, Amsterdam: Amsterdam University Press, pp. 85–99.

Gellner, Ernest (1983), *Nations and Nationalism*, Cornell: Cornell University Press.

Gellner, Ernest (1994), "Nations and nationalism," in J. Hutchinson and A. D. Smith (eds), *Ethnicity*, Oxford: Oxford University Press, pp. 55–63.

Geoffroy-Schneitter, Bérénice (2004), *Fayum Portraits*, New York: Assouline.

Gerstin, Julian (2010), "Tangled roots: Kalenda and other neo-African dances in the circum-Caribbean," in S. Sloat (ed.), *Making Caribbean Dance: Continuity and Creativity in Island Cultures*, Tallahassee: University of Press of Florida, pp. 11–34.

Gerth, H. H. and C. Wright Mills (1946), *From Max Weber: Essay in Sociology* (trans., ed. and with an introd. H. H. Gerth and C. Wright Mills), New York: Oxford University Press.

Gholami, Saloumeh (2016), "The history of dance in Iran," in S. Gholami (ed.), *Dance in Iran: Past and Present*, Wiesbaden: Reichert Verlag, pp. 35–90.

Giersdorf, Jens Richard (2013), *The Body of the People: East German Dance since 1945*, Madison: University of Wisconsin Press.

Gilliland, Mary Kay (1995), "Nationalism and ethnogenesis in the former Yugoslavia," in L. Romanucci-Ross and G. DeVos (eds), *Ethnic Identity: Creation, Conflict, and Accommodation*, 3rd ed., Walnut Creek: AltaMira Press, pp. 197–221.

Gillett, Andrew (ed.) (2002), *On Barbarian Identity: Critical Approaches to Ethnicity in the Early Middle Ages*, Turnhout, Belgium: Brepols.
Gillis, John R. (ed.) (1994), *Commemorations: The Politics of National Identity*, Princeton: Princeton University Press.
Giruchescu, Anca and Bloland, Sunni (1995), *Romanian Traditional Dance: A Contextual and Structrual Approach*, Mill Valley, CA: Wild Flower Press.
Gladell, Malcolm (2008), *Outliers: The Story of Success*, New York: Little, Brown.
Glazer, Nathan and Moynihan, Daniel E. (1975), "Introduction," in *Ethnicity: Theory and Experience*, Cambridge: Harvard University Press, pp. 1–26.
Glenny, Misha (1996), *The Fall of Yugoslavia*, 3rd ed., London: Penguin.
Glenny, Misha (2001), *The Balkans: Nationalism, War, and the Great Powers, 1804–1999*, New York and London: Penguin Books.
Goetz, Hans-Werner (1996), *Life in the Middle Ages: from the Seventh to the Thirteenth Century*, Notre Dame and London: Notre Dame University Press.
Goldstein, Ivo (1999), *Croatia: A History*, Montreal and Kingston: McGill-Queen's University Press.
Goldsworthy, Vesna (1998), *Inventing Ruritania: The Imperialism of the Imagination*, New Haven, CT: Yale University Press.
Goldsworthy, Vesna (2002), "Invention and in/ter/ventions: The rhetoric of Balkanization," in D. I. Bjelić and O. Savić (eds), *Balkan as Metaphor: Between Globalization and Fragmentation*, Cambridge: MIT Press, pp. 25–38.
Gottschild, Brenda Dixon (1996), *Digging the Africanist Presence in American Performance: Dance and Other Contexts*, Westport, CT: Praeger.
Gray, Laurel Victoria (1998), "Uzbekistan," in S. J. Cohen (ed.), *International Encyclopedia of Dance*, New York: Oxford University Press, vol. 6, pp. 304–307.
Greenfeld, Liah (2016), *Advanced Introduction to Nationalism*, Cheltenham: Edward Elgar.
Gross, Jo-Ann (1992), "Approaches to the problem of identity formation," in J.-A. Gross (ed.), *Muslims in Central Asia: Expressions of Identity and Change*, Durham, NC: Duke University Press, pp. 1–23.
Gruen, Erich S. (1992), *Cultural and National Identity in Republican Rome*, Ithaca, NY: Cornell University Press.
Gunst, Péter (1989), *The Origins of Backwardness in Eastern Europe: Economics and Politics from the Middle Ages until the Early Twentieth Century* (ed. Daniel Chirot), Berkeley and Los Angeles: University of California Press.
Gušić, Marjana (1955), *Tumač Izložene Građe. Commentary on the Exhibited Material*, Zagreb: Etnografski Muzej.
Guss, David M. (2000), *The Festive State: Race, Ethnicity, and Nationalism as Cultural Performance*, Berkeley: University of California Press.
Hāfez, Shams Ad-din Mohammad (1994–95), *Hāfez be sa'i-ye sāyeh*, Tehran: Tus.

Hahn, Hans Peter (2017), "Ethnicity as a form of social organization: Notes on the multiplicity of understandings of a contested concept," in M. Gori and M. Ivanova (eds), *Balkan Dialogues: Negotiating Identity between Prehistory and the Present*, London and New York: Routledge, pp. 38–51.

Hahn, Tomie (2007), *Sensational Knowledge: Embodying Culture through Japanese Dance*, Middletown, CT: Wesleyan University Press.

Hale, Henry (1994), "Islam, state-building and Uzbekistan foreign policy," in A. Bauazizi and M. Weiner (eds), *The New Geopolitics of Central Asia and Its Borderlands*, Bloomington: Indiana University Press, pp. 136–72.

Hall, Edith (1989), *Inventing the Barbarian: Greek Self-Definition through Tragedy*, Oxford: Clarendon Press.

Hall, Edith (2014), *Introducing the Ancient Greeks: From Bronze Age Seafarers to Navigators of the Western Mind*, New York: Norton.

Hall, Jonathan M. (1997), *Ethnic Identity in Greek Antiquity*, Cambridge: Cambridge University Press.

Hall, Jonathan M. (2001), "Contested ethnicities: Perceptions of Macedonia within evolving definitions of Greek identity," in I. Malkin (ed.), *Ancient Perceptions of Greek Ethnicity*, Washington, DC: Center for Hellenic Studies, Trustees for Harvard University, pp. 159–86.

Hall, Jonathan M. (2002), *Hellenicity: Between Ethnicity and Culture*, Chicago: University of Chicago Press.

Hall, Jonathan M. (2007), "Polis, community, and ethnic identity," in H. A. Shapiro (ed.), *Archaic Greece*, New York: Cambridge University Press, pp. 40–60.

Hallinan, Victoria Anne (2013), "Cold war cultural exchange and the Moiseyev dance company: American perception of Soviet peoples," Ph.D. dissertation, Northeastern University.

Halpern, Joel M. and Kideckel, David A. (eds) (2000), *Neighbors at War: Anthropological Perspectives on Yugoslav Ethnicity, Culture, and History*, University Park: Pennsylvania State University Press.

Hamby, Gavin (ed.) (1966), *Central Asia*, New York: Delacorte Press.

Hartlyn, Jonathan (1998), "The Trujillo regime in the Dominican Republic," in H. E. Chehabi and J. J. Linz (eds), *Sultanistic Regimes*, Baltimore: John Hopkins University Press, pp. 85–112.

Hemmasi, Farzaneh (2020), *Tehrangeles Dreaming: Intimacy and Imagination in Southern California's Iranian Pop Music*, Durham, NC: Duke University Press.

Herzfeld, Michael (1997), *Cultural Intimacy: Social Poetics in the Nation-State*, New York and London: Routledge.

Hernandez, Benjamin (1999), "Mexican dance in the Los Angeles public schools, 1970–1999," MA thesis, UCLA.

Hiro, Dilip (2011), *Inside Central Asia: A Political and Cultural History of Uzbekistan, Turkmenistan, Khazkhstan, Kyrgystan, Tajikistan, Turkey, and Iran*, New York and London: Overlook Duckworth.

Hobsbawm, Eric and Terence Ranger (eds) (1983), *The Invention of Tradition*, Cambridge: Cambridge University Press.

Hoetink, Harry (1967), *The Two Variants in Caribbean Race Relations: A Contribution to the Sociology of Segmented Societies*, Oxford: Oxford University Press.

Holguín, Sandie (2019), *Flamenco Nation: The Construction of Spanish National Identity*, Madison: University of Wisconsin Press.

Hovannisian, Richard G. and Georges Sabagh (1998), *The Persian Presence in the Islamic World*, Cambridge: Cambridge University Press.

Hutchinson, John and Smith, Anthony D. (1994), "Introduction," in J. Hutchinson and A. D. Smith (eds), *Ethnicity*, Oxford: Oxford University Press, pp. 3–14.

Hutchinson, Sydney (2016), *Tigers of a Different Stripe: Performing Gender in Dominican Music*, Chicago: University of Chicago Press.

Inalcik, Halil (2000), *The Ottoman Empire: The Classical Age, 1300–1600*, London: Phoenix.

Isaac, Benjamin (2004), *The Invention of Racism in Classical Antiquity*, Princeton: Princeton University Press.

Isager, Signe and Jens Erik Skydsgaard (1992), *Ancient Greek Agriculture: An Introduction*, London: Routledge.

Ivančan, Ivan (1981), *Narodni Plesovi I Igre u Lici*, Zagreb: Prosvjetni Sabor Hrvatske.

Ivančan Ivan (1996), *Narodni Plesni Običaji u Hrvata*, Zagreb: Institut za Etnologiju i Folkloristiku.

Ivanković, Ivica and Vladimir Šimunić (2001), *Hrvatske narodne nošnje. Croatian National Costumes*, Zagreb: Multigraf.

Jackson, Naomi and Toni Shapiro-Phim (2008), *Dance, Human Rights, and Social Justice: Dignity in Motion*, Lanham, MD: Scarecrow Press.

Jelavich, Barbara (1983a), *History of the Balkans: Eighteenth and Nineteenth Centuries*, Cambridge: Cambridge University Press.

Jelavich Barbara (1983b), *History of the Balkans: Twentieth Century*, vol. 2, Cambridge: Cambridge University Press.

Jelavich, Barbara and Charles (1977), *The Establishment of the Balkan National States, 1804–1920*, Seattle: University of Washington Press.

Jenkins, Richard (1997), *Rethinking Ethnicity: Arguments and Explorations*, London: Sage.

Jeschke, Claudia and Gabi Vettermann (2000), "Germany: Between institutions and aesthetics: Choreographing Germanness?" in A. Grau and S. Jordan (eds), *Europe Dancing: Perspectives on Theatre Dance and Cultural Identity*, London: Routledge, pp. 55–78.

Jones, Siân (1997), *The Archeaeology of Ethnicity: Constructing Identities in the Past and Present*, London and New York: Routledge.

Jory, E. J. (1996), "The drama of the dance: Prolegomena to an iconography of imperial pantomime," in W. J. Slater (ed.), *Roman Theater and Society*: E. Togo Salmon Papers I, Ann Arbor: University of Michigan Press, pp. 1–27.

Just, Roger (1989), "Triumph of the Ethnos," in E. Tonkin, M. McDonald and M. Chapman (eds), *History and Ethnicity*, London: Routledge, pp. 71–88.

Kaeppler, Adrienne L. (1983), *Polynesian Dance with a Selection for Contemporary Performances*, Honolulu, HI: Privately printed by Alpha Delta Kappa.

Kaeppler, Adrienne L. (1985), "Structured movement systems in Tonga," in P. Spencer (ed.), *Society and the Dance*, New York: Cambridge University Press, pp. 233–54.

Kaiser, Robert J. (1994), "Ethnic demography and interstate relations in Central Asia," in R. Szporluk (ed.), *National Identity and Ethnicity in Russia and the New States of Eurasia*, Armonk, NY: M.E. Sharpe, pp. 230–65.

Kantor, Marvin (1993), "A question of language: Church Slavonic and the West Slavs," in R. A. Maguire and A. Timberlake (eds), *American Contributions to the Eleventh International Congress of Slavists, Bratislava, August-September, 1993. Literature. Linguistics. Poetics*, Columbus, OH: Slavica, pp. 320–29.

Karayanni, Stavros Stavrou (2005), "Dismissal veiling desire: Kuchuk Hanem and imperial masculinity," in A. Shay and B. Sellers-Young (eds), *Belly Dance: Orientalism, Transnationalism, and Harem Fantasy*, Costa Mesa, CA: Mazda, pp. 114–44.

Karimova, Roziya (1973), *Ferganskii Tanets*, Tashkent: Ghafur Ghulom Press.

Karimova, Roziya (1975), *Khorezmskii Tanets*, Tashkent: Ghafur Ghulom Press.

Karimova, Roziya (1977), *Bukhaskii Tanets*, Tashkent: Ghafur Ghulom Press.

Karimova, Roziya (1979), *Tantsy Ansambl'a Bakhor*, Tashken: Literatura I Iskusstvo.

Karina, Lilian and Marion Kant (2003 [2004]), *Hitler's Dancers: German Modern Dance and the Third Reich* (trans. J. Steinberg), New York: Beghahn Books.

Katouzian, Homa (1998), "The Pahlavi Regime in Iran," in H. E. Chehabi and J. J. Linz (eds), *Sutlanistic Regimes*, Baltimore: John Hopkins University Press, pp. 182–205.

Katzew, Ilona (2004), *Casta Painting: Images of Race in Eighteenth-Century Mexico*, New Haven, CT and London: Yale University Press.

Kaufmann, Eric P. (ed.) (2004), *Rethinking Ethnicity: Majority Groups and Dominant Minorities*, London and New York: Routledge.

Kealiinohomoku, Joann (1970), "An anthropologist looks at Ballet as a form of ethnic dance," *Impulse*, 24–33 (reprinted in *Moving History/Dancing Cultures: A Dance History Reader*, Ann Dils and Ann Cooper Albright (eds), Middletown, CT: Wesleyan University Press, pp. 33–43).

Kedourie, Elie (1994), "Nationalism and self-determination," in John Hutchinson and Anthony D. Smith (eds), *Ethnicity*, Oxford: Oxford University Press, pp. 49–55.

Kellas, James G. (1998), *The Politics of Nationalism and Ethnicity*, 2nd ed., London: Macmillan.

Kennedy, Rebecca F., C. Sydnor Roy, and Max L. Goldman (eds) (2013), *Race and Ethnicity in the Classical World: An Anthology of Primary Sources in Translation*, Indianapolis: Hackett.

Kershaw, Ian (1987), *The "Hitler Myth": Image and Reality in the Third Reich*, Oxford: Oxford University Press.

Keyder, Caglar (1997), "Whither the project of modernity?: Turkey in the 1990s," in S. Bodogan and R. Kasaba (eds), *Rethinking Modernity and National Identity in Turkey*, Seattle: University of Washington Press, pp. 37–51.

Khaleqi, Ruhallah (1974), *Sar gozasht-e musiqi-ye Iran*, Tehran: Safiali Shah.

Khalid, Adeeb (2015), *Making Uzbekistan: Nation, Empire, and Revolution in the Early USSR*, Ithaca, NY: Cornell University Press.

Khayyam, Omar (1956), *Robāiyyāt-khayyām*, Tehran: Gravarsazi Zanichkhah.

Kiann, Nima (2016), "The history of ballet in Iran," in S. Gholami (ed.), *Dance in Iran: Past and Present*, Wiesbaden: Reichert Verlag, pp. 91–176.

Kinzer, Stephen (2008), *All the Shah's Men: An American Coup and the Roots of Middle East Terror*, New York: John Wiley.

Kiossev, Alexander (2002), "The dark intimacy: Maps, identities, acts of identifications," in D. I. Bjelić and O. Savić (eds), *Balkan as Metaphor: Between Globalization and Fragmentation*, Cambridge: MIT Press, pp. 165–90.

Klein, George (1996), "Socialist crises and national politics," in G. Augustinos (ed.), *The National Idea in Eastern Europe: The Politics of Ethnic and Civic Community*, Lexington, MA: D. C. Heath, pp. 96–109.

Klenke, Kerstin (2019), *The Sound State of Uzbekistan: Popular Music and Politics in the Karimov Era*, London and New York: Routledge.

Kolb, Alexandra (2011), "About this book," in A. Kolb (eds), *Dance and Politics*, Bern: Peter Lang AG, International, pp. xiii–xix.

Kolb, Alexandra (2017), "Dance and politics in China," in R. J. Kowal, G. Sigmund, and R. Martin (eds), *The Oxford Handbook of Dance and Politics*, New York: Oxford University Press, pp. 347–70.

Konstan, David (2001), "To Hellēnikon ethnos: Ethnicity and the construction of Ancient Greek identity," in I. Malkin (ed.), *Ancient Perceptions of Greek Ethnicity*, Washington, DC: Center for Hellenic Studies, Trustees for Harvard University, pp. 29–50.

Koroteyeva and Ekaterina Makarova (1998), "The assertion of Uzbek national identity: Nativization or state-building process?" in T. Atabaki and J. O'Kane (eds), *Post-Soviet Central Asia*, London and New York: Tauris Academic Studies in Association with The International Institute for Asian Studies, Brill and Amsterdam, pp. 137–43.

Kowal, Rebekah J., Sigmund, Gerald, and Martin, Randy (2017), "Introduction," in R. J. Kowal, G. Sigmund, and R. Martin (eds), *The Oxford Handbook of Dance and Politics*, New York: Oxford University Press, pp. 1–24.

Kramer, Heinz (2000), *Changing Turkey: The Challenge to Europe and the United States*, Washington, DC: Brookings Institute.

Kruger, Julie A. (2000), "'In Our Blood': Merengue and Dominican Identity," MA Thesis, Laramie: University of Wyoming.

Lada-Richards, Ismene (2007), *Silent Eloquence: Lucian and Pantomime Dancing*, London: Duckworth.

Lado (1959), *1949–1959 Souvenir Program*, Zagreb: Lado.

Lado (1979), *1949–1979 Trideset Godina*, Zagreb: Lado.

Lado (2019), *Godišnjak: 70 Godina Ansambla Lado*, Zagreb: Ansambl Narodnih Plesova i Pjesama Hrvatske Lado.

Lampe, John R. (2000), *Yugoslavia as History: Twice There Was a Country*, Cambridge: Cambridge University Press.

Landau, Jacob M. and Barbara Kellner-Heinkele (2001), *Politics of Language in the Ex-Soviet Muslim States*, Ann Arbor: University of Michigan Press.

Laušević, Mirjana (2007), *Balkan Fascination: Creating an Alternative Music Culture in America*, Oxford: Oxford University Press.

Lawler, Lillian (1964), *The Dance in Ancient Greece*, Middletown, CT: Wesleyan University Press.

Lazard, Gilbert (1975), "The rise of the new Persian language," in R. N. Frye (ed.), *Cambridge History of Iran*, vol. 4, Cambridge: Cambridge University Press, pp. 595–632.

Lazzerini, Edward J. (1992), "Beyond renewal: The *Jadid* response to pressure for change in the Modern Age," in J.-A. Gross (ed.), *Muslims in Central Asia: Expressions of Identity and Change*, Durham, NC: Duke University Press, pp. 151–66.

Leppin, Hartmut (2011), "Between marginality and celebrity: Entertainers and entertainments in Roman society," in M. Peachin (ed.), *The Oxford Handbook of Social Relations in the Roman World*, Oxford: Oxford University Press, pp. 660–78.

Levin, Theodore (1993), *Shashmaqam: The Bukharan Jewish Ensemble, 1993–1994 Tour*, program notes.

Levin, Theodore (1996), *The Hundred Thousand Fools of God: Musical Travels in Central Asia (and Queens, New York*, Bloomington: Indiana University Press.

Levin, Theodore (2016), "Music in Central Asia: An overview," in T. Levin, S. Daukeyeva, and E. Köchümkulova (eds), *The Music of Central Asia*, Bloomington: Indiana University Press, pp. 3–25.

Levitsky, Steven and Lucan A. Way (2010), *Authoritarianism: Hybrid Regimes after the Cold War*, New York: Cambridge University Press.

Levy, Shawn (2005), *The Last Playboy: The High Life of Porfirio Rubirosa*, New York: Harper.

Lim, Jae-Cheon (2015), *Leader Symbols and Personality Cult in North Korea*, London and New York: Routledge.

Lindholm, Charles (1993), *Charisma*, Oxford: Blackwell.

Livi-Bacci, Massimo (1992), *A Concise History of World Population* (trans. C. Ipsen), Cambridge: Blackwell.

Lixfeld, Hannjost (1994), *Folklore and Fascism: The Reich Institute for German Volkskunde* (ed. and trans. J. R. Dow), Bloomington: Indiana University Press.

Longinović, Tomislav Z. (2002), "Vampires like us: Gothic imaginary and 'the serbs,' " in D. I. Bjelić and O. Savić (eds), *Balkan as Metaphor: Between Globalization and Fragmentation*, Cambridge: MIT Press, pp. 39–60.

Loutzaki, Irene (2008), "Dance as propaganda: The metaxas regime's stadium ceremonies, 1937–1940," in A. Shay (ed.), *Balkan Dance: Essays on Characteristics, Performance and Teaching*, Jefferson, NC: McFarland, pp. 89–115.

Lowenthal, David (1985), *The Past Is a Foreign Country*, Cambridge: Cambridge University Press.

MacFayden, David (2006), *Russian Culture in Uzbekistan: One Language in the Middle of Nowhere*, London and New York: Routledge.

Machin-Autenrieth, Matthew (2017), *Flamenco, Regionalism and Musical Heritage in Southern Spain*, London and New York: Routledge.

Magaš, Branka (1993), *The Destruction of Yugoslavia: Tracking the Break-Up 1990–1992*, London and New York: Verso.

Magaš, Branka (2007), *Croatia Through History*, London: Saqi.

Magaš, Branka and Ivo Žanić (eds) (2001), *The War in Croatia and Bosnia-Herzegovina, 1991–1995* (foreword by Noel Malcolm), London: Frank Cass.

Malcolm, Noel (2001), "Foreword," in B. Magaš and I. Žanić (eds), *War in Croatia and Bosnia-Herzegovina, 1991–1995*, London: Frank Cass, pp. xvii–xx.

Malešević, Siniša (2006), *Identity as Ideology: Understanding Ethnicity and Nationalism*, Basingstoke and New York: Palgrave Macmillan.

Malkin, Irad (2001), "Introduction," in I. Malkin (ed.), *Ancient Perceptions of Greek Ethnicity*, Washington, DC: Center for Hellenic Studies, Trustees for Harvard University, pp. 1–28.

Malm, William P. (1998), "Bugaku," in S. J. Cohen (ed.), *International Encyclopedia of Dance*, vol. 2, New York: Oxford University Press, pp. 5–6.

Maners, Lynn S. (1995), "The Social Lives of Dances in Bosnia and Hercegovina: Cultural Performance and the Anthropology of Aesthetic Phenomena," Ph.D. dissertation, Los Angeles: UCLA.

Maners, Lynn S. (2000), "Clapping for serbs: Nationalism and performance in Bosnia and Herzegovina," in J. M. Halpern and D. A. Kideckel (eds), *Neighbors at War: Anthropological Perspectives on Yugoslav Ethnicity, Culture, and History*, University Park: Pennsylvania State University Press, pp. 302–15.

Maners, Lynn S. (2008), "Clapping for serbs: Nationalism and performance in Bosnia and Herzegovina" (reprint of Maners 2000), in Anthony Shay (ed), *Balkan Dance: Essays on Characteristics, Performance and Teaching*, Jefferson, NC: McFarland, pp. 145–60.

Manning, Susan (2006), *Ecstasy and the Demon: The Dances of Mary Wigman* (with a New Introduction), Minneapolis: University of Minnesota Press.

Manuel, Peter (2006), *Caribbean Currents: Caribbean Music from Rumba to Reggae*, responded and expanded edition with K. Bilby and M. Largey, Philadelphia: Temple University Press.

Manz, Beatrice Forbes (1992), "The development and meaning of Chaghatay identity," in J.-A. Gross (ed.), *Muslims of Central Asia: Expressions of Identity and Change*, Durham, NC: Duke University Press, pp. 27–46.

March, Richard Anthony-Daniel (1983), "The Tamburitza tradition," Ph.D. dissertation, Bloomington: University of Indiana.

Marković, Predrag J. and Miloš Ković, Nataša Milićević (2004), *(Re)writing History: Historiography in Southeast Europe after Socialism* (ed. U. Brunnbauer), Münster: Lit Verlag, pp. 277–316.

Martínez Del Fresno, Beatriz (2013), "Women, land, and nation: The dances of the Falange's women's section in the political map of Franco's Spain (1939–1952)," in G. P. Zalduonda and G. G. Quesada (eds), *Music and Francoism*, Turnhout: Brepols, pp. 99–126.

Martínez Del Fresno, Beatriz (2014), "Las armas de Terpsícore en la recuperación diplomática del franquismo: Coros y Danzas in España en la Argentina de Perón (1948)," in M. Sala (ed.), *Music and Propaganda in the Short Twentieth Century*, Tournhut: Brepols, pp. 243–64.

Matin-Asgari, Afshin (2014), "The Pahlavi era: Iranian modernity in global context," in T. Daryaee (ed.), *Oxford Handbook of Iranian History*, Oxford: Oxford University Press, pp. 346–64.

Mayes, April J. (2014), *The Mulatto Republic: Class, Race, and Dominican National Identity*, Tallahassee: University Press of Florida.

Mazower, Mark (2002), *The Balkans: A Short History*, New York: Modern Library.

McCray, Thomas R. (2004), *Uzbekistan*, Philadelphia: Chelsea House.

McInerny, Jeremy (2001), "Ethnos and ethnicity in early Greece," in I. Malkin (ed.), *Ancient Perceptions of Greek Ethnicity*, Washington, DC: Center for Hellenic Studies, Trustees for Harvard University, pp. 51–73.

Meftahi, Ida (2007), "Rethinking the history of dance in 20th century Iran: Nationalizing dance to exhibit Iranian identity," *Proceedings, Society of Dance History Scholars International Conference*, Paris, pp. 149–52.

Meftahi, Ida (2016a), *Gender and Dance in Modern Iran: Biopolitics on Stage*, New York: Routledge.

Meftahi, Ida (2016b), "Dancing angels and princesses: The invention of an ideal female national dancer in twentieth-century Iran," in A. Shay and B. Sellers-Young (eds), *The Oxford Handbook of Dance and Ethnicity*, New York: Oxford University Press, pp. 210–35.

Meftahi, Ida (2019), Personal communication, February.

Meltzer, Milton (1993), *Slavery: A World History*, updated ed., Boston: Da Capo Press.

Mendoza-Garcia, Gabriela (2016), "The Jarabe Tapatio: Imagining race, nation, class, and gender in 1920s Mexico," in A. Shay and B. Sellers-Young (eds), *The Oxford Handbook of Dance and Ethnicity*, New York: Oxford University Press, pp. 319–43.

Menges, Karl H. (1994), "People, languages, and migrations," in E. Allworth (ed.), *Central Asia: 130 Years of Russian Dominance, A Historical Overview*, 3rd ed., Durham, NC: Duke University Press, pp. 60–91.

Mertens, Joan R. (2010), *How to Read Greek Vases*, New York: Metropolitan Museum of Art.

Mesić, Stjepan (2001), "The road to war," in B. Magaš and I. Žanić (eds), *War in Croatia and Bosnia-Herzegovina, 1991–1995*, London: Frank Cass, pp. 3–13.

Michnik, Adam (1996), "Dignity and fear: Letter to a friend," in R. Caplan and J. Feffer (eds), *Europe's New Nationalism: States and Minorities in Conflict*, New York and Oxford: Oxford University Press, pp. 15–22.

Microsoft Encarta College Dictionary (2001), New York: St. Martins Press.
Miller, Frank J. (1990), *Folklore for Stalin: Russian Folklore and Pseudofolklore of the Stalin Era*, Armonk, NY: M. E. Sharpe.
Mitchell, J. Clyde (1956), The Kalela Dance, Rhodes-Livingstone Paper No. 27, Manchester. Manchester University Press.
Moats, Alice Leone (1977), *The Million Dollar Studs*, New York: Delacorte Press.
Moiseyev, Igor (1996), *Ya Vspominaiu: Gastrol' Dlinolu v Zhizn'*, Moscow: Soglasie.
Monés, Nèlida, Maria Carrasco, Estrella Casero-García, and Delfín Colomé (2000), "Spain: Between tradition and innovation: Two ways of understanding the history of dance in Spain," in A. Grau and S. Jordan (eds), *Europe Dancing: Perspectives on Theatre Dance and Cultural Identity*, London: Routledge, pp. 144–67.
Morgan, Catherine (2001), "Ethne, ethnicity, and early Greek State, ca. 1200–480 B.C: An Archaeological Perspective," in I. Malkin (ed.), *Ancient Perceptions of Greek Ethnicity*, Washington, DC: Center for Hellenic Studies, Trustees for Harvard University, pp. 75–112.
Morony, Michael G. (2005), *Iraq after the Islamic Conquest*, Piscataway, NJ: Giorgias Press.
Mosse, George L. (1975), *The Nationalization of the Masses: Political Symbolism and Mass Movements in Germany from the Napoleanic Wars through the Third Reich*, New York: Howard Fertig.
Moya Pons, Frank (2010), *The Dominican Republic: A National History*, 3rd ed., Princeton: Markus Wiener.
Naby, Eden (1994), "The emerging Central Asia: Ethnic and religious factions," in M. Mesbahi (ed.), *Central Asia and the Caucasus after the Soviet Union*, Gainesville: University Press of Florida, pp. 34–55.
Nagata, J. A. (1981), "In defense of ethnic boundaries: The changing myths and charters of Malay identity," in C. Keyes (ed.), *Ethnic Change*, Seattle: University of Washington Press, pp. 87–116.
Najmabadi, Afsaneh (2005), *Women with Mustaches and Men without Beards: Gender and Sexual Anxieties of Iranian Modernity*, Berkeley and Los Angeles: University of California Press.
Naumkin, Vitaly (1993), *Bukhara: Caught in Time: Great Photographic Archives*, Compiler Andrei G. Nedvvetsky, intro. D. Y. Arapov, Reading, GB: Garnet.
Nevile, Jennifer (2008), "Introduction and overview," in Jennifer Nevile (ed.), *Dance, Spectacle and the Body Politick, 1250–1750*, Bloomington: Indiana University Press, pp. 1–64.
Nichols, Johanna (1993), "The linguistic geography of the Slavic expansion," in R. A. Maguire and A. Timberlake (eds), *American Contributions to the Eleventh International Congress of Slavists, Bratislava, August-September, 1993. Literature. Linguistics. Poetics*, Columbus, OH: Slavica, pp. 377–91.
Nichols, Johanna (2011), "The Eurasian spread zone and the Indo-European dispersal," in R. Blench and M. Spriggs (eds), *Archaeology and Language II: Archaeological Data and*

Linguistic Hypotheses. Part II: Migration and Expansion and Their Linguistic Correlations: Eurasian Case Studies, London and New York: Routledge, pp. 220–66.

Nielsen, Erica (2008), "Bulgarian dance culture: From censorship to Chalga," in A. Shay (ed.), *Balkan Dance: Essays on Characteristics, Performance and Teaching*, Jefferson, NC: McFarland, pp. 130–44.

Nooshin, Laudan (2005), "Subversion and countersubversion, power, control and meaning in the New Iranian pop music," in A. J. Randell (ed.), *Music, Power, and Politics*, New York: Routledge, pp. 238–72.

Olcott, Martha Brill (1994), "Nation building and ethnicity in the foreign policies of the New Central Asian states," in R. Szporluk (ed.), *National Identity and Ethnicity in Russia and the New States of Eurasia*, Armonk, NY: M.E. Sharpe, pp. 209–29.

Olson, Laura J. (2004), *Performing Russia: Folk Revival and Russian Identity*, New York and London: Routledge Curzon.

Olzak, Susan (1992), *The Dynamics of Ethnic Competition and Conflict*, Stanford, CA: Stanford University Press.

Ortolani, Benito (1998), "Japan: An overview," in S. J. Cohen (ed.), *International Encyclopedia of Dance*, vol. 3, New York: Oxford University Press, pp. 578–83.

O'Shea, Janet (2020), "Roots/routes of dance studies," in A. Carter and J. O'Shea (eds), *Dance Studies Reader*, 2nd ed., pp. 1–15.

Ostler, Nicholas (2005), *Empire of the Word: A Language History of the World*, New York: Harper Perennial.

Öztürkmen, Arzu (1993), "Folklore and nationalism in Turkey," Ph.D. dissertation, University of Pennsylvania.

Öztürkmen, Arzu (1992), "Folk dance and nationalism in Turkey," *Proceedings. 17th Symposium of the Study Group on Ethnochoreology*, Nafplion, Greece, July 2– 10, pp. 83–86.

Pahlen, K. K. (1964), *Mission to Turkestan: Being the Memoirs of Count K. K. Pahlen, 1908–09* (ed. and intro. R. A. Pierce; trans. N. J. Couriss), London: Oxford University Press.

Partsch-Bergsohn and Harold Bergsohn (2003), *The Makers of Modern Dance in Germany: Rudolf Laban, Mary Wigman, Kurt Jooss*, Heightstown, NJ: Princeton Book.

Payne, Stanley G. (2012), *The Spanish Civil War*, New York: Cambridge University Press.

Pérez, Xiomarita (2010), "How to dance son and the style of a Dominican Sonero," in S. Sloat (ed.), *Making Caribbean Dance: Continuity and Creativity in Island Cultures*, Tallahassee: University of Press of Florida, pp. 198–207.

Pérez Zalduondo, Gemma (2017), " 'Spain is a Fiesta'/'Spain is a festival': Music and dance in Spanish festivals (1953–1963)," in B. M. del Fresno and B. V. Pichaco (eds), *Dance, Ideology and Power in Francoist Spain (1938–1968)*, Turnhout: Bepols, pp. 139–74.

Perica, Vjekoslav (2002), *Balkan Idols: Religion and Nationalism in Yugoslav States*, Oxford and New York: Oxford University Press.

Petkovski, Filip (2016), "Professional folk dance ensembles in Eastern Europe and the presentation of folk dance on stage," in L. Mellish, N. Green and M. Zakić (eds), *Fourth Symposium of the ICTM Study Group on Music and Dance in Southeastern Europe*, pp. 173–78.

Petrone, Karen (2000), *Life Has Become More Joyous, Comrades: Celebrations in the Time of Stalin*, Bloomington: Indiana University Press.

Plokhy, Serhii (2006), *The Origins of the Slavic Nations: Premodern Identities in Russia, Ukraine, and Belarus*, Caembridge: Cambridge University Press.

Pohl, Walter (2002), "Ethnicity, theory, and tradition: A response," in A. Gillett (ed.), *On Barbarian Identity: Critical Approaches to Ethnicity in the Early Middle Ages*, Turnhout, Belgium: Brepols, pp. 221–39.

Pohl, Walter (2018), *The Avars: A Steppe Empire in Central Europe, 567–822*, Ithaca, NY: Cornell University Press.

Potter, David (2011), "The Roman army," in M. Peachin (ed.), *The Oxford Handbook of Social Relations in the Roman World*, Oxford: Oxford University Press, pp. 516–34.

Potter, Pamela M. (2016), *Art of Suppression: Confronting the Nazi Past in Histories of the Visual and Performing Arts*, Oakland: University of California Press.

Poulton, Hugh (1995), *Who Are the Macedonians?* Bloomington: Indiana University Press.

Pourshariati, Parvaneh (2017), *Decline and Fall of the Sasanian Empire: The Sasanian- Parthian Confederacy and the Arab Conquest of Iran*, London and New York: I.B. Tauris.

Povijest Hrvata (2007), Treća knjiga. *Od 1918 do dancas*, Zagreb: Školska Knjiga.

Prest, Julia (2008), "The politics of Ballet at the court of Louis XIV," in J. Neville (ed.), *Dance, Spectacle, and the Body Politick, 1250–1750*, Bloomington: Indiana University Press, pp. 229–40.

Pronko, Leonard and Hall, Jonathan M. (2016), "To call dance Japanese: Nihon Buyô as Ethnic dance," in A. Shay and B. Sellers-Young (eds), *The Oxford Handbook of Dance and Ethnicity*, New York: Oxford University Press, pp. 131–59.

Quigley, Colin (1992), "Reflections on the hearing to 'designate the square dance as the American folk dance of the United States' cultural politics and the American vernacular form," *Proceedings. 17th Symposium of the Study Group on Ethnochoreology*, Nafplion, Greece, July, pp. 87–97.

Quigley, Colin (2014), "The Hungarian dance house movement and the revival of Transylvanian string band music," in C. Bithell and J. Hill (eds), *The Oxford Handbook of Music Revival*, New York: Oxford University Press, pp. 182–202.

Radelić, Zdenko, Davor Marijan, Nikica Barić, Albert Bing, and Dražen Živić (2006), *Stvaranje hrvatske države i Domovinski rat*, Zagreb: Školska Knijga.

Ramazani, Nesta (2002), *The Dance of the Rose and the Nightingale*, Syracuse: Syracuse University Press.

Ramet, Pedro (1984), *Nationalism and Federalism in Yugoslavia, 1963–1983*, Bloomington: Indiana University Press.

Ramet, Sabrina P. (2006), *The Three Yugoslavias: State-Building and Legitimation, 1918–2005*, Washington, DC; Bloomington: Woodrow Wilson Center Press and Indiana University Press.

Ramet, Sabrina P. (2007), "What's love (of country) got to do with it?: Civic values in democratic transition," in Sabrina P. Ramet and Davorka Matić (eds), *Democratic Transition in Croatia: Value Transformation, Education and Media*, College Station: Texas A & M University, pp. 1–27.

Ramet, Sabrina and Matić, Davorka (eds) (2007), *Democratic Transition in Croatia: Value Transformation, Education and Media*, College Station: Texas A & M University.

Randell, A. J. (ed.) (2005), *Music, Power, and Politics*, New York: Routledge.

Rastovac-Akbarzadeh, Heather (2016), "Performing (trans)national Iranianness: The choreographic cartographies of diasporic Iranian dancers and performance artists," Ph.D. dissertation, Berkeley: University of California.

Rastovac-Akbarzadeh, Heather (2020), "Do Iranian dancers need saving?: Savior spectatorship and the production of Iranian Bodies as 'objects of rescue'," in S. Manning, J. Ross, and R. Schnieder (eds), *Future of Dance Studies*, Madison: University of Wisconsin Press, pp. 453–70.

Rees, Laurence (2012), *Hitler's Charisma: Leading Millions into the Abyss*, New York: Vintage Books.

Revell, Louise (2016), *Ways of Being Roman: Discourses of Identity in the Roman West*, Oxford and Philadelphia: Oxbow Books.

Reynolds, Nancy and Malcolm McCormick (2003), *No Fixed Points: Dance in the Twentieth Century*, New Haven, CT: Yale University Press.

Rezvani, Medjid (1962), *Le theâtre et la danse en Iran*, Paris: G. P. Maisonneuve et Larose.

Rice, Timothy (1994), *May It Fill Your Soul: Experiencing Bulgarian Music*, Chicago: University of Chicago Press.

Richmond, Kathleen (2003), *Women and Spanish Fascism: The Women's Section of the Falange, 1934–1959*, London and New York: Routledge.

Rivera-Servera, Ramón H. (2002), "A Dominican York in Andrhra," in S. Sloat (ed.), *Caribbean Dance From Abakuá to Zouk: How Movement Shapes Identity*, Gainsville: University Press of Florida, pp. 152–61.

Roach, Joseph (2007), *It*, Ann Arbor: University of Michigan Press.

Romanucci-Ross, Lola and George A. De Vos (1995), "Preface," in L. Romanucci-Ross and G. DeVos (eds), *Ethnic Identity: Creation, Conflict, and Accommodation*, 3rd ed., Walnut Creek: AltaMira Press, pp. 11–14.

Roosens, Eugeen E. (1989), *Creating Ethnicity: The Process of Ethnogenesis*, Newbury Park, CA: Sage.

Root, Margaret Cool (1979), *The King and Kingship in Achaemenid Art*, Acta Iranica, Troisième Série, Volume IX, Leiden: Brill.

Roudemetof, Victor (2001), *Nationalism, Globalization, and Orthodoxy: The Social Origins of Ethnic Conflict in the Balkans*, Westport, CT: Greenwood.

Royce, Anya Peterson (1977), *Anthropology of Dance*, Bloomington: University of Indiana Press.

Roymans, Nico (2009), "Hercules and the construction of Batavian identity in the context of the Roman Empire," in T. Derks and N. Roymans (eds), *Ethnic Constructs in Antiquity: The Role of Power and Tradition*, Amsterdam: Amsterdam University Press, pp. 219–238.

Rumbaut, Rubén G. and Alejandro Portes (eds) (2001), *Ethnicities: Children of Immigrants in America*, Berkeley and Los Angeles: University of California Press.

Rusinow, Dennison (1977), *The Yugoslav Experiment, 1948–1974*, Berkeley: University of California Press.

Rusinow, Dennison (1996), "From empire to nation: The national idea triumphant," in G. Augustinos (ed.), *The National Idea in Eastern Europe: The Politics of Ethnic and Civic Community*, Lexington, KY: D. C. Heath, pp. 1–14.

Rutherford, Adam (2017), *A Brief History of Everyone Who Ever Lived: The Human Story Retold through Our Genes*, New York: The Experiment.

Ruyter, Nancy Lee Chalfa (2008), "Dvoransko Kolo from the 1840s to the twentieth century," in A. Shay (ed.), *Balkan Dance: Essays on Characteristics, Performance and Teaching*, Jefferson, NC: McFarland, pp. 239–49.

Rywkin, Michael (1994), *Moscow's Lost Empire*, Armonk, NY: M. E. Sharpe.

Sa'adi, Mushrefedin (2017), *The Gulistan of Sa'di* (trans. W. M. Thackston), Bethesda, MD: Ibex.

Said, Edward (1978), *Orientalism*, New York: Vintage.

Saïd, Suzanne (2001), "The discourse of identity in Greek rhetoric from Isocrates to Aristides," in I. Malkin (ed.), *Ancient Perceptions of Greek Ethnicity*, Washington, DC: Center for Hellenic Studies, Trustees for Harvard University, pp. 275–300.

Saikal, Amin (2008), *The Rise and Fall of the Shah: Iran From Autocracy to Religious Rule*, Princeton: Princeton University Press.

Sánchez Ekiza, Karlos (2017), " 'Cuando en Castilla sepan que se toca el chistu': La Participción vasca en los concursos de Danza de la Sección Femenina y en sus vijaes," in B. M. del Fresno and B. V. Pichaco (eds), *Dance, Ideology and Power in Francoist Spain (1938–1968)*, Turnhout: Bepols, pp. 31–66.

Sancisi-Weerdenburg, Heleen (2001), "*Yauna* by the sea and across the sea," in I. Malkin (ed.), *Ancient Perceptions of Greek Ethnicity*, Washington, DC: Center for Hellenic Studies, Trustees for Harvard University, pp. 323–46.

Savigliano, Marta (1995), *Tango and the Political Economy of Passion*, Boulder, CO: Westview Press.

Schauert, Paul (2015), *Staging Ghana: Artistry and Nationalism in State Dance Ensembles*, Bloomington: Indiana University Press.

Scheff, Thomas J. (1994), " 'Emotions and identity: A theory of ethnic nationalism," in C. Calhoun (ed.), *Social Theory and the Politics of Identity*, Oxford: Blackwell, pp. 277–303.

Schmidt, Alexander and Urban, Markus (2009), *The Nazi Party Rally Grounds in Nuremberg. A Short Guide* (trans. J. Jenkins), Nuremberg: Geschichte Für Alle e. V.

Schumacher, Leonhard (2011), "Slaves in Roman society," in M. Peachin (ed.), *The Oxford Handbook of Social Relations in the Roman World*, New York: Oxford University Press, pp. 589–608.

Schuyler, Eurgene (1885), *Turkkistan: Notes of a Journey in Russian Turkestan, Khokand, Bukhara, and Kuldja*, vol. I, 3rd American ed., New York: Charles Scribner's Sons.

Sell, Louis (2002), *Slobodan Milosevic and the Destruction of Yugoslavia*, Durham, NC: Duke University Press.

Sellars, Julie A. (2004), *Merengue and Dominican Identity: Music as National Identity*, Jefferson, NC: McFarland.

Sellers-Young, Barbara (1993), *Teaching Personality and Gracefulness: Transmission of Japanese Cultural Values through Dance*, Lanham, MD: University Press of America.

Seton-Watson, Hugh (1994), "Old and new nations," in J. Hutchinson and A. D. Smith (eds), *Ethnicity*, Oxford: Oxford University Press, pp. 134–38.

Shahbazi, A. Saphur (1991), *Ferdowsī: A Critical Biography*, Costa Mesa: Mazda.

Shay, Anthony (1994), "Is a picture worth of thousand words? Iconographic sources of Middle Eastern dance," *Society of Dance Historians Conference*, Minneapolis: University of Minnesota.

Shay, Anthony (1997), "In search of traces: Linkages of dance and visual and performative expression in the Iranian world," *Visual Anthropology*, 10, pp. 335–60.

Shay, Anthony (1999), *Choreophobia: Solo Improvised Dance in the Iranian World*, Costa Mesa, CA: Mazda.

Shay, Anthony (2000), "The 6/8 beat goes on: Persian popular music from *Bazm-e Qāajariyyeh* to Beverly Hills garden parties," in W. Armbrust (ed.), *Mass Mediations: New Approaches to Popular Culture in the Middle East and Beyond*, Berkeley and Los Angeles: University of California Press, pp. 61–87.

Shay, Anthony (2002), *Choreographic Politics: State Folk Dance Companies, Representation, and Power*, Middletown: Wesleyan University Press.

Shay, Anthony (2005), "The male oriental dancer," in A. Shay and B. Sellers-Young (eds), *Belly Dance: Orientalism, Transationalism & Harem Fantasy*, Costa Mesa, CA: Mazda, pp. 85–113.

Shay, Anthony (2006), *Choreographing Identities: Folk Dance, Ethnicity and Festival in the United States and Canada*, Jefferson, NC: McFarland.

Shay, Anthony (2008a), *Dancing Across Borders: The American Fascination with Exotic Dance Forms*, Jefferson, NC: McFarland.

Shay, Anthony (2008b), "Dance and human rights in the Middle East, North Africa, and Central Asia," in N. Jackson and T. Shapiro-Phim (eds), *Dance Human Rights and Social Justice: Dignity in Motion*, London and Lanham, MD: Scarecrow Press, pp. 67–85.

Shay, Anthony (2008c), "Introduction: Choreographing the Balkans," in A. Shay (ed.), *Balkan Dance: Essays on Characteristics, Performance and Teaching*, Jefferson, NC: McFarland, pp. 12–33.

Shay, Anthony (2008d), "Choreographing hypermasculinity in Egypt, Iran, and Uzbekistan," *Dance Chronicle*, 31:2, pp. 211–38.

Shay, Anthony (2013), "Dance as the international language: The search for an American cultural voice at the height of the Cold War," in T. Hagood and L. Kallich (eds), *The Impulse Project: A Digital Preservation and Contemporary Analysis of the West Coast Annual 1950–1970*, Boyer College of Music and Dance, Temple University, Philadelphia: Temple University Press, pp. 289–312.

Shay, Anthony (2014a), *The Dangerous Lives of Public Performers: Dancing, Sex, and Entertainment in the Islamic World*, New York: Palgrave Macmillan.

Shay, Anthony (2014b), "Reviving the reluctant art of Iranian dance in Iran and in the American diaspora," in C. Bithell and J. Hill (eds), *The Oxford Handbook of Music Revival*, Oxford and New York: Oxford University Press, pp. 618–43.

Shay, Anthony (2015), "Fandangos and Bailes: Dance and dance events in early California," in K. M. Goldberg, N. D. Bennahum, and M. H. Hayes (eds), *Flamenco on the Global State: Historical Critical and Theoretical Perspectives*, Jefferson, NC: McFarland.

Shay, Anthony (2016a), *Ethno Identity Dance for Sex, Fun and Profit: Staging Popular Dances Around the World*, London: Palgrave Macmillan.

Shay, Anthony (2016b), "The spectacularization of Soviet/Russian Folk dance," in A. Shay and B. Sellers-Young (eds), *The Oxford Handbook of Dance and Ethnicity*, New York: Oxford University Press, pp. 236–55.

Shay, Anthony (2016c), "Lado, the state ensemble of Croatian folk dances and songs: Icon of Croatian identity," in Anthony and B. Sellers-Young (eds), *The Oxford Handbook of Dance and Ethnicity*, New York: Oxford University Press, pp. 256–78.

Shay, Anthony (2019a), "In the moment: Improvisation in traditional dance," in V. Midgelow (ed.), *The Oxford Handbook of Dance and Improvisation*, Oxford and London: Oxford University Press, pp. 705–18.

Shay, Anthony (2019b), *The Igor Moiseyev Dance Company: Dancing Diplomats*, Bristol: Intellect Books.

Shay, Anthony (forthcoming), "Introduction," in A. Shay (ed.), *Solo Improvised Dance in the Persianate World*, Costa Mesa, CA: Mazda.

Shay, Anthony and Barbara Sellers-Young (eds) (2005), *Belly Dance: Orientalism, Transnationalism and Harem Fantasy*, Costa Mesa: Mazda.

Shay, Anthony and Barbara Sellers-Young (2016), *The Oxford Handbook of Dance and Ethnicity*, New York: Oxford University Press.

Shirokaya, O. I. (1973), *Tamara Khanum: Eastern Folk Dances*, Tashkent: Gafur Gulyam Literature and Art Publishing House.

Shiva, Shahram T. (1995), *Rending the Veil: Literal and Poetic Translations of Rumi*, Prescott, AZ: Hohm Press.

Siamdoust, Nahid (2017), *Sound Track of the Revolution: The Politics of Music in Iran*, Stanford: Stanford University Press.

Slobin, Mark (1996), "Introduction," in M. Slobin (ed.), *Returning Culture: Musical Changes in Central and Eastern Europe*, Durham, NC: Duke University Press, pp. 1–13.

Smith, Julia M. H. (2005), *Europe after Rome: A New Cultural History 500–1000*, Oxford: Oxford University Press.

Smith, Anthony D. (1986), *The Ethnic Origins of Nations*, Oxford: Blackwell.

Smith, Anthony D. (2003), *Chosen Peoples: Sacred Sources of National Identity*, Oxford: Oxford University Press.

Smith, Anthony D. (2008), *The Cultural Foundations of Nations: Hierarchy, Covenant, and Republic*, Oxford: Blackwell.

Smith, Graham (1996), "The Soviet state and nationalities policy," in G. Smith (ed.), *The Nationalities Question in the Post-Soviet States*, London and New York: Longman, pp. 2–22.

Smith, Julia M. H. (2005), *Europe after Rome: A New Cultural History*, Oxford: Oxford University Press.

Smith, Michael E. (1996), *The Aztecs*, Oxford: Blackwell.

Snyder, Richard (1998), "Paths out of Sultanistic regimes: Confronting structural and voluntarist perspecitves," in H. E. Chehabi and Juan J. Linz (eds), *Sultanistic Regimes*, Baltimore: John Hopkins University Press, pp. 49–81.

Soberg, Marius (2007), "Croatia since 1989: The HDZ and the politics of transition," in S. P. Ramet and D. Matić (eds), *Democratic Transition in Croatia: Value Transformation, Education and Media*, College Station, TX: Texas A & M University Press, pp. 31–62.

Soucek, Svat (2000), *A History of Inner Asia*, Cambridge: Cambridge University Press, *Spanish Songs and Dances, 1957*, 10th ed., Madrid: Sección Femenina de F.E.T. y de la J.O.N.S.

Spanish Songs and Folk Dances (1957), 10th ed., Souvenir program. Madrid: Seccion Femenina de F. E.T. y de Las J. O. N. S.

Spector, Johanna (1994), "Musical tradition and innovation," in E. Allworth (ed.), *Central Asia: 130 Years of Russian Dominance, A Historical Overview*, 3rd ed., Durham, NC: Duke University Press, pp. 434–84.

Špegelj, Martin (2001), "The first phase, 1990–1992: the JNA prepares for aggression and Croatia for defence," in B. Magaš and I. Žanić (eds), *War in Croatia and Bosnia-Herzegovina, 1991–1995*, London: Frank Cass, pp. 14–40.

Spooner, Brian and William Hanaway L. (2012), "Preface," in B. Spooner and W. L. Hanaway (eds), *Literacy in the Persianate World: Writing and the Social Order*, Philadelphia: University of Pennsylvania Museum of Archaeology and Anthropology.

Spuler, Berthold (2015), *Iran in the Early Islamic Period: Politics, Culture, Administration and Public Life between the Arab and the Seljuk Conquests, 633–1055* (ed. R. G. Hoyland, trans. G. Goldbloom, and B. Walburg), Leiden: Brill.

Sremac, Stjepan (2001), "Folklorni Ples u Hrvata od Izvora do Pozornice: Izmedu drustvene I kulturne potrebe, politike, kulturnog I nacionalnog identiteta," Ph.D. dissertation, University of Zagreb.

Sremac, Stjepan (2009), "Povjest lada/the history of Lado," in Z. Vitez and M. Vučić (eds), *Lado: Hrvatsko Nacionalno Blago, 1949–2009*, Zagreb: Ansambl Narodnih Plesova i Pjesama Hrvatske Lado and Školska Knjiga, pp. 93–117.

Stall, Bill (2006), "Where's Tantu Tuva?," *Los Angeles Times*, E1, E8, 27 May.

Starr, S. Frederick (2018), "Change and continuity in Uzbekistan, 1991–2016," in S. F. Starr and S. E. Cornell (eds), *Uzbekistan's New Face*, Lanham, MD: Rowman and Littlefield, pp. 18–40.

Starr, S. Frederick and Svante E. Cornell (eds) (2018), *Uzbekistan's New Face*, Lanham, MD: Rowman and Littlefield.

Steele, Claude M. (2011), *Whistling Vivaldi: And Other Clues How Stereotypes Affect Us*, New York: Norton.

Steinberg, Stephen (2001), "Preface to the updated edition," in *The Ethnic Myth: Race, Ethnicity, and Class in America*, 3rd ed., Boston: Beacon Press, xi–xii.

Stellar, Zeinab (2011), "From 'evil-inciting' dance to chaste 'rhythmic movements': A genealogy of Modern Islamic dance theatre in Iran," in K. van Nieuwkerk (ed.), *Muslim Rap, Halal Soaps, and Revolutionary Theater: Artistic Developments in the Muslim World*, Austin: University of Texas Press, pp. 231–56.

Stern, Stephen and John Allan Cicala (eds) (1991), *Creative Ethnicity: Symbols and Strategies of Contemporary Ethnic Life*, Logan: Utah State University Press.

Stevens, Robert (1952), *Music in Mexico: A Historical Survey*, New York: Thomas Y. Crowell.

Stuart, Kathy (1999), *Defiled Trades and Social Outcasts: Honor and Ritual Pollution in Early Modern Germany*, Cambridge: Cambridge University Press.

Svolik, Milan W. (2012), *The Politics of Authoritarian Rule*, Cambridge: Cambridge University Press.

Sweers, Britta (2005), "The power to influence minds: German folk music during the Nazi era and after," in A. J. Randall (ed.), *Music, Power, and Politics*, New York: Routledge, pp. 65–86.

Sweet, Jill D. (2004), *Dances of the Tewa Pueblo Indians: Expressions of New Life*, 2nd ed., Santa Fe, New Mexico: School of American Research Press.

Swift, Mary Grace (1968), *The Art of the Dance in the U.S.S.R.*, Notre Dame: University of Notre Dame Press.

Szporluk, Roman (1994), "Introduction and nation building in post-Soviet space," in R. Szporluk (ed.), *National Identity and Ethnicity in Russia and the New States of Eurasia*, Armonk, NY: M.E. Sharpe, pp. 3–17.

Talbot, Margaret (2018), "Color blind," *New Yorker*, October 29, pp. 44–51.

Tanner, Marcus (2001), *Croatia: A Nation Forced into War*, 2nd ed., New Haven and London: Yale Nota Bene.

Tanner, Marcus (2019), *Croatia: A History from the Middle Ages to the Present Day*, 4th ed., New Haven and London: Yale University Press.

Tapper, Richard (1989), "Ethnic identities and social categories in Iran and Afghanistan," in E. Tonkin, M. McDonald, and M. Chapman (eds), *History and Ethnicity*, ASA Monographs 27, London and New York: Routledge, pp. 232–46.

Tavakoli-Targhi, Mohamad (2001), *Refashioning Iran: Orientalism, Occidentalism and Historiography*, Basingstoke and New York: Palgrave.

Thomas, Rosalind (2001), "Ethnicity, genealogy, and hellenism in Herodotus," in I. Malkin (ed.), *Ancient Perceptions of Greek Ethnicity*, Washington, DC: Center for Hellenic Studies, Trustees for Harvard University, pp. 213–33.

Thompson, Mark R. (1998), "The marcos regime in the Philippines," in H. E. Chehabi and J. J. Linz (eds), *Sutlanistic Regimes*, Baltimore: John Hopkins University Press, pp. 206–29.

Tismaneanu, Vladimir (1998), *Fantasies of Salvation: Democracy, Nationalism and Myth in Post-Communist Europe*, Princeton: Princeton University Press.

Tismaneanu, Vladimir (2012), *The Devil in History: Communism, Fascism and Some Lessons of the Twentieth Century*, Berkeley and Los Angeles: University of California Press.

Tkachenko, Tamara (1954), *Nardony Tanets*, Moscow: Isskustvo.

Todorova, Maria (1997), *Imagining the Balkans*, New York and London: Oxford University Press.

Tonkin, Elizabeth, Maryon McDonald, and Malcolm Chapman (eds) (1989), *History and Ethnicity*, London: Routledge.

Tsirtsoni, Zoi (2017), "Let's stop speaking 'culture'! Alternative means to assess historical development in the prehistoric Balkans," in M. Gori and M. Ivanova (eds), *Balkan Dialogues: Negotiating Identity between Prehistory and the Present*, London and New York: Routledge, pp. 64–84.

Turits, Richard Lee (2003), *Foundations of Despotism: Peasants, the Trujillo Regime, and Modernity in Dominican Republic*, Stanford: Stanford University Press.

Turner, Bryan S. (2008), *The Body and Society*, 3rd ed., London: Sage.

Tus, Anton (2001), "The war in Slovenia and Croatia up to the Sarajevo ceasefire," in B. Magaš and I. Žanić (eds), *War in Croatia and Bosnia-Herzegovina, 1991–1995*, London: Frank Cass, pp. 41–66.

Uebel, Michael (2003), "Re-orienting desire: Writing on gender trouble in fourteenth-century Egypt," in S. Farmer and C. B. Pasternak (eds), *Gender and Difference in the Middle Ages*, Minneapolis: University of Minnesota Press, pp. 230–57.

Ugresić, Dubravka (1998), *The Culture of Lies: Antipolitical Essays*, University Park: Pennsylvania State University Press.

Van der Spek, Bert (2009), "Multi-ethnicity and ethnic segregation in Babylon," in T. Derks and N. Roymans (eds), *Ethnic Constructs in Antiquity: The Role of Power and Tradition*, Amsterdam: Amsterdam University Press, pp. 101–16.

Van Steen, Gonda (2015), *Stage of Emergency: Theater and Public Performance under the Greek Military Dictatorship of 1967–1974*, Oxford: Oxford University Press.

Ventura, Johnny (2014), "Johnny ventura," in E. P. Roorda, L. Derby, and R. González (eds), *The Dominican Republic Reader: History, Culture, Politics*, Durham, NC: Duke University Press, pp. 435–38.

Verdery, Katherine (1996), "Why national ideology under socialism?" in G. Augustinos (ed.), *The National Idea in Eastern Europe: The Politics of Ethnic and Civic Community*, Lexington, MA: D. C. Heath, pp. 109–17.

Vitez, Zorica and Miroslava Vučić (eds) (2009), *Lado: Hrvatsko Nacionalno Blago, 1949–2009*, Zagreb: Ansambl Narodnih Plesova i Pjesama Hrvatske Lado and Školska Knjiga.

Von Bibra, Anne Louise (1987), *Continuity and Change in the Dance Events of Two Lower Franconian Villages During the Twentieth Century*, Los Angeles: UCLA MA Thesis.

Von Bibra, Anne Louise (2001), "Folk Dance Revival in Germany during 1930–1940: In proceedings of the 21st symposium of the ICTM Study Group on Ethnochoreology," Korčula, Croatia, and Institute of Ethnolgy and Folklore Research, Zagreb, pp. 262–67.

Vujačić, Veljko (2015), *Nationalism, Myth, and the State in Russia and Serbia: Antecedents of the Dissolution of the Soviet Union and Yugoslavia*, Cambridge and New York: Cambridge University Press.

Wachtel, Andrew Baruch (1998), *Making a Nation, Breaking a Nation: Literature and Cultural Politics in Yugoslavia*, Stanford, CA: Stanford University Press.

Wachtel, Andrew Baruch (2008), *The Balkans in World History*, Oxford and New York: Oxford University Press.

Wade, Peter (2010), *Race and Ethnicity in Latin America*, 2nd ed., London: Pluto Press.

Waters, Mary C. (1990), *Ethnic Options: Choosing Identities in America*, Berkeley and Los Angeles: University of California Press.

Weber, Eugen (1976), *Peasants into Frenchmen: The Modernization of Rural France, 1870–1914*, Stanford: Stanford University Press.

Wedeen, Lisa (2019), *Authoritarian Apprehensions: Ideology, Judgment, and Mourning in Syria*, Chicago: University of Chicago Press.

Wells, Peter S. (2001), *Beyond Celts, Germans and Scythians: Archeology and Identity in Iron Age Europe*, London: Duckworth.

West, Rebecca [1940, 1941] 1966, *Black Lamb and Grey Falcon: A Journey through Yugoslavia*, New York: Viking.

Wickham, Chris (2005), *Framing the Early Middle Ages: Europe and the Mediterranean, 400–800*, Oxford: Oxford University Press.

Wilcox, Emily (2019), *Revolutionary Bodies: Chinese Dance and the Socialist Legacy*, Berkeley: University of California Press.

Wimmer, Andreas (2013), *Ethnic Boundary Making: Institutions, Power, Networks*, New York: Oxford University Press.

Winland, Daphne N. (2007), *We Are Now a Nation: Croats between "Home" and "Homeland"*, Toronto: University of Toronto Press.

Winnant, Howard (1994), "Racial formation and hegemony: Global and local developments," in A. Rattansi and S. Westwood (eds), *Racism, Modernity, and Identity*, Cambridge: Polity Press, pp. 266–89.

Wolff, Larry (1994), *Inventing Eastern Europe: The Map of Civilization on the Mind of the Enlightenment*, Stanford: Stanford University Press.

Woolf, Greg (2009), "Cruptorix and his kind: Talking ethnicity on the middle ground," in T. Derks and N. Roymans (eds), *Ethnic Constructs in Antiquity: The Role of Power and Tradition*, Amsterdam: Amsterdam University Press, pp. 207–17.

Yar-Shater, Ehsan (1998), "The Persian presence in the Islamic world," in R. G. Hovannisian and G. Sabagh (eds), *The Persian Presence in the Islamic World*, Cambridge: Cambridge University Press, pp. 4–125.

Yavari, Neguin (2014), "Medieval Iran," in T. Daryaee (ed.), *The Oxford Handbook of Iranian History*, New York: Oxford University Press, pp. 227–42.

Yntema, Douwe (2009), "Material culture and plural identity in Early Roman Southern Italy," in T. Derks and N. Roymans (eds), *Ethnic Constructs in Antiquity: The Role of Power and Tradition*, Amsterdam: Amsterdam University Press, pp. 145–66.

Yugoslavian Folk Dances (1950), Program of joint appearances of Lado (then the newly established State Ensemble of Folk Dances and Songs), the State Folk Dance Ensemble of Serbia and the villagers of Lazarpolje, Macedonia, Belgrad: Jugoslavia.

Zebec, Trvtko (2001), "Folklorni Ples," in Z. Vitez and A. Muraj (eds), *Hrvatska Tradicija Kultura: na razmeđu svetova i epoha*, Zagreb: Ministarsto Kultura Republike Hrvatske, Ministarstvo Zananosti I tehnologije Republike Hrvatske, pp. 441–49.

Zemtsovsky, Izaly and Alma Kunanbaeva (1994), "Communism and folklore," in J. Porter (ed.), *Folklore and Traditional Music in the Former Soviet Union and Eastern Europe: Proceedings of a One-day Conference*, Department of Ethnomusicology, May 16, pp. 3–23.

Žganec, Vinko and Sremec, Nada (1950), *Hrvatske Narodnje Pjesme I Plesovi*, Svezak I. Zagreb: Tisak Grafičog Zavoda Hrvatske.

Zhornitskaya, M. Ia (1979), "The study of folk dancing in the Soviet Union: Its state and tasks," in J. Blacking and J. W. Kealiinohomoku (eds), *The Performing Arts: Music and Dance*, Mouton: The Haague: Mouton Publishers, pp. 79–90.

Zoka, Yahya (1978), "Tarikh-e raqs dar Iran," *Honar va mardom*, vol. XVI, part 1, pp. 188, 2–12; part 2, pp. 189, 2–7; part 3, pp. 191, 38–41; part 4, pp. 192, 22–28.

Žunec, Ozren (2001), "Operations flash and storm," in B. Magaš and I. Žanić (eds), *War in Croatia and Bosnia-Herzegovina, 1991–1995*, London: Frank Cass, pp. 67–83.

VIDEOLOG

American Aloha: Hula Beyond Hawaii. Directed by Lisette Marie Flanery and Evan Bluestocking Films, 2006.

Avaz-e bi sarzamin (Song without a Country). Directed by Ayat Najafi, 2016.

Beijing Olympics Opening Ceremony, NBC, 2008.
Cold War. Directed by Pawel Pawilkowski. Kino Swiat, Poland, 2018.
Dances of Life. Produced by Shana Palusi Seggar and Catherine Tatge, Pacific Islanders in Communication and KQED, 2005.
Dancing. Video produced by WNET in association with RM Arts and BBC-TV. Created by Rhoda Grauer, Executive Producer. Program 3.
"Dragi Naš Kaj." Annual Concert. Zagreb: LADO, 2005.
Iran's Magnificent Party: Decadence and Downfall. BBC Storyville, 1974.
Kumu Hula: Keepers of a Culture. Directed by Robert Mugge, 1999.
"LADO in Concert." Zagreb: Lado, 2005.

Index

Z